Flavor Fusion

Unleashing the Power of Indoor and Outdoor Grilling

John Pennwright

TABLES OF CONTENTS

INTRODUCTION

Imagine your family sitting around a big picnic table, talking and laughing, and enjoying a feast of pulled pork, smoked turkey, twice baked potatoes, grilled fish and chocolate brownies. Now imagine you're not on vacation at a 5-star restaurant, but you're in your own backyard and you've cooked everything on one great appliance.

The Grill is the one-stop-shop you've been waiting for. Known as the premier wood pellet grill, the is also of the best smokers and barbeques on the market. It can be used as a smoker, grill and oven, and will quickly become your ultimate favourite appliance.

A wood pellet smoker-grill is a barbecue pit that smokes, grills, roasts, and bakes using compressed hardwood sawdust such as apple, cherry, hickory, maple, mesquite, oak, and other wood pellets. Only hardwood cooking can provide the flavor profiles and moisture that the wood pellet smoker grill can give. On several types, grill temperatures range from 150°F to well over 600°F, depending on the manufacturer and model. The days of not being able to sear and grill on a wood pellet smoker-grill are over! Wood pellet smoker-grills offer a level of flavor, convenience, and safety that neither charcoal nor gas grills can equal. The smoke profile is gentler than you might be used to from other smokers. They have the adaptability and benefits of a convection oven due to its design. Wood pellet smoker-grills are easy to use and safe.

So, how exactly does the smoker grill work? When you turn on the appliance, the motor begins to rotate a screw-like device known as the auger, which feeds the burn pot. The pellets are then ignited, and the exhaust is expelled through the chimney.

Pellet grills also have air convection, which feeds air to the burning pellets. This ensures that the heat is distributed efficiently and that the air around the food is filled with smoke. The heat is moved around the meat in the same way that it is in a convection oven.

Most other types of grills use charcoal, natural gas, or propane as a fuel source. In the case of these fuel sources, the user must be familiar with the grill type and be present to 'babysit' the grill.

Smoker grills, on the other hand, use all-natural wood pellets. In a controlled environment, these pellets can burn well and provide flavorful food. Furthermore, these pellets are FDA-approved and suitable for both indoor and outdoor use.

When burned, they do not harm the environment and can be used to create a new range of individual flavors.

Wood pellets come in many different varieties, including pecan, apple, mesquite, and hickory. Aside from infusing delicious flavor into the meat, they can also be used to bake sweets such as pie and cookies.

CHAPTER 1: WOOD PELLET GRILL ESSENTIAL

It is not necessary for anyone to say how important an easy griller is. Anyone can use it without much involvement along with professional help. It is a convenient, compact, and comfortable griller. It is very versatile and can be used for creating a BBQ Menu in a relatively short time. You don't require any freestanding gas or propane tanks which makes it very friendly to the environment. It requires very little effort for light, temperature, and comfort. It is the best answer for easy grilling and it is the appetizing kind of grill.

Here are some essentials for every grill owner's tool kit.

1. Gourmet Rubs & Spices

If you've ever smeared a pork roast with supermarket barbecue sauce making your meat tasteless and loaded with sugar, then you immediately understand the importance of making your own seasonings and sauces.

While it's awesome to have access to the authentic, high-quality ingredients (and cheap, too!), you don't have to give up your everyday cheat list either.

2. Premium Wood Pellets

There are two big reasons why wood pellets are at the top of the food chain: A) They have zero additives, and B) they smoke up like a pro. It might look like hard work, but woods like hickory, oak, apple, cherry, and maple are the best tree breeds for the tastier grilling. Never settle for convenience store chips again!

3. Pink Butcher Paper

The light-colored surface of the Signature Pink Butcher Paper acts as a natural buffer to protect the meat from the direct heat source. It has low permeability, dissolves quickly and can reflect infrared rays to prevent over-drying. The difference is that you will eat more meat you paid for instead of throwing away a crunchy, dry surface.

4. Flexible Stainless-Steel Skewers

Looking to master your kebab game? Then your grill shouldn't be without stainless-steel skewers. They're almost odorless, won't scratch your grill like wooden ones, and the flavor-converting ability is way better than regular metal skewers. Plus, building your own kebabs will allow you to master your creative side.

5. Stainless Steel Meat Shredding Claw

Get that juicy pulled chicken and pork you've always dreamed of, every time. The meat claw makes it easy to use your hands (and fingers) to finish chopping up a huge amount of meat, vegetables, cheese, pasta, or whatever the situation calls for.

6. Drip Tray Liners

They make maintenance of the grill child's play. They are made of aluminum, light, heat resistant. They are also disposable.

Make sure they rest completely on the grease tray without covering other external areas as it could affect the performance of the grill.

7. Stuffed Burger Press

Have you tried making hamburgers stuffed with bacon or stuffed with cheese? The burger filling options are unlimited and they are delicious! But, whether you're a tacos or burger filling wizard, the Ball Stuffed Burger Press makes it easy to add all the delicacy inside the meat.

8. Dexter Large Cut Slicing Knife

Engraving a brisket is not an easy task, especially if you opt for a single-pointed blade. Most likely, you will end up sawing from side to side and shredding your meat. That's why we love Dexter Large Cut Slicing Knife. It has a serrated edge and a comfortable grip that will make harder cuts look like child's play.

9. Barbecue, Smoking & Grilling Cookbooks

Barbecue cookbooks are not one-size-fits-all, but we rounded up a list of the best barbecuing recipes out there. Whether you're a smoker-meister or a rotisserie-rager, you'll find something that suits your preferences.

10. Spray Bottles

If you want value-added to your food, then you need a spray bottle. Whether you're spraying a fresh burst or a light mist of flavor, these bottles are the perfect tools for your perfect meal.

11. Vacuum Sealer

Vacuum sealers keep your food wholesome and tasty. They lock in all the juices that are lost when wrapped in plastic wrap or aluminum foil and make keeping meats, veggies, and snacks fresh and delicious.

12. Magnetic & Clamp Grill Light

If you're a grill master, then you're a daytime grill master. This explains why you need a clamp light.

13. Food Saver Jar Sealer

If you vacuum your food, then you are also a daytime vacuum sealer. Food Saver Jar Sealer allows you to extend the shelf life of meats, vegetables and snacks with an airtight, watertight seal. It blocks deep flavors and keeps air, bacteria and other contaminants out.

14. High Heat Baking Pans + Lids

Bring out the grill master in you. High heat baking pans and lids are two tools that work great for grilling food indoors. You can even stack your pans for a unique presentation.

15. Grill-Shaped Cake Pan

Cake for dinner? A grill-shaped cake pan is perfect for sweeping up all the flavors of your favorite grilled meals.

CHAPTER 2: CLEANING AND MAINTENANCE

In comparison to similar barbecues, grills are simple to clean. It would only need to be cleaned every five usage, which is fantastic. Cleaning traditional grills can be a pain and can quickly become filthy.

1.   Open the grill lid and wipe the grates with a paper towel or damp cloth. If your grates have more residue, you can use a grill mark brush instead. Use a scraper to remove debris at the back wall of the grill then let all the dirt fall on the bottom of the drip tray.

2.   Brush or wipe the inside of the smoke exhaust and empty the grease bucket.

3.   Take out the drip pan and replace it with fresh aluminum foil.

4.   Siphon the ash beneath the heat deflector and on the inside of the fire pot using a vacuum.

5.   Use a grease cleaner or soapy water on a spray bottle to clean the exterior of the grill. Spray it while carefully avoiding the electronic controls. Leave it on for 1 minute, then wipe it down with a clean cloth.

More Tips:

• Before cleaning, make sure the grill has completely cooled down.

• While cleaning, visually inspect the parts to ensure they are in good operating order.

• Follow the top to bottom cleaning method.

• Vacuum the insides of the hopper to remove any ash or dust.

• If the temperature probes become dirty, you may need to clean them. Do these gently by using a clean damp cloth.

• When removing the grate, be careful not to damage or scrape the temperature probe.

A barbecue grill can be quite a significant investment. It can cost $1000 or more. You need to take some time to learn how to take care of your investment when you spend that much. When it comes to barbecue, taking care of them needs to become a habit. After every use, you should ensure that your grill is thoroughly cleaned. It doesn't matter if you're using an indoor electric grill like the Breville Smart Grill, a barbecue model like a Weber grill, or even a gas grill; most of the maintenance tips that you follow will not change.

Phase 1: Use the right equipment

You don't have to go to the hardware store and spend hundreds of dollars to find the right tools to clean your barbecue. All you need are:

• Some steel wool sheets.

• A mild dish cleaner.

• Baking soda.

• Spray cooking oil.

• A grill brush.

• Aluminum foil.

• Cloth.

Take a few moments to pick and keep these things close to your barbecue, but note that you should store them inside so that the weather does not harm them.

Phase 2: Give A Good Brushing to Your Grill

You should provide your grill with a regular brushing after every single use. One thing you were supposed to get when you gathered materials earlier was a grill brush. They are commonly made of brass wires that can be used to brush the grilling surface to remove all of the unpleasant accumulation so that it won't become permanent. The longer that all grease and stuck-on food is left on the grilling board, the more difficult it will be to clean.

Phase 3: Use the other products

Mix a little bit of baking soda with water to make the nasty bits nice and clean, and put it on your wire brush. You can clean every part of your barbecue with this baking soda combination. Next, tear up some aluminum foil and wipe down the grill surfaces in a light circular motion to make it really clean. Spray the cooking oil on your grill after it has cooled and cleaned. This is vital because it prevents the grilling surface from rusting.

Phase 4: Don't think about the soap

Get the soap out and wash your shelves. You can combine a bit of soap and water in a bucket and use a tissue to clean your racks. This may seem like a lot of work, but if you spent a lot of money on your grill, you would certainly want it to be always perfect. It can make them last longer. On top of that, the soap's anti-bacterial properties will help kill off any bacteria that has been left on your food. The steel wool pads can also be used to remove some of the residual grime.

CHAPTER 3: WOOD PELLET

Wood Pellet Grill is a grill that has a set of digital controls that allows the user to control the cooking temperature. The grill uses a wood pellet fuel that causes it to smoke. The different types of wood pellets that the grill uses to smoke food are Apple wood pellets, Hickory wood pellets, Mesquite wood pellets, Cherry wood pellets, Alder wood pellets, and others. The wood pellets can be used to grill or smoke chicken, turkey, fish, oysters, cow beef, and many other types of poultry and other foods such as pizza and vegetables. The wood pellets are made using recycled wood materials. The food cooked on this grill has a consistent smoky flavor because of the wood pellets.

The wood pellet grill is easy to use and can be used indoors as well as outdoors. The user can check the temperature to make sure that the food is cooked perfectly. The grill is an automatic cooker, meaning that it conserves the heat that it produces and doesn't lose it.

One of the popular features of the wood pellet grill is the result of its smoke from the wood pellet. Many customers are amazed by the wood pellet smoker. There are hundreds of positive and amazing testimonials about the grill. It allows users to smoke and grill their food and the meat can be smoked for up to 15 hours. The grill is also very durable because its body is made of cast iron. It's easy to install and is easy to maintain.

Using a wood pellet smoker-grill has various advantages. It not only improves the taste of your meal, but it also has a number of other advantages. Here are some of the most important benefits of using a wood pellet smoker-grill!

Saves Time It goes without saying that anything that saves time and effort, particularly when it comes to cooking, is a good thing. One of the most major benefits of using wood pellet grills is the amount of time they save you. You can prepare smoked dishes considerably more quickly and with greater ease and comfort. You can immediately pre-heat them, saving you a lot of time.

For a long time, having a barbeque at home meant you had a stainless steel box connected to either your gas line or a propane tank, that works similar to your oven at home – it heats stainless steel rods via a fire in the bottom and then your food cooks on those rods. This is okay for basic cooking, but it doesn't impart any flavour and makes it incredibly easy to burn your food. It is also true than when cooking this way, you need to add lots of oil to your food to prevent it from sticking, thus making what was a healthy dinner of grilled fish and vegetables, less healthy.

In addition, with a traditional grill, there is very little control over what parts of your grill will get the hottest, and virtually impossible to control flare ups of hot spots caused by fat dripping down from the surface to the fire raging below. Even on the lowest setting, it is possible (and even likely) to dry out lean meats using this traditional grill.

If you're someone who had desired real barbeque flavour from your outdoor cooking experience, you may have switched from this outdated model to a charcoal grill... which is one step better but you will still run into the same problems with hot spots and having very little control over the heat distribution within your grill. A charcoal grill does indeed impart the smoky flavour you are craving if you're a barbeque enthusiast but is fairly high maintenance – they take a long time to heat up and then it is very difficult to maintain the same temperature over the course of a few hours. They take constant attention to keep the embers burning and then you have to deal with ash and dirty coals.

If you're someone who doesn't like to create a massive mess to clean up every time you cook, a charcoal barbeque is definitely not for you. But, you might have considered an electric smoker. These are great for keeping mess to a minimum but the flavour you'll achieve with these machines in nothing compared to the real thing. Most electric smokers on the market reach a maximum temperature of 225F which is not nearly enough heat to penetrate past the surface of a large cut of meat. The flavour can also become artificial or even chemical, which will miss the mark if you're trying to achieve true barbeque flavour.

Barbeque purists may take it one step further than coal and decide to burn their own hardwood in these grills. You'll run into similar problems here with making an absolute mess of your outdoor space, but you will also have to deal with fire hazards! When using raw hardwood, it's difficult to manage the amount of smoke, and you can wind up with a product that's too smoky to eat. You will have to make sure the wood you are using is completely dry (but not too dry,) and that it's not too green. Basically, it's a lot of guesswork. Even if you do get a great log of hardwood, it is difficult or near impossible to maintain the temperature once you hit it, or to control the rate of burning on the wood. You will end up opening the grill a lot, making the temperature fluctuate even more and wasting valuable time and heat.

When wood pellets entered the scene, everything changed for the home grilling enthusiast! A by-product of sawmills, these wood pellets are made from material that would otherwise go to waste (another reason to love this grill!) The by-product is ground up finely and then sends into a die that forms it into a small puck. The production technique does not require the use of glues or chemicals, making wood pellets fully natural and chemical-free. This is part of the reason they make food taste so good! The only added ingredient in wood pellets is a food-grade soybean oil, which is used to help form the ground up wood into a puck shape.

These tiny wood pellets burn just like a real log of hardwood but are much cleaner, more predictable and easier to maintain. You will find a variety of wood pellets at your local hardware store or you can order them in bulk online, but basically once you have your bag, you will just empty it into the hopper on the side of your Grill and away you go! There is no need to soak, stir or mix. The pellets provided by come in a variety of flavours which we will outline later, but just know that they are specifically designed to work with grills. They are developed in American mills and designed specifically for a remarkably consistent burn and result in perfect smoked results, every time! No fuss, no mess, just great authentic wood flavour.

CHAPTER 4: LAMB RECIPES

Lamb Kabobs

Preparation Time: 8 minutes

Cooking Time: 35 minutes

Servings: 6

Ingredients:

- 1 ¼ cup of olive oil
- 1 ¼ cup of sherry
- 1 or 2 red onions, medium
- 1 Heaped tablespoon of GMG Wild Game Rub
- 1 Heaped tablespoon of ground black pepper
- 5 Garlic cloves
- A leg of lamb

Directions:

1. Trim the fat from the lamb; then cut the lamb into cubes of about 1 ½ inch
2. Place in a large bowl; then sprinkle the rub over the meat and toss until your ingredients are very well combined
3. If you don't have an already prepared rub; just combine 1 teaspoon of brown sugar with 1 teaspoon of salt, ¼ teaspoon of turmeric; and ¼ teaspoon of ginger.
4. Peel the garlic and press to mash it
5. Chop the onion into rough dices in a small bowl; then chop a few sprigs of parsley
6. Add the liquid to the onion; then; mix and pour the mixture of the onion over the cubed lamb and place in the refrigerator for an overnight
7. Skewer the lamb chunks into wooden skewers
8. Grill the kabobs at a temperature of about 360-380° for about 25 to 35 minutes
9. Remove the meat from the grill
10. Serve and enjoy your dish!

Nutrition Calories: 200, Fat: 11g, Protein: 22g

Glorious Pork Back Ribs

Servings: 16

Cooking Time: 5 Hours

Ingredients:

- ¼ C. yellow honey mustard
- ¼ C. brown sugar
- 1/3 C. paprika
- ¼ C. garlic powder
- ¼ C. onion powder
- 2 tbsp. chipotle chili pepper flakes
- 1 tbsp. ground cumin
- Salt and freshly ground black pepper, to taste
- 2 tbsp. dried parsley flakes
- 8 lb. pork baby back ribs, silver skin removed

Directions:

1. In a bowl, add all ingredients except for ribs and mix well.

2. Rub the pork ribs with spice mixture generously.

3. Set the temperature of Grill to 200 degrees F and preheat with closed lid for 15 minutes, using charcoal.

4. Arrange the ribs onto the grill and cook for about 2 hours.

5. Remove the ribs from grill and wrap in heavy duty foil.

6. Cook for about 2 hours.

7. Remove the foil and cook for about 1 hour more.

8. Remove the ribs from grill and place onto a cutting board for about 10-15 minutes before serving.

Nutrition Info: Calories per serving: 659; Carbohydrates: 7.8g; Protein: 61.1g; Fat: 40.7g; Sugar: 4.4g; Sodium: 186mg; Fiber: 1.5g

Sriracha Lamb Chops

Preparation time: 15 minutes

Cooking time: 10 to 20 minute | **Serves** 4 to 6

½ cup rice wine vinegar

1 teaspoon liquid smoke

2 tablespoons extra-virgin olive oil

2 tablespoons dried minced onion

1 tablespoon chopped fresh mint

8 (4-ounce / 113-g) lamb chops

½ cup hot pepper jelly

1 tablespoon Sriracha

1 teaspoon salt

1 teaspoon freshly ground black pepper

1. In a small bowl, whisk together the rice wine vinegar, liquid smoke, olive oil, minced onion, and mint. Place the lamb chops in an aluminum roasting pan. Pour the marinade over the meat, turning to coat thoroughly. Cover with plastic wrap and marinate in the refrigerator for 2 hours.

2. Supply your smoker with wood pellets and follow the manufacturer's specific start-up procedure. Preheat, with the lid closed, to 165°F (74°C), or the "Smoke" setting.

3. On the stove top, in a small saucepan over low heat, combine the hot pepper jelly and Sriracha and keep warm.

4. When ready to cook the chops, remove them from the marinade and pat dry. Discard the marinade.

5. Season the chops with the salt and pepper, then place them directly on the grill grate, close the lid, and smoke for 5 minutes to "breathe" some smoke into them.

6. Remove the chops from the grill. Increase the pellet cooker temperature to 450°F (232°C), or the "High" setting. Once the grill is up to temperature, place the chops on the grill and sear, cooking for 2 minutes per side to achieve medium-rare chops. A meat thermometer inserted in the thickest part of the meat should read 145°F (63°C). Continue grilling, if necessary, to your desired doneness.

7. Serve the chops with the warm Sriracha pepper jelly on the side.

Herb-Crusted Rack Of Lamb With Parsley And Mint Chimichurri

(TOTAL COOK TIME 45 MINUTES)

INGREDIENTS FOR 4 SERVINGS

THE MEAT

· 1 rack of lamb, cleaned and Frenched

THE RUB

· 1 garlic clove, peeled and chopped

· Fresh rosemary, chopped – 1 teaspoon

· Fresh thyme, chopped – 1 teaspoon

· Canola oil – 1 tablespoon

· Salt and black pepper

THE CHIMICHURRI

· Fresh parsley, packed– ½ cup

· Fresh mint, packed – ½ cup

· 2 garlic cloves, peeled and chopped

· Extra-virgin olive oil – ½ cup

· Red wine vinegar - ⅛ cup

· Red pepper flakes – ½ teaspoon

· Kosher salt – ½ teaspoon

· Red onion, peeled and diced – ¼ cup

THE WOOD PELLET GRILL

· The grill grates will need to be cleaned and oiled

· Preheat your pellet grill until hot

· Choose your favorite wood pellets

METHOD

1. First, prepare the mint chimichurri. In a food blender, combine the parsley with the mint, garlic, oil, vinegar, red pepper flakes, and salt. On the pulse setting,

process until well chopped. You will need to scrape the sides of the bowl down using a spatula to ensure the mixture is chopped evenly.

2. Spoon the sauce into a bowl, and stir in the red onion.

3. Season with salt, vinegar, and red pepper flakes to taste.

4. Cover the bowl with kitchen wrap and transfer to the fridge until needed.

5. To prepare the rub in a bowl, combine the garlic with the thyme, rosemary, and oil.

6. Rub the mixture all over the meat and set aside to come to room temperature.

7. Season the lamb liberally with salt and black pepper.

8. First, bone side facing downwards, and second, rib bones facing away from the heat, sear the lamb. Do this with the lid closed over a moderate heat part of the grill for around 5 minutes on each side.

9. When grill marks have appeared on the meat, move the rack to indirect heat, and cook until the internal temperature registers 120-125°F (52-49°C) for medium-rare. Set the lamb aside to rest for 12-15 minutes on a chopping board. Tent the meat with aluminum foil.

10. Remove the foil and slice between the rib bones.

11. Season the lamb with salt, and serve with the chimichurri.

Crown Rack Of Lamb

Servings: 6

Cooking Time: 30 Minutes

Ingredients:

- 2 racks of lamb, frenched
- 1 tbsp garlic, crushed
- 1 tbsp rosemary, finely chopped
- 1/4 cup olive oil
- 2 feet twine

Directions:

1. Rinse the racks with cold water then pat them dry with a paper towel.

2. Lay the racks on a flat board then score between each bone, about 1/4 inch down.

3. In a mixing bowl, mix garlic, rosemary, and oil then generously brush on the lamb.

4. Take each lamb rack and bend it into a semicircle forming a crown-like shape.

5. Use the twine to wrap the racks about 4 times starting from the base to the top. Make sure you tie the twine tightly to keep the racks together.

6. Preheat the wood pellet to 400-450F then place the lamb racks on a baking dish. Plac ethe baing dish on the pellet grill.

7. Cook for 10 minutes then reduce temperature to 300F. cook for 20 more minutes or until the internal temperature reaches 130F.

8. Remove the lamb rack from the wood pellet and let rest for 15 minutes.

9. Serve when hot with veggies and potatoes. Enjoy.

Nutrition Info: Calories 390, Total fat 35g, Saturated fat 15g, Total Carbs 0g, Net Carbs 0g, Protein 17g, Sugar 0g, Fiber 0g, Sodium: 65mg.

Lamb Chops

Preparation Time: 10 minutes

Cooking Time: 12 minutes

Servings: 6

Ingredients:

- 6 (6-ounce) lamb chops
- 3 tablespoons olive oil
- Ground black pepper

Directions:

1. Preheat the pallet grill to 450 degrees F.
2. Coat the lamb chops with oil and then, season with salt and black pepper evenly.

3. Arrange the chops in a pallet grill grate and cook for about 4-6 minutes per side.

Nutrition:

Calories: 376 Cal Fat: 19.5 g

Carbohydrates: 0 g Protein: 47.8 g

Fiber: 0 g

Lamb Meatball And Tuscan Sauce Casserole

(TOTAL COOK TIME 2 HOURS 15 MINUTES)
INGREDIENTS FOR 2-4 SERVINGS
THE MEAT
· Ground lamb (1-lb, 0.5-kgs)
· Nonstick cooking spray
· Rotini noodles, cooked al dente, drained, to serve– 6 cups
· Parmesan cheese, freshly grated, to serve – ¼ cup
THE INGREDIENTS
· 1 egg, lightly beaten
· ½ onion, peeled and diced small
· 3 cloves garlic, peeled and minced
· Fresh parsley, minced – ¼ cup
· Kosher salt flakes – 1 ½ teaspoons
· Freshly ground black pepper – 1 teaspoon
· Oregano – 1 teaspoon
· Dried basil – 1 teaspoon
· Ground rosemary – ½ teaspoon
· Panko breadcrumbs – ¼ cup
THE SAUCE
· Olive oil – 2 tablespoons
· ½ onion, peeled and minced
· 2 garlic cloves, peeled and minced
· 8 plum tomatoes, peeled and chopped
· Tomato sauce – 2 cups
· Dried oregano – 1 teaspoon
· Dried basil - 1 teaspoon
· Ground rosemary – ½ teaspoon
· Dried black olives, pitted and chopped – ¼ cup
· Salt and freshly ground black pepper
THE WOOD PELLET GRILL
· Preheat your pellet grill to 325°F (163°C)
· Choose your favorite wood pellets
METHOD

1. For the sauce, in a skillet, heat the oil.
2. Add the onions to the pan and cook until softened and translucent.
3. Add the garlic to the pan and sauté for an additional 60 seconds.
4. Stir in the tomatoes, tomato sauce, oregano, basil, and rosemary. Simmer the mixture while occasionally stirring for 30 minutes. If the sauce is too thick, add a splash of water.
5. Stir in the olives, taste, and season with salt and black pepper.
6. To prepare the meatballs: In a large bowl, combine the ingredients (ground lamb, beaten egg, onion, garlic, parsley, kosher salt flakes, ground pepper, oregano, dried basil, ground rosemary, and breadcrumbs).
7. With damp hands, form the lamb mixture into even-sized meatballs, approximately 2-ins (5-cms) in diameter.
8. Over moderate to high heat, heat 2 tablespoons of oil.
9. In batches, if necessary, in the pan, fry the meatballs, rolling them as needed until browned all over. The internal temperature of the meatballs should register 350°F (177°C).
10. Cook the noodles until al dente, and drain well.
11. Using nonstick cooking spray, spritz a baking or casserole dish.
12. To assemble the casserole in a large bowl, toss the cooked pasta with 1 cup of the tomato sauce to coat evenly. Spoon the mixture into the prepared baking dish.
13. Arrange the meatballs around the top of the noodle and sauce mixture.
14. Pour the remaining sauce over the meatballs to cover.
15. Scatter over Parmesan cheese.
16. Transfer the baking dish to the middle of your wood pellet's lower rack, and bake for 30 minutes.
17. Enjoy.

Lamb with Pitas

Preparation time: 20 minute

Cooking time: 40 minute | **Serves** 4

1 pound (454 g) ground lamb

2 teaspoons salt

1 teaspoon freshly ground black pepper

2 tablespoons chopped fresh oregano

1 tablespoon minced garlic

1 tablespoon onion powder

4 to 6 pocketless pitas

Tzatziki sauce, for serving

1 tomato, chopped, for serving

1 small onion, thinly sliced, for serving

1. In a medium bowl, combine the lamb, salt, pepper, oregano, garlic, and onion powder; mix well. Cover with plastic wrap and refrigerate overnight.

2. Supply your smoker with wood pellets and follow the manufacturer's specific start-up procedure. Preheat, with the lid closed, to 300°F (149°C).

3. Remove the meat mixture from the refrigerator and, on a Frogmat or a piece of heavy-duty aluminum foil, roll and shape it into a rectangular loaf about 8 inches long by 5 inches wide.

4. Place the loaf directly on the grill, close the lid, and smoke for 35 minutes, or until a meat thermometer inserted in the center reads 155°F (68°C).

5. Remove the loaf from the heat and increase the temperature to 450°F (232°C).

6. Cut the loaf into ⅛-inch slices and place on a Frogmat or a piece of heavy-duty foil.

7. Return the meat (still on the Frogmat or foil) to the smoker, close the lid, and continue cooking for 2 to 4 minutes, or until the edges are crispy.

8. Warm the pitas in the smoker for a few minutes and serve with the lamb, tzatziki sauce, chopped tomato, and sliced onion.

Lamb Shank

Servings: 6
Cooking Time: 4 Hours
Ingredients:

- 8-ounce red wine
- 2-ounce whiskey
- 2 tablespoons minced fresh rosemary
- 1 tablespoon minced garlic
- Black pepper
- 6 (1¼-pound) lamb shanks

Directions:

1. In a bowl, add all ingredients except lamb shank and mix till well combined.
2. In a large resealable bag, add marinade and lamb shank.
3. Seal the bag and shake to coat completely.
4. Refrigerate for about 24 hours.
5. Preheat the pallet grill to 225 degrees F.
6. Arrange the leg of lamb in pallet grill and cook for about 4 hours.

Nutrition Info: Calories: 1507 Cal Fat: 62 g Carbohydrates: 68.7 g Protein:163.3 g Fiber: 6 g

Classic Lamb Chops

Preparation Time: 10 minutes

Cooking Time: 30 minutes

Servings: 4

Ingredients:

- Wood Pellet Flavor: Alder
- 4 (8-ounce) bone-in lamb chops
- 2 tablespoons olive oil
- 1 batch Rosemary-Garlic Lamb Seasoning

Directions:

1. Supply your smoker with wood pellets and follow the manufacturer's specific start-up procedure. Preheat the grill to 350°F. Close the lid

2. Rub the lamb generously with olive oil and coat them on both sides with the seasoning.

3. Put the chops directly on the grill grate and grill until their internal temperature reaches 145°F. Remove the lamb from the grill and serve immediately.

Nutrition: Calories: 50 Carbs: 4g Fiber: 2g Fat: 2.5g Protein: 2g

Grilled Lamb and Apricot Kabobs

Prep time: 15 minutes

Cook time: 8 to 10 minutes | **Serves** 4

½ cup olive oil

½ cup lemon juice

2 tablespoons minced fresh mint

1 tablespoon lemon zest

½ tablespoon finely chopped cilantro

½ tablespoon salt

2 teaspoons black pepper

1 teaspoon cumin

3 pounds (1.4 kg) boneless leg of lamb, cut into 2-inch cubes

15 whole dried apricots

2 whole red onions, cut into ⅛-inch thick

1. In a medium bowl, stir together the olive oil, lemon juice, mint, lemon zest, cilantro, salt, pepper and cumin. Add the lamb shoulder to the bowl and toss to coat. Set in the refrigerator and marinate overnight.

2. Remove the lamb from the marinade and thread lamb, apricots, and red onion alternately until the skewer is full.

3. When ready to cook, set temperature to 400°F (204°C) and preheat, lid closed for 15 minutes.

4. Lay the skewers on the grill grate and cook for 8 to 10 minutes, or until the onions are lightly browned and the lamb is cooked to the desired temperature.

5. Remove the skewers from the grill and serve immediately.

Lamb Skewers

Servings: 6

Cooking Time: 8-12 Minutes

Ingredients:

- One lemon, juiced
- Two crushed garlic cloves
- Two chopped red onions
- One t. chopped thyme
- Pepper
- Salt
- One t. oregano
- 1/3 c. oil
- ½ t. cumin
- Two pounds cubed lamb leg

Directions:

1. Refrigerate the chunked lamb.

2. The remaining ingredients should be mixed together. Add in the meat. Refrigerate overnight.

3. Pat the meat dry and thread onto some metal or wooden skewers. Wooden skewers should be soaked in water.

4. Add wood pellets to your smoker and follow your cooker's startup procedure. Preheat your smoker, with your lid closed, until it reaches 450.

5. Grill, covered, for 4-6 minutes on each side.

6. Serve.

Nutrition Info: Calories: 201 Cal Fat: 9 g Carbohydrates: 3 g Protein: 24 g Fiber: 1 g

Leg of a Lamb

Preparation Time: 10 minutes

Cooking Time: 2 hours and 30 minutes

Servings: 10

Ingredients:

- 1 (8-ounce) package softened cream cheese
- ¼ cup cooked and crumbled bacon
- 1 seeded and chopped jalapeño pepper
- 1 tablespoon crushed dried rosemary; 2 teaspoons garlic powder
- 1 teaspoon onion powder; 1 teaspoon paprika
- 1 teaspoon cayenne pepper; Salt, to taste
- 1 (4-5-pound) butterflied leg of lamb; 2-3 tablespoons olive oil

Directions:

1. For filling in a bowl, add all ingredients and mix till well combined.
2. For spice mixture in another small bowl, mix all ingredients.
3. Place the leg of lamb onto a smooth surface. Sprinkle the inside of the leg with some spice mixture.
4. Place filling mixture over the inside surface evenly. Roll the leg of lamb tightly and with a butcher's twine, tie the roll to secure the filling
5. Coat the outer side of the roll with olive oil evenly and then sprinkle with spice mixture. Preheat the pallet grill to 225-240 degrees F.
6. Arrange the leg of lamb in a pallet grill and cook for about 2-2½ hours. Remove the leg of lamb from the pallet grill and transfer it onto a cutting board. Cover leg loosely and transfer onto a cutting board for about 20-25 minutes before slicing with a piece of foil.
7. With a sharp knife, cut the leg of lamb in desired sized slices and serve.

Nutrition: Calories: 715Cal Fat: 38.9g Carbohydrates: 2.2g Protein: 84.6 g

Smoked Lamb Meatballs

Servings: 5
Cooking Time: 1 Hour
Ingredients:

· 1 lb lamb shoulder, ground
· 3 garlic cloves, finely diced
· 3 tbsp shallot, diced
· 1 tbsp salt
· 1 egg
· 1/2 tbsp pepper
· 1/2 tbsp cumin
· 1/2 tbsp smoked paprika
· 1/4 tbsp red pepper flakes
· 1/4 tbsp cinnamon, ground
· 1/4 cup panko breadcrumbs

Directions:

1. Set the wood pellet smoker to 250F using a fruitwood.
2. In a mixing bowl, combine all meatball ingredients until well mixed.
3. Form small-sized balls and place them on a baking sheet. Place the baking sheet in the smoker and smoke until the internal temperature reaches 160F.
4. Remove from the smoker and serve. Enjoy.

Nutrition Info: Calories 73, Total fat 5.2g, Saturated fat 1.6g, Total Carbs 1.5g, Net Carbs 1.4g, Protein 4.9g, Sugar 0g, Fiber 0.1g, Sodium: 149mg, Potassium 72mg

Lemon Mint Smoked Lamb Leg with Apricot Honey Glaze

(Cooking Time 7 hours 10 minutes)
Ingredients for 10 servings
· Boneless lamb leg (5-lb., 2.3-kg.)
The Marinade
· Lemon juice - 1 cup
· Grated lemon zest - 1 tablespoon
· Diced fresh mint leaves - ¼ cup
· Chopped fresh basil - 3 tablespoons
· Oregano - 2 tablespoons
· White vinegar - ¼ cup
· Olive oil - 2 tablespoons
· Minced garlic - 2 tablespoons
The Glaze
· Apricot jam - 3 tablespoons
· Honey - 2 tablespoons
· Lemon juice - 1 tablespoon
· Olive oil - 2 tablespoons
· Salt - a pinch
· Black pepper - ½ teaspoon
The Spray
· Apple cider vinegar - 1 cup
The Heat
· Cherry wood pellet
Method

1. Add the entire marinade mixture--lemon juice, lemon zest, mint leaves, basil, oregano, white vinegar, olive oil, and minced garlic to a container with a lid. Stir until combined.
2. Score the lamb leg at several places and put it into the marinade mixture.
3. Marinate the lamb leg for at least 4 hours and store it in the fridge to keep the lamb leg fresh.

4. After 4 hours, take the marinated lamb leg out of the marinade and thaw it at room temperature.

5. Next, plug the wood pellet smoker then fill the hopper with the wood pellet. Turn the switch on and set the wood pellet smoker for indirect heat.

6. Adjust the temperature to 250°F (121°C) and let the wood pellet smoker reaches the desired temperature.

7. Wait until the wood pellet smoker reaches the desired temperature and place the lamb leg in it.

8. Smoked the lamb leg for 7 hours and spray apple cider vinegar over the lamb leg once every hour.

9. Regularly check the internal temperature of the smoked lamb leg and once it reaches 195°F (91°C), remove it from the wood pellet smoker.

10. Quickly combine the apricot jam with honey, lemon juice, olive oil, salt, and pepper. Stir until incorporated.

11. Baste the glaze mixture over the smoked lamb leg and repeat it until the glaze mixture is completely applied.

12. Once it is done, remove the smoked lamb leg from the wood pellet smoker and transfer it to a serving dish.

13. Serve and enjoy!

Grilled Lamb Leg

Prep time: 10 minutes

Cook time: 30 to 40 minutes | **Serves** 8

5 pounds (2.3 kg) leg of lamb, butterflied and boneless

1 whole onion, sliced into rings

Marinade:

1 whole lemon, juiced and rinds reserved

4 cloves garlic, minced

1 cup olive oil

¼ cup red wine vinegar

2½ teaspoons minced rosemary

1 teaspoon thyme

1 teaspoon salt

1 teaspoon ground black pepper

1. In a mixing bowl, whisk together all the ingredients for the marinade.

2. Remove any netting from the lamb and place into a large resealable plastic bag. Pour the marinade into the bag and add the onion. Massage the bag to distribute the marinade and herbs. Refrigerate for several hours or overnight.

3. Remove the lamb from the marinade and pat dry with paper towels. Discard the marinade.

4. When ready to cook, set the to High and preheat, lid closed for 15 minutes.

5. Arrange the lamb on the grill grate, fat-side down. Grill for 30 to 40 minutes per side, or until the internal temperature reaches 135°F (57°C) for medium-rare.

6. Let the lamb leg cool for 5 minutes before slicing. Serve warm.

Elegant Lamb Chops

Servings: 4

Cooking Time: 30 Minutes

Ingredients:

- 4 lamb shoulder chops
- 4 C. buttermilk
- 1 C. cold water
- ¼ C. kosher salt
- 2 tbsp. olive oil
- 1 tbsp. Texas-style rub

Directions:

1. In a large bowl, add buttermilk, water and salt and stir until salt is dissolved.

2. Add chops and coat with mixture evenly.

3. Refrigerate for at least 4 hours.

4. Remove the chops from bowl and rinse under cold running water.

5.   Coat the chops with olive oil and then sprinkle with rub evenly.

6.   Set the temperature of Grill to 240 degrees F and preheat with closed lid for 15 minutes, using charcoal.

7.   Arrange the chops onto grill and cook for about 25-30 minutes or until desired doneness.

8.   Meanwhile, preheat the broiler of oven. Grease a broiler pan.

9.   Remove the chops from grill and place onto the prepared broiler pan.

10. Transfer the broiler pan into the oven and broil for about 3-5 minutes or until browned.

11. Remove the chops from oven and serve hot.

Nutrition Info: Calories per serving: 414; Carbohydrates: 11.7g; Protein: 5.6g; Fat: 22.7g; Sugar: 11.7g; Sodium: 7000mg; **Fiber:** 0g

Coffee Rub Smoked Lamb Shank with Coconut Sugar

(Cooking Time 5 hours 10 minutes)

Ingredients for 10 servings

·   Lamb shank (6-lb., 2.7-kg.)

The Brine

·   Cold water - 1 quart
·   Kosher salt - 3 tablespoons
·   Coconut sugar - ¼ cup
·   Peppercorns - 2 tablespoons
·   Allspice - 1 teaspoon
·   Garlic powder - 1 tablespoon
·   Dried thyme - 1 teaspoon
·   Ground clove - 4
·   Bay leaves - 2

The Rub

·   Ground black coffee - ¼ cup
·   Kosher salt - 1 ½ teaspoon
·   Smoked paprika - 2 tablespoons
·   Paprika - 1 tablespoon
·   Coconut sugar - ¼ cup
·   Ground cumin - 1 tablespoon
·   Ground mustard - 1 tablespoon
·   Coriander - 1 tablespoon
·   Onion powder - 2 tablespoons
·   Garlic powder - 2 tablespoons
·   Olive oil - ¼ cup

The Spray

·   Apple cider vinegar - ½ cup
·   Apple juice - ½ cup

The Heat

·   A mix of Hickory and Apple wood pellet

Method

1.   Pour cold water into a container with a lid.

2.   Add kosher salt, coconut sugar, peppercorns, allspice, garlic powder, dried thyme, ground clove, and bay leaves to the brine. Stir until dissolved.

3.   Put the lamb shank into the brine mixture and soak it overnight. Store it in the fridge to keep the lamb shank fresh.

4.   On the next day, remove the lamb shank from the fridge and take it out of the brine. Thaw it at room temperature.

5.   Wash and rinse the lamb shank then pat it dry.

6.   Next, mix the rub ingredients--ground black coffee, kosher salt, smoked paprika, paprika, coconut sugar, ground cumin, mustard, coriander, onion powder, and garlic powder.

7.   Drizzle olive oil over the spices and mix until becoming a paste.

8.   Apply the spice mixture over the lamb shank and set aside.

9.   After that, plug the wood pellet smoker then fill the hopper with the wood pellet. Turn the switch on and set the wood pellet smoker for indirect heat.

10. Adjust the temperature to 250°F (121°C) and let the wood pellet smoker reaches the desired temperature.

11. Wait until the wood pellet smoker reaches the desired temperature and place the seasoned lamb shank on the grill grate inside the wood pellet smoker. Smoke the lamb shank for 5 hours.

12. Spray apple juice and apple cider vinegar over the lamb shank and repeat it once every 30 minutes to an hour.

13. Once the internal temperature of the smoked lamb shank reaches 190°F (88°C), take the smoked lamb shank out of the wood pellet smoker and transfer it to a serving dish.

14. Serve and enjoy.

Roasted Leg of Lamb

Preparation Time: 10 minutes
Cooking Time: 2 hours
Servings: 6
Ingredients:

·   2 teaspoons extra virgin olive oil

·   1 tablespoon crushed garlic

·   7 pounds bone-in leg of lamb

·   4 cloves of garlic, sliced lengthwise

·   4 sprig rosemary, cut into 1-inch pieces

·   2 lemons, sliced

·   Salt and pepper to taste

Directions:

1.   Combine olive oil and crushed garlic. Rub the mixture on the leg of the lamb. Make small perforations in the lamb using a sharp knife and stuff the slivered garlic and rosemary sprigs. Zest and juice the lemons and sprinkle over the lamb. Season with salt and pepper to taste. When ready to cook, fire the Grill to 500oF. Use desired wood pellets when cooking. Close the lid and preheat for 15 minutes. Place the seasoned leg of lamb on the grill grate and reduce the grill to 350oF. Cook for 2 hours. Let the lamb rest for 15 minutes before carving.

Nutrition: Calories per serving: 439; Protein: 74.1g; Carbs: 2g; Fat: 14.9g Sugar: 0.6g

Rosemary Lamb Seasoning

Prep time: 5 minutes
Cook time: 0 minute | Makes 2 tablespoons

2 teaspoons dried rosemary leaves

2 teaspoons coarse kosher salt

1 teaspoon garlic powder

1 teaspoon freshly ground black pepper

½ teaspoon onion powder

½ teaspoon dried minced onion

1.   In a small airtight container or zip-top bag, combine the rosemary, salt, garlic powder, black pepper, onion powder, and minced onion.

2.   Close the container and shake to mix. Unused seasoning will keep in an airtight container for months.

Bourbon Molasses Brine Smoked Lamb Rack with Brown Sugar Glaze

(Cooking Time 3 hours 10 minutes)

Ingredients for 10 servings

·   Lamb rack (6-lb., 2.7-kg.)

The Brine

·   Cold water - 1 quart

·   Bourbon - ½ cup

·   Kosher salt - ¼ cup

·   Molasses - ¼ cup

·   Brown sugar - 2 tablespoons

·   Worcestershire sauce - 2 tablespoons

·   Vanilla extract - 2 teaspoons

The Glaze

·   Brown sugar - ½ cup

- Unsalted butter - 1 tablespoon
- Chicken broth - ¼ cup
- Soy sauce - 1 tablespoon
- Dijon mustard - 1 tablespoon
- Kosher salt - A pinch
- Ground nutmeg - ¼ teaspoon
- Ground cinnamon - ¼ teaspoon
- Dried thyme - ½ teaspoon
- Dried rosemary - ½ teaspoon
- Rum - 2 tablespoons

The Heat

- Apple wood pellet

Method

1. Add bourbon, kosher salt, molasses, brown sugar, Worcestershire sauce, and vanilla extract to the cold water. Stir until dissolved.

2. Put the lamb rack into the brine mixture and soak it overnight. Store it in the fridge to keep the lamb rack fresh.

3. On the next day, remove the lamb rack from the fridge and take it out of the brine. Thaw it at room temperature.

4. Wash and rinse the lamb rack then pat it dry.

5. Next, plug the wood pellet smoker then fill the hopper with the wood pellet. Turn the switch on and set the wood pellet smoker for indirect heat.

6. Adjust the temperature to 250°F (121°C) and let the wood pellet smoker reaches the desired temperature.

7. Wait until the wood pellet smoker reaches the desired temperature and arrange the lamb rack on the grill grate inside the wood pellet smoker. Smoke the lamb rack for an hour.

8. In the meantime, place brown sugar, butter, and chicken broth in a saucepan and bring it to a simmer.

9. Season the glaze mixture with soy sauce, Dijon mustard, kosher salt, ground nutmeg, ground cinnamon, dried thyme, dried rosemary, and rum. Stir well.

10. After an hour of smoking, baste the glaze mixture over the lamb rack and continue smoking for another 2 hours.

11. Once the internal temperature of the smoked lamb rack reaches 140°F (60°C), remove the smoked lamb rack from the wood pellet smoker and transfer it to a serving dish.

12. Baste the remaining glaze mixture over the smoked lamb rack and serve.

13. Enjoy!

Wood Pellet Smoked Lamb Shoulder

Servings: 7

Cooking Time: 1hour 30 Minutes;

Ingredients:

- For Smoked Lamb Shoulder
- 5 lb lamb shoulder, boneless and excess fat trimmed
- 2 tbsp kosher salt
- 2 tbsp black pepper
- 1 tbsp rosemary, dried
- The Injection
- 1 cup apple cider vinegar
- The Spritz
- 1 cup apple cider vinegar
- 1 cup apple juice

Directions:

1. Preheat the wood pellet smoker with a water pan to 225 F.

2. Rinse the lamb in cold water then pat it dry with a paper towel. Inject vinegar to the lamb.

3. Pat the lamb dry again and rub with oil, salt black pepper and rosemary. Tie with kitchen twine.

4. Smoke uncovered for 1 hour then spritz after every 15 minutes until the internal temperature reaches 195 F.

5.   Remove the lamb from the grill and place it on a platter. Let cool before shredding it and enjoying it with your favorite side.

Nutrition Info: Calories 243, Total fat 19g, Saturated fat 8g, Total Carbs 0g, Net Carbs 0g, Protein 17g, Sugar 0g, Fiber 1g, Sodium: 63mg, Potassium 234mg

Brown Sugar Lamb Chops

Preparation Time: 2 hours

Cooking Time: 10-15 minutes

Servings: 4

Ingredients:

- Pepper; Salt
- One t. garlic powder
- Two t. tarragon
- One t. cinnamon
- ¼ c. brown sugar
- 4 lamb chops
- Two t. ginger

Directions:

1. Combine the salt, garlic powder, pepper, cinnamon, tarragon, ginger, and sugar. Coat the lamb chops in the mixture and chill for two hours.
2. Add wood pellets to your smoker and follow your cooker's startup procedure. Preheat your smoker, with your lid closed, until it reaches 450.
3. Place the chops on the grill, cover, and smoke for 10-15 minutes per side. Serve.

Nutrition:

- Calories: 210 Cal
- Fat: 11 g
- Carbohydrates: 3 g
- Protein: 25 g
- Fiber: 1 g

Braised Lamb Shank

Preparation time: 15 minutes

Cooking Time: 4 hours

Servings: 4-6

Ingredients:

- 4 whole Lamb, shanks
- 1 cup red wine
- Prime Rib Rub
- 4 sprig fresh thyme or rosemary
- 1 cup beef broth

Instructions:

1. Start seasoning the lamb shanks thoroughly with Prime Rib Rub.

2. When you are ready for cooking, set the temperature to approximately 225F, add the wood pallets and let it preheat, make sure to close the lid for approximately 15 minutes. For maximum flavor, use may like to use the Super Smoke option.

3. Now, spread the shanks on grill and cook them approximately for 20 minutes or the exterior turned brown.

4. Carefully, place the shanks to oven and pour the beef broth, red wine, and the add herbs. Cover with air tight lid, and then place it back on grill, make use to reduce the temperature approximately to 332F.

5. Now, braise the lamb around 3-4 hours.

6. Now, transfer the lamb carefully along with any of accumulated juices to flat platter or shallow plates.

Recommended Side Dish: Peas in Mint Cream

Alcoholic Drinks to accompany: red wines

Nutrition: Calories: 14, Fat: 0g, Carbs: 2.55g, Protein: 1.16g, Sodium: 16mg

Smoked Lamb Meatballs

Preparation Time: 10 Minutes

Cooking Time: 1 Hour

Servings: 20 Meatballs

Ingredients:

- 1 lb. lamb shoulder, ground
- 3 garlic cloves, finely diced
- 3 tbsp. shallot, diced
- 1 tbsp. salt
- 1 egg
- ½ tbsp. pepper
- ½ tbsp. cumin
- ½ tbsp. smoked paprika
- ¼ tbsp. red pepper flakes
- ¼ tbsp. cinnamon
- ¼ cup panko breadcrumbs

Directions:

1. Set your to 250°F.

2. Combine all the ingredients in a small bowl then mix thoroughly using your hands.

3. Form golf ball-sized meatballs and place them on a baking sheet.

4. Place the baking sheet in the smoker and smoke until the internal temperature reaches 160°F.

5. Remove the meatballs from the smoker and serve when hot.

Nutrition:

- Calories: 93
- Fat: 5.9g
- Carbs: 4.8g
- Protein: 5g
- Sugars: 0.3g
- Fiber: 0.3g
- Sodium: 174.1mg
- Potassium: 82.8mg

Whole Rack of Lamb

Preparation time: 10 minutes

Cooking Time: 30 minutes

Servings: 4-6

Ingredients:

- 8 cloves of garlic
- 2-pound Lamb, Racks
- 1 bunch fresh thyme
- 2 teaspoon extra-virgin olive oil
- 1 teaspoon sherry vinegar
- 1 tablespoon kosher salt

Instructions:

1.Start the process by putting fresh garlic and thyme leaves in food processor along with salt, olive oil & vinegar. Thoroughly rub this prepared paste all over the lamb.

2.When you are ready for cooking, set the temperature to approximately 450F, add the wood pallets and let it preheat, make sure to close the lid for approximately 15 minutes. For maximum flavor, use may would like to use the Super Smoke option.

3.Spread the rack of lamb with fat-side facing down grill and then cook it for around 20 minutes. Now flip to the other side so that the fat side is facing up now and then cook it for another 10 minutes.

4.Let the lamb rests for at least 10 minutes. Slice them carefully in chops & serve.

Recommended Side Dish: Peas in Mint Cream

Alcoholic Drinks to accompany: Scotch

Nutrition: Calories: 2394, Fat: 156.59g, Carbs: 7.98g, Protein: 224.01g, Sodium: 7748mg

Grilled Lamb Chops with Rosemary

Preparation Time: 10 minutes

Cooking Time: 12 minutes

Servings: 4

Ingredients:

- ½ cup extra virgin olive oil
- ¼ cup coarsely chopped onion
- 2 cloves of garlic, minced
- 2 tablespoons soy sauce
- 2 tablespoons balsamic vinegar
- 1 tablespoon fresh rosemary
- 2 teaspoons Dijon mustard
- 1 teaspoon Worcestershire sauce
- Salt and pepper to taste
- 4 lamb chops (8 ounces each)

Directions:

1. Heat oil in a saucepan over medium flame and sauté the onion and garlic until fragrant. Place in a food processor together with the soy sauce, vinegar, rosemary, mustard, Worcestershire sauce, salt, and pepper. Pulse until smooth. Set aside.

2. Fire the Grill to 5000F. Use desired wood pellets when cooking. Close the lid and preheat for 15 minutes. Brush the lamb chops on both sides with the paste. Place on the grill grates and cook for 6 minutes per side or until the internal temperature reaches 1350F for medium-rare. Serve with the paste if you have leftovers.

Nutrition: Calories per serving: 442; Protein: 16.7g; Carbs: 6.1g; Fat:38.5 g Sugar: 3.7g

- 1 tbsp kosher salt
- 1 tbsp black pepper
- 1 tbsp smoked paprika
- 1 tbsp garlic powder
- 1 tbsp rosemary, dried
- 1 tbsp onion powder
- 1tbsp cumin
- 1/2 tbsp cayenne pepper
- Roasted Carrots
- 1 bunch rainbow carrots
- Olive oil
- Salt
- pepper

Directions:

1. Heat the wood pellet grill to 375 F.

2. Trim any excess fat from the lamb.

3. Combine all the rub ingredients and rub all over the lamb. Place the lamb on the grill and smoke for 2 hours.

4. Toss the carrots in oil, salt, and pepper then add to the grill after the lamb has cooked for 1-1/2 hour.

5. Cook until the roast internal temperature reaches 135 F. Remove the lamb from the grill and cover with foil. Let rest for 30 minutes.

6. Remove the carrots from the grill once soft and serve with the lamb. Enjoy.

Nutrition Info: Calories 257, Total fat 8g, Saturated fat 2g, Total Carbs 6g, Net Carbs 5g, Protein 37g, Sugar 3g, Fiber 1g, Sodium: 431mg, Potassium 666mg

Wood Pellet Grilled Aussie Leg Of Lamb Roast

Servings: 8

Cooking Time: 2 Hours

Ingredients:

- 5 lb Aussie leg of lamb, boneless
- Smoked Paprika Rub
- 1 tbsp raw sugar

Simple Grilled Lamb Chops

Preparation Time: 10 Minutes

Cooking Time: 20 Minutes

Servings: 6

Ingredients:

- ¼ cup white vinegar, distilled

- 2 tbsp. olive oil
- 2 tbsp. salt
- ½ tbsp. black pepper
- 1 tbsp. minced garlic
- 1 onion, thinly sliced
- 2 lb. lamb chops

Directions:

1. In a resealable bag, mix vinegar, oil, salt, black pepper, garlic, and sliced onions until all salt has dissolved.

2. Add the lamb and toss until evenly coated. Place in a fridge to marinate for 2 hours.

3. Preheat your grill.

4. Remove the lamb from the resealable bag and leave any onion that is stuck on the meat. Use an aluminum foil to cover any exposed bone ends.

5. Grill until the desired doneness is achieved. Serve and enjoy when hot.

Nutrition:

- Calories: 519
- Fat: 44.8g
- Carbs: 2.3g
- Protein: 25g
- Sugars: 0.8g
- Fiber: 0.4g
- Sodium: 861mg
- Potassium: 358.6mg

Wood Pellet Grill Dale's Lamb

Servings: 8
Cooking Time: 50 Minutes
Ingredients:
- 2/3 cup lemon juice
- 1/2 cup brown sugar
- 1/4 cup Dijon mustard
- 1/4 cup soy sauce
- 1/4 cup olive oil
- 2 garlic cloves, minced
- 1 piece ginger root, freshly sliced

- 1 tbsp salt
- 1/2 tbsp black pepper, ground
- 5 lb leg of lamb, butterflied

Directions:

1. In a mixing bowl, mix lemon juice, sugar, dijon mustard, sauce, oil, garlic cloves, ginger root, salt, and pepper.

2. Place the lamb in a dish and pour the seasoning mixture over it. Cover the dish and put in a fridge to marinate for 8 hours.

3. Preheat a wood pellet grill to medium heat. Drain the marinade from the dish and bring it to boil in a small saucepan.

4. Reduce heat and let simmer while whisking occasionally.

5. Oil the grill grate and place the lamb on it. Cook for 50 minutes or until the internal temperature reaches 145 F while turning occasionally.

6. Slice the lamb and cover with the marinade. Serve and enjoy.

Nutrition Info: Calories 451, Total fat 27.2g, Saturated fat 9.5g, Total Carbs 17.8g, Net Carbs 17.6g, Protein 32.4g, Sugar 14g, Fiber 0.2g, Sodium: 1015mg, Potassium 455mg.

Greek Lamb Leg

Preparation Time: 15 minutes
Cooking Time: 25 minutes
Servings: 12
Ingredients:
- 2 tablespoons fresh rosemary, chopped
- 1 tablespoon ground thyme
- 5 garlic cloves, minced
- 2 tablespoons salt
- 1 tablespoon fresh ground pepper
- Butcher's string
- 1 whole boneless (6-8 pounds) leg of lamb
- ¼ cup extra virgin olive oil
- 1 cup red wine vinegar
- ½ cup canola oil

Directions:

1. Take a small bowl and add rosemary, thyme, garlic, salt, pepper and keep it on the side

2.   Use butcher's string and tie leg of lamb in the shape of the roast
3.   Rub lamb generously with olive oil mix and spice mix
4.   Transfer to plate and cover with plastic wrap
5.   Chill for 4 hours
6.   Remove lamb from the fridge
7.   Preheat your Smoker to 325 degrees F
8.   Take a small bowl and add red wine vinegar and canola oil
9.   Place lamb directly on the grill and close lid, smoke for 20-25 minutes per pound, making sure to keep basing after every 30 minutes
10. Once the thickest part reaches 145 degrees F, the lamb is ready
11. Let it rest for a while and serve
12. Enjoy!
Nutrition Calories: 590 Fats: 50g Carbs: 3g Fiber: 1g

Easy-to-prepare Lamb Chops

Servings: 6
Cooking Time: 12 Minutes
Ingredients:
·   6 (6-oz.) lamb chops
·   3 tbsp. olive oil
·   Salt and freshly ground black pepper, to taste
Directions:
1.   Set the temperature of Grill to 450 degrees F and preheat with closed lid for 15 minutes.
2.   Coat the lamb chops with oil and then, season with salt and black pepper evenly.
3.   Arrange the chops onto the grill and cook for about 4-6 minutes per side.
4.   Remove the chops from grill and serve hot.
Nutrition Info: Calories per serving: 376; Carbohydrates: 0g; Protein: 47.8g; Fat: 19.5g; Sugar: 0g; Sodium: 156mg; Fiber: 0g

Grilled Leg of Lamb Steak

Preparation Time: 10 Minutes
Cooking Time: 10 Minutes
Servings: 4
Ingredients:
·   4 reaches lamb steaks, bone-in
·   1/4 cup olive oil
·   Four garlic cloves, minced
·   1 tbsp rosemary, freshly chopped
·   Salt and pepper to taste
Directions:
1.   Arrange the steak in a dish in a single layer. Cover the meat with oil, garlic, fresh rosemary, salt, and pepper.
2.   Flip the meat to coat on all sides and let it marinate for 30 minutes.
3.   Preheat your and lightly oil the grates. Cook the meat on the grill until well browned on both sides, and the internal temperature reaches 140F. Serve and enjoy.
Nutrition:
·   Calories 327.3
·   Total fat 21.9g
·   Total carbs 1.7g
·   Protein 29.6g
·   Sugars 0.1g
·   Fiber 0.2g
·   Sodium 112.1mg
·   Potassium 409.8mg

Lamb Ribs Rack

Servings: 2
Cooking Time: 2 Hours
Ingredients:
·   2 tablespoons fresh sage
·   2 tablespoons fresh rosemary
·   2 tablespoons fresh thyme
·   2 peeled garlic cloves
·   1 tablespoon honey
·   Black pepper
·   ¼ cup olive oil
·   1 (1½-pound) trimmed rack lamb ribs
Directions:
1.   Combine all ingredients. While motor is running, slowly add oil and pulse till a smooth paste is formed. Coat the rib rack with paste

generously and refrigerate for about 2 hours. Preheat the pallet grill to 225 degrees F. Arrange the rib rack in pallet grill and cook for about 2 hours.

2. Remove the rib rack from pallet grill and transfer onto a cutting board for about 10-15 minutes before slicing. With a sharp knife, cut the rib rack into equal sized individual ribs and serve.

Nutrition Info: Calories: 826 Cal Fat: 44.1 g Carbohydrates: 5.4 g Protein: 96.3 g Fiber: 1 g

Garlic Rack Lamb

Preparation Time: 45 Minutes
Cooking Time: 3 Hours
Servings: 4
Ingredients:
· Lamb Rack; Basil – 1 teaspoon
· Oregano – 1 teaspoon; Peppermill – 10 cranks
· Marsala wine – 3 oz.; Cram Sherry – 3 oz.
· Olive oil; Madeira wine – 3 oz
· Balsamic vinegar – 3 oz.; Rosemary – 1 teaspoon

Directions:
1. Add all of the ingredients into a zip bag the mix well to form an emulsion.
2. Place the rack lamb into the bag the release all of the air as you rub the marinade all over the lamb.
3. Let it stay in the bag for about 45 minutes
4. Get the wood pellet grill preheated to 250F, cook the lamb for 3 hours as you turn on both sides.
5. Ensure that the internal temperature is at 165F before removing it from the grill.
6. Allow to cool for a few minutes, then serve and enjoy.

Nutrition:
· Calories: 291 Cal
· Protein: 26 g
· Fat: 21 g

Spicy & Tangy Lamb Shoulder

Preparation Time: 45 minutes
Servings: 6
Cooking Time: 5¾ Hours
Ingredients:
• 1 (5-lb.) bone-in lamb shoulder, trimmed
• 3-4 tbsp. Moroccan seasoning
• 2 tbsp. olive oil
• 1 C. water
• ¼ C. apple cider vinegar

Instructions:
1. Set the temperature of Grill to 275 degrees F and preheat with closed lid for 15 minutes, using charcoal.
2. Coat the lamb shoulder with oil evenly and then rub with Moroccan seasoning generously.
3. Place the lamb shoulder onto the grill and cook for about 45 minutes.
4. In a food-safe spray bottle, mix vinegar and water.
5. Spray the lamb shoulder with vinegar mixture evenly.
6. Cook for about 4-5 hours, spraying with vinegar mixture after every 20 minutes.
7. Remove the lamb shoulder from grill and place onto a cutting board for about 20 minutes before slicing.
8. With a sharp knife, cut the lamb shoulder in desired sized slices and serve.

Nutrition: Calories: 563, Carbohydrates: 3.1g, Protein: 77.4g, Fat: 25.2g, Sugar: 1.4g, Sodium: 1192mg, Fiber: 0g

Spicy Chinese Cumin Lamb Skewers

Preparation Time: 20 minutes
Cooking Time: 6 minutes
Servings: 10
Ingredients:
· 1 lb. lamb shoulder, cut into 1/2-inch pieces
· 10 skewers
· 2 tbsp ground cumin
· 2 tbsp red pepper flakes
· 1 tbsp salt
Intolerances:
· Gluten-Free

· Egg-Free
· Lactose-Free

Directions:
1. Thread the lamb pieces onto skewers.
2. Preheat the wood pellet grill to medium heat and lightly oil the grill grate.
3. Place the skewers on the grill grate and cook while turning occasionally. Sprinkle cumin, pepper flakes, and salt every time you turn the skewer.
4. Cook for 6 minutes or until nicely browned. Serve and enjoy.

Nutrition:
Calories: 77 Fat: 5g
Carbs: 2g Protein: 6g

Pistachio Roasted Lamb

Preparation Time: 20 minutes
Cooking Time: 40 minutes
Servings: 6
Ingredients:
Pellets: Cherry
· 1 tablespoon vegetable oil
· 2 lamb racks
· 3 carrots, peeled and chopped
· 1 lb. potatoes
· 1 tablespoon olive oil
· 1/2 teaspoon salt
· 1/2 teaspoon pepper
· 1 clove garlic, minced
· 2 teaspoons thyme
· 3 cups pistachios
· 2 tablespoons breadcrumbs
· 1 tablespoon butter
· 1 teaspoon olive oil
· 3 tablespoons Dijon mustard

Instructions:
1. When ready to cook, set your smoker to 450F and preheat.
2. Place a large pan on the grill and add vegetable oil.
3. Pat the lamb dry and then season each rack of lamb with salt and black pepper.
4. Add the carrots to a mixing bowl with the salt, potatoes, garlic, olive oil, pepper, and thyme. Set aside.

5. Place lamb in the pan and cook for eight minutes. Transfer lamb from the grill to rest before mixing the pistachios, butter, salt, bread crumbs, and olive oil
6. Spread mustard on the fat-side of each rack of lamb. Pat pistachio mixture on top of the mustard.
7. Place the carrots and lamb onto the pan and then cook them alongside the lamb for 15 minutes.
8. Open the lid and cook for ten more minutes before serving.

Nutrition: Calories: 50 Carbs: 4g Fiber: 2g Fat: 2.5g Protein: 2g

Smoked Leg

Prep Time: 15 minutes
Cooking Time: 3 hours
Temperature: 250F
Servings: 6
Ingredients:
- 1 leg of lamb, boneless
- 2 tbsp oil
- 4 garlic cloves, minced
- 2 tbsp oregano
- 1 tbsp thyme
- 2 tbsp salt
- 1 tbsp black pepper, freshly ground

Directions:
1. In a bowl, mix oil, garlic, and all the spices. Rub the mixture all over the lamb, then cover with a plastic wrap.
2. Place the lamb in a fridge and marinate for 1 hour.
3. Transfer the lamb on a smoker rack and set the to smoke at 250F.
4. Smoke the meat for 4 hours or until the internal temperature reaches 145F.
5. Remove from the and serve.

Nutrition:
Calories: 356|Fat: 16g| Carb: 3g| Protein: 49g

Greek-Style Roast Leg of Lamb

Preparation Time: 25 minutes
Cooking Time: 1 hour and 30 minutes
Servings: 12
Ingredients:
- 7 pounds leg lamb, bone-in, fat trimmed
- 2 lemons, juiced
- 8 cloves garlic, peeled, minced
- Salt as needed
- Ground black pepper as needed
- 1 tsp. dried oregano
- 1 tsp. dried rosemary
- 6 tbsp. olive oil

Directions:
1. Make a small cut into the meat of lamb by using a paring knife, then stir together garlic, oregano, and rosemary and stuff this paste into the slits of the lamb meat.
2. Take a roasting pan, place lamb in it, then rub with lemon juice and olive oil, cover with a plastic wrap and let marinate for a minimum of 8 hours in the refrigerator.
3. When ready to cook, switch on the grill, fill the grill hopper with oak flavored grills, power the grill on by using the control panel, select 'smoke' on the temperature dial, or set the temperature to 400°F and let it preheat for a minimum of 15 minutes.
4. Meanwhile, remove the lamb from the refrigerator, bring it to room temperature, uncover it and then season well with salt and black pepper.
5. When the grill has preheated, open the lid, place food on the grill grate, shut the grill, and smoke for 30 minutes.
6. Change the smoking temperature to 350°F and then continue smoking for 1 hour until the internal temperature reaches 140°F.
7. When done, transfer lamb to a cutting board, let it rest for 15 minutes, then cut it into slices and serve.

Nutrition:
- Calories: 168
- Fat: 10 g
- Carbs: 2 g
- Protein: 17 g
- Fiber: 0.7 g

Aromatic Herbed Rack of Lamb

Prep Time: 15 minutes
Cooking Time: 2 hours
Temperature: 225F
Servings: 3
Ingredients:
- 2 tbsp. fresh sage
- 2 tbsp. fresh rosemary
- 2 tbsp. fresh thyme
- 2 garlic cloves, peeled
- 1 tbsp. honey
- Salt and ground black pepper, to taste
- ¼ cup olive oil
- 1 (1½-lb.) rack of lamb, trimmed

Directions:
1. In a food processor, add all ingredients except for oil and rack of lamb rack and pulse until mixed.
2. While the motor is running, slowly add oil and pulse until smooth.
3. Coat the rib rack with paste well and refrigerate for 2 hours.
4. Set the temperature of to 225F and preheat with a closed lid for 15 minutes.
5. Arrange the rack of lamb onto the grill and cook for 2 hours.
6. Remove the rack of lamb from the grill and place onto a cutting board. Rest for 15 minutes.
7. Slice and serve.

Nutrition:
Calories: 566|Fat: 33.5g| Carb: 9.8g| Protein: 46.7g

Grilled Aussie Leg of Lamb

Prep Time: 30 minutes
Cooking Time: 2 hours
Temperature: 350F
Servings: 8
Ingredients:
0 5 lb. Aussie Boneless Leg of lamb
Smoked Paprika Rub
- 1 tbsp raw sugar
- 1 tbsp salt
- 1 tbsp black pepper
- 1 tbsp smoked paprika

- 1 tbsp garlic powder
- 1 tbsp rosemary
- 1 tbsp onion powder
- 1 tbsp cumin
- 1/2 tbsp cayenne pepper

Roasted Carrots
- 1 bunch rainbow carrots
- Olive oil as needed
- Salt and pepper to taste

Directions:

1. Preheat the to 350F.
2. Combine the paprika rub ingredients and rub the meat with this mixture.
3. Place the lamb on the preheated over indirect heat and smoke for 2 hours.
4. Meanwhile, toss the carrots in oil, salt, and pepper.
5. Add the carrots to the grill after 1 ½ hour or until the internal temperature has reached 90F.
6. Cook until the meat's internal temperature reaches 135F.
7. Remove the lamb from the and cover it with the foil for 30 minutes.
8. Serve.

Nutrition:

Calories: 257|Fat: 8g| Carb: 6g| Protein: 37g

Wine Braised Lamb Shank

Prep Time: 15 minutes
Cooking Time: 10 hours
Temperature: 250F
Servings: 2
Ingredients:

- 2 (1¼-lb.) lamb shanks
- 1-2 cup of water
- ¼ cup brown sugar
- 1/3 cup rice wine
- 1/3 cup soy sauce
- 1 tbsp. dark sesame oil
- 4 (1½x½-inch) orange zest strips
- 2 (3-inch long) cinnamon sticks
- 1½ tsp. Chinese five-spice powder

Directions:

1. Set the temperature of to 250F and preheat with a closed lid for 15 minutes.
2. Pierce each lamb shank at many places.
3. In a bowl, add all remaining ingredients and mix until sugar is dissolved.
4. In a large foil pan, place the lamb shanks and top with sugar mixture evenly.
5. Place the foil pan onto the grill and cook for 8 to 10 hours, flipping after every 30 minutes. If needed, add more water.
6. Remove from the grill and serve.

Nutrition:

Calories: 120 |Fat:48.4g | Carb:9.7g | Protein:61.9g

Grilled Lamb Liver

Prep Time: 5 minutes | **Cooking Time**: 15 minutes | **Temperature:** 400F| **Servings:** 3
Ingredients:

- 1 lb. of lamb liver; chopped into thin slices
- ½ cup of olive oil
- 1 crushed garlic clove
- 1 tbsp of finely chopped mint
- 1 tsp of salt
- ¼ tsp of black pepper ground

Directions:

1. Preheat the grill to 400F.
2. Rinse the liver under cold running water.
3. Pat the liver dry with a clean paper towel. Remove the tough veins with a knife, then cut into thin slices.
4. In a bowl, combine the olive oil with the crushed garlic, mint, salt, and pepper.
5. Mix well and generously brush the slices of the liver with the mixture and grill for 5 to 7 minutes on each side.
6. Serve.

Nutrition:

Calories: 141|Fat: 3.8g| Carb: 0g| Protein: 21.1g

Smoked Lamb Leg with Salsa Verde

Prep Time: 10 minutes | **Cooking Time**: 3 hours | **Temperature**: 500F| **Servings**: 6

Ingredients:

- 2 tbsp. oil
- 1 whole leg of lamb, fat trimmed and cut into chunks
- Salt to taste
- 6 cloves green garlic, unpeeled
- 1-pound tomatillos, husked and washed
- 1 small yellow onion, quartered
- 5 whole serrano chili peppers
- 1 tbsp. capers, drained
- ¼ cup cilantro, finely chopped
- ½ tsp. sugar
- 1 cup chicken broth
- 3 tbsp. lime juice, freshly squeezed

Directions:

1. Preheat the to 500F with the lid closed for 15 minutes.
2. Place a Dutch oven on the grill grate and add oil.
3. Put the lamb in the Dutch oven and season with salt. Mix and close the lid.
4. Place the garlic, tomatillos, onion, serrano peppers, and capers in a parchment-lined baking tray. Season with salt and drizzle with olive oil.
5. Place in the grill and cook for 15 minutes.
6. Remove the vegetables from the grill and transfer to a blender. Add the cilantro and sugar. Add more salt if needed. Pulse until smooth, then set aside.
7. Pour the mixture into the Dutch oven and add in chicken broth and lime juice.
8. Cook for 3 hours and serve.

Nutrition:

Calories: 430|Fat: 18.4g| Carb: 7.8g| Protein: 56.4g

Smoked Lamb Sausage

Preparation Time: 2 hours

Cooking Time: 6 hours

Servings: 6

Ingredients:

- 1 tsp. cumin
- ½ tsp. cayenne pepper
- 1 tbsp. parsley
- 1 tsp. black pepper
- 1 Hog Casing
- 1 tbsp. garlic
- 1 tsp. paprika
- 2 tbsp. salt
- 2 tbsp. fennel, diced
- 1 tbsp. cilantro
- 2 lbs. lamb shoulders
- Cherry

Yogurt sauce:

- 3 cup yogurt
- Lemon juice to taste
- 1 clove garlic, minced
- Salt and pepper
- 1 cucumber, diced
- 1 onion, minced

Directions:

1. Chop the lamb into pieces before grinding the meat in a meat grinder.
2. Mix the lamb with all of the spices and refrigerate.
3. Then use a sausage horn to attach the hog casing and begin pushing the sausage through the grinder and into the casing, twisting into links. Make holes in the casing before refrigerating.
4. Mix all ingredients for the yogurt sauce and set aside.
5. When ready to cook, set your smoker to 225F and preheat.
6. Lay the sausage on the grill and smoke it for one hour.
7. Then, take the links off the grill and increase the grill's temperature to 500°F.
8. Put the links back on the grill for 5 minutes on each side, and then serve with the yogurt sauce.

Nutrition:

- Calories: 50
- Carbs: 4g
- Fiber: 2g

- Fat: 2.5g
- Protein: 2g

Nutrition:
Calories: 227|Fat: 21g| Carb: 0g| Protein: 49g

Mouthwatering Lamb Chops

Prep Time: 15 minutes
Cooking Time: 20 minutes
Temperature: 165F and 450F
Servings: 4
Ingredients:
For Marinade
- ½ cup of rice wine vinegar
- 1 tsp. liquid smoke
- 2 tbsp. extra virgin olive oil
- 2 tbsp. dried onion, minced
- 1 tbsp. fresh mint, chopped

Lamb Chops
- 8 (4 ounces) lamb chops
- ½ cup hot pepper jelly
- 1 tbsp. Sriracha
- 1 tsp. salt
- 1 tsp. ground black pepper

Directions:
1. In a bowl, whisk in the rice wine vinegar, liquid smoke, olive oil, minced onion, and mint.
2. Add lamb chops in an aluminum roasting pan. Pour marinade over the meat and coat well.
3. Cover with plastic wrap and marinate for 2 hours.
4. Preheat the smoker to 165F.
5. Heat a saucepan over low heat. Add hot pepper jelly and sriracha. Keep it warm.
6. Remove the lamb chops from the marinade and pat dry. Discard marinade.
7. Season chops with salt, pepper, and transfer to the grill grate.
8. Close and smoke for 5 minutes.
9. Remove chops from grill and increase the temperature to 450F.
10. Transfer chops to grill and sear for 2 minutes per side or until internal temperature reaches 145F.
11. Serve.

Rosemary Lamb

Preparation Time: 10 minutes
Cooking Time: 3 hours
Servings: 2
Ingredients:
- 1 rack of lamb rib, membrane removed
- 12 baby potatoes
- 1 bunch of asparagus, ends trimmed
- Ground black pepper, as needed
- Salt, as needed
- 1 teaspoon dried rosemary
- 2 tablespoons olive oil
- 1/2 cup butter, unsalted

Directions:
1. Switch on the Pellet grill, fill the grill hopper with flavored wood pellets, power the grill on by using the control panel, select 'smoke' on the temperature dial, or set the temperature to 225 degrees F and let it preheat for a minimum of 5 minutes.
2. Meanwhile, drizzle oil on both sides of lamb ribs and then sprinkle with rosemary.
3. Take a deep baking dish, place potatoes in it, add butter and mix until coated.
4. When the grill has preheated, open the lid, place lamb ribs on the grill grate along with potatoes in the baking dish, shut the grill and smoke for 3 hours until the internal temperature reaches 145 degrees F.
5. Add asparagus into the baking dish in the last 20 minutes and, when done, remove baking dish from the grill and transfer lamb to a cutting board.
6. Let lamb rest for 15 minutes, cut it into slices, and then serve with potatoes and asparagus.

Nutrition: Calories: 355 Cal Fat: 12.5 g Carbs: 25 g Protein: 35 g Fiber: 6 g

Braised Lamb Tacos

Preparation Time: 2 hours

Cooking Time: 5 hours

Servings: 4

Ingredients:

- ¼ tbsp. cumin seeds
- ¼ tbsp. coriander seeds
- ¼ tbsp. pumpkin seeds
- 2 oz. guajillo peppers
- 1 tbsp. paprika
- 1 tbsp. lime juice
- 1 tbsp. fresh oregano, diced
- 3 cloves garlic, minced
- 2 tbsp. olive oil
- 1 tbsp. salt
- 3 lbs. lamb shoulders

Directions:

1. Grind all of the seeds together before microwaving the chili with water for two minutes on high.
2. Mix the seeds, lime juice, paprika, garlic cloves, salt, oil, and oregano with the chili.
3. Put the meat in a pan, and then rub the seasoning mixture over it. Leave for two hours in the fridge.
4. When ready to cook, turn your smoker to 325F and preheat.
5. Pour ½ cup of water into the pan and cover with foil. Cook the lamb for two hours, adding water when needed.
6. Discard the foil and cook for 2 hours more, then leave for 20 minutes before shredding.
7. Serve on corn tortillas.

Nutrition:

Calories: 328

Carbs: 11g

Protein: 19g

Fat: 24g

Smoked Lamb Shoulder

Preparation Time: 10 minutes

Cooking Time: 4 hours

Servings: 6

Ingredients:

- 8 pounds lamb shoulder, fat trimmed
- 2 tbsp. olive oil
- Salt as needed

For the Rub:

- 1 tbsp. dried oregano
- 2 tbsp. salt
- 1 tbsp. crushed dried bay leaf
- 1 tbsp. sugar
- 2 tbsp. dried crushed sage
- 1 tbsp. dried thyme
- 1 tbsp. ground black pepper
- 1 tbsp. dried basil
- 1 tbsp. dried rosemary
- 1 tbsp. dried parsley

Directions:

1. Switch on the grill, fill the grill hopper with cherry flavored, power the grill on by using the control panel, select 'smoke' on the temperature dial, or set the temperature to 250°F and let it preheat for a minimum of 5 minutes.

2. Meanwhile, prepare the rub and for this, take a small bowl, place all of its ingredients in it and stir until mixed.

3. Brush lamb with oil and then sprinkle with prepared rub until evenly coated.

4. When the grill has preheated, open the lid, place lamb should on the grill grate fat-side up, shut the grill, and smoke for 3 hours.

5. Then change the smoking temperature to 325°F and continue smoking for 1 hour until fat renders, and the internal temperature reaches 195°F.

6. When done, wrap lamb should in aluminum foil and let it rest for 20 minutes.

7. Pull lamb shoulder by using two forks and then serve.

Nutrition:

- Calories: 300
- Fat: 24 g
- Carbs: 0 g
- Protein: 19 g

- Fiber: 0 g

Chicken Fajitas On A Wood Pellet Grill

Servings: 10
Cooking Time: 20 Minutes
Ingredients:
- Chicken breast - 2 lbs, thin sliced
- Red bell pepper - 1 large
- Onion - 1 large
- Orange bell pepper - 1 large
- Seasoning mix
- Oil - 2 tbsp
- Onion powder - ½ tbsp
- Granulated garlic - ½ tbsp
- Salt - 1 tbsp

Directions:
1. Preheat the grill to 450 degrees.
2. Mix the seasonings and oil.
3. Add the chicken slices to the mix.
4. Line a large pan with a non-stick baking sheet.
5. Let the pan heat for 10 minutes.

6. Place the chicken, peppers, and other vegetables in the grill.
7. Grill for 10 minutes or until the chicken is cooked.
8. Remove it from the grill and serve with warm tortillas and vegetables.

Nutrition Info: Carbohydrates: 5 g Protein: 29 g Fat: 6 g Sodium: 360 mg Cholesterol: 77 mg

Spicy BBQ Chicken

Ingredients:
- 1 Whole Chicken
- 6 Thai Chiles
- 2 Tbsp Sweet Paprika
- 1 Scotch Bonnet
- 2 Tbsp Sugar
- 3 Tbsp Salt
- 1 White Onion
- 5 Garlic Cloves
- 4 Cups Grape Seed Oil

Instructions:
- Puree the Thai chilies, paprika, scotch bonnet, sugar, salt, onion, garlic, and grape seed oil together until smooth.
- Smother the chicken with mixture and let rest in fridge overnight.
- When ready to cook, set the to 300°F and preheat, lid closed for 15 minutes.
- Place chicken on grill breast side up and smoke for 3 hours or until it reaches an internal temperature of 165°F in the breast.
- Remove from grill and allow to rest for 10 to 15 minutes before slicing.Serve with sides of choice. Enjoy!

Hickory Smoked Chicken

Servings: 4
Cooking Time: 30 Minutes
Ingredients:
- 4 chicken breasts
- ¼ cup olive oil
- 1 teaspoon pressed garlic
- 1 tablespoon Worcestershire sauce
- Kirkland Sweet Mesquite Seasoning as needed
- 1 button Honey Bourbon Sauce

Directions:
1. Place all ingredients in a bowl except for the Bourbon sauce. Massage the chicken until all parts are coated with the seasoning.
2. Allow to marinate in the fridge for 4 hours.
3. Once ready to cook, fire the Grill to 350F. Use Hickory wood pellets and close the lid. Preheat for 15 minutes.
4. Place the chicken directly into the grill grate and cook for 30 minutes. Flip the chicken halfway through the cooking time.

5. Five minutes before the cooking time ends, brush all surfaces of the chicken with the Honey Bourbon Sauce.
6. Serve immediately.
Nutrition Info: Calories per serving: 622; Protein: 60.5g; Carbs: 1.1g; Fat: 40.3g Sugar: 0.4g

Easy Smoked Chicken Breasts

Preparation Time: 20 minutes
Cooking Time: 30 minutes
Servings: 4
Ingredients:
• 4 large chicken breasts, bones and skin removed
• 1 tbsp. olive oil
• 2 tbsp. brown sugar:
• 2 tbsp. maple syrup
• 1 tsp. celery seeds
• 2 tbsp. paprika
• 2 tbsp. salt
• 1 tsp. black pepper
• 2 tbsp. garlic powder
• 2 tbsp. onion powder
Directions:
1. Place all ingredients in a bowl and massage the chicken with your hands. Place in the fridge to marinate for at least 4 hours.
2. Fire the Grill to 350°F and use maple. Close the lid and allow to preheat to 15 minutes.
3. Place the chicken on the grill and cook for 15 minutes with the lid closed.
4. Turn the chicken over and cook for another 10 minutes.
5. Insert a thermometer into the thickest part of the chicken and make sure that the temperature reads 165°F.
6. Remove the chicken from the grill and allow to rest for 5 minutes before slicing.
Nutrition:
• Calories: 327
• Protein: 40 g
• Carbs: 23g
• Fat: 9g
• Sugar: 13g

Peppered Bbq Chicken Thighs

Servings: 6
Cooking Time: 35 Minutes
Ingredients:
• 6 bone-in chicken thighs
• Salt and pepper to taste
• Big Game Rub to taste, optional
Directions:
1. Place all ingredients in a bowl and allow to marinate in the fridge for at least 4 hours.
2. When ready to cook, fire the Grill to 350F. Use apple wood pellet. Close the lid and preheat for 15 minutes.
3. Place the chicken directly on the grill grate and cook for 35 minutes. To check if the chicken is cooked thoroughly, insert a meat thermometer, and make sure that the internal temperature reads at 165F.
4. Serve the chicken immediately.
Nutrition Info: Calories per serving: 430; Protein: 32g; Carbs: 1.2g; Fat: 32.1g; Sugar: 0.4g

Barbecued Chicken Legs

(TOTAL COOK TIME 2 HOURS 15 MINUTES)
INGREDIENTS FOR 2 SERVINGS
THE MEAT
· 4 chicken leg quarters, visible excess fat removed, patted dry
· Olive oil – 1 tablespoon
THE RUB
· Paprika – 2 tablespoons
· Thyme – 1 tablespoon
· Chili powder – 2 tablespoons
· Cayenne pepper – 1 tablespoon
· Garlic powder – 1 tablespoon
· Onion powder – 1 tablespoon
· Kosher salt – 1 tablespoon
· Freshly ground black pepper – 2 tablespoons
THE WOOD PELLET GRILL
· Preheat your wood pellet grill to 220°F (104°C)
· Use your favorite flavor wood pellets
METHOD

1. Brush a fine layer of olive oil over the chicken skin.

2. In a small bowl, combine the rub ingredients (paprika, thyme, chili powder, cayenne pepper, garlic powder, onion powder, salt, and black pepper). Rub the seasoning mix all over the chicken, rubbing it in thoroughly.

3. Place the chicken legs on your smoker's rack and cook with the lid closed for approximately 2 hours. The chicken is ready when it registers an internal temperature of 165°F (74°C). When this temperature is achieved, turn the heat up to moderate heat, and continue to cook for 2-3 minutes more, regularly flipping over. Doing this will help you achieve crisp outer skin.

4. Enjoy.

Smoked Chicken and Potatoes

Preparation Time: 30 minutes
Cooking Time: 1 hour 30 minutes
Servings: 4
Ingredients:
- 2.5-pounds rotisserie chicken
- 2 tbsp. coconut Sugar:
- 1 tbsp. onion powder
- 2 tbsp. garlic powder
- 1 tsp. cayenne pepper powder
- 2 tsp. kosher salt
- 4 tbsp. olive oil
- 2 pounds creamer potatoes, scrubbed and halved
- A dash of black pepper powder

Directions:
1. Place the chicken in a bowl. In a smaller bowl, combine the coconut sugar, onion powder, garlic powder, cayenne pepper powder, and salt. Add in the olive oil. Rub the mixture into the chicken and allow to marinate for 4 hours in the fridge.

2. Fire the Grill to 400°F and close the lid. Preheat to 15 minutes.

3. Place the seasoned chicken in a heat-proof dish and place the potatoes around the chicken. Season the potatoes with salt.

4. Place in the grill and cook for 30 minutes. Lower the heat to 250°F and cook for another hour.

5. Insert a meat thermometer in the thickest part of the chicken and make sure that the temperature reads 165°F. Flip the chicken halfway through the cooking time for even browning.

Nutrition:
- Calories: 991
- Protein: 79.7g
- Carbs: 49.8g
- Fat: 73.6g
- Sugar: 6.5g

Chili Barbecue Chicken

Servings: 4
Cooking Time: 2 Hours And 10 Minutes
Ingredients:
- 1 tablespoon brown sugar
- 1 tablespoon lime zest
- 1 tablespoon chili powder
- 1/2 teaspoon ground cumin
- 1/2 tablespoon ground espresso
- Salt to taste
- 2 tablespoons olive oil
- 8 chicken legs
- 1/2 cup barbecue sauce

Directions:
1. Combine sugar, lime zest, chili powder, cumin, ground espresso and salt.

2. Drizzle the chicken legs with oil.

3. Sprinkle sugar mixture all over the chicken.

4. Cover with foil and refrigerate for 5 hours.

5. Set the wood pellet grill to 180 degrees F.

6. Preheat it for 15 minutes while the lid is closed.

7. Smoke the chicken legs for 1 hour.

8. Increase temperature to 350 degrees F.

9. Grill the chicken legs for another 1 hour, flipping once.

10. Brush the chicken with barbecue sauce and grill for another 10 minutes.

11.   Tips: You can also add chili powder to the barbecue sauce.

Sweet and Sour Chicken

Preparation Time: 20 minutes
Cooking Time: 35 minutes
Servings: 6
Ingredients:
* 6 cups water
* ⅓ cup salt
* ¼ cup brown Sugar:
* ¼ cup soy sauce
* 6 chicken breasts, boneless
* 1 cup granulated white sugar:
* ½ cup ketchup
* 1 cup apple cider vinegar
* 2 tbsp. soy sauce
* 1 tsp. garlic powder

Directions:
1.   Place the water, salt, brown sugar, and soy sauce in a large bowl. Stir until well combined. Add the chicken breasts into the brine and let soak for 24 hours in the refrigerator.
2.   Fire the Grill to 350°F. Use maple flavour. Close the grill lid and preheat for 15 minutes.
3.   Place the breasts on the grill grate and cook for 35 minutes on each side with the lid closed. Flip the chicken halfway through the cooking time.
4.   Meanwhile, place the remaining ingredients in a bowl and stir until combined.
5.   Ten minutes before the chicken breasts are cooked, brush with the sauce.
6.   Serve immediately.

Nutrition:
* Calories: 675
* Protein: 61.9g
* Carbs: 35.8g
* Fat: 29.7g
* Sugar: 32.7g

Smoked Chicken Thighs

Servings: 6
Cooking Time: 24 Minutes.
Ingredients:
* 6 chicken thighs
* ½ cup commercial BBQ sauce of your choice
* 1 ½ tablespoon poultry spice
* 4 tablespoons butter

Directions:
1.   Place all ingredients in a bowl except for the butter. Massage the chicken to make sure that the chicken is coated with the marinade.
2.   Place in the fridge to marinate for 4 hours.
3.   Fire the Grill to 350F. Use hickory wood pellets. Close the lid and preheat for 15 minutes.
4.   When ready to cook, place the chicken on the grill grate and cook for 12 minutes on each side.
5.   Before serving the chicken, brush with butter on top.
Nutrition Info: Calories per serving: 504; Protein: 32.4g; Carbs: 2.7g; Fat: 39.9g Sugar: 0.9g

Lemon Rosemary and Beer Marinated Chicken

Preparation Time: 20 minutes
Cooking Time: 35 minutes
Servings: 6
Ingredients:
* 1 whole chicken
* 1 lemon, zested and juiced
* 1 tsp. salt
* 1 tsp. ground black pepper
* 1 tsp. rosemary, chopped
* 12-ounce beer, apple-flavored

Directions:
1.   Place all ingredients in a bowl and allow the chicken to marinate for at least 12 hours in the fridge.

2.   When ready to cook, fire the Grill to 350°F. Use preferred flavour. Close the grill lid and preheat for 15 minutes.

3.   Place the chicken on the grill grate and cook for 55 minutes.

4.   Cook until the internal temperature reads 165°F.

5.   Take the chicken out and allow to rest before carving.

Nutrition:

- Calories: 288
- Protein: 36.1g
- Carbs: 4.4g
- Fat: 13.1g
- Sugar: 0.7g

Wood Pellet Chicken Wings With Spicy Miso

Servings: 6
Cooking Time: 25 Minutes
Ingredients:

- 2-pound chicken wings
- 3/4 cup soy
- 1/2 cup pineapple juice
- 1 tbsp sriracha
- 1/8 cup miso
- 1/8 cup gochujang
- 1/2 cup water
- 1/2 cup oil
- Togarashi

Directions:

1.   Mix all ingredients then toss the chicken wings until well coated. Refrigerate for 12 minutes.

2.   Preheat your wood pellet grill to 375°F. Place the chicken wings on the grill grates and close the lid. Cook until the internal temperature reaches 165°F. Remove the wings from the grill and sprinkle with togarashi. Serve when hot and enjoy.

Nutrition Info: Calories: 704 Cal Fat: 56 g Carbohydrates: 24 g Protein: 27 g Fiber: 1 g

Easy Rapid-fire Roast Chicken

Servings: 4
Cooking Time: 1 To 2 Hours
Ingredients:

- 1 (4-pound) whole chicken, giblets removed
- Extra-virgin olive oil, for rubbing
- 3 tablespoons Greek seasoning
- Juice of 1 lemon
- Butcher's string

Directions:

1.   Supply your smoker with wood pellets and follow the manufacturer's specific start-up procedure. Preheat, with the lid closed, to 450°F.

2.   Rub the bird generously all over with oil, including inside the cavity.

3.   Sprinkle the Greek seasoning all over and under the skin of the bird, and squeeze the lemon juice over the breast.

4.   Tuck the chicken wings behind the back and tie the legs together with butcher's string or cooking twine.

5.   Put the chicken directly on the grill, breast-side up, close the lid, and roast for 1 hour to 1 hour 30 minutes, or until a meat thermometer inserted in the thigh reads 165°F.

6.   Let the meat rest for 10 minutes before carving.

Sweet Smoked Chicken in Black Tea Aroma

Preparation Time: 30 minutes
Cooking Time: 10 Hours
Servings: 1
Ingredients:

- Chicken breast (6-lbs., 2.7-kgs)
- The Rub
- ¼ cup Salt
- 2 tbsp. Chili powder
- 2 tbsp. Chinese five-spice
- 1 ½ cups Brown Sugar:
- 2 cups Black tea

Directions:

1.   Place salt, chili powder, Chinese five-spice, and brown Sugar: in a bowl then stir to combine.
2.   Rub the chicken breast with the spice mixture then marinate overnight. Store in the refrigerator to keep it fresh.
3.   In the morning, preheat a smoker to 225°F (107°C) with charcoal and hickory wood chips. Prepare indirect heat.
4.   Pour black tea into a disposable aluminum pan then place in the smoker.
5.   Remove the chicken from the refrigerator then thaw while waiting for the smoker.
6.   Once the smoker has reached the desired temperature, place the chicken on the smoker's rack.
7.   Smoke the chicken breast for 2 hours then check whether the internal temperature has reached 160°F (71°C).
8.   Take the smoked chicken breast out from the smoker and transfer it to a serving dish.
9.   Serve and enjoy immediately.

Nutrition:
- Carbs: 27 g
- Protein: 19 g
- Sodium: 65 mg
- Cholesterol: 49 mg

Chile-lime Rubbed Chicken

Servings: 6
Cooking Time: 40 Minutes
Ingredients:
- 3 tablespoons chili powder
- 2 tablespoons extra virgin olive oil
- 2 teaspoons lime zest
- 3 tablespoons lime juice
- 1 tablespoon garlic, minced
- 1 teaspoon ground coriander
- 1 teaspoon ground cumin
- 1 teaspoon dried oregano
- 1 ½ teaspoons salt
- 1 teaspoon ground black pepper
- A pinch of cinnamon
- 1 chicken, spatchcocked

Directions:
1.   In a bowl, place the chili powder, olive oil, lime zest, juice, garlic, coriander, cumin, oregano, salt, pepper, cinnamon, and cinnamon in a bowl. Mix to form a paste.
2.   Place the chicken cut-side down on a chopping board and flatten using the heel of your hand. Carefully, break the breastbone to flatten the chicken.
3.   Generously rub the spices all over the chicken and make sure to massage the chicken with the spice rub. Place in a baking dish and refrigerate for 24 hours in the fridge.
4.   When ready to cook, fire the Grill to 400F. Use maple wood pellets. Close the grill lid and preheat for 15 minutes.
5.   Place the chicken breastbone-side down on the grill grate and cook for 40 minutes or until a thermometer inserted in the thickest part reads at 165F.
6.   Make sure to flip the chicken halfway through the cooking time.
7.   Once cooked, transfer to a plate and allow to rest before carving the chicken.

Nutrition Info: Calories per serving: 213; Protein: 33.1g; Carbs: 3.8g; Fat: 7g Sugar: 0.5g

Buffalo Chicken Thighs

Preparation Time: 30 minutes
Cooking Time: 6 Hours
Servings: 1
Ingredients:
- 4–6 skinless, boneless chicken thighs
- Pork and poultry rub
- 4 tbsp. butter
- 1 cup sauce; buffalo wing
- Bleu cheese crumbles
- Ranch dressing

Directions:
1.   Set the grill to preheat by keeping the temperature to 450°F and keeping the lid closed.
2.   Now season the chicken thighs with the poultry rub and then place it on the grill grate.
3.   Cook it for 8 to 10 minutes while making sure to flip it once midway.

4.   Now take a small saucepan and cook the wing sauce along with butter by keeping the flame on medium heat. Make sure to stir in between to avoid lumps.

5.   Now take the cooked chicken and dip it into the wing sauce and the butter mix. Make sure to coat both the sides in an even manner.

6.   Take the chicken thighs that have been sauced to the grill and then cook for further 15 minutes. Do so until the internal temperature reads 175°F.

7.   Sprinkle bleu cheese and drizzle the ranch dressing.

8.   Serve and enjoy.

Nutrition:
- Carbs: 29 g
- Protein: 19 g
- Sodium: 25 mg
- Cholesterol: 19 mg

Lemon Rosemary And Beer Marinated Chicken

Servings: 6
Cooking Time: 55 Minutes
Ingredients:
- 1 whole chicken
- 1 lemon, zested and juiced
- 1 teaspoon salt
- 1 teaspoon ground black pepper
- 1 teaspoon rosemary, chopped
- 12-ounce beer, apple-flavored

Directions:

1.   Place all ingredients in a bowl and allow the chicken to marinate for at least 12 hours in the fridge.

2.   When ready to cook, fire the Grill to 350F. Use preferred wood pellets. Close the grill lid and preheat for 15 minutes.

3.   Place the chicken on the grill grate and cook for 55 minutes.

4.   Cook until the internal temperature reads at 165F.

5.   Take the chicken out and allow to rest before carving.

Nutrition Info: Calories per serving: 288; Protein: 36.1g; Carbs: 4.4g; Fat: 13.1g Sugar: 0.7g

Grilled Sweet And Sour Chicken

Servings: 6
Cooking Time: 35 Minutes
Ingredients:
- 6 cups water
- 1/3 cup salt
- ¼ cup brown sugar
- ¼ cup soy sauce
- 6 chicken breasts, boneless
- 1 cup granulated white sugar
- ½ cup ketchup
- 1 cup apple cider vinegar
- 2 tablespoons soy sauce
- 1 teaspoon garlic powder

Directions:

1.   Place the water, salt, brown sugar, and soy sauce in a large bowl. Stir until well combined. Add in the chicken breasts into the brine and allow to soak for 24 hours in the refrigerator.

2.   Fire the Grill to 350F. Use maple wood pellets. Close the grill lid and preheat for 15 minutes.

3.   Place the breasts on the grill grate and cook for 35 minutes on each side with the lid closed. Flip the chicken halfway through the cooking time.

4.   Meanwhile, place the remaining ingredients in a bowl and stir until combined.

5.   Ten minutes before the chicken breasts are cooked, brush with the sauce.

6.   Serve immediately.

Nutrition Info: Calories per serving: 675 ; Protein: 61.9g; Carbs: 35.8g; Fat: 29.7g Sugar: 32.7g

Beer-Braised Chicken Tacos with Jalapenos Relish

Preparation Time: 30 minutes
Cooking Time: 3 Hours
Servings: 1
Ingredients:
- For the braised chicken
- 2 lbs. chicken thighs; boneless, skinless
- ½ small-sized diced onion
- 1 de-seeded and chopped jalapeno
- 1 (12 oz.) can Modelo beer
- 1 tbsp. olive oil
- 1 EA chipotle Chile in adobo
- 1 clove minced garlic
- 4 tbsp. adobo sauce
- 1 tsp. chili powder
- 1 tsp. garlic powder
- 1 tsp. salt
- 1 tsp. black pepper
- Juice 2 limes
- For the tacos
- 8–12 tortillas; small flour
- Hot sauce
- Cilantro
- Cotija cheese
- For the jalapeno relish
- ¼ cup finely diced red onion
- 3 seeded and diced jalapenos
- 1 clove minced garlic
- 1/3 cup water
- 1 tbsp. Sugar:
- 2/3 cup white wine vinegar
- 1 tbsp. salt
- For pickled cabbage
- 2 cups red cabbage; shredded
- ½ cup white wine vinegar
- 1 tbsp. Sugar:
- 1 tbsp. salt

Directions:
1. For the jalapeño relish: take all the ingredients and mix them in a non-reactive dish and then keep it aside to be used.
2. For the pickled cabbage: take another non-reactive dish and mix all its respective ingredients and keep it aside
3. Now, transfer both the relish along with the pickled cabbage to your refrigerator and allow it to see for a couple of hours or even overnight if you so desire
4. Take the chicken thighs and season them with an adequate amount of salt and pepper
5. Take a Dutch oven and keep the flame over medium-high heat. Heat 1 tbsp. of olive oil in it
6. Now place the chicken thighs skin side down and brown
7. Remove them from the heat and then set them aside
8. Now, add 1 tbsp. of butter and keep the flame to medium-high
9. When the butter has melted, add jalapeno along with onion and sauté it for 3 to 5 minutes until they turn translucent
10. Add minced garlic to it and sauté it for 30 more seconds
11. Now add adobo sauce along with lime juice, chili powder, and chipotle chile.
12. Add the chicken thighs in the oven and pour in the beer
13. Now set the grill to pre-heat by keeping the temperature to 350°F
14. Place the oven on the grill and let it braise for 30 minutes
15. Remove the chicken from the braising liquid and slowly shred it
16. For the tacos: place the shredded part of chicken on the tortillas. Top it with jalapeno relish along with cotija, cabbage, and cilantro, and pour the hot sauce
17. Serve and enjoy

Nutrition:
- Carbs: 29 g
- Protein: 19 g
- Sodium: 25 mg
- Cholesterol: 19 mg

Grilled Chicken

Preparation Time: 10 minutes
Cooking Time: 30 minutes
Servings: 8
Ingredients:
- Whole chicken (4–5 lbs.)
- Grilled chicken mix

Directions:

1.   Preheat the grill with the 'smoke' option for 5 minutes.
2.   Preheat another 10 minutes and keep the temperature on high until it reaches 450°F.
3.   Use baker's twine to tie the chicken's legs together.
4.   Keep the breast side up when you place the chicken in the grill.
5.   Grill for 70 minutes. Do not open the grill during this process.
6.   Check the temperature of your grilled chicken. Make sure it is 165 degrees. If not, leave the chicken in for longer.
7.   Carefully take the chicken out of the grill.
8.   Set aside for 15 minutes.
9.   Cut and serve.

Nutrition:
- Carbs: 0 g
- Protein: 107 g
- Fat: 0 g
- Sodium: 320 mg
- Cholesterol: 346 mg

Wood Pellet Grilled Chicken Kabobs

Servings: 6
Cooking Time: 12 Minutes
Ingredients:
- 1/2 cup olive oil
- 2 tbsp white vinegar
- 1 tbsp lemon juice
- 1-1/2 tbsp salt
- 1/2 tbsp pepper, coarsely ground
- 2 tbsp chives, freshly chopped
- 1-1/2 tbsp thyme, freshly chopped
- 2 tbsp Italian parsley freshly chopped
- 1tbsp garlic, minced
- Kabobs
- 1 each orange, red, and yellow pepper
- 1-1/2 pounds chicken breast, boneless and skinless
- 12 mini mushrooms

Directions:

1.   In a mixing bowl, add all the marinade ingredients and mix well. Toss the chicken and mushrooms in the marinade then refrigerate for 30 minutes.
2.   Meanwhile, soak the skewers in hot water. Remove the chicken from the fridge and start assembling the kabobs.
3.   Preheat your wood pellet to 450°F.
4.   Grill the kabobs in the wood pellet for 6 minutes, flip them and grill for 6 more minutes.
5.   Remove from the grill and let rest. Heat up the naan bread on the grill for 2 minutes.
6.   Serve and enjoy.

Nutrition Info: Calories: 165 Cal Fat: 13 g Carbohydrates: 1 g Protein: 33 g Fiber: 0 g

Grilled Chicken Kebabs

Preparation Time: 10 minutes
Cooking Time: 40 minutes
Servings: 8
Ingredients:
For Marinade
- ½ cup Olive oil
- 1 tbsp. lemon, juiced
- 2 tbsp. White vinegar
- 1 ½ tbsp. Salt
- 1 tbsp. Minced garlic
- 1 ½ tbsp. Fresh thyme
- 2 tbsp. Fresh Italian parsley
- 2 tbsp. Fresh chives
- ½ tbsp. Ground pepper

For Kebabs
- Orange, yellow, and red bell peppers
- 1 ½ Chicken breasts, boneless and skinless
- 10–12 medium-sized mushrooms of your choice

Directions:

1.   Mix all the ingredients for the marinade.
2.   Add the chicken and mushrooms to the marinade and put them in the refrigerator.
3.   Preheat your grill to 450°F.
4.   Remove the marinated chicken from the refrigerator and place it on the grill.

5.   Grill the kebabs on one side for 6 minutes. Flip to grill on the other side.
6.   Serve with a side dish of your choice.
Nutrition:
*   Carbs: 1 g
*   Fat: 2 g
*   Sodium: 582 mg

Smoked Cornish Chicken In Wood Pellets

Servings: 6
Cooking Time: 1 Hour 10 Minutes
Ingredients:
*   Cornish hens - 6
*   Canola or avocado oil - 2-3 tbsp
*   Spice mix - 6 tbsp

Directions:
1.   Preheat your wood pellet grill to 275 degrees.
2.   Rub the whole hen with oil and the spice mix. Use both of these ingredients liberally.
3.   Place the breast area of the hen on the grill and smoke for 30 minutes.
4.   Flip the hen, so the breast side is facing up. Increase the temperature to 400 degrees.
5.   Cook until the temperature goes down to 165 degrees.
6.   Pull it out and leave it for 10 minutes.
7.   Serve warm with a side dish of your choice.
Nutrition Info: Carbohydrates: 1 g Protein: 57 g Fat: 50 g Sodium: 165 mg Cholesterol: 337 mg

Chicken Wings

Preparation Time: 10 minutes
Cooking Time: 50 minutes
Servings: 1
Ingredients:
*   6–8 lbs. Chicken wings
*   1/3 cup Canola oil
*   1 tbsp. Barbeque seasoning mix

Directions:
1.   Combine the seasonings and oil in one large bowl.
2.   Put the chicken wings in the bowl and mix well.
3.   Turn your to the 'smoke' setting and leave it on for 4–5 minutes.
4.   Set the heat to 350°F and leave it to preheat for 15 minutes with the lid closed.
5.   Place the wings on the grill with enough space between the pieces.
6.   Let it cook for 45 minutes or until the skin looks crispy.
7.   Remove from the grill and serve with your choice of sides.
Nutrition:
*   Protein: 33 g
*   Fat: 8 g
*   Sodium: 134 mg
*   Cholesterol: 141 mg

Lemon Chicken

Servings: 6
Cooking Time: 10 Minutes
Ingredients:
*   2 teaspoons honey
*   1 tablespoon lemon juice
*   1 teaspoon lemon zest
*   1 clove garlic, coarsely chopped
*   2 sprigs thyme
*   Salt and pepper to taste
*   ½ cup olive oil
*   6 chicken breast fillets

Directions:
1.   Mix the honey, lemon juice, lemon zest, garlic, thyme, salt and pepper in a bowl.
2.   Gradually add olive oil to the mixture.
3.   Soak the chicken fillets in the mixture.
4.   Cover and refrigerate for 4 hours.
5.   Preheat the wood pellet grill to 400 degrees F for 15 minutes while the lid is closed.
6.   Grill the chicken for 5 minutes per side.
7.   Tips: You can also make additional marinade to be used for basting during grill time.

Hot and Spicy Smoked Chicken Wings

Preparation Time: 30 minutes
Cooking Time: 3 Hours
Servings: 1
Ingredients:
* Chicken wings (6 lbs., 2.7 kgs)
* 3 tbsp. Olive oil
* 2 ½ tbsp. Chili powder
* 3 tbsp. Smoked paprika
* ½ tsp. Cumin
* 2 tsp. Garlic powder
* 1 ¾ tsp. Salt
* 1 tbsp. Pepper
* 2 tsp. Cayenne

Directions:
1. Divide each chicken wing into two then place in a bowl. Set aside.
2. Combine olive oil with chili powder, smoked paprika, cumin, garlic powder, salt, pepper, and cayenne then mix well.
3. Rub the chicken wings with the spice mixture then let them sit for about an hour.
4. Meanwhile, preheat a smoker to 225°F (107°C) with charcoal and hickory wood chips. Prepare indirect heat.
5. When the smoker is ready, arrange the spiced chicken wings on the smoker's rack.
6. Smoke the chicken wings for 2 hours or until the internal temperature of the chicken wings has reached 160°F (71°C).
7. Take the smoked chicken wings from the smoker and transfer to a serving dish.
8. Serve and enjoy immediately.

Nutrition:
* Carbs: 27 g
* Protein: 19 g
* Sodium: 65 mg
* Cholesterol: 49 mg

Grill Bbq Chicken Breasts

Servings: 4
Cooking Time: 30 Minutes
Ingredients:
* 4 whole chicken breasts, deboned
* ¼ cup olive oil
* 1 teaspoon pressed garlic
* 1 teaspoon Worcestershire sauce
* 1 teaspoon cayenne pepper powder
* ½ cup 'Que BBQ Sauce

Directions:
1. In a bowl, combine all ingredients except for the 'Que BBQ Sauce and make sure to rub the chicken breasts until coated with the mixture. Allow to marinate in the fridge for at least overnight.
2. Place the preferred wood pellets into the Grill and fire the grill. Allow the temperature to rise to 500F and preheat for 5 minutes. Reduce the temperature to 165F.
3. Place the chicken on the grill grate and cook for 30 minutes.
4. Five minutes before the chicken is done, glaze the chicken with BBQ sauce.
5. Serve immediately.

Nutrition Info: Calories per serving: 631; Protein: 61g; Carbs: 2.9g; Fat: 40.5g Sugar: 1.5g

Asian Miso Chicken wings

Preparation Time: 15 minutes
Cooking Time: 25 minutes
Servings: 6
Ingredients:
* 2 lb. chicken wings
* ¾ cup soy
* ½ cup pineapple juice
* 1 tbsp. sriracha
* ⅛ cup miso
* ⅛ cup gochujang
* ½ cup water
* ½ cup oil
* Togarashi

Directions:
1. Preheat the to 375°F
2. Combine all the ingredients except togarashi in a Ziploc bag. Toss until the chicken wings are well coated. Refrigerate for 12 hours

3.   Pace the wings on the grill grates and close the lid. Cook for 25 minutes or until the internal temperature reaches 165°F

4.   Remove the wings from the and sprinkle Togarashi.

Nutrition:

* Calories: 703,
* Fat: 56g,
* Protein: 27g,
* Fiber: 1g,
* Sodium: 1156mg

Cinco De Mayo Chicken Enchiladas

Servings: 6
Cooking Time: 45 Minutes
Ingredients:

* 6 cups diced cooked chicken
* 3 cups grated Monterey Jack cheese, divided
* 1 cup sour cream
* 1 (4-ounce) can chopped green chiles
* 2 (10-ounce) cans red or green enchilada sauce, divided
* 12 (8-inch) flour tortillas
* ½ cup chopped scallions
* ¼ cup chopped fresh cilantro

Directions:

1.   Supply your smoker with wood pellets and follow the manufacturer's specific start-up procedure. Preheat, with the lid closed, to 350°F.

2.   In a large bowl, combine the cooked chicken, 2 cups of cheese, the sour cream, and green chiles to make the filling.

3.   Pour one can of enchilada sauce in the bottom of a 9-by-13-inch baking dish or aluminum pan.

4.   Spoon ⅓ cup of the filling on each tortilla and roll up securely.

5.   Transfer the tortillas seam-side down to the baking dish, then pour the remaining can of enchilada sauce over them, coating all exposed surfaces of the tortillas.

6.   Sprinkle the remaining 1 cup of cheese over the enchiladas and cover tightly with aluminum foil.

7.   Bake on the grill, with the lid closed, for 30 minutes, then remove the foil.

8.   Continue baking with the lid closed for 15 minutes, or until bubbly.

9.   Garnish the enchiladas with the chopped scallions and cilantro and serve it.

Paprika Chicken

Preparation Time: 20 minutes
Cooking Time: 2–4 hours
Servings: 7
Ingredients:

* 4–6 chicken breast
* 4 tbsp. olive oil
* 2 tbsp. smoked paprika
* ½ tbsp. salt
* ¼ tsp. pepper
* 2 tsp. garlic powder
* 2 tsp. garlic salt
* 2 tsp. pepper
* 1 tsp. cayenne pepper
* 1 tsp. rosemary

Directions:

1.   Preheat your smoker to 220°F using your favorite flavours

2.   Prepare your chicken breast according to your desired shapes and transfer to a greased baking dish

3.   Take a medium bowl and add spices, stir well

4.   Press the spice mix over the chicken and transfer the chicken to the smoker

5.   Smoke for 1–1 and a half hour

6.   Turn-over and cook for 30 minutes more

7.   Once the internal temperature reaches 165°F

8.   Remove from the smoker and cover with foil

9.   Allow it to rest for 15 minutes

Nutrition:

* Calories: 237
* Fats: 6.1g

- Carbs: 14g
- Fiber: 3g mmediately.

Smoked Chicken Drumsticks

Servings: 5
Cooking Time: 2 Hours 30 Minutes
Ingredients:
- 10 chicken drumsticks
- 2tsp garlic powder
- 1tsp salt
- 1tsp onion powder
- 1/2 tsp ground black pepper
- ½ tsp cayenne pepper
- 1tsp brown sugar
- 1/3 cup hot sauce
- 1tsp paprika
- ½ tsp thyme

Directions:
1. In a large mixing bowl, combine the garlic powder, sugar, hot sauce, paprika, thyme, cayenne, salt, and ground pepper. Add the drumsticks and toss to combine.
2. Cover the bowl and refrigerate for 1 hour.
3. Remove the drumsticks from the marinade and let them sit for about 1 hour until they are at room temperature.
4. Arrange the drumsticks into a rack.
5. Start your pellet grill on smoke, leaving the lid open for 5 minutes for the fire to start.
6. Close the lid and preheat grill to 250°F, using hickory or apple hardwood pellets.
7. Place the rack on the grill and smoke drumsticks for 2 hours, 30 minutes, or until the drumsticks' internal temperature reaches 180°F.
8. Remove drumsticks from heat and let them rest for a few minutes.
9. Serve.

Nutrition Info: Calories: 167 Total Fat: 5.4 g Saturated Fat: 1.4 g Cholesterol: 81 mg Sodium: 946 mg Total Carbohydrate: 2.6 g Dietary Fiber: 0.5 g Total Sugars: 1.3 g Protein: 25.7 g

Smoked and Fried Chicken wings

Preparation Time: 10 minutes
Cooking Time: 2 hours
Servings: 4
Ingredients:
- 3 lb. chicken wings
- 1 tbsp. Goya adobo seasoning
- Your favorite sauce

Directions:
1. Fire up your to smoke setting
2. Generously coat the wings with adobo seasoning then place them on the grill.
3. Smoke them for 2 hours turning them at least once during smoking.
4. Remove the wings from the smoker and heat oil to 3750F.
5. Drop the wings in the hot oil and fry for 5 minutes or until the skin is crispy.
6. Remove the wings from the oil and drain them. Toss in your favorite sauce then serve.

Nutrition:
- Calories: 75
- Fat: 55g
- Protein: 39g
- Fiber: 1g
- Sodium: 1747mg

Smoked Fried Chicken

Servings: 6
Cooking Time: 3 Hours
Ingredients:
- 3.5 lb. chicken
- Vegetable oil
- Salt and pepper to taste
- 2 tablespoons hot sauce
- 1 quart buttermilk
- 2 tablespoons brown sugar
- 1 tablespoon poultry dry rub
- 2 tablespoons onion powder
- 2 tablespoons garlic powder
- 2 1/2 cups all-purpose flour
- Peanut oil

Directions:
1. Set the wood pellet grill to 200 degrees F.

2. Preheat it for 15 minutes while the lid is closed.

3. Drizzle chicken with vegetable oil and sprinkle with salt and pepper.

4. Smoke chicken for 2 hours and 30 minutes.

5. In a bowl, mix the hot sauce, buttermilk and sugar.

6. Soak the smoked chicken in the mixture.

7. Cover and refrigerate for 1 hour.

8. In another bowl, mix the dry rub, onion powder, garlic powder and flour.

9. Coat the chicken with the mixture.

10. Heat the peanut oil in a pan over medium heat.

11. Fry the chicken until golden and crispy.

12. Tips: Drain chicken on paper towels before serving.

Smoked Chicken Leg Quarters

Preparation Time: 15 minutes
Cooking Time: 2 hours
Servings: 8
Ingredients:
- 8 chicken leg quarters
- 2 tbsp. olive oil
- 1 tsp. salt or to taste
- ½ tsp. chili powder
- ½ tsp. paprika
- ½ tsp. ground thyme
- 1 tsp. dried rosemary
- ½ tsp. cayenne pepper
- 1 tsp. garlic powder
- 1 tsp. onion powder

Directions:

1. To make the rub, combine cayenne, rosemary, garlic, onion powder, chili, paprika, salt, thyme.

2. Drizzle oil over the chicken leg quarters and season the quarters generously with rub mix.

3. Preheat the grill to 180°F with the lid closed for 15 minutes, using apple hard flavours.

4. Arrange the chicken onto the grill grate. Smoke for 1 hour, flipping halfway through.

5. Increase the grill temperature to 350°F. Cook for an additional 1 hour, or until the temperature of the chicken quarters reaches 165°F.

6. Remove chicken from grill, let it rest for about 15 minutes.

Nutrition:
- Calories: 34
- Fat 3.6g
- Carbs: 0.9g
- Fiber: 0.3g
- Protein: 0.2g

Peach And Basil Grilled Chicken

Servings: 4
Cooking Time: 35 Minutes
Ingredients:
- 4 boneless chicken breasts
- ½ cup peach preserves, unsweetened
- ½ cup olive oil
- ¼ cup apple cider vinegar
- 3 tablespoons lemon juice
- 2 tablespoons Dijon mustard
- 1 garlic clove, crushed
- ½ teaspoon red hot sauce
- ½ cup fresh basil leaves, chopped
- Salt to taste
- 4 peaches, halved, pit removed

Directions:

1. Place chicken in a bowl and stir in the peach preserves, olive oil, vinegar, lemon juice, Dijon mustard, garlic, red hot sauce, and basil leaves.

2. Massage the chicken until all surfaces are coated with the marinade. Marinate in the fridge for 4 hours.

3. Once ready to cook, fire the Grill to 400F. Use apple wood pellets. Close the lid and preheat for 15 minutes.

4. Place the chicken directly on the grill grate and cook for 35 minutes.

5. Flip the chicken halfway through the cooking time.

6.   Ten minutes before the cooking time ends, place the peach halves and grill.

7.   Serve with the chicken.

Nutrition Info: Calories per serving: 777; Protein: 61g; Carbs: 9.8g; Fat: 54.2g Sugar: 8g

Chicken Fajitas

Preparation Time: 0 minutes
Cooking Time: 20 minutes
Servings: 10
Ingredients:
• Chicken breast - 2 lbs., thin sliced
• Red bell pepper - 1 large
• Onion - 1 large
• Orange bell pepper - 1 large
• Seasoning mix
• Oil - 2 tbsp
• Onion powder - ½ tbsp
• Granulated garlic - ½ tbsp
• Salt - 1 tbsp

Instructions:
1. Preheat the grill to 450 degrees.
2. Mix the seasonings and oil.
3. Add the chicken slices to the mix.
4. Line a large pan with a non-stick baking sheet.
5. Let the pan heat for 10 minutes.
6. Place the chicken, peppers, and other vegetables in the grill.
7. Grill for 10 minutes or until the chicken is cooked.
8. Remove it from the grill and serve with warm tortillas and vegetables.

Recommended Side Dish: Avocado Salad
Alcoholic Drinks to accompany: chardonnay
Nutrition: Carbohydrates: 5g, Protein: 29g, Fat: 6g, Sodium: 360mg, Cholesterol: 77mg

Honey Baked Mustard Chicken

Preparation Time: 15 minutes
Cooking Time: 35 minutes
Servings: 4

Ingredients:
•   4 boneless skinless chicken breasts (4 ounces each)
•   1 tbsp. grainy mustard
•   4 tbsp. honey
•   ½ tsp. white vinegar
•   ½ tsp. paprika
•   2 tbsp. Dijon mustard
•   1 tbsp. + 2 tsp. olive oil
•   1 tsp. salt
•   1 tsp. ground black pepper or to taste
•   1 tbsp. freshly chopped parsley
•   1 tsp. dried basil

Directions:
1.   Preheat the grill to 375°F with the lid closed for 15 minutes.
2.   Grease a baking dish with a non-stick cooking spray.
3.   Season both sides of the chicken breasts with pepper and salt.
4.   Place a cast-iron skillet on the grill and add 2 tsp. olive oil.
5.   Once the oil is hot, add the seasoned chicken breast, sauté until both sides of the chicken breasts are browned.
6.   Use a slotted spoon to transfer the fried chicken breast to a paper towel lined plate.
7.   Combine the Dijon mustard, honey, vinegar, basil, grainy mustard, remaining oil, paprika in a mixing bowl. Mix until the ingredients are well combined.
8.   Pour half of the honey mixture into the prepared baking dish, spread it to cover the bottom of the dish.
9.   Arrange the chicken breast into the dish and pour the remaining honey mixture over the chicken.
10.   Cover the baking dish with foil and place it on the grill. Cook on grill for about 20 minutes.
11.   Remove the foil cover and cook, uncovered, for 15 minutes.
12.   Remove the baking dish from the grill and let the chicken cool for a few minutes.

Nutrition:
•   Calories: 320
•   Fat 12.4g
•   Carbs: 18.5g
•   Fiber: 0.6g
•   Protein: 33.4g

Korean Chicken Wings

Servings: 6
Cooking Time: 1 Hour
Ingredients:
- 3 pounds of chicken wings
- 2 tablespoons olive oil
- For the Brine:
- 1 head garlic, halved
- 1 lemon, halved
- 1/2 cup sugar
- 1 cup of sea salt
- 4 sprigs of thyme
- 10 peppercorns
- 16 cups of water
- For the Sauce:
- 2 teaspoons minced garlic
- 1/2 cup gochujang hot pepper paste
- 1 tablespoon grated ginger
- 2 tablespoons of rice wine vinegar
- 1/3 cup honey
- 1/4 cup soy sauce
- 2 tablespoons lime juice
- 2 tablespoons toasted sesame oil
- 1/4 cup melted butter

Directions:

1. Prepare the brine and for this, take a large stockpot, place it over high heat, pour in water, stir in salt and sugar until dissolved, and bring to a boil.

2. Then remove the pot from heat, add remaining ingredients for the brine, and bring the brine to room temperature.

3. Add chicken wings, submerge them completely, cover the pot and let wings soak for a minimum of 4 hours in the refrigerator.

4. When ready to cook, switch on the grill, fill the grill hopper with flavored wood pellets, power the grill on by using the control panel, select 'smoke' on the temperature dial, or set the temperature to 375 degrees F and let it preheat for a minimum of 15 minutes.

5. Meanwhile, remove chicken wings from the brine, pat dry with paper towels, place them in a large bowl, drizzle with oil and toss until well coated.

6. When the grill has preheated, open the lid, place chicken wings on the grill grate, shut the grill, and smoke for 1 hour until the internal temperature reaches 165 degrees F.

7. Meanwhile, prepare the sauce and for this, take a medium bowl, place all of the sauce ingredients in it and whisk until smooth.

8. When done, transfer chicken wings to a dish, top with prepared sauce, toss until coated, and then serve.

Nutrition Info: Calories: 137 Cal ;Fat: 9 g ;Carbs: 4 g ;Protein: 8 g ;Fiber: 1 g

Honey Garlic Chicken Wings

Preparation Time: 30 minutes
Cooking Time: 1 hour and 15 minutes
Servings: 4
Ingredients:
- 2 1/2 lb. chicken wings
- Poultry dry rub
- 4 tablespoons butter
- 3 cloves garlic, minced
- 1/2 cup hot sauce
- 1/4 cup honey

Instructions:

1. Sprinkle chicken wings with dry rub.
2. Place on a baking pan.
3. Set the wood pellet grill to 350 degrees F.
4. Preheat for 15 minutes while the lid is closed.
5. Place the baking pan on the grill.
6. Cook for 50 minutes.
7. Add butter to a pan over medium heat.
8. Sauté garlic for 3 minutes.
9. Stir in hot sauce and honey.
10. Cook for 5 minutes while stirring.
11. Coat the chicken wings with the mixture.
12. Grill for 10 more minutes.

Recommended Side Dish: Super-Crispy Oven Fries
Alcoholic Drinks to accompany: Lager
Nutrition: Calories: 530, Fat: 21.67g, Carbs: 18.73g, Protein: 62.76g, Fiber: 0.2g

Tandoori Chicken Wings

Preparation Time: 20 minutes
Cooking Time: 1 hour 20 minutes
Servings: 4–6
Ingredients:
- ¼ Cup Yogurt
- 1 Whole Scallion, minced
- 1 tbsp. minced cilantro leaves
- 2 tsp. ginger, minced
- 1 tsp. Masala
- 1 tsp. salt
- 1 tsp. ground black pepper
- 1 ½ pound chicken wings
- ¼ cup yogurt
- 2 tbsp. mayonnaise
- 2 tbsp. Cucumber
- 2 tsp. lemon juice
- ½ tsp. cumin
- ½ tsp. salt
- ⅛ cayenne pepper

Directions:
1. Combine yogurt, scallion, ginger, garam masala, salt, cilantro, and pepper ingredients in the jar of a blender and process until smooth.
2. Put chicken and massage the bag to cat all the wings
3. Refrigerate for 4 to 8 hours. Remove the excess marinade from the wings; discard the marinade
4. Set the temperature to 350°F and preheat, lid closed, for 10 to 15 minutes. Brush and oil the grill grate
5. Arrange the wings on the grill. Cook for 45 to 50 minutes, or until the skin is brown and crisp and meat is no longer pink at the bone. Turn once or twice during cooking to prevent the wings from sticking to the grill.
6. Meanwhile, combine all sauce ingredients; set aside and refrigerate until ready to serve.
7. When wings are cooked through, transfer to a plate or platter. Serve with yogurt sauce

Nutrition:
- Calories: 241
- Carbs: 11g
- Protein: 12g
- Fat: 16g
- Saturated Fat: 3g

Chicken Lollipops

Preparation time: 30 minutes
Cooking Time: 2 hours
Serving: 6
Ingredients:
12 chicken lollipops
Chicken seasoning
10 tablespoons butter, sliced into 12 cubes
1 cup barbecue sauce
1 cup hot sauce
Instructions:
1. Turn on your wood pellet grill.
2. Set it to 300 degrees F.
3. Season the chicken with the chicken seasoning.
4. Arrange the chicken in a baking pan.
5. Put the butter cubes on top of each chicken.
6. Cook the chicken lollipops for 2 hours, basting with the melted butter in the baking pan every 20 minutes.
7. Pour in the barbecue sauce and hot sauce over the chicken.
8. Grill for 15 minutes.
Serving Suggestion: Serve with blue cheese dressing.
Nutrition: Calories: 2559, Fat: 75.38g, Carbs: 22.36g, Protein: 421.48g, Fiber: 1.2g

Bbq Sauce Smothered Chicken Breasts

Servings: 4
Cooking Time: 30 Minutes
Ingredients:
- 1 tsp. garlic, crushed
- ¼ C. olive oil
- 1 tbsp. Worcestershire sauce
- 1 tbsp. sweet mesquite seasoning
- 4 chicken breasts
- 2 tbsp. regular BBQ sauce
- 2 tbsp. spicy BBQ sauce

- 2 tbsp. honey bourbon BBQ sauce

Directions:

1. Set the temperature of Grill to 450 degrees F and preheat with closed lid for 15 minutes.

2. In a large bowl, mix together garlic, oil, Worcestershire sauce and mesquite seasoning.

3. Coat chicken breasts with seasoning mixture evenly.

4. Place the chicken breasts onto the grill and cook for about 20-30 minutes.

5. Meanwhile, in a bowl, mix together all 3 BBQ sauces.

6. In the last 4-5 minutes of cooking, coat breast with BBQ sauce mixture.

7. Serve hot.

Nutrition Info: Calories per serving: 421; Carbohydrates: 10.1g; Protein: 41,2g; Fat: 23.3g; Sugar: 6.9g; Sodium: 763mg; Fiber: 0.2g

Lemon Chicken in Foil Packet

Preparation time: 15 minutes
Cooking Time: 15 minutes
Servings: 4
Ingredients:
4 chicken fillets
3 tablespoon melted butter
1 garlic, minced
1-1/2 teaspoon dried Italian seasoning
Salt and pepper to taste
1 lemon, sliced
Instructions:
1. Turn on your wood pellet grill.
2. Keep the lid open while burning for 5 minutes.
3. Preheat it to 450 degrees F.
4. Add the chicken fillet on top of foil sheets.
5. In a bowl, mix the butter, garlic, seasoning, salt, and pepper.
6. Brush the chicken with this mixture.
7. Put the lemon slices on top.
8. Wrap the chicken with the foil.
9. Grill for 7 to 10 minutes per side.
Tip: You can also add broccoli or beans to cook along with the chicken.

Recommended Side Dish: cilantro-lime potato salad
Alcoholic Drinks to accompany: India Pale Ales
Nutrition: Calories: 1144, Fat: 34.45g, Carbs: 2.2g, Protein: 194.33g, Fiber: 0.3g

Buttermilk Brine Smoked Whole Chicken with Brown Sugar Chili Rub

(Cooking Time 3 hours 10 minutes)
Ingredients for 10 servings
- Whole Chicken (5-lb., 2.3-kg.)
The Brine
- Buttermilk - 3 cups
- Kosher salt - 1 teaspoon
- Pepper - 1 teaspoon
- Oregano - 1 tablespoon
The Rub
- Brown sugar - ½ cup
- Sweet paprika - ¼ cup
- Chili powder - 2 teaspoons
- Cayenne pepper - 2 teaspoons
The Spray
- Apple cider vinegar - 1 cup
The Heat
- Mesquite wood pellet
Method
1. Season the buttermilk with salt, pepper, and oregano. Stir until incorporated.
2. Add the chicken to the brine mixture and rub the mixture over the chicken including the chicken cavity.
3. Soak the chicken in the brine mixture for at least 4 hours to overnight and store it in the fridge to keep the chicken fresh.
4. On the next day, take the chicken out of the fridge and thaw it at room temperature.
5. In the meantime, mix brown sugar with sweet paprika, chili powder, and cayenne powder. Stir until combined.
6. Apply the spice mixture over the chicken and set aside.
7. Next, plug the wood pellet smoker then fill the hopper with the wood pellet. Turn the

switch on and set the wood pellet smoker for indirect heat.

8. Adjust the temperature to 275°F (135°C) and let the wood pellet smoker reaches the desired temperature.

9. Wait until the wood pellet smoker is ready and insert the seasoned chicken into the wood pellet smoker.

10. Smoke the chicken for 3 hours and spray apple cider vinegar over it once every 20 to 25 minutes.

11. Regularly check the internal temperature of the smoked chicken and once it reaches 165°F (74°C), take the smoked chicken out of the wood pellet smoker.

12. Transfer the smoked chicken to a serving dish and serve.

13. Enjoy!

Roasted Chicken With Pimenton Potatoes

Servings: 16
Cooking Time: 1 Hour
Ingredients:
- 2 whole chicken
- 6 clove garlic, minced
- 2 tablespoons salt
- 3 tablespoons pimento (smoked paprika)
- 3 tablespoons extra virgin olive oil
- 2 bunch fresh thyme
- 3 pounds Yukon gold potatoes

Directions:
1. Season the whole chicken with garlic, salt, paprika, olive oil, and thyme. Massage the chicken to coat all surface of the chicken with the spices. Tie the legs together with a string. Place in a baking dish and place the potatoes on the side. Season the potatoes with salt and olive oil.

2. Allow the chicken to rest in the fridge for 4 hours.

3. When ready to cook, fire the Grill to 300F. Use preferred wood pellets. Close the grill lid and preheat for 15 minutes.

4. Place the chicken and potatoes in the grill and cook for 1 hour until a thermometer inserted in the thickest part of the chicken comes out clean.

5. Remove from the grill and allow to rest before carving.

Nutrition Info: Calories per serving: 210; Protein: 26.1g; Carbs: 15.3g; Fat: 4.4g Sugar: 0.7g

Chipotle Smoked Chicken Wings with Pineapple and Coconut Sugar

(Cooking Time 1 hour 15 minutes)
Ingredients for 10 servings
- Chicken wings (5-lb., 2.3-kg.)

The Rub
- Coconut sugar - ¼ cup
- Onion powder - 1 tablespoon
- Paprika - 1 tablespoon
- Chili powder - 1 teaspoon
- Chipotle powder - 1 teaspoon
- Ground cinnamon - 1 teaspoon
- Mustard seeds - 1 teaspoon
- Kosher salt - 1 teaspoon
- Pepper - ½ teaspoon

The Sauce
- Olive oil - 2 tablespoons
- Diced onion - ¼ cup
- Minced garlic - 1 teaspoon
- Pineapple juice - 1 cup
- Teriyaki sauce - 3 tablespoons
- Worcestershire sauce - 1 tablespoon
- Lemon juice - 2 tablespoons
- Whisky - 1 tablespoon
- Cayenne pepper - ¼ teaspoon
- Coconut sugar - 2 tablespoons

The Heat
- Cherry wood pellet

Method
1. Mix the rub ingredients--coconut sugar, onion powder, paprika, chili powder, chipotle powder, ground cinnamon, mustard seeds, kosher salt, and pepper.

2. Rub the chicken wings with the spice mixture and set them aside.

3.   Next, plug the wood pellet smoker then fill the hopper with the wood pellet. Turn the switch on and set the wood pellet smoker for indirect heat.

4.   Adjust the temperature to 275°F (135°C) and let the wood pellet smoker reaches the desired temperature.

5.   Arrange the seasoned chicken wings on the grill grate inside the wood pellet smoker and smoke it for an hour to an hour and 15 minutes.

6.   In the meantime, pour olive oil into a saucepan and preheat it over low heat.

7.   Stir in diced onion and minced garlic then sauté until wilted and aromatic.

8.   Pour pineapple juice together with teriyaki sauce, Worcestershire sauce, lemon juice, and whisky.

9.   Season the sauce with cayenne pepper and coconut sugar then stir until incorporated.

10. Bring the sauce to a simmer and remove it from heat.

11. Check the internal temperature of the smoked chicken wings and once it reaches 165°F (74°C), remove the smoked chicken wings from the wood pellet smoker.

12. Take a smoked chicken wing and dip it into the sauce.

13. Repeat with the remaining smoked chicken wings and arrange them on a serving dish.

14. Serve and enjoy.

Sweet Sriracha Bbq Chicken

Servings: 5
Cooking Time: 1 And ½-2 Hours
Ingredients:
- 1cup sriracha
- ½ cup butter
- ½ cup molasses
- ½ cup ketchup
- ¼ cup firmly packed brown sugar
- 1teaspoon salt
- 1teaspoon fresh ground black pepper
- 1whole chicken, cut into pieces
- ½ teaspoon fresh parsley leaves, chopped

Directions:
1.   Preheat your smoker to 250 degrees Fahrenheit using cherry wood

2.   Take a medium saucepan and place it over low heat, stir in butter, sriracha, ketchup, molasses, brown sugar, mustard, pepper and salt and keep stirring until the sugar and salt dissolves

3.   Divide the sauce into two portions

4.   Brush the chicken half with the sauce and reserve the remaining for serving

5.   Make sure to keep the sauce for serving on the side, and keep the other portion for basting

6.   Transfer chicken to your smoker rack and smoke for about 1 and a ½ to 2 hours until the internal temperature reaches 165 degrees Fahrenheit

7.   Sprinkle chicken with parsley and serve with reserved BBQ sauce

8.   Enjoy!

Nutrition Info: Calories: 148 Fats: 0.6g Carbs: 10g Fiber: 1g

The Grilled Chicken Challenge

Preparation Time: 15 minutes
Cooking Time: 1 hour and 10 minutes
Servings: 4–6
Ingredients:
- 1 (4-lbs.) whole chicken
- As needed chicken rub

Directions:
1.   When ready to cook, set temperature to 375°F then preheat, close the lid for 15 minutes.

2.   Rinse and dry the whole chicken (remove and discard giblets, if any). Season the entire chicken, including the inside of the chicken using chicken rub.

3.   Place the chicken on the grill and cook for 1 hour and 10 minutes.

4.   Remove chicken from grill when the internal temperature of breast reaches 160°F. Check heat periodically throughout as cook

times will vary based on the weight of the chicken.

5. Allow chicken to rest until the internal temperature of breast reaches 165°F, 15-20 minutes. Enjoy!

Nutrition:
- Calories: 212
- Carbs: 42.6g
- Protein: 6.1g
- Fat: 2.4g
- Saturated Fat: 0.5g
- Fiber: 3.4g
- Sugar: 2.9g

Perfect Smoked Chicken Patties

Preparation Time: 20 minutes
Cooking Time: 50 minutes
Servings: 6
Ingredients:
- 2 lb. ground chicken breast
- 2/3 cup minced onion
- 1 tbsps. cilantro (chopped)
- 2 tbsp. fresh parsley, finely chopped
- 2 tbsp. olive oil
- 1/8 tsp crushed red pepper flakes
- 1/2 tsp ground cumin
- 2 tbsps. fresh lemon juice
- 3/4 tsp kosher salt
- 2 tsp paprika
- Hamburger buns for serving

Directions:
1. In a bowl combine all ingredients from the list.
2. Using your hands, mix well. Form mixture into 6 patties. Refrigerate until ready to grill (about 30 minutes).
3. Start your grill on SMOKE with the lid open until the fire is established). Set the temperature to 350°F and preheat for 10 to 15 minutes.
4. Arrange chicken patties on the grill rack and cook for 35 to 40 minutes turning once.
5. Serve hot with hamburger buns and your favorite condiments.

Nutrition:
- Calories: 258

- Carbs: 2.5g
- Fat: 9.4g
- Fiber: 0.6g
- Protein: 39g

Grilled Chicken with Pineapple

Preparation Time: 1 hour
Cooking Time: 1 hr. 15 mins
Servings: 6
Ingredients:
- 2 lbs. Chicken tenders
- 1 cup sweet chili sauce
- ¼ cup fresh pineapple juice
- ¼ cup honey

Directions:
1. Combine the honey, pineapple juice, and sweet chili sauce in a medium bowl. Whisk together thoroughly.
2. Put ¼ cup of the mixture to one side.
3. Coat the chicken in the sauce.
4. Place a lid over the bowl and leave it in the fridge for 30 minutes to marinate.
5. Heat the grill to high heat.
6. Separate the chicken from the marinade and grill for 5 minutes on each side.
7. Use the reserved sauce to brush over the chicken.
8. Continue to grill for a further 1 minute on each side.
9. Take the chicken off the grill and let it rest for 5 minutes before servings.

Nutrition:
- Calories: 270
- Fat: 2 g,
- Carbs: 25 g,
- Protein: 33 g

South-East-Asian Chicken Drumsticks

Preparation Time: 15 minutes
Cooking Time: 2 hours
Servings: 6
Ingredients:

- 1 cup fresh orange juice
- ¼ cup honey
- 2 tbsp. sweet chili sauce
- 2 tbsp. hoisin sauce
- 2 tbsp. fresh ginger, grated finely
- 2 tbsp. garlic, minced
- 1 tsp. Sriracha
- ½ tsp. sesame oil
- 6 chicken drumsticks

Directions:

1. Set the temperature of Grill to 225°F and preheat with closed lid for 15 mins, using charcoal.
2. Mix all the ingredients except for chicken drumsticks and mix until well combined.
3. Set aside half of honey mixture in a small bowl.
4. In the bowl of remaining sauce, add drumsticks and mix well.
5. Arrange the chicken drumsticks onto the grill and cook for about 2 hours, basting with remaining sauce occasionally.
6. Serve hot.

Nutrition:

- Calories: 385
- Carbs: 22.7g
- Protein: 47.6g
- Fat: 10.5g
- Sugar: 18.6g
- Sodium: 270mg
- Fiber: 0.6g

Budget Friendly Chicken Legs

Preparation Time: 15 minutes
Cooking Time: 1 hour and 30 minutes
Servings: 6
Ingredients:

For Brine:
- 1 cup kosher salt
- ¾ cup light brown Sugar:
- 16 cup water
- 6 chicken leg quarters

For Glaze:
- ½ cup mayonnaise
- 2 tbsp. BBQ rub
- 2 tbsp. fresh chives, minced
- 1 tbsp. garlic, minced

Directions

1. For brine: in a bucket, dissolve salt and brown Sugar: in water.
2. Place the chicken quarters in brine and refrigerate, covered for about 4 hours.
3. Set the temperature of Grill to 275°F and preheat with closed lid for 15 mins.
4. Remove chicken quarters from brine and rinse under cold running water.
5. With paper towels, pat dry chicken quarters.
6. For glaze: in a bowl, add all ingredients and mix till well combined.
7. Coat chicken quarters with glaze evenly.
8. Place the chicken leg quarters onto grill and cook for about 1–1½ hours.
9. Serve immediately.

Nutrition:

- Calories: 399
- Carbs: 17.2g
- Protein: 29.1g
- Fat: 24.7g
- Sugar: 14.2g
- Sodium: 15000mg
- Fiber: 0g

CHAPTER 6: PORK RECIPES

Pork Back Ribs

Prep Time: 15 minutes
Cooking Time: 5 hours
Temperature: 200F
 Servings: 16
Ingredients:
- ¼ cup yellow honey mustard
- ¼ cup brown sugar
- 1/3 cup paprika
- ¼ cup garlic powder
- ¼ cup onion powder
- 2 tbsp. chipotle chili pepper flakes
- 1 tbsp. ground cumin
- Salt and ground black pepper, to taste
- 2 tbsp. dried parsley flakes
- 8 lb. pork baby back ribs, silver skin removed

Directions:
1. In a bowl, add all ingredients except for ribs and mix well.
2. Rub the pork ribs with spice mixture.
3. Set the temperature of to 200F and preheat with a closed lid for 15 minutes.
4. Arrange the ribs onto the grill and cook for 2 hours.
5. Remove the ribs from the grill and wrap in heavy-duty foil.
6. Cook for 2 hours.
7. Remove the foil and cook for 1 hour more.
8. Remove from the grill and rest for 15 minutes.
9. Slice and serve.

Nutrition:
Calories: 659 |Fat: 40.7g| Carb: 7.8g| Protein: 61.1g

Summertime Pork Chops

Prep Time: 15 minutes
Cooking Time: 1 hour 35 minutes
Temperature: 250F
Servings: 4
Ingredients:
For Brine:
- 8 cups apple juice
- 1 cup light brown sugar
- ½ cup kosher salt
- ½ cup BBQ rub

For Pork Chops:
- 4 thick-cut pork loin chops
- 2 tbsp. BBQ rub
- 1 tbsp. Montreal steak seasoning

Directions:
1. For the brine: in a pan, add 4 cups of apple juice and cook until heated completely.
2. Add sugar, salt, and dry rub and cook until dissolved, stirring continuously.
3. Remove the pan from the heat and stir in the remaining apple juice. Set aside to cool completely.
4. In a large zip lock bag, add brine mixture and chops.
5. Seal the bag and refrigerate for about 2 hours.
6. Set the temperature of to 250F and preheat with a closed lid for 15 minutes.
7. Remove the chops from brine and set aside for 15 minutes.
8. Now, season the chops with BBQ rub and steak seasoning evenly.
9. Place the chops onto the grill and cook for 1 ½ hour.
10. Remove the chops from the grill and set aside for about 5 minutes before serving.
11. Serve.

Nutrition:
Calories: 609|Fat: 12.6g| Carb: 92.6g| Protein: 29.5g

Pork Loin

Prep Time: 15 minutes
Cooking Time: 1 hour 40 minutes
Temperature: 350F| **Servings**: 8
Ingredients:
- 1 (12-oz.) bottle German lager
- 1/3 cup honey
- 2 tbsp. Dijon mustard
- 1 tsp. dried thyme
- 1 tsp. caraway seeds
- 1 (3-lb.) pork loin, silver skin removed
- 1 large Vidalia onion, chopped
- 3 garlic cloves, minced
- 3 tbsp. dry seasoned pork rub

Directions:
1. In a bowl, add the lager, honey, mustard, thyme, and caraway seeds and mix well.
2. In a Ziploc bag, place pork loin, onion, garlic, and honey mixture.
3. Seal the bag and shake to coat well. Refrigerate to marinate overnight.
4. Set the temperature of to 350F and preheat with a closed lid for 15 minutes.
5. Remove the pork loin, onions, and garlic from the bag and place onto a plate.
6. Rub the pork loin with pork rub evenly.
7. Place the seasoned pork, onions, and garlic into a large roasting pan.
8. Arrange the pork tenderloin, fat side pointing up.
9. Place the marinade into a pan over medium heat and bring to a boil.
10. Cook for 3 to 5 minutes or until the liquid reduces by half.
11. Remove from the heat and set aside.
12. Place the roasting pan onto the grill and cook for 1 hour.
13. Carefully pour the reduced marinade on top of the pork loin evenly.
14. Cook for 30 to 60 minutes more, basting the meat with marinade occasionally.
15. Remove from the grill and cool for 10 minutes.
16. Slice and serve.

Nutrition:
Calories: 492|Fat: 23.9g| Carb: 16.3g| Protein: 47.2g

Fajita Favorite Pork Shoulder

Prep Time: 15 minutes
Cooking Time: 10 hours| **Temperature**: 160F & 250F
Servings: 20
Ingredients:
For Brine:
- 4 cup hot water
- 1 cup kosher salt
- ¼ cup brown sugar
- 2 tbsp. black peppercorn
- 12 cups cold water
- 8 cups apple cider
- ¼ cup apple cider vinegar
- ¼ cup Worcestershire sauce

For Pork:
- 8½ pounds pork shoulder roast, trimmed
- ¼-½ cup pork rub

Directions:
1. For the brine: in a container, add hot water, salt, brown sugar, and peppercorn and mix until dissolved.
2. Add the cold water, apple cider, vinegar, and Worcestershire sauce and mix until well combined.
3. Score the pork on both sides with a knife, then place it in the brine.
4. Cover the container and refrigerate for 24 hours.
5. Remove the pork from the container and discard the brine.
6. Rinse the pork shoulder under running cold water.
7. Pat dry the pork shoulder completely.
8. Place the pork shoulder onto a baking sheet and refrigerate for 2 hours or up to overnight.
9. Set the temperature of to 160F and preheat with a closed lid for 15 minutes.
10. Place the pork shoulder onto the grill and cook for 4 hours.
11. Now, set the temperature of the gill to 250F and cook for 4 to 6 hours.
12. Remove the pork shoulder from the grill and place onto a baking sheet for about 40 to 60 minutes.
13. Shred the meat and serve.

Nutrition:

Calories: 626|Fat: 41.4g| Carb: 15g| Protein: 45g

Pork Belly Burnt Ends

Preparation Time: 15 minutes
Cooking Time: 6 hours
Servings: 3
Ingredients:
•1kg pork belly
•Finest No. 7 by Spacebar
•Chili & horseradish from BBQED
•Butter
•Honey
Instructions:
1.   Remove the bones from the pork belly and cut off the rind. Cut into 1-2 finger-thick cubes and season generously with the Finest No.7 Rub. Place the finished cubes in the fridge for a few hours to marinate. Prepare the grill indirectly to 105 degrees, put the pork belly cubes on the grill and smoke for 3 hours.
2.   After 3 hours, put the burnt ends together with BBQ sauce, butter, and honey in an aluminum dish. Seal the dish airtight with aluminum foil and raise the grill temperature to 160 degrees.
3.   Burnt ends with BBQED.
4.   After another 2 hours, remove the dish from the grill and remove the aluminum foil. Adjust the grill to 105 degrees and reset the aluminum dish for another hour. Let the Pork Belly Burnt Ends cool briefly and eat them straight away.
Recommended Side Dish: Cheddar And Jalapeño Skillet Cornbread
Alcoholic Drinks to accompany: Beer
Nutrition: Calories: 1727 Fats: 176.7g, Carbs: 0g, Fiber: 0g, Sodium: 107mg

Grilled Pork Chops

Prep Time: 15 minutes
Cooking Time: 20 minutes **Temperature**: 450F

Servings: 6
Ingredients:
•   6 thick-cut pork chops
•   BBQ rub as needed
Directions:
1.   Preheat the to 450F.
2.   Season the pork chops with the BBQ rub.
3.   Place the chops on the and cook for 6 minutes on each side or until the internal temperature reaches 145F.
4.   Remove the chops from the and cool for 5 minutes.
5.   Serve.
Nutrition:
Calories: 398|Fat: 19g| Carb: 8g| Protein: 46g

Pulled Pork, Brisket

Preparation Time: 4 hours
Cooking Time: 20 hours
Servings: 12
Ingredients:
•Creekstone brisket from don carne
•Boston butt or pork neck, for example from don carne
•Baby back ribs from don carne
•Apple juice
•Pickled onions
•Pickled cucumbers
•Pickled jalapenos
•BBQ sauce of your choice
•Cornbread recipe
•Ankerkraut steak and BBQ salt flakes
•Ankerkraut 9 pepper symphony
•Ankerkraut pull that piggy
Instructions:
1.   Set the Timberline to 80 degrees "Super Smoke" and season the pork neck generously with Ankerkraut Pull that Piggy. Place the pork neck on the grill and parry the brisket in the meantime. You can watch how this works on the YouTube channel "BBQ with Franklin", for example.
2.   As soon as the meat is parried, it is seasoned with salt & pepper; the pepper should not be too coarse and not too fine. Put

the brisket in the carrier Timberline and smoke overnight for approx. 10-12 hours. The temperature remains at 80 degrees and "Super Smoke".

3. The ribs can parry (remove silver skin) and also season with Pull that Piggy (can happen the night before). As soon as the first 12 hours are through, the brisket is packed in pink paper, wired with a thermometer (between flat and point) and the grill temperature is increased to 120 degrees. The ribs can now be placed on the carrier for the next 3 hours and sprayed with a little apple juice in between.

4. After 3 hours the ribs are wrapped in aluminum foil together with a good dash of apple juice, and are now steamed for 2 hours. In the meantime, check the core temperature of the brisket and pork neck from time to time.

5. If one of the two pieces already have a core temperature of around 90 degrees, it is packed in pink paper (the brisket can remain packed) and left to rest in the oven at room temperature for one hour. After the rest phase, set the oven to 60 degrees and keep the meat warm.

6. Now the side dishes such as cornbread and Coleslaw can be prepared, the corresponding recipes can be found here on the blog. After another 2 hours, the ribs are removed from the aluminum foil and glazed in the last phase with BBQ sauce and grilled on the carrier for another hour. If the ribs are ready before the other two pieces of meat, these can be wrapped in aluminum foil and kept warm in the oven.

7. As soon as the meat is completely finished and has rested, the pork neck is plucked and the brisket cut. Then everything is arranged and served together with the ribs and the side dishes on a tray. If you like, serve a few slices of toast and BBQ sauce.

Recommended Side Dish: Jalapeno Cornbread

Alcoholic Drinks to accompany: Shiner Bock

Nutrition: Calories: 348 Fats: 23.31g, Carbs: 4.67g, Protein: 30.4g, Sodium: 89mg

Blackened Pork Chops

Prep Time: 5 minutes
Cooking Time: 20 minutes
Temperature: 375F
Servings: 6
Ingredients:
- 6 pork chops
- ¼ cup blackening seasoning
- Salt and pepper to taste

Directions:
1. Preheat the to 375F.
2. Season the pork chops with the blackening seasoning, salt, and pepper.
3. Place the chops on the grill and cook for 8 minutes on one side, then flip.
4. Cook until the internal temperature reaches 142F.
5. Rest for 10 minutes. Serve.

Nutrition:
Calories: 333|Fat:18g| Carb: 1g| Protein: 40g

Smoked Pork Tenderloin - Recipe

Preparation Time: 15-45 minutes
Cooking Time: 2 and ½ hours
Servings: 4
Ingredients:
•2 pork fillets (about 500g each)
For the marinade:
•1/2 cup apple juice
•3 teaspoons honey
•3 teaspoons spice for meat
•1/4 cup brown sugar
•2 teaspoon thyme leaves
•1/2 teaspoon black pepper

Instructions:
1. Mix all the ingredients in a bowl and add the pork fillets checking that they are all drizzled with the marinade.
2. Leave to rest in the refrigerator for about 3 hours.
3. Place the smoking grill with the lid open until the fire stabilizes, about 5 minutes, then set the temperature to 248 °F and close the lid, leaving it to preheat for about 15 minutes.
4. In the meantime, remove the meat from the fridge and place it directly on the grill until

the meat reaches the internal temperature of 140 °F, it will take about 2 and a half hours.

5. Before cutting into slices, leave to rest for 5 minutes and serve!

Recommended Side Dish: Garlic Mashed Cauliflower

Alcoholic Drinks to accompany: Mojito

Nutrition: Calories: 348, Fats: 23.31g, Carbs: 4.67g, Protein: 30.4g, Sodium: 89mg

Grilled Pork Tenderloin with Herb Sauce

Prep Time: 10 minutes

Cooking Time: 15 minutes **Temperature**: 400F

Servings: 4

Ingredients:

*   1 pork tenderloin, silver skin removed and pat dry
*   BBQ seasoning

Fresh Herb Sauce

*   1 handful basil, fresh
*   1/2 handful flat-leaf parsley, fresh
*   1/4 tbsp garlic powder
*   1/3 cup olive oil
*   1/2 tbsp kosher salt

Directions:

1. Preheat the to 400F.

2. Generously rub the pork with BBQ seasoning, then cook over indirect heat in the while turning occasionally.

3. Cook until the internal temperature reaches 145F. Remove the pork from the and rest for 10 minutes.

4. Meanwhile, add all the fresh herb sauce ingredients to a food processor and pulse a few times.

5. Slice the pork and serve with sauce.

Nutrition:

Calories: 300|Fat: 22g| Carb: 13g| Protein: 14g

Smoked Pulled Pork

Preparation time: 10 minutes

Cooking time: 20 minutes

Serving: 8

Ingredients:

*   6-9 lb. of whole pork shoulder
*   2 cups of apple cider
*   Big game rub

Instructions:

1. Set the temperature to 250 degrees F and put it on preheat by keeping the lid closed for 15 minutes.

2. Now take off the excess fat from the butt of the pork and season it with big game rub on all sides.

3. Put the pork butt on the grill grate making sure to keep the fat side up.

4. Smoke it till the internal temperature reaches 160 degrees F. This should take approx. 3 to 5 hours.

5. Remove it from the grill and keep aside.

6. Now take a large baking sheet and keep 4 large pieces of aluminum foil one on top of the other. This should be wide enough to wrap the pork butt entirely.

7. Keep the pork butt in the very center of the foil and bring up the sides a little

8. Pour apple cider on top of the pork and wrap the foil tightly around it.

9. Keep it back on the grill again having the fat side up and cook till the internal temperature reaches 200 degrees F. This should take 3 to 4 hours.

10. Remove it from the grill and let it rest for 45 minutes inside the foil packet.

11. Take off the foil and pour off the extra liquid.

12. Now keep the pork in a dish and remove the bones and excess fat.

13. Add the separated liquid back to the pork and season it again with big game rub.

14. Serve and enjoy.

Nutrition: Calories: 543, Fats: 22.96g, Carbs: 13.04g, Fiber: 0.1g, Sodium: 4791mg, Protein: 72.61g

Togarashi Pork Tenderloin

Prep Time: 5 minutes
Cooking Time: 25 minutes **Temperature**: 400F
Servings: 4
Ingredients:
o   1 pork tenderloin
o   1/2 tbsp. kosher salt
o   1/4 cup Togarashi seasoning
Directions:
1.   Trim off any silver skin on the pork, then sprinkle salt and seasoning evenly.
2.   Preheat the to 400F.
3.   Cook the pork for 25 minutes or until the internal temperature reaches 145F.
4.   Remove the pork and rest for 10 minutes.
5.   Slice and serve.
Nutrition:
Calories: 390|Fat: 19g| Carb: 14g| Protein: 40g

Smoked Pork Tenderloin

Preparation time: 10 minutes
Cooking time: 1 hour & 45 minutes
Serving: 3
Ingredients:
•2 1-1/4 to 1-1/2 lb. silver skin removed pork tenderloins
•2 tbsp of thyme leaves
•1/4 cup of brown sugar
•1/2 cup of apple juice
•3 tbsp of pork & poultry rub
•3 tbsp of warmed honey
•1/2 tbsp of black pepper
Instructions:
1.   Take a large bowl and add apple juice along with honey and black pepper. Also add thyme leaves, pork, and poultry rub, and brown sugar.
2.   Whisk well to mix thoroughly.
3.   Now add the pork loins to this bowl containing the marinade.
4.   Turn it over to coat it well, and then cover the bowl with the help of a plastic wrap.
5.   Marinate it in the fridge for a couple of hours.
6.   Now put the smoker to preheat by pushing the temperature to 225 degrees F.
7.   Place the pork loin on the grates of the grill and smoke it well till the internal temperature reaches 145 degrees F.
8.   Let it rest for 5 minutes, and then slice it.
9.   Serve.
Recommended Side Dish: Cherry Farro Salad with Sweet Vinaigrette
Alcoholic Drinks to accompany: oaked Chardonnay
Nutrition: Calories: 420, Fats: 7.52g, Carbs: 41.1g, Fiber: 0.6g, Sodium: 1023mg, Protein: 46.3g

Smoked Pork Ribs

Prep Time: 15 minutes | **Cooking Time**: 5 hours| **Temperature:** 180F   &   350F|
Servings: 7
Ingredients:
•   3 rack baby back ribs
•   3/4 cup pork and poultry rub
•   3/4 cup BBQ Sauce
Directions:
1.   Season the pork with the rub.
2.   Preheat the grill to 180F for 15 minutes with the lid closed.
3.   Place the pork ribs on the grill and smoke them for 5 hours.
4.   Remove the pork from the grill and wrap them in a foil with the BBQ sauce.
5.   Place back the pork and increase the temperature to 350F. Cook for 45 minutes.
6.   Remove the pork and rest for 20 minutes.
7.   Serve.
NUTRITION:
Calories: 762|Fat: 57g| Carb: 23g | Protein: 39g

Smoked Stuff Pork Loin

Preparation time: 10 minutes
Cooking time: 1 hour
Serving: 2
Ingredients:
•1 3 lb. of pork loin
•6 diced sliced of bacon
•4 oz. of chopped Cremini mushroom
•1 ½ cup of arugula
•1/3 cup of grated parmesan cheese
•2 tsp of fresh, chopped thyme
•1 tbsp of divided sweet rib rub
Instructions:
1.   Fire up the smoker and preheat it to 225 degrees F.
2.   Now take the pork loin and place it on the cutting board.
3.   Push a long knife inside the right side of the loin and cut it an inch deep.
4.   Curve the knife and push the loin to the left. While doing so, the loin should be unrolled and rectangular.
5.   Season it with sweet rib rub.
6.   Now heat an iron skillet over medium flame.
7.   Add bacon to it and cook till it turns slightly golden brown.
8.   Add mushroom and then sauté it for 3 minutes while making sure to stir in between.
9.   Turn off the heat and then add parsley, arugula, and thyme.
10.   Transfer this whole mixture to pork loin slowly.
11.   Make sure to distribute it evenly and leave a 1-inch gap on the right side.
12.   Top it with an adequate amount of parmesan cheese.
13.   Now roll the pork loin gently from left to right and secure it well.
14.   Place it in the skillet along with the bacon fat in it and move to the grill.
15.   Smoke it at 225 degrees F for an hour and then flip it and raise the temperature to 350 degrees.
16.   Cook for half an hour.
17.   Remove it from the grill and allow it to rest for 15 minutes.
18.   Place it on the cutting board, slice well, and serve.

Recommended   Side   Dish: Baked Macaroni and Cheese III
Alcoholic   Drinks   to   accompany: Burgundy wine
Nutrition: Calories: 1300, Fats: 69.79g, Carbs: 99.46g, Fiber: 5.2g, Sodium: 5617mg, Protein: 68.2g

Grill Pork Crown Roast

Prep Time: 5 minutes | **Cooking Time**: 1 hour | **Temperature**: 375F| **Servings**: 5
Ingredients:
•   13 ribs pork
•   1/4 cup favorite rub
•   1 cup apple juice
•   1 cup Apricot BBQ sauce
Directions:
1.   Preheat the grill to 375F for 15 minutes with lid closed.
2.   Meanwhile, season the pork with the rub, then let sit for 30 minutes.
3.   Wrap the tips of each crown roast with foil to prevent the meat from turning black.
4.   Place the meat on the grill grate and cook for 90 minutes. Spray apple juice every 30 minutes.
5.   When the meat has reached an internal temperature of 125F, remove the foil.
6.   Spray the roast with apple juice again and let cook until the internal temperature has reached 135F.
7.   In the last 10 minutes of cooking, baste the roast with BBQ sauce.
8.   Remove from the grill and wrap with foil. Let rest for 15 minutes before serving. Serve.
NUTRITION:
Calories: 240 |Fat: 16g| Carb: 0g| Protein: 23g

Cocoa Crusted Pork Tenderloin

Prep Time: 30 minutes | **Cooking Time:** 25 minutes | **Temperature**: 400F & 350F | **Servings**: 5
Ingredients:

- 1 pork tenderloin
- 1/2 tbsp fennel, ground
- 2 tbsp cocoa powder, unsweetened
- 1 tbsp smoked paprika
- 1/2 tbsp kosher salt
- 1/2 tbsp black pepper
- 1 tbsp extra virgin olive oil
- 3 green onion

Directions:

1. Combine everything in a bowl, except for the pork loin.
2. Rub the mixture on the pork and refrigerate for 30 minutes.
3. Preheat the grill to 400F for 15 minutes with lid closed.
4. Sear all sides of the loin at the front of the grill, then reduce the temperature to 350F and move the pork to the center grill.
5. Cook for 15 more minutes or until the internal temperature reaches 145F.
6. Remove from the grill and rest for 10 minutes.
7. Slice and serve.

NUTRITION:

Calories: 264|Fat: 13.1g| Carb: 4.6g| Protein: 33g

3.In an oven skillet, heat oil until smoking. Add the pork and sear on all sides until golden brown.

4.Set the skillet in the grill and cook for 20 minutes or until the meat is no longer pink and the internal temperature is 150°F.

5.Remove the pork from the grill and let rest for 10 minutes.

6.Add berries to the skillet and sear over the stovetop for a minute. Remove the strawberries from the skillet.

7.Add vinegar in the same skillet and scrape any browned bits from the skillet bottom. Bring it to boil, then reduce heat to low. Stir in sugar and cook until it has reduced by half.

8.Slice the meat and place the strawberries on top, then drizzle vinegar sauce. Enjoy.

Nutrition:

Calories: 244
Total Fat: 9g
Saturated Fat: 3g
Total Carbs: 15g
Net Carbs: 13g
Protein: 25g
Sugar: 12g
Fiber: 2g
Sodium: 159mg

Roasted Pork with Balsamic Strawberry Sauce

Preparation Time: 15 minutes
Cooking Time: 35 minutes
Servings: 3
Ingredients:

- 2 lb. pork tenderloin
- Salt and pepper to taste
- 2 tbsp rosemary, dried
- 2 tbsp olive oil
- 12 strawberries, fresh
- 1 cup balsamic vinegar
- 4 tbsp sugar

Instructions:

1.Set the wood pellet grill to 350°F and preheat for 15 minutes with a closed lid.

2.Meanwhile, rinse the pork and pat it dry. Season with salt, pepper, and rosemary.

BBQ Pork Ribs

Preparation Time: 10 minutes | **Cooking Time**: 2 hours | **Temperature**: 225F|
Servings: 6
Ingredients:

- 2 racks of St. Louis-style ribs
- 1 cup Pork and Poultry Rub
- 1/8 cup brown sugar
- 4 tbsp. butter
- 4 tbsp. agave
- 1 bottle Sweet and Heat BBQ Sauce

Directions:

1. In a bowl, combine the Pork and Poultry Rub, brown sugar, butter, and agave. Mix well.
2. Massage the rub onto the ribs and allow them to rest in the fridge for minimum of 2 hours.

3.   Fire the Grill to 225F. Close the lid and preheat for 15 minutes.
4.   Place the ribs on the grill grate and close the lid. Smoke for 1 hour and 30 minutes. Flip the ribs halfway through the cooking time.
5.   Brush the ribs with the BBQ sauce ten minutes before the cooking time ends.
6.   Remove from the grill and allow to rest before slicing.
NUTRITION:
Calories: 399|Fat:20.5g | Carb: 3.5g| Protein: 47.2g

Wet-Rubbed St. Louis Ribs

Preparation Time: 15 minutes
Cooking Time: 4 hours
Servings: 3
Ingredients:
- 1/2 cup brown sugar
- 1 tbsp cumin, ground
- 1 tbsp Ancho Chile powder
- 1 tbsp smoked paprika
- 1 tbsp garlic salt
- 3 tbsp balsamic vinegar
- 1 Rack St. Louis style ribs
- 2 cup apple juice

Instructions:
1.Add all the ingredients except ribs in a mixing bowl, and mix until well mixed. Place the rub on both sides of the ribs and let sit for 10 minutes.
2.Set the wood pellet temperature to 180°F and preheat for 15 minutes. Smoke the ribs for 2 hours.
3.Increase the temperature to 250°F and wrap the ribs and apple juice with foil or tinfoil.
4.Place back the pork, and cook for another 2 hours.
5.Remove from the grill, and let rest for 5 minutes before serving. Enjoy.
Recommended Side Dish: Coleslaw
Alcoholic Drinks to accompany: Beer
Nutrition:
Calories: 210
Total fat: 13g
Saturated fat: 4g

Total Carbs: 0g
Net Carbs: 0g
Protein: 24g
Sodium: 85mg

Citrus-Brained Pork Roast

Prep Time: 10 minutes | **Cooking Time**: 45 minutes | **Temperature**: 300F| **Servings**: 6
Ingredients:
- ½ cup of salt
- ¼ cup brown sugar
- 3 cloves of garlic, minced
- 2 dried bay leaves
- 6 peppercorns
- 1 lemon, juiced
- ½ tsp. dried fennel seeds
- ½ tsp. red pepper flakes
- ½ cup of apple juice
- ½ cup of orange juice
- 5 pounds pork loin
- 2 tbsp. extra virgin olive oil

Directions:
1.   In a bowl, combine the salt, brown sugar, garlic, bay leaves, peppercorns, lemon juice, fennel seeds, pepper flakes, apple juice, and orange juice.
2.   Mix to form a paste rub.
3.   Rub the mixture onto the pork loin and marinate for at least 2 hours.
4.   Add in the oil and fire the Grill to 300F. Close the lid and preheat for 15 minutes.
5.   Place the seasoned pork loin on the grill grate and close the lid. Cook for 45 minutes. Flip the pork halfway through the cooking time.
6.   Serve.
NUTRITION:
Calories: 869 |Fat: 43.9g| Carb: 15.2g| Protein: 97.2g

Wood Pellet Grilled Pork Chops

Preparation Time: 20 minutes

Cooking Time: 10 minutes
Servings: 6
Ingredients:
•Six pork chops, thickly cut
•BBQ rub
Instructions:
1.Preheat the wood pellet to 450°F.
2.Season the pork chops generously with the BBQ rub. Place the pork chops on the grill and cook for 6 minutes or until the internal temperature reaches 145°F.
3.Remove from the grill and let sit for 10 minutes before serving.
4.Enjoy.
Recommended Side Dish: Parmesan Pesto Roasted Potatoes
Alcoholic Drinks to accompany: red wines
Nutrition:
Calories: 264
Total fat: 13g
Saturated fat: 6g
Total Carbs: 4g
Net Carbs: 1g
Protein: 33g
Fiber: 3g
Sodium: 66mg

Smoked Pork Loin

Prep Time: 15 minutes | **Cooking Time**: 3 hours | **Temperature**: 250F | **Servings**: 6
Ingredients:
- ½ quart apple juice
- ½ quart apple cider vinegar
- ½ cup of sugar
- ¼ cup of salt
- 2 tbsp. fresh ground pepper
- 1 pork loin roast
- ½ cup Greek seasoning

Directions:
1.	Take a large container and make the brine mix by adding apple juice, vinegar, salt, pepper, sugar, liquid smoke, and mix.
2.	Keep stirring until the sugar and salt dissolved, and add the loin.

3.	Add more water if needed to submerge the meat.
4.	Cover and chill overnight.
5.	Preheat the grill to 250F.
6.	Coat the meat with the Greek seasoning and transfer it to your smoker.
7.	Smoke for 3 hours or until the internal temperature of the thickest part reaches 160F.
8.	Serve and enjoy.
NUTRITION:
Calories: 169 |Fat: 5g| Carb: 3g | Protein: 77g

Teriyaki Pineapple Pork Tenderloin Sliders

Preparation Time: 20 minutes
Cooking Time: 20 minutes
Servings: 6
Ingredients:
- 1-1/2 lb. pork tenderloin
- 1 can pineapple ring
- 1 package king's Hawaiian rolls
- 8 oz teriyaki sauce
- 1-1/2 tbsp salt
- 1 tbsp onion powder
- 1 tbsp paprika
- 1/2 tbsp garlic powder
- 1/2 tbsp cayenne pepper

Instructions:
1.Add all the fixings for the rub in a mixing bowl and mix until well mixed. Generously rub the pork loin with the mixture.
2.Heat the pellet to 325°F. Place the meat on a grill and cook while you turn it every 4 minutes.
3.Cook until the internal temperature reaches 145°F. Remove from the grill and let it rest for 5 minutes.
4.Meanwhile, open the pineapple can and place the pineapple rings on the grill. Flip the crews when they have a dark brown color.
5.At the same time, half the rolls, place them on the grill, and grill them until toasty browned.
6.Assemble the slider by putting the bottom roll first, followed by the pork tenderloin,

pineapple ring, a drizzle of sauce, and top with the other roll half. Serve and enjoy.

Recommended Side Dish: Cheese Grits Casserole

Alcoholic Drinks to accompany: Burgundy wine

Nutrition:

Calories: 243

Total fat: 5g

Saturated fat: 2g

Total Carbs: 4g

Net Carbs: 15g

Protein: 33g

Sugar: 10g

Fiber: 1g

Sodium: 2447mg

Easy Pork Chunk Roast

Prep Time: 15 minutes | **Cooking Time**: 4 hours | **Temperature**: 225F| **Servings**: 6

Ingredients:

- 1 whole 4-5 pounds chuck roast
- ¼ cup olive oil
- ¼ cup firm packed brown sugar
- 2 tbsp. Cajun seasoning
- 2 tbsp. paprika
- 2 tbsp. cayenne pepper

Directions:

1.   Preheat the grill to 225F.
2.   Rub chuck roast all over with olive oil.
3.   In a small bowl, add the brown sugar, paprika, Cajun seasoning, cayenne, and mix.
4.   Coat the roast well with the spice mix.
5.   Transfer the chuck roast to the grill rack and smoke for 4 to 5 hours, or until the internal temperature reaches 165F.
6.   Rest and enjoy.

NUTRITION:

Calories: 219|Fat: 16g| Carb: 0g| Protein: 59g

BBQ Spareribs with Mandarin Glaze

Prep Time: 10 minutes | **Cooking Time**: 60 minutes | **Temperature**: | **Servings**: 6

Ingredients:

- 3 large spareribs, membrane removed
- 3 tbsp. yellow mustard
- 1 tbsp. Worcestershire sauce
- 1 cup honey
- 1 ½ cup brown sugar
- 13 ounces Mandarin Glaze
- 1 tsp. sesame oil
- 1 tsp. soy sauce
- 1 tsp. garlic powder

Directions:

1.   In a bowl, mix everything except for the meat.
2.   Massage the spice mixture onto the spareribs. Rest in the fridge for at least 3 hours.
3.   Fire the to 300F. Close the lid and preheat for 15 minutes.
4.   Place the seasoned ribs on the grill grate and cover the lid.
5.   Cook for 60 minutes.
6.   Rest. Slice and serve.

NUTRITION:

Calories: 123|Fat:36.9g | Carb: 10.3g| Protein: 76.8g

Grilled BBQ Ribs

Prep time: 15 minutes | **Cook time**: 6 hours | **Serves** 6

⅓ cup yellow mustard

½ cup apple juice, divided, plus more as needed

1 tablespoon Worcestershire sauce

2 rack baby back pork ribs, membrane removed

Pork &Poultry Rub, to taste

½ cup dark brown sugar

⅓ cup honey, warmed

1 cup 'Que BBQ sauce

1.   Stir together the mustard, ¼ cup of apple juice, and Worcestershire sauce in a

small bowl. Spread the mustard mixture thinly on both sides of the ribs and season to taste with Pork & Poultry Rub.

2. When ready to cook, set temperature to 180°F (82°C) and preheat, lid closed for 15 minutes. Smoke the ribs for 3 hours, meat-side up.

3. Once complete, transfer the ribs to a rimmed baking sheet and increase the grill temperature to 225°F (107°C).

4. Tear off four long sheets of heavy-duty aluminum foil. Top with a rack of ribs and pull up the sides to keep the liquid enclosed. Scatter the rack with half the brown sugar, then top with half the honey and half the remaining apple juice. If you want more tender ribs, you can use a bit more apple juice. Lay another piece of foil on top and tightly crimp the edges so there is no leakage. Repeat with the remaining rack of ribs.

5. Return the foiled ribs to the grill and cook for another 2 hours.

6. Remove the foil from the ribs and brush the ribs with 'Que Sauce on both sides. Discard the foil.

7. Place the ribs directly on the grill and continue to grill for 30 to 60 minutes more, or until the sauce has tightened.

8. Allow the ribs to cool for 5 to 10 minutes and serve.

Classic Pulled Pork

Preparation Time: 15 minutes
Cooking Time: 16-20 hours
Servings: 8-12
Ingredients:

- 1 (6- to 8-pound) bone-in pork shoulder
- 2 tablespoons yellow mustard
- 1 batch Not-Just-for-Pork Rub

Directions:

1. Supply your smoker with wood pellets and follow the manufacturer's specific start-up procedure.

2. Coat the pork shoulder all over with mustard and season it with the rub.

3. Place the shoulder on the grill grate and smoke until its internal temperature reaches 195°F.

4. Pull the shoulder from the grill and wrap it completely in aluminum foil or butcher paper. Place it in a cooler, cover the cooler, and let it rest for 1 or 2 hours.

5. Remove the pork shoulder from the cooler and unwrap it. Remove the shoulder bone and pull the pork apart using just your fingers. Serve immediately as desired. Leftovers are encouraged.

Nutrition:

- Calories: 414 Cal
- Fat: 29 g
- Carbohydrates: 1 g
- Protein: 38 g
- Fiber: 0 g

Smoked Marinated Pork Tenderloins

Prep time: 5 minutes | **Cook time**: 3 hours | **Serves** 4

Marinade:
½ cup apple juice
¼ cup brown sugar
3 tablespoons Pork & Poultry Rub
3 tablespoons honey, warmed
2 tablespoons thyme leaves
½ tablespoon black pepper
Pork:
2 (1½-pound / 680-g) pork tenderloins, silver skin removed

1. In a large bowl, whisk all the ingredients for the marinade to combine. Add the pork tenderloins, turning to coat well on all sides. Cover the bowl with plastic wrap. Let marinate for 2 to 3 hours in the refrigerator.

2. When ready to cook, set temperature to 225°F (107°C) and preheat, lid closed for 15 minutes. For optimal flavor, use Super Smoke if available.

3. Put the marinated pork tenderloins directly on the grill and smoke for about 2½ to 3 hours, or until the internal temperature 145°F (63°C) on a meat thermometer.

4.   Remove the pork from the grill and cool for 5 minutes before slicing and serving.

Apple-Smoked Pork Tenderloin

Preparation Time: 15 minutes
Cooking Time: 4-5 hours
Servings: 4-6
Ingredients:
- 2 (1-pound) pork tenderloins
- 1 batch Not-Just-for-Pork Rub

Directions:
1.   Supply your smoker with wood pellets and follow the manufacturer's specific start-up procedure. Preheat the grill
2.   Generously season the tenderloins with the rub. W
3.   Put tenderloins on the grill and smoke for 4 or 5 hours, until their internal temperature reaches 145°F.
4.   The tenderloins must be put out of the grill and let rest for 5-10 minutes then begin slicing into thin pieces before serving

Nutrition:
- Calories: 180 Cal
- Fat: 8 g
- Carbohydrates: 3 g
- Protein: 24 g
- Fiber: 0 g

Barbecue Baby Back Ribs

Prep time: 15 minutes | **Cook time**: 5 to 6 hours | **Serves** 12 to 15
2 full slabs baby back ribs, back membranes removed
1 cup prepared table mustard
1 cup Pork Rub
1 cup apple juice, divided
1 cup packed light brown sugar, divided
1 cup of The Ultimate BBQ Sauce, divided
1.   Supply your with wood pellets and follow the manufacturer's specific start-up procedure. Preheat, with the lid closed, to 150°F (66°C) to 180°F (82°C), or to the "Smoke" setting.
2.   Coat the ribs with the mustard to help the rub stick and lock in moisture.
3.   Generously apply the rub.
4.   Place the ribs directly on the grill, close the lid, and smoke for 3 hours5. Increase the temperature to 225°F (107°C).
5.   Remove the ribs from the grill and wrap each rack individually with aluminum foil, but before sealing tightly, add ½ cup apple juice and ½ cup brown sugar to each package.
6.   Return the foil-wrapped ribs to the grill, close the lid, and smoke for 2 more hours.
7.   Carefully unwrap the ribs and remove the foil completely. Coat each slab with ½ cup of barbecue sauce and continue smoking with the lid closed for 30 minute to 1 hour, or until the meat tightens and has a reddish bark. For the perfect rack, the internal temperature should be 190°F (88°C).

Lovable Pork Belly

Preparation Time: 15 Minutes
Cooking Time: 4 Hours and 30 Minutes
Servings: 4
Ingredients:
- 5 pounds of pork belly; 1 cup dry rub
- 3 tablespoons olive oil
For Sauce
- Two tablespoons honey
- Three tablespoons butter
- 1 cup BBQ sauce

Directions:
1.   Take your drip pan and add water. Cover with aluminum foil.
2.   Pre-heat your smoker to 250 degrees F
3.   Add pork cubes, dry rub, olive oil into a bowl and mix well
4.   Use water fill water pan halfway through and place it over the drip pan.
5.   Add wood chips to the side tray
6.   Transfer pork cubes to your smoker and smoke for 3 hours (covered)

7. Remove pork cubes from the smoker and transfer to foil pan, add honey, butter, BBQ sauce, and stir
8. Cover the pan with foil and move back to a smoker, smoke for 90 minutes more
9. Remove foil and smoke for 15 minutes more until the sauce thickens
10. Serve and enjoy!

Nutrition:
Calories: 1164 Fat: 68g Carbohydrates: 12g Protein: 104g

Classic Pulled Pork Shoulder

Prep time: 15 minutes | **Cook time:** 16 to 20 hours | **Serves** 8 to 12

1 (6- to 8-pound / 2.7- to 3.6-kg) bone-in pork shoulder
2 tablespoons yellow mustard
1 batch Pork Rub

Supply your smoker with wood pellets and follow the manufacturer's specific start-up procedure. Preheat the grill, with the lid closed, to 225°F (107°C).

Coat the pork shoulder all over with mustard and season it with the rub. Using your hands, work the rub into the meat.

Place the shoulder on the grill grate and smoke until its internal temperature reaches 195°F (91°C).

Pull the shoulder from the grill and wrap it completely in aluminum foil or butcher paper. Place it in a cooler, cover the cooler, and let it rest for 1 or 2 hours.

Remove the pork shoulder from the cooler and unwrap it. Remove the shoulder bone and pull the pork apart using just your fingers. Serve immediately as desired. Leftovers are encouraged.

Wow-Pork Tenderloin

Preparation Time: 15 Minutes
Cooking Time: 3 Hours
Servings: 4

Ingredients:
• One pork tenderloin
• ¼ cup BBQ sauce
• Three tablespoons dry rub

Directions:
1. Take your drip pan and add water. Cover with aluminum foil.
2. Pre-heat your smoker to 225 degrees F
3. Rub the spice blend all finished the pork tenderloin
4. Use water fill water pan halfway through and place it over the drip pan.
5. Add wood chips to the side tray
6. Transfer pork meat to your smoker and smoke for 3 hours until the internal temperature reaches 145 degrees F
7. Brush the BBQ sauce over pork and let it rest
8. Serve and enjoy!

Nutrition:
• Calories: 405
• Fat: 9g
• Carbohydrates: 15g
• Protein: 59g

Barbecued Pork Belly Burnt Ends

Prep time: 30 minute | **Cook time**: 6 hours | **Serves** 8 to 10

1 (3-pound / 1.4-kg) skinless pork belly (if not already skinned, use a sharp boning knife to remove the skin from the belly), cut into 1½- to 2-inch cubes
1 batch Sweet Brown Sugar Rub
½ cup honey
1 cup The Ultimate BBQ Sauce
2 tablespoons light brown sugar

Supply your smoker with wood pellets and follow the manufacturer's specific start-up procedure. Preheat the grill, with the lid closed, to 250°F (121°C).

2. Generously season the pork belly cubes with the rub. Using your hands, work the rub into the meat.

3. Place the pork cubes directly on the grill grate and smoke until their internal temperature reaches 195°F (91°C).

4. Transfer the cubes from the grill to an aluminum pan. Add the honey, barbecue sauce, and brown sugar. Stir to combine and coat the pork.

5. Place the pan in the grill and smoke the pork for 1 hour, uncovered. Remove the pork from the grill and serve immediately.

Herbed Prime Rib

Preparation Time: 15 Minutes
Cooking Time: 4 Hours
Servings: 4
Ingredients:
- 5 pounds prime rib; Two tablespoons black pepper
- ¼ cup olive oil; Two tablespoons salt Herb Paste
- ¼ cup olive oil
- One tablespoon fresh sage
- One tablespoon fresh thyme
- One tablespoon fresh rosemary
- Three garlic cloves

Directions:
1. Take a blender and add herbs, blend until thoroughly combined
2. Take your drip pan and add water. Cover with aluminum foil.
3. Pre-heat your smoker to 225 degrees F
4. Use water fill water pan halfway through and place it over the drip pan.
5. Add wood chips to the side tray
6. Coat rib with olive oil and season it well with salt and pepper
7. Transfer seasoned rib to your smoker and smoke for 4 hours
8. Remove rib from the smoker and keep it on the side. Let it cool for 30 minutes. Cut into slices and serve. Enjoy!

Nutrition:
Calories: 936 Fat: 81g Carbohydrates: 2g Protein: 46g

Stuffed Pork Loin wwith Bacon

Prep time: 20 minute | **Cook time**: 1 hour | **Serves** 4 to 6
Ingredients:
3 pound (1.4 kg) pork loin, butterflied
As needed pork rub
¼ cup Walnuts, chopped
⅓ cup Craisins
1 tablespoon oregano, fresh
1 tablespoon fresh thyme
6 pieces Asparagus, fresh
6 slices Bacon, sliced
1/3 cup Parmesan cheese, grated
As needed bacon grease

1. Lay down 2 large pieces of butcher's twine on your work surface. Place butterflied pork loin perpendicular to twine.
2. Season the inside of the pork loin with the pork rub.
3. On one end of the loin, layer in a line all of the ingredients, beginning with the chopped walnuts, craisins, oregano, thyme, and asparagus.
4. Add bacon and top with the parmesan cheese.
5. Starting at the end with all of the fillings, carefully roll up the pork loin and secure on both ends with butcher's twine.
6. Roll the pork loin in the reserved bacon grease and season the outside with more Pork Rub.
7. When ready to cook, set temperature to 180°F (82°C) and preheat, lid closed for 15 minutes. Place stuffed pork loin directly on the grill grate and smoke for 1 hour.
8. Remove the pork loin; increase the temperature to 350°F (177°C) and allow to preheat.
9. Place the loin back on the and grill for approximately 30 to 45 minutes or until the temperature reads 135°F (57°C) on an instant-read thermometer.
10. Move the pork loin to a plate and tent it with aluminum foil. Let it rest for 15 minutes before slicing and serving. Enjoy!

Alabama Pulled Pig Pork

Preparation Time: 1 Hour
Cooking Time: 12 Hours
Servings: 8
Ingredients:

- 2 cups of soy sauce
- 1 cup of Worcestershire sauce
- 1 cup of cranberry grape juice
- 1 cup of teriyaki sauce
- One tablespoon of hot pepper sauce
- Two tablespoons of steak sauce
- 1 cup of light brown sugar
- ½ a teaspoon of ground black pepper
- 2 pounds of flank steak cut up into ¼ inch slices

Directions:

1. Take a non-reactive saucepan and add cider, salt, vinegar, brown sugar, cayenne pepper, black pepper, and butter
2. Bring the mix to a boil over medium-high heat
3. Add in water and return the mixture to a boil
4. Carefully rub the pork with the sauce
5. Take your drip pan and add water. Cover with aluminum foil.
6. Pre-heat your smoker to 225 degrees F
7. Use water fill water pan halfway through and place it over the drip pan.
8. Add wood chips to the side tray
9. Smoke meat for about 6-10 hours. Make sure to keep basting it with the sauce every hour or so
10. After the first smoking is done, take an aluminum foil and wrap up the meat forming a watertight seal
11. Place the meat in the middle of your foil and bring the edges to the top, cupping up the meat complete
12. Pour 1 cup of sauce over the beef and tight it up
13. Place the package back into your smoker and smoke for 2 hours until the meat quickly pulls off from the bone
14. Once done, remove it from the smoker and pull off the pork, discarding the bone and fat
15. Place the meat chunks in a pan and pour 1 cup of sauce for every4 pound of meat
16. Heat until simmering and serve immediately!

Nutrition:

- Calories: 1098
- Fats: 86g
- Carbs: 38g
- Fiber: 3g

BBQ St. Louis-Style Ribs

Prep time: 5 minutes | **Cook time**: 6 hours 10 minutes | **Serves** 4
2 racks of St. Louis-style ribs
¼ cup Pork & Poultry Rub
1 cup apple juice
1 bottle Sweet & Heat BBQ Sauce

1. Trim the ribs and peel off the membrane from the back of the ribs. Brush the Pork & Poultry Rub all over the ribs. Let marinate for 20 minutes and up to 4 hours if refrigerated.
2. When ready to cook, set temperature to 225°F (107°C) and preheat, lid closed for 15 minutes.
3. Place the ribs, bone-side down, on the grill grate. Pour the apple juice in a spray bottle and spritz the ribs evenly. Smoke for 3 hours.
4. Remove the ribs from the grill and wrap in aluminum foil. Leave an opening at one end, pour in the remaining apple juice into the foil and wrap tightly.
5. Place the ribs back on the grill, meat-side down. Smoke for an additional 3 hours.
6. After 1 hour, start checking the internal temperature of the ribs. The ribs are done when the internal temperature reaches 203°F (95°C).
7. When done, remove from the foil and brush the Sweet & Heat BBQ Sauce all over the ribs.
8. Return to the grill and cook for an additional 10 minutes to set the sauce.
9. After sauce has set, take the ribs off the grill and let rest for 10 minutes.
10. Slice the ribs in between the bones and serve warm

Juicy BBQ Ribs

Prep time: 10 minutes | Cook time: 2 hours 20 minutes | **Serves** 6

4 rack baby back ribs
½ cup white grape juice
½ cup apple juice
Honey, as needed
BBQ Sauce, as needed
Rub:
⅔ cup brown sugar
½ cup paprika
⅓ cup garlic powder
2 tablespoons chili powder
2 tablespoons onion powder
1 tablespoon freshly ground white pepper
1 tablespoon cayenne pepper
1 tablespoon ground black pepper
1½ teaspoons ground cumin
1½ teaspoons dried oregano

1. In a bowl, stir together all the ingredients for the rub. Season the ribs with the rub on both sides.
2. When ready to cook, set temperature to 275°F (135°C) and preheat, lid closed for 15 minutes.
3. Place the seasoned ribs on the grill and cook for 45 minutes.
4. Meanwhile, combine the grape and apple juices in a small bowl and set aside.
5. Remove the ribs from the grill and place them, bone-side down, on a large disposable foil pan. Pour the juice mixture over the ribs.
6. Drizzle with the honey. Wrap up the ribs completely with the foil and seal the edges. Return the ribs to the grill and cook for 1 hour.
7. Remove the ribs from the foil and place directly on the grill grate. Set the temperature to 350°F (177°C) and cook for 30 additional minutes.
8. Rub the ribs with the BBQ Sauce and cook for an additional 5 minutes to set the sauce.
9. Transfer the ribs to a cutting board. Slice into single serving-size pieces and serve.

Smoked Avocado Pork Ribs

Preparation Time: 20 minutes
Cooking Time: 4 hours
Servings: 5
Ingredients:
- 2 lbs. pork spareribs
- 1 cup avocado oil
- 1 tsp. garlic powder
- 1 tsp. onion powder
- 1 tsp. sweet pepper flakes
- Salt and pepper, to taste

Directions:
1. In a bowl, combine the avocado oil, garlic salt, garlic powder, onion powder, sweet pepper flakes, and salt and pepper.
2. Place pork chops in a shallow container and pour evenly avocado mixture.
3. Arrange pork chops on the grill rack and smoke for about 3 to 4 hours.
4. Transfer pork chops to serving plate, let them rest for 15 minutes, and serve.

Nutrition:
- Calories: 677
- Carbs: 0.9g
- Fat: 64g
- Fiber: 0.14g
- Protein: 28.2g

Smoked Pork Chops Marinated with Tarragon

Preparation Time: 20 minutes
Cooking Time: 3 hours
Servings: 4
Ingredients:
- ½ cup olive oil
- 4 tbsp. fresh tarragon chopped
- 2 tsp. fresh thyme, chopped
- Salt and grated black pepper
- 2 tsp. apple cider vinegar
- 4 pork chops or fillets

Directions:
1. Whisk the olive oil, tarragon, thyme, salt, pepper, apple cider and stir well.
2. Place the pork chops in a container and pour with tarragon mixture.
3. Refrigerate for 2 hours.

4.   Start grill on, lid open, until the fire is established (4–5 minutes). Increase the temperature to 225°F and allow to pre-heat, lid closed, for 10–15 minutes.
5.   Remove chops from marinade and pat dry on kitchen towel.
6.   Arrange pork chops on the grill rack and smoke for about 3 to 4 hours.
7.   Transfer chops on a serving platter and let's rest 15 minutes before serving.
Nutrition:
- Calories: 528.8
- Carbs: 0.6g
- Fat: 35g
- Fiber: 0.14g
- Protein: 51g

BBQ Honey Pork Belly

Prep time: 5 minutes | **Cook time**: 4 hours | **Serves** 8
1 (about 5- to 7-pound / 2.3- to 3.2-kg) skinless pork belly, cut into 1-inch cubes
Meat Church Honey Hog, as needed
1 cup apple juice, for spritzing
1½ cups Apricot BBQ Sauce
½ cup clover honey
1.   When ready to cook, set temperature to 275°F (135°C) and preheat, lid closed for 15 minutes.
2.   In a large bowl, toss together the pork belly cubes and Meat Church Honey Hog until well coated. Let sit for at least 15 minutes.
3.   Place the pork belly cubes, fat-side down, on the grill. Cook for 3 hours, spritzing with apple juice every 45 minutes or whenever it starts to look dry.
4.   Remove the pork when the internal temperature of the meat reaches 195°F (91°C) on a meat thermometer.
5.   Transfer the cubes to a half-size aluminum pan. Season with more Meat Church Honey Hog.
6.   Cover the cubes with the Apricot BBQ Sauce. Drizzle clover honey over the top. Toss the cubes thoroughly until completely coated.

7.   Place the pan back to the grill and cook uncovered for 1 more hour, or until all liquid has reduced and caramelized.
8.   Let cool for 15 minutes before serving. Serve warm.

Smoked Pork Cutlets with Caraway and Dill

Preparation Time: 15 minutes
Cooking Time: 1 hour 30 minutes
Servings: 4
Ingredients:
- 4 pork cutlets
- 2 lemons freshly squeezed
- 2 tbs. fresh parsley finely chopped
- 1 tbsp. ground caraway
- 3 tbsp. fresh dill finely chopped
- ¼ cup olive oil
- salt and ground black pepper

Directions:
1.   Place the pork cutlets in a large resealable bag along with all remaining ingredients; shake to combine well.
2.   Refrigerate for at least 4 hours.
3.   Remove the pork cutlets from the marinade and pat dry on a kitchen towel.
4.   Start the grill (recommended maple flavour) on SMOKE with the lid open until the fire is established. Set the temperature to 250°F and preheat, lid closed, for 10 to 15 minutes.
5.   Arrange pork cutlets on the grill rack and smoke for about 1 and a half hours.
6.   Allow cooling at room temperature before serving.
Nutrition:
- Calories: 308
- Carbs: 2.4g
- Fat: 18.5g
- Fiber: 0.36g
- Protein: 32g

Chile Verde Braised Pork Shoulder

Prep time: 20 minutes | **Cook time**: 2 hours | **Serves** 6

1 pork shoulder, bone removed and cut into 1½-inch cubes (about 2 to 3 pounds / 0.9 to 1.4 kg)
1 tablespoon all-purpose flour
Salt, to taste
Black pepper, to taste
1 pound (454 g) tomatillos, husked and washed
1 medium yellow onion, peeled and cut into 1-inch chunks
2 jalapeños
4 cloves garlic
4 tablespoons olive oil, divided
2 cans green chiles
2 cups chicken stock
1 tablespoon cumin
1 tablespoon dried oregano
¼ cup chopped cilantro
½ lime, juiced

1. In a medium bowl, toss the pork shoulder with the flour, salt and pepper until well coated.
2. When ready to cook, set temperature to 500°F (260°C) and preheat, lid closed for 15 minutes.
3. Place a large cast iron skillet directly on the bottom rack of the grill and let preheat for 20 minutes.
4. Place the tomatillos, onion, jalapeños and garlic on a parchment-lined sheet tray. Drizzle with 2 tablespoons of the olive oil and season with salt and pepper. Stir to coat.
5. Pour the remaining 2 tablespoons of the olive oil in the cast iron skillet and add the pork shoulder. Spread the meat out evenly.
6. Place the sheet tray on the top rack. Close the lid and cook for 20 minutes, undisturbed. The pork should be evenly browned on the bottom and the veggies should be tender and lightly browned.
7. Remove the vegetables from the grill and transfer to a blender. Pulse until smooth. Pour the puréed vegetables into the skillet with the pork along with the green chiles, chicken stock, cumin and oregano.
8. Close the lid and reduce the temperature to 325°F (163°C). Cook for 60 to 90 minutes, or until the liquid has reduced and the pork is fork tender.
9. Remove from the grill. Top with the chopped cilantro and drizzle with the lime juice. Serve immediately.

Smoked Pork Ribs with Fresh Herbs

Preparation Time: 20 minutes
Cooking Time: 3 hours
Servings: 6
Ingredients:
- ¼ cup olive oil
- 1 tbs. garlic minced
- 1 tbs. crushed fennel seeds
- 1 tsp. fresh basil leaves finely chopped
- 1 tsp. fresh parsley finely chopped
- 1 tsp. fresh rosemary finely chopped
- 1 tsp. fresh sage finely chopped
- Salt and ground black pepper to taste
- 3 lbs. pork rib roast bone-in

Directions:
1. Combine the olive oil, garlic, fennel seeds, parsley, sage, rosemary, salt, and pepper in a bowl; stir well.
2. Coat each chop on both sides with the herb mixture.
3. Start the grill (recommended hickory flavour) on SMOKE with the lid open until the fire is established. Set the temperature to 225°F and preheat, lid closed, for 10 to 15 minutes.
4. Smoke the ribs for 3 hours.
5. Transfer the ribs to a serving platter and serve hot.

Nutrition:
- Calories: 459.2
- Carbs: 0.6g
- Fat: 31.3g
- Fiber: 0.03g
- Protein: 41g

Butter-Sugar Glazed BBQ Pork Ribs

Prep time: 5 minutes | Cook time: 4 hours 50 minutes| **Serves** 6

2 rack St. Louis-style ribs, membrane removed
1 cup Pork & Poultry Rub
4 tablespoons agave, divided
4 tablespoons butter, divided
2 tablespoons brown sugar, divided
1 bottle Sweet & Heat BBQ Sauce

1. When ready to cook, set temperature to 225°F (107°C) and preheat, lid closed for 15 minutes.
2. Brush the ribs all over with the Pork & Poultry Rub. Let marinate for 15 to 20 minutes.
3. Place the ribs, bone-side down, on the grill and cook for 3 hours.
4. Meanwhile, prepare the brown sugar wrap. Spread 2 tablespoons of the agave, 2 tablespoons of the butter and 1 tablespoon of the brown sugar on top of a double layer of aluminum foil. Repeat for the second foil.
5. After 3 hours, place one rack of ribs, meat-side down, in the prepared foil and wrap. Repeat with the second rack.
6. Increase the temperature of the grill to 250°F (121°C) and place the wrapped ribs, meat-side down, on the grill. Cook for another 1½ hours, or until an instant-read thermometer inserted in the meat registers 205°F (96°C).
7. Remove the ribs from the grill and discard the foil. Return the unwrapped ribs to the grill and cook for 10 more minutes.
8. Remove from the grill and rub with the Sweet & Heat BBQ Sauce. Return the ribs to the grill and cook for another 10 minutes.
9. Let cool for 10 minutes before slicing. Serve warm.

Smoked Spicy Pork Medallions

Preparation Time: 15 minutes
Cooking Time: 1 hour 30 minutes
Servings: 6
Ingredients:

- 2 lbs. pork medallions
- ¾ cup chicken stock
- ½ cup tomato sauce (organic)
- 2 tbs. smoked hot paprika (or to taste)
- 2 tbsp. fresh basil finely chopped
- 1 tbsp. oregano
- Salt and pepper to taste

Directions:

1. In a bowl, combine together the chicken stock, tomato sauce, paprika, oregano, salt, and pepper.
2. Brush generously over the outside of the tenderloin.
3. Start the grill on Smoke with the lid open until the fire is established (4 to 5 minutes). Set the temperature to 250°F and preheat, lid closed, for 10 to 15 minutes.
4. Place the pork on the grill grate and smoke until the internal temperature of the pork is at least medium-rare (about 145°F), for 1 and a half hours.
5. Let meat rest for 15 minutes and serve.

Nutrition:

- Calories: 364.2
- Carbs: 4g
- Fat: 14.4g
- Fiber: 2g
- Protein: 52.4g

Apricot BBQ Smoked Pork Tenderloin

Prep time: 5 minutes | **Cook time**: 48 minutes | **Serves** 4

2 pounds (907 g) pork tenderloin, trimmed
3 ounces (85 g) Big Game Rub
1 cup Apricot BBQ Sauce

1. Brush the pork tenderloin all over with the Big Game Rub and let marinate for 30 minutes.
2. When ready to cook, set temperature to 180°F (82°C) and preheat, lid closed for 15 minutes.
3. Arrange the pork tenderloin on the grill grate and smoke for 45 minutes.

4. Remove the pork from the grill. Set temperature to High and preheat, lid closed for 15 minutes.

5. Place the pork back to the grill grate and grill each side of the pork tenderloin for 90 seconds, or until an instant-read thermometer inserted in the thickest part of the meat registers 145°F (63°C).

6. Brush the pork with the Apricot BBQ Sauce. Transfer to a plate and let cool for 20 minutes before serving.

Smoked Apple Pork Tenderloin

Preparation Time: 25 minutes
Cooking Time: 3 hours
Servings: 8
Ingredients:
* ½ cup apple juice
* 3 tbsp. honey
* 3 tbsp. Pork and Poultry Rub
* ¼ cup brown Sugar:
* 2 tbsp. thyme leaves
* ½ tbsp. black pepper
* 2 pork tenderloin roasts, skin removed

Directions:
1. In a bowl, mix together the apple juice, honey, pork and poultry rub, brown sugar, thyme, and black pepper. Whisk to mix everything.

2. Add the pork loins into the marinade and allow to soak for 3 hours in the fridge.

3. Once ready to cook, fire the Grill to 225°F. Use hickory flavours when cooking the ribs. Close the lid and preheat for 15 minutes.

4. Place the marinated pork loin on the grill grate and cook until the temperature registers to 145°F. Cook for 2 to 3 hours on low heat.

5. Meanwhile, place the marinade in a saucepan. Place the saucepan in the grill and allow to simmer until the sauce has reduced.

6. Before taking the meat out, baste the pork with the reduced marinade.

7. Let rest for 10 minutes before slicing.

Nutrition:
* Calories: 203

* Protein: 26.4g
* Carbs: 15.4g
* Fat: 3.6g
* Sugar: 14.6g

Pork Collar with Rosemary Marinade

Preparation Time: 15 minutes
Cooking Time: 30 minutes
Servings: 6
Ingredients:
* 1 Pork Collar (3 - 4lb.)
* 3 tbsp. Rosemary, fresh
* 3 minced Shallots
* 2 tbsp. chopped Garlic
* ½ cup of Bourbon
* 2 tsp. Coriander, ground
* 1bottle of Apple Ale
* 1 tsp. ground Black pepper
* 2 tsp. Salt
* 3 tbsp. oil

Directions:
1. In a zip lock bag, combine the black pepper, salt, canola oil, apple ale, bourbon, coriander, garlic, shallots, and rosemary.

2. Cut the meat into slabs (2 inches) and marinate in the refrigerator overnight.

3. Preheat the grill to 450F with the lid closed. Grill the meat for 5 minutes and lower the temperature to 325F. Pour the marinade over the meat. Cook 25 minutes more.

4. Cook until the internal temperature of the meat is 160F.

5. Serve and enjoy!

Nutrition: Calories: 420 Proteins: 30g Carbohydrates: 4g Fat: 26g

Smoked Honey - Garlic Pork Chops

Preparation Time: 15 minutes
Cooking Time: 1 hour
Servings: 4
Ingredients:

- ¼ cup lemon juice freshly squeezed
- ¼ cup honey (preferably a darker honey)
- 3 cloves garlic, minced
- 2 tbs. soy sauce (or tamari sauce)
- Salt and pepper to taste
- 24 ounces center-cut pork chops boneless

Directions:
1. Combine honey, lemon juice, soy sauce, garlic, and salt and pepper in a bowl.
2. Place pork in a container and pour marinade over pork.
3. Cover and marinate in a fridge overnight.
4. In a meantime, heat the remaining marinade in a small saucepan over medium heat to simmer.
5. Transfer pork chops on a serving plate, pour with the marinade, and serve hot.

Nutrition:
- Calories: 301.5
- Carbs: 17g
- Fat: 6.5g
- Fiber: 0.2g
- Protein: 41g

Pork Collar and Rosemary Marinade

Preparation Time: 15 minutes + marinate time
Cooking Time: 30 minutes
Servings: 4
Ingredients:
- 1 pork collar, 3-4 pounds
- 3 tablespoons rosemary, fresh
- 3 shallots, minced
- 2 tablespoons garlic, chopped
- ½ cup bourbon
- 2 teaspoons coriander, ground
- 1 bottle of apple ale
- 1 teaspoon ground black pepper
- 2 teaspoons salt
- 3 tablespoons oil

Directions:
1. Take a zip bag and add pepper, salt, canola oil, apple ale, bourbon, coriander, garlic, shallots, rosemary, and mix well.
2. Cut meat into slabs and add them to the marinade; let it refrigerate overnight
3. Pre-heat your smoker to 450 degrees F
4. Transfer meat to smoker and smoke for 5 minutes, lower temperature to 325 degrees F
5. Pour marinade all over and cook for 25 minutes more until the internal temperature reaches 160 degrees F
6. Serve and enjoy!

Nutrition: Calories: 420 Fats: 26g Carbohydrates: 4g Fiber: 2g

Smoked Pork Shoulder

Preparation Time: 30 minutes
Cooking Time: 1 hour 30 minutes
Servings: 6
Ingredients:
- 3 pounds pork shoulder, roasts

Shoulder Rub Ingredients:
- ¼ cup brown sugar
- ¼ cup white sugar
- 1 tbsp. paprika
- 1 tbsp. garlic powder
- Salt, to taste
- ½ tbsp. chili powder
- 1 tsp. cayenne pepper
- ¼ tsp. black pepper
- 2 tsp. dried oregano
- 2 tsp. cumin

Liquid Ingredients to Be Injected
- ¾ cup apple juice
- 1 cup water
- ½ cup Sugar:
- Salt, to taste
- 6 tbsp. Worcestershire sauce

Directions:
1. Take a large bowl and add all the shoulder spice rub ingredients and mix well.
2. Take a separate bowl and add all the liquid ingredients.
3. Now use an injector to inject the mixed liquid into the meat.

4.   Pat dry it from the top with a paper towel.

5.   Rub the spice mixture on top and left for a few hours before cooking.

6.   Preheat the smoker grill for 50 minutes at 220°F.

7.   Put the meat onto the grill grate and cook for 2 hours at 225 degrees.

8.   Serve and enjoy.

Nutrition:

- Calories: 236
- Protein: 17 g
- Fat: 18 g

Zesty Herbal Smoke Pork Tenderloin

Preparation Time: 30 minutes
Cooking Time: 3 hours
Servings: 4
Ingredients:

- 2–4 pork tenderloins
- 6 tbsp. BBQ sauce

Pork Rub Ingredients:

- ½ cup cane sugar
- 1⁄3 tsp. chili powder
- ¼ tbsp. granulated onion
- ½ tbsp. granulated garlic
- 1 tbsp. dried chilies
- 1 tbsp. dill weed
- 1 tbsp. lemon powder
- 1 tbsp. mustard powder

Directions:

1.   Take a large mixing bowl and combine all the poke rub ingredients in it.

2.   Now preheat the smoker grill at 225°F until the smoke started to form

3.   **Cooking Time** for 3 hours, until the internal temperature reaches 150°F.

4.   After 3 hours a brush generous amount of the barbecue sauce and then left it to sit for 20 minutes before serving.

5.   Serve and enjoy.

Nutrition:

- Calories: 147
- Protein: 26 g
- Fat: 4 g

Pineapple Pork BBQ

Preparation Time: 10 minutes
Cooking Time: 60 minutes
Servings: 4
Ingredients:

- 1-pound pork sirloin
- 4 cups pineapple juice
- 3 cloves garlic, minced
- 1 cup carne asada marinade
- 2 tablespoons salt
- 1 teaspoon ground black pepper

Directions:

1. Place all ingredients in a bowl and massage the pork sirloin to coat. Place inside the fridge to marinate for at least 2 hours.

2.   When ready to cook, fire the Grill to 3000F. Use desired wood pellets when cooking the ribs. Close the lid and preheat for 15 minutes.

3. Place the pork sirloin on the grill grate and cook for 45 to 60 minutes. Make sure to flip the pork halfway through the cooking time.

4.   At the same time, when you put the pork on the grill grate, place the marinade in a pan and place it inside the smoker. Allow the marinade to cook and reduce.

5.   Baste the pork sirloin with the reduced marinade before the cooking time ends.

6.   Allow resting before slicing.

Nutrition: Calories per serving: 347; Protein: 33.4 g; Carbs: 45.8 g; Fat: 4.2g Sugar: 36g

Pork Sirloin Tip Roast Three Ways

Preparation Time: 20 minutes
Cooking Time: 1½ to 3 hours
Servings: 4 to 6
Ingredients:

Flavour: Apple, Hickory

- Apple-injected Roasted Pork Sirloin Tip Roast
- 1 (1½ to 2 pounds) pork sirloin tip roast
- ¾ cup 100% apple juice
- 2 tbsp. roasted garlic–seasoned extra-virgin olive oil

- 5 tbsp. Pork Dry Rub or a business rub, for example, Plowboys BBQ Bovine Bold

Directions:

1. Dry the roast with a piece of paper
2. Utilize a flavor/marinade injector to infuse all zones of tip roast with the apple juice.
3. Rub the whole roast with the olive oil and afterward cover generously with the rub.
4. Utilize 2 silicone nourishment grade cooking groups or butcher's twine to support the roast.
5. Roast the meat until the internal temperature arrives at 145°F, about 1 and a half hours.
6. Rest the roast under a free foil tent for 15 minutes.
7. Remove the cooking groups or twine and cut the roast contrary to what would be expected.

Nutrition:

- Calories: 354
- Protein: 22 g
- Fat: 30 g

Hickory-Smoked Pork Sirloin Tip Roast

Preparation Time: 30 minutes

Cooking Time: 3 hours

Servings: 3

Ingredients:

- 1 (1½ to 2 pounds) pork sirloin tip roast
- 2 tbsp. roasted garlic-seasoned extra-virgin olive oil
- 5 tbsp. Jan's Original Dry Rub, Pork Dry Rub, or your preferred pork rub

Directions:

1. Pat the roast dry with a paper towel.
2. Rub the whole roast with olive oil. Coat the roast with the rub.
3. Support the roast utilizing 2 to 3 silicone nourishment grade cooking groups or butcher's twine to ensure the roast keeps up its shape during cooking.
4. Wrap the tip roast in plastic wrap and refrigerate medium-term.

5. Place the roast directly on the grill grates and smoke the roast until the internal temperature, at the thickest part of the roast, arrives at 145°F, around 3 hours.
6. Rest the roast under a free foil tent for 15 minutes.
7. Remove the cooking groups or twine and cut the roast contrary to what would be expected.

Nutrition:

- Calories: 276
- Protein: 28 g
- Fat: 12 g

Bourbon Honey Glazed Smoked Pork Ribs

Preparation Time: 15 minutes

Cooking Time: 5 hours

Servings: 10

Ingredients:

- Pork Ribs (4-lbs., 1.8-kg.)
- The Marinade
- Apple juice – 1 ½ cups
- Yellow mustard – ½ cup
- The Rub
- Brown sugar – ¼ cup
- Smoked paprika – 1 tablespoon
- Onion powder – ¾ tablespoon
- Garlic powder – ¾ tablespoon
- Chili powder – 1 teaspoon
- Cayenne pepper – ¾ teaspoon
- Salt – 1 ½ teaspoon
- The Glaze
- Unsalted butter – 2 tablespoons
- Honey – ¼ cup
- Bourbon – 3 tablespoons

Directions:

1. Place apple juice and yellow mustard in a bowl, then stir until combined.
2. Apply the mixture over the pork ribs, then marinates for at least an hour.
3. In the meantime, combine brown sugar with smoked paprika, onion powder, garlic powder, chili powder, black pepper, cayenne pepper, and salt, then mix well.

4. After an hour of the marinade, sprinkle the dry spice mixture over the marinated pork ribs, then let it rest for a few minutes.
5. Plug the wood pellet smoker, then fill the hopper with the wood pellet. Turn the switch on.
6. Set the wood pellet smoker for indirect heat, then adjust the temperature to 250°F (121°C).
7. When the wood pellet smoker is ready, place the seasoned pork ribs in the wood pellet smoker and smoke for 3 hours.
8. Meanwhile, place unsalted butter in a saucepan, then melt over very low heat.
9. Once it is melted, remove it from heat, and then add honey and bourbon to the saucepan. Stir until incorporated and set aside.
10. After 3 hours of smoking, baste the honey bourbon mixture over the pork ribs and wrap it with aluminum foil.
11. Return the wrapped pork ribs to the wood pellet smoker and continue smoking for another 2 hours.
12. Once the smoked pork ribs reach 145°F (63°C), remove the smoked pork ribs from the wood pellet smoker.
13. Unwrap the smoked pork ribs and serve.
Nutrition: Calories: 313 Carbs: 5g Fat: 20g Protein: 26g

Italian seasoning – ½ teaspoon
Onion powder – 1 teaspoon
Directions:
1. Pour apple juice into a container, then stir in honey, brown sugar, dried thyme, black pepper, chili powder, Italian seasoning, and onion powder. Mix well.
2. Rub the pork tenderloin with the spice mixture, then let it rest for an hour.
3. Plug the wood pellet smoker, then fill the hopper with the wood pellet. Turn the switch on.
4. Set the wood pellet smoker for indirect heat, then adjust the temperature to 250°F (121°C).
5. When the wood pellet smoker has reached the desired temperature, place the seasoned pork tenderloin in the wood pellet smoker and smoke for 3 hours.
6. After 3 hours of smoking, increase the wood pellet smoker's temperature to 350°F (177°C) and continue smoking the pork tenderloin for another 30 minutes.
7. Once the smoked pork tenderloin's internal temperature has reached 165°F (74°C), remove it from the wood pellet smoker and transfer it to a serving dish.
8. Cut the smoked pork tenderloin into thick slices, then serve.
Nutrition: Calories: 318 Carbs: 7g Fat: 10g Protein: 8g

Chili Sweet Smoked Pork Tenderloin

Preparation Time: 10 minutes
Cooking Time: 3 hours 30 minutes
Servings: 8
Ingredients:
- Pork Tenderloin (3-lb., 1.4-kg.)
- The Rub
- Apple juice – 1 cup
- Honey – ½ cup
- Brown sugar – ¾ cup
- Dried thyme – 2 tablespoons
- Black pepper – ½ tablespoon
- Chili powder – 1 ½ teaspoon

Tender Grilled Loin Chops

Preparation Time: 10 minutes
Cooking Time: 12 to 15 minutes
Servings: 6
Ingredients:
Flavour: Any
- 6 boneless focus cut midsection pork cleaves, 1 to 1½ inches thick 2 quarts Pork Brine
- 2 tbsp. roasted garlic-seasoned extra-virgin olive oil
- 2 tsp. black pepper
Directions:

1. Trim abundance fat and silver skin from the pork slashes.
2. Place the pork slashes and brine in a 1-gallon sealable pack and refrigerate for in any event 12 hours or medium-term.
3. Remove the pork slashes from the brine and pat them dry with paper towels.
4. Brined pork hacks cook quicker than un-brined cleaves, so be mindful so as to screen internal temperatures.
5. Rest the pork slashes under a foil tent for 5 minutes before serving.

Nutrition:
- Calories: 211
- Protein: 17 g
- Fat: 21 g

Bacon-Wrapped Pork Tenderloin

Preparation Time: 15 minutes
Cooking Time: 40 minutes
Servings: 4
Ingredients:
- 1 pork tenderloin.
- 4 strips of bacon.
- Rub:
- 8 tablespoons of brown sugar.
- 3 tablespoons of kosher salt to taste.
- 1 tablespoon of chili powder.
- 1 teaspoon of black pepper to taste.
- 1 teaspoon of onion powder.
- 1 teaspoon of garlic powder.

Directions:
1. Using a small mixing bowl, add sugar, chili powder, onion powder, garlic powder, salt, and pepper to taste, mix properly to combine, and set aside. Use a sharp knife to trim off fats present on the pork, then coat with 1/4 of the prepared rub. Make sure you coat all sides.
2. Roll each pork tenderloin with a piece of bacon, lay the meat on a cutting board, then pound with a meat mallet to give an even thickness, secure the ends of the bacon with toothpicks to hold still. Coat the meat again with just a little more of the rub spice, then set aside.

3. Preheat a Wood Pellet Smoker and Grill to 350 degrees F, place the pork tenderloin on the grill, and grill for about fifteen minutes. Increase the temperature of the grill to 400 degrees F and cook for another fifteen minutes until it is cooked through and reads an internal temperature of 145 degrees F.
4. Once cooked, let the pork rest for a few minutes, slice, and serve.

Nutrition: Calories 236 Fat 8g Carbohydrates 10g Protein 29g

Buttermilk Pork Sirloin Roast

Preparation Time: 20 minutes
Cooking Time: 3 to 3½ hours
Servings: 4 to 6
Ingredients:
Flavour: Apple, Cherry
· 1 (3 to 3½-pound) pork sirloin roast

Directions:
1. Trim all fat and silver skin from the pork roast.
2. Place the roast and buttermilk brine in a 1-gallon sealable plastic sack or brining holder.
3. Refrigerate medium-term, turning the roast like clockwork whenever the situation allows.
4. Remove the brined pork sirloin roast from the brine and pat dry with a paper towel.
5. Supplement a meat probe into the thickest part of the roast.
6. Design the smoker-grill for non-direct cooking and preheat to 225°F utilizing apple or cherry flavours.
7. Smoke the roast until the internal temperature arrives at 145°F, 3 to 3 and a half hours.
8. Rest the roast under a free foil tent for 15 minutes, at that point cut contrary to what would be expected.

Nutrition:
Calories: 311
Protein: 25 g
Fat: 18 g

BBQ Breakfast Grist

Preparation Time: 20 minutes
Cooking Time: 30 to 40 minutes
Servings: 8
Ingredients:
- 1 cup of water
- 1 cup quick-cooking grits
- 3 tablespoons unsalted butter
- 2 tablespoons minced garlic
- 1 medium onion, chopped
- 1 jalapeño pepper, stemmed, seeded, and chopped
- 1 teaspoon cayenne pepper
- 2 teaspoons red pepper flakes
- 1 tablespoon hot sauce
- 1 cup shredded Monterey Jack cheese
- 1 cup sour cream
- Salt
- Freshly ground black pepper
- 2 eggs, beaten
- ⅓ cup half-and-half
- 3 cups leftover pulled pork (preferably smoked)

Directions:
1. Supply your smoker with wood pellets and follow the manufacturer's specific start-up procedure. Preheat, with the lid, closed, to 350°F.
2. On your kitchen stovetop, in a large saucepan over high heat, bring the chicken stock and water to a boil.
3. Add the grits and reduce the heat to low, then stir in the butter, garlic, onion, jalapeño, cayenne, red pepper flakes, hot sauce, cheese, and sour cream. Season with salt and pepper, then cook for about 5 minutes.
4. Temper the beaten eggs and incorporate them into the grits. Remove the saucepan from the heat and stir in the half-and-half and pulled pork.
5. Pour the grits into a greased grill-safe 9-by-13-inch casserole dish or aluminum pan.
6. Transfer to the grill, close the lid, and bake for 30 to 40 minutes, covering with aluminum foil toward the end of cooking if the grits start to get too brown on top.

Nutrition: Calories per serving: 1263; Protein: 36.9g; Carbs: 110.3g; Fat: 76.8g Sugar: 107g

Sweet & Spicy Pork Kabobs

Preparation Time: 24 Hours
Cooking Time: 10 minutes
Servings: 6
Ingredients:
- 2 lbs. boneless pork, 1-inch cubes
- ¾ cup olive oil
- 1 tbsp. Worcestershire sauce
- 1 tsp. dried thyme
- 2 tsp. black pepper
- ½ tsp. cayenne
- ¾ cup cider vinegar
- ¼ cup sugar
- 4 tbsp. lemon juice
- 1 tbsp. oregano
- 2 cloves garlic, minced
- 1 tsp. salt

Directions:
1. Mix together the first 11 ingredients, place in a sealable bag and refrigerate 24 hours: thread onto skewers.
2. Grill on high heat, basting with reserved marinade, for 4–5 minutes; turn and grill another 4–5 minutes.
3. Sprinkle with salt and serve.

Nutrition:
- Calories: 160
- Carbs: 2g
- Fat: 5g
- Protein: 28g

Party Pulled Pork Shoulder

Preparation Time: 30 minutes
Cooking Time: 8 to 9 minutes
Servings: 10
Ingredients:
- 1 (5-pound) Boston butt (pork shoulder)
- ¼ cup prepared table mustard
- ½ cup Our House Dry Rub or your favorite rub, divided
- 2 cups apple juice
- ½ cup of salt

Directions:
1. Slather the meat with the mustard and coat with ¼ cup of the dry rub

2. In a spray bottle, mix the apple juice and salt and shake until the salt is dissolved

3. Supply your smoker with wood pellets and follow the manufacturer's specific start-up procedure. Preheat, with the lid, closed, to 225°F.

4. Place the pork fat-side up in an aluminum pan, transfer to the grill, close the lid, and smoke for 8 to 9 hours, spritzing well all over with the salted apple juice every hour, until a meat thermometer inserted in the thickest part of the meat reads 205°F. Cover the pork loosely with aluminum foil toward the end of cooking, if necessary, to keep the top from blackening.

5. Drain the liquid from the pan, cover, and allow the meat to cool for a few minutes before using two forks to shred it.

6. Sprinkle the remaining rub over the meat and serve with barbecue sauce.

Nutrition: Calories: 426; Protein: 65.3g; Carbs: 20.4g; Fat: 8.4g Sugar: 17.8g

Asian Pork Sliders

Preparation Time: 24 Hours
Cooking Time: 15 minutes
Servings: 8
Ingredients:
- 2 lbs. ground pork
- 1 cup diced green onion
- 2 tsp. garlic powder
- 2 tbsp. soy sauce
- 2 tsp. brown sugar:
- 1 cup shredded lettuce
- 1 tsp. cornstarch
- Honey-mustard dressing
- 16 sesame rolls, split

Directions:

1. Mix all ingredients (except soy sauce) and form 16 equal patties. Brush each patty with soy sauce, and grill over high heat, turning once.

2. Serve with honey mustard and cucumber spears.

3. I like to chill the seasoned meat and then spread it on an oiled cutting board, using a rolling pin for an even ¼-inch thickness.

4. Then, I just grab a biscuit cutter, and voila...perfectly round sliders!

Nutrition:
- Calories: 280
- Carbs: 31g
- Fat: 9g
- Protein: 26g

Carolina Pork Ribs

Preparation Time: 12 Hours
Cooking Time: 3 Hours
Servings: 6
Ingredients:
- 2 racks pork spareribs
- ½ cup "Burning' Love" Rub
- 1 cup Carolina Basting Sauce
- 1 cup Carolina BBQ Sauce

Directions:

1. Prepare ribs by removing the membrane from the underside. Trim off any loose fat, and season ribs with rub, wrap in plastic wrap and refrigerate overnight.

2. Allow ribs to warm for 1 hour. Preheat grill to 280°F.

3. If you want to sauce the ribs, do so 5 minutes before they're done, turning every minute, and observe.

Nutrition:
- Calories: 290
- Carbs: 5g
- Fat: 23g
- Protein: 15g

Rub-Injected Pork Shoulder

Preparation Time: 15 minute
Cooking Time: 16 to 20 hours
Servings: 8 to 12
Ingredients:
- 1 (6- to 8-pound) bone-in pork shoulder

- 2 cups Tea Injectable made with Not-Just-for-Pork Rub
- 2 tablespoons yellow mustard
- 1 batch Not-Just-for-Pork Rub

Directions:

1. Supply your smoker with wood pellets and follow the manufacturer's specific start-up procedure. Preheat the grill, with the lid closed, to 225°F.
2. Inject the pork shoulder throughout with the tea injectable.
3. Coat the pork shoulder all over with mustard and season it with the rub. Using your hands, work the rub into the meat.
4. Place the shoulder directly on the grill grate and smoke until its internal temperature reaches 160°F and a dark bark has formed on the exterior.
5. Pull the shoulder from the grill and wrap it completely in aluminum foil or butcher paper.
6. Increase the grill's temperature to 350°F.
7. Return the pork shoulder to the grill and cook until its internal temperature reaches 195°F.
8. Pull the shoulder from the grill and place it in a cooler. Cover the cooler and let the pork rest for 1 or 2 hours.
9. Remove the pork shoulder from the cooler and unwrap it. Remove the shoulder bone and pull the pork apart using just your fingers. Serve immediately.

Nutrition: Calories per serving: 688; Protein: 58.9g; Carbs: 2.7g; Fat: 47.3g

Chinese BBQ Pork

Preparation Time: 10 minutes
Cooking Time: 20 minutes
Servings: 6
Ingredients:
- Pork & Marinade
- 2 Pork Tenderloins, Silver Skin Removed
- 1/4 Cup Hoisin Sauce
- 1/4 Cup Honey
- 1 1/2 Tbsp. Brown Sugar
- 3 Tbsp. Soy Sauce
- 1 Tbsp. Asian Sesame Oil
- 1 Tbsp. Oyster Sauce, Optional
- 1 Tsp Chinese Five Spice
- 1 Garlic Clove, Minced
- 2 Tsp Red Food Coloring, Optional
- Five Spice Dipping Sauce
- 1/4 Cup Ketchup
- 3 Tbsp. Brown Sugar
- 1 Tsp Yellow Mustard
- 1/4 Tsp Chinese Five Spice

Directions:

1. In a medium bowl, whisk together marinade thoroughly, making sure brown sugar is dissolved. Add pork and marinade to a glass pan or resealable plastic bag and marinate for at least 8 hours or overnight, occasionally turning to ensure all pork sides are well coated.
2. When ready to cook, set the temperature to 225°F and preheat, lid closed for 15 minutes.
3. Remove pork from marinade and boil marinade in a saucepan over medium-high heat on the stovetop for 3 minutes to use for basting pork. Cool slightly, then whisk in 2 additional Tablespoons of honey.
4. Arrange the tenderloins on the grill grate and smoke pork until the internal temperature reaches 145°F.
5. Baste pork with reserved marinade halfway through cooking. Remove pork from grill and, if desired, increase the temperature to High and return pork to grill for a few minutes per side to slight char and set the sauce. Alternatively, you can broil in the oven, just a couple of minutes per side.
6. For the 5 Spice Sauce: In a small saucepan over low heat, mix ketchup, brown sugar, mustard, and five-spice until sugar is dissolved and sauce is smooth. Let cool, and serve chilled or at room temperature.
7. Serve pork immediately with Jasmine rice, or cool and refrigerate for future use as an appetizer, served with Five Spice dipping sauce and toasted sesame seeds. Enjoy!
8. In a medium bowl, whisk together marinade thoroughly, making sure brown sugar is dissolved. Add pork and marinade to a glass pan or resealable plastic bag and marinate for at least 8 hours or overnight,

occasionally turning to ensure all sides of pork are well coated.

9. When ready to cook, set the temperature to 225°F and preheat, lid closed for 15 minutes.

10. Remove pork from marinade and boil marinade in a saucepan over medium-high heat on the stovetop for 3 minutes to use for basting pork. Cool slightly, then whisk in 2 additional Tablespoons of honey.

11. Arrange the tenderloins on the grill grate and smoke pork until the internal temperature reaches 145°F.

12. Baste pork with reserved marinade halfway through cooking. Remove pork from grill and, if desired, increase the temperature to High and return pork to grill for a few minutes per side to slight char and set the sauce. Alternatively, you can broil in the oven, just a couple of minutes per side.

13. For the 5 Spice Sauce: In a small saucepan over low heat, mix ketchup, brown sugar, mustard, and five-spice until sugar is dissolved and sauce is smooth. Let cool, and serve chilled or at room temperature.

14. Serve pork immediately with Jasmine rice, or cool and refrigerate for future use as an appetizer, served with Five Spice dipping sauce and toasted sesame seeds. Enjoy!

Nutrition: Calories: 324 Total Fat: 11.6g Cholesterol: 6mg Sodium: 1029mg

Lime Barbecue Smoked Pork Shoulder Chili

Preparation Time: 20 minutes
Cooking Time: 6 hours 10 minutes
Servings: 8
Ingredients:
· Pork Shoulder (3.5-lb., 1.6-kg.)
The Rub
· 3 tbsp. Brown sugar
· 1 tbsp. Garlic powder
· 1 tbsp. Smoked paprika
· 1 tbsp. Ground cumin
· 1 tsp. Salt
· 1 ½ tsp. Chili powder
· 1 tsp. Black pepper
The Glaze
· 1 tbsp. Red chili flakes
· 2 tbsp. Vegetable oil
· 1 tbsp. Minced garlic
· 1 ½ tsp. Ground coriander
· 1 ½ cups Tomato ketchup
· ¼ cup White sugar
· ½ cup Apple juice
The Topping
· 2 Fresh limes

Directions:
1. Place brown sugar, garlic powder, smoked paprika, ground cumin, salt, chili powder, and black pepper in a bowl, then stir until combined.

2. Rub the spices mixture over and side by side of the pork shoulder, then let it rest for approximately an hour.

3. In the meantime, pour vegetable oil into a saucepan, then preheat over medium heat.

4. Once the oil is hot, stir in minced garlic and sauté until wilted and aromatic. Remove the saucepan from heat.

5. Stir in red chili flakes, ground coriander, and white Sugar: into the saucepan, then pour apple juice and tomato ketchup over the sauce. Mix well and set aside.

6. Plug the grill smoker, then fill the hopper with the wood pellet. Turn the switch on.

7. Set the smoker for indirect heat, then adjust the temperature to 250°F (121°C).

8. Place the seasoned pork shoulder in the smoker and smoke for 3 hours. The internal temperature should be 165°F (74°C).

9. Take the pork shoulder out of the grill smoker, then place it on a sheet of aluminum foil.

10. Baste the glaze over the pork shoulder, then arrange sliced limes over the pork shoulder.

11. Wrap the pork shoulder with aluminum foil, then return it to the grill smoker.

12. Smoke the wrapped smoked pork shoulder for another 3 hours or until the internal temperature has reached 205°F (96°C).

13. Once it is done, remove the smoked pork shoulder from the smoker and let it rest for approximately 15 minutes.

14. Unwrap the smoked pork shoulder and place it on a serving dish.
Nutrition:
· Calories: 220
· Carbs: 1g
· Fat: 18g
· Protein: 16g

Pigs in a Blanket

Preparation Time: 10 minutes
Cooking Time: 45 minutes
Servings: 4
Ingredients:
· Pork sausages - 1 pack
· Biscuit dough - 1 pack
Directions:
1. Preheat your wood pellet grill to 350 degrees.
2. Cut the sausages and the dough into thirds.
3. Wrap the dough around the sausages. Place them on a baking sheet.
4. Grill with a closed lid for 20-25 minutes or until they look cooked.
5. Take them out when they are golden brown.
6. Serve with a dip of your choice.
Nutrition: Protein: 9 g Fat: 22 g Sodium: 732 mg Cholesterol: 44 mg

Smoked Apple Barbecue Ribs

Preparation Time: 25 minutes
Cooking Time: 2 hours
Servings: 6
Ingredients:
· 2 racks St. Louis-style ribs
· ¼ cup Wood Pellet Grill Smoker Big Game Rub
o cup apple juice
· A bottle of Wood Pellet Grill Smoker BARBECUE Sauce
Directions:

1. Place the ribs on a working surface and remove the film of connective tissues covering it.
2. In another bowl, mix the Game Rub and apple juice until well-combined.
3. Massage the rub on to the ribs and allow to rest in the fridge for at least 2 hours.
4. When ready to cook, fire the Wood Pellet Grill Smoker Grill to 2250F. Use apple Wood Pellet Grill Smokers when cooking the ribs. Close the lid and preheat for 15 minutes.
5. Place the ribs on the grill grate and close the lid. Smoke for 1 hour and 30 minutes. Make sure to flip the ribs halfway through the cooking time.
6. Ten minutes before the cooking time ends, brush the ribs with BARBECUE sauce.
7. Remove from the grill and allow to rest before slicing.
Nutrition: Calories: 337; Protein: 47.1g; Carbs: 4.7 g; Fat: 12.9g Sugar: 4g

Delicious Parmesan Roast Pork

Preparation Time: 10 minutes
Cooking Time: 3 hours 45 minutes
Servings: 10
Ingredients:
· 4 chopped garlic cloves.
· 2 tbsp. olive oil.
· 1 tbsp. minced dried basil.
· 1 tbsp. dried and crushed oregano.
· 1 pound boneless pork loin.
· 1 cup bread crumbs.
· ¼ cup grated Parmesan cheese.
Directions:
1. Using a small mixing bowl, add in the garlic, olive oil, basil, and oregano, then mix properly to combine. Rub the mixture on the pork loin, coating all sides, then place in the large bowl. Cover the bowl with plastic wrap, then place in the refrigerator for about two hours to overnight.
2. In another mixing bowl, add in the bread crumbs and cheese, then mix properly to combine. Dredge the pork in the cheese mixture, then set aside. Preheat a smoker and

Grill to 225°F, place the pork on the grill, cover the lid and smoke the pork for about three to four hours until an inserted thermometer reads 155°F.

3. Wrap the pork in aluminum foil and let stand for about ten minutes. Slice and serve.

Nutrition:

- Calories: 250
- Fat 10g
- Carbs: 3g
- Protein: 34g

Stuffed Pork Crown Roast

Preparation Time: 10 minutes
Cooking Time: 3 hours 5 minutes
Servings: 4
Ingredients:

- 12-14 ribs or 1 Snake River Pork Crown Roast
- Apple cider vinegar - 2 tablespoon
- Apple juice - 1 cup
- Dijon mustard - 2 tablespoon
- Salt - 1 teaspoon
- Brown sugar - 1 tablespoon
- Freshly chopped thyme or rosemary - 2 tablespoon
- Cloves of minced garlic - 2
- Olive oil - ½ cup
- Coarsely ground pepper - 1 teaspoon
- Your favorite stuffing - 8 cups

Directions:

1. Set the pork properly in a shallow roasting pan on a flat rack. Cover both ends of the bone with a piece of foil.

2. To make the marinade, boil the apple cider or apple juice on high heat until about half its quantity. Remove the content from the heat and whisk in the mustard, vinegar, thyme, garlic, brown sugar, pepper, and salt. Once all that is properly blended, whisk in the oil slowly.

3. Use a pastry brush to apply the marinade to the roast. Ensure that you coat all the surfaces evenly. Cover it on all sides using plastic wrap. Allow it to sit for about 60 minutes until the meat has reached room temperature.

4. At this time, feel free to brush the marinade on the roast again. Cover it and return it to the refrigerator until it is time to cook it. When you are ready to cook it, allow the meat to reach room temperature, then put it on the pellet grill. Ensure that the grill is preheated for about 15 minutes before you do.

5. Roast the meat for 30 minutes, then reduce the temperature of the grill. Fill the crown loosely with the stuffing and mound it at the top. Cover the stuffing properly with foil. You can also bake the stuffing separately alongside the roast in a pan.

6. Roast the pork thoroughly for 90 more minutes. Get rid of the foil and continue to roast the stuffing for 30-90 minutes until the pork reaches an internal temperature of 150 degrees Fahrenheit. Ensure that you do not touch the bone of the meat with the temperature probe or get a false reading.

7. Remove the roast from the grill. Allow it to rest for around 15 minutes so that the meat soaks in all the juices. Remove the foil covering the bones. Leave the butcher's string on until you are ready to carve it. Now, transfer it to a warm platter, carve between the bones, and enjoy!

Nutrition: Carbohydrates: 37 g Protein: 9 g Sodium: 565 mg Cholesterol: 49 mg

Braised Pork Carnitas

Preparation Time: 20 minutes
Cooking Time: 3 hours and 30 minutes
Servings: 6
Ingredients:

- 4 pounds Pork shoulder, boneless, fat trimmed, marbled
- 12 ounces Beer
- 2 tsp. Salt
- ½ tsp. Ground cumin
- 2 tbsp. Vegetable shortening

Directions:

1. Meanwhile, cut pork into 2-inch pieces and then place them in a Dutch oven.

2.   Add salt and cumin, pour in beer, and then pour in water until pork pieces are covered.
3.   Place the pot over medium-high heat and then bring the mixture to a boil.
4.   When the grill has preheated, place the pot on the grilling rack and let smoke for 3 hours or until pork pieces have turned tender.
5.   Check the fire after one hour of smoking and add more wood pallets if required.
6.   When done, remove the pot from the grill, drain the cooking liquid, and break it into bite-size pieces using two forks.
7.   Add shortening into the pot, return it onto the grilling rack, switch the temperature of the grill to 400°F, and continue cooking for 20 minutes until pork has turned nicely brown, stirring frequently.
8.   When done, divide pork evenly among tortillas, add **servings** as desired, and then serve.

Nutrition:
- Calories: 343
- Carbs: 6g
- Protein: 29g
- Fat: 21g

Porchetta

Preparation Time: 30 minutes
Cook time: 3 hours
Servings: 12
Ingredients:
- 6 pounds' skin-on pork belly
- 4 pounds' center-cut pork loin
- 4 tbsp. olive oil
- 1 cup apple juice
- 2 garlic cloves (minced)
- 1 onion (diced)
- 1 ¼ cups grated pecorino Romano cheese
- 1 tsp ground black pepper
- 2 tsp kosher salt - 3 tbsp. fennel seeds
- 1 tbsp. freshly chopped rosemary
- 1 tbsp. freshly chopped sage
- 1 tbsp. freshly chopped thyme
- 1 tbsp. grated lemon zest

Rub:
- 1 tbsp. chili powder - 2 tsp grilling seasoning
- 1 tsp salt or to taste
- ½ tsp cayenne
- 1 tsp oregano - 1 tsp paprika
- 1 tsp mustard powder

Directions:
1.   Butterfly the pork loin and place it in the middle of two plastic wraps. On a flat surface, pound the pork evenly until it is ½ inch thick.
2.   Combine all the rub ingredients in a small mixing bowl.
3.   Place the butterflied pork on a flat surface, cut side up. Season the cut side generously with 1/3 of the rub.
4.   Heat 1 tbsp. olive oil in a frying pan over medium to high heat. Add the onion, garlic, and fennel seed. Sauté until the veggies are tender.
5.   Stir the black pepper, 1 tsp kosher salt, rosemary, sage, thyme, and lemon zest. Cook for 1 minute and stir in the cheese.
6.   Put the sautéed ingredients on the flat pork and spread evenly. Roll up the pork like you are rolling a burrito.
7.   Brush the rolled pork loin with 1 tbsp. oil and season with the remaining rub. The loin with butcher's string at the 1-inch interval.
8.   Roll the pork belly around the pork, skin side out. Brush the pork belly with the remaining oil and season with 1 tsp salt.
9.   Set a rack into a roasting pan and place the Porchetta on the rack. Pour the wine into the bottom of the roasting pan.
10. Start your grill on smoke mode, leaving the lid opened for 5 minutes until the fire starts.
11. Close the lid and preheat the grill to 325°F, using maple or apple hardwood pellets.
12. Place the roasting pan on the grill and roast Porchetta for about 3 hours or until the Porchetta's internal temperature reaches 155°F.
13. Remove the Porchetta from heat and let it rest for a few minutes to cool.
14. Remove the butcher's string. Slice Porchetta into sizes and serve.

Nutrition: Calories: 611 Fat: 22.7g Cholesterol: 252mg Carbohydrate: 6.6g Protein: 89.4g

Maplewood Bourbon BBQ Ham

Preparation Time: 15 minutes
Cook time: 2 hours 30 minutes
Servings: 8
Ingredients:
· 1 large ham
· ½ cup brown Sugar:
· 3 tbsp. bourbon
· 2 tbsp. lemon
· 2 tbsp. Dijon mustard
· ¼ cup apple juice
· ¼ cup maple syrup
· 1 tsp salt
· 1 tsp freshly ground garlic
· 1 tsp ground black pepper

Directions:
1. Start your grill on a smoke setting, leaving for 5 minutes, until the fire starts.
2. Close the lid and preheat the grill to 325°F.
3. Place the ham on a smoker rack and place the rack on the grill. Smoke for 2 hours or until the internal temperature of the ham reaches 125°F.
4. Combine the sugar, bourbon, lemon, mustard, apple juice, salt, pepper, and maple in a saucepan over medium to high heat.
5. Bring mixture to a boil, reduce the heat and simmer until the sauce thickens.
6. Glaze the ham with maple mixture.
7. Increase the grill temperature to 375°F and continue cooking until the internal temperature of the ham reaches 140°F.
8. Remove the glazed ham from the grill and let it rest for about 15 minutes.
9. Cut ham into small sizes and serve.

Nutrition:
· Calories: 163
· Fat: 4.6g
· Cholesterol: 29mg
· Carbohydrate: 19g
· Protein: 8.7g

Sauced Up Pork Spares

Preparation Time: 5 hours
Cooking Time: 4 hours
Serving: 6

Ingredients:
· 6 pound of pork spareribs
For Dry Rub
· ½ a cup of packed brown sugar
· 2 tablespoons of chili powder
· 1 tablespoon of paprika
· 1 tablespoon of freshly ground black pepper
· 2 tablespoons of garlic powder
· 2 teaspoons of onion powder
· 2 teaspoons of kosher salt
· 2 teaspoons of ground cumin
· 1 teaspoon of ground cinnamon
· 1 teaspoon of jalapeno seasoning salt
· 1 teaspoon of Cayenne pepper
For Mop Sauce
· 1 cup of apple cider
· ¾ cup of apple cider vinegar
· 1 tablespoon of onion powder
· 1 tablespoon of garlic powder
· 2 tablespoon of lemon juice
· 1 jalapeno pepper, chopped
· 3 tablespoon of hot pepper sauce
· Kosher salt as needed
· Black pepper as needed
· 2 cups of soaked wood chips

Directions:
1. Take a medium-sized bowl and add brown sugar, chili powder, 2 tablespoons of garlic powder, 2 teaspoons of onion powder, cumin, cinnamon, kosher salt, cayenne pepper, jalapeno seasoning
2. Mix well and rub the mixture over the pork spare ribs
3. Allow it to refrigerate for 4 hours
4. Take your drip pan and add water; cover with aluminum foil. Pre-heat your smoker to 225 degrees F
5. Use water fill water pan halfway through and place it over drip pan. Add wood chips to the side tray
6. Take a medium bowl and stir in apple cider, apple cider vinegar, 1 tablespoon of onion powder, jalapeno, 1 tablespoon of garlic powder, salt, pepper, and lemon juice
7. Add a handful of soaked wood chips and transfer the ribs to your smoker middle rack
8. Smoke for 3-4 hours, making sure to keep adding chips after every hour
9. Take the meat out and serve!

Strawberry and Jalapeno Smoked Ribs

Preparation Time: 15 minutes
Cooking Time: 90 minutes
Serving: 8
Ingredients:

- 3 tbsp. Kosher Salt
- 2 tbsp. Ground Cumin
- 1 tbsp. Dried Oregano
- 1 tbsp. garlic, minced
- 2 tsp. chili powder
- 1 tsp. ground black pepper
- 1 tsp. celery seed
- 1 tsp. dried thyme
- 1 rack spareribs
- 2 slabs baby back pork ribs
- 1 cup apple juice
- 2 jalapeno peppers. cut in half lengthwise and deseeded
- ½ a mug beer
- ½ onion, chopped
- ¼ cup sugar-free strawberry
- 3 tbsp. BBQ sauce
- 1 tbsp. olive oil
- 2 cloves garlic
- Sea salt as needed
- Ground pepper as needed

Directions:

1. Take a bowl first and blend in your salt, oregano, cumin, minced garlic, 1 tsp. of ground black pepper, chili powder, ground thyme, and celery seed ad toss them in a food processor
2. Place your baby back rib slabs and spare rib rack on sheets of aluminum foil and rub the spice mix all over their body
3. Fold up the foil around each of them
4. Divide and pour the apple juice amongst the foil packets and foil the edges together to seal them up
5. Let them marinate for about 8 hours or overnight
6. Prepare your oven rack and place it about 6 inches away from the heat source, and pre-heat your oven's broiler
7. Line up a baking sheet with the aluminum foil and place your jalapeno pepper on top of it, with the cut upsides down
8. Cook Jalapeno peppers for 8 minutes under the broiler until the skin is blackened
9. Toss them and seal them up using a plastic wrap
10. Let the peppers steam off for 20 minutes
11. Remove them and discard the skin
12. Blend the jalapeno peppers, onion, beer, strawberry preserve, olive oil, BBQ sauce, sea salt, and just a pinch of ground black pepper altogether in a blender until the sauce is fully smoothened out
13. Transfer the sauce to a container and let cover it up with a lid; let it chill for 8 hours or overnight
14. Take your drip pan and add water; cover with aluminum foil. Pre-heat your smoker to 225°F
15. Use water fill water pan halfway through and place it over drip pan. Add wood chips to the side tray
16. Smoke for 60 minutes
17. Increase the temp to 225°Fahrenheit or 110°F Celsius and keep cooking for another 2–3 hours
18. Preheat your smoker to a temperature of 250°F or 120°C
19. Unwrap your cooked ribs and toss away the apple juice
20. Place them on top of your smoker
21. Cook on your smoker until the surface of your meat is finely dried up; it should take about 5–10 minutes
22. After which, continue cooking, making sure to brush it up with the sauce after every 15 minutes
23. Turn it around after 30 minutes
24. Repeat and cook for 1 hour
25. Serve hot when tender

Nutrition:

- Fats: 41.2g
- Carbs: 8.2g
- Fiber: 0.7g

Porky Onion Soup

Preparation Time: 2 hours
Cooking Time: 4 hours 30 minutes
Serving: 6
Ingredients:
· 1 full rack of pork spare ribs
· 2 packs onion soup mix of your choice
· BBQ Pork Rub
· 4 cups of water

Directions:
1. Remove the white membrane of the pork meat and trim off any excess fat
2. Take your drip pan and add water; cover with aluminum foil. Pre-heat your smoker to 225 degrees F
3. Use water fill water pan halfway through and place it over drip pan. Add wood chips to the side tray
4. Prepare your rub mixture by mixing salt, garlic powder, pepper, and paprika in a bowl
5. Rub the rib with the mixture
6. Transfer to the smoker and smoker for 2 hours
7. Blend 2 packs of onion soup with 4 cups of water
8. Once smoking is complete, take a heavy aluminum foil and transfer the meat to the foil, pour the soup mix all over
9. Seal the ribs
10. Smoke for another 1 and a ½ hours
11. Gently open the foil and turn the rib, seal it up and smoke for 1 hour more
12. Slice and serve!

Nutrition: Calories: 461 Fats: 22g Carbs: 17g Fiber: 4g

Wood Pellet Grilled Shredded Pork Tacos

Preparation Time: 15 Minutes
Cooking Time: 7 Hours
Servings: 8
Ingredients:
• 5 lb. pork shoulder, bone-in
• 3 tbsp. brown sugar
• 1 tbsp. salt
• 1 tbsp. garlic powder
• 1 tbsp. paprika
• 1 tbsp. onion powder
• 1/4 tbsp. cumin
• 1 tbsp. cayenne pepper

Directions:
1. Mix all the dry rub ingredients and rub on the pork shoulder.
2. Preheat the grill to 275°F and cook the pork directly for 6 hours or until the internal temperature has reached 145°F.
3. If you want to fall off the bone tender pork, then cook until the internal temperature is 190°F.
4. Let rest for 10 minutes before serving. Enjoy

Nutrition: Calories 566 Total fat 41g Saturated fat 15g Total Carbs 4g Net Carbs 4g Protein 44g Sugar 3g Fiber 0g Sodium: 659mg

CHAPTER 7: BEEF RECIPES

· Protein: 32.38g

Grilled Beef Steak with Peanut Oil and Herbs

Preparation Time: 4 hours and 45 minutes
Cooking Time: 55 minutes
Servings: 6
Ingredients:
· 3 lbs. beef steak, preferably flank
· 1 tsp. sea salt
· 2 tbsp. peanut oil
· ¼ olive oil
· 2 tbsp. fresh mint leaves, finely chopped
· 2 tsp. peppercorn black
· 2 tsp. peppercorn green
· ½ tsp. cumin seeds
· 1 pinch of chili flakes
Directions:
1. Rub the beef steaks with coarse salt and place in a large dish.
2. Make a marinade; in a bowl, combine peanut oil, olive oil, fresh mint leave, peppercorn, cumin, and chili flakes.

3. Cover and refrigerate for 4 hours.
4. Bring the meat to room temperature 30 minutes before you put it on the grill.
5. Start your grill, set the temperature on High and preheat, lid closed, for 10 to 15 minutes.
6. As a general rule, you should grill steaks on high heat (450–500°F).
7. Grill about 7–10 minutes per side at high temperatures or 15–20 minutes per side at the lower temperatures, or to your preference for doneness.
8. Remove flank steak from the grill and let cool before slicing for 10 -15 minutes.
9. Slice and serve.
Nutrition:
· Calories: 346.3
· Fat 15.15g
· Carbs: 0.21g
· Fiber: 0.07g

Fully Loaded Brisket Fries

(TOTAL COOK TIME 8 HOURS 40 MINUTES)
INGREDIENTS FOR 18 SERVINGS
THE MEAT
· Brisket flat (8-lbs, 3.6-kgs)
THE BRISKET
· Beef stock – 1 cup
· Dijon mustard – ¼ cup
· Worcestershire sauce – ¼ cup
· Tri-tip seasoning, as needed
THE FRIES
· Russet potatoes, peeled and sliced into wedges (2-lbs, 0.9-kgs)
· Panko breadcrumbs – ½ cup
· Parmesan, finely grated – ¼ cup
· Steak rub of choice – 1 tablespoon
· Olive oil, as needed
THE SAUCE
· Heavy cream – ½ cup
· Truffle pecorino cheese – ¼ cup
· Provolone cheese, grated – ¼ cup
· Hot sauce, of choice – 1 teaspoon
THE TOPPINGS
· Cheese sauce, warmed
· Caramelized onions
· Fresh chives, chopped
· Spicy dill pickles, sliced
· BBQ sauce, any brand
THE WOOD PELLET GRILL
· Preheat your wood pellet grill for smoking to 250°F (121°C)
· Use your favorite wood pellets
METHOD
1. First, prepare the injection for the brisket. Combine the beef stock, mustard, and Worcestershire sauce. Set half a cup of the mixture to one side and transfer the remaining mixture to a kitchen syringe.
2. Use the syringe to inject the brisket at even intervals. Season the surface of the brisket with the tri-tip seasoning.

3. Transfer the brisket to the grill and smoke for approximately 6 hours. The meat is ready when it registers an internal temperature of 160°F (71°C).
4. Lay the brisket on a double-layered sheet of aluminum foil and pour over the reserved injection liquid. Cover tightly with the foil and return to the heat.
5. Continue to cook the meat until the internal temperature reaches at least 204°F (95°C). Take brisket off the grill and leave it to rest, still wrapped in the foil.
6. Increase the grill temperature to 425°F (218°C).
7. Place the potatoes on a parchment-lined sheet pan and drizzle with olive oil. Toss to combine.
8. In a small bowl, combine the breadcrumbs, Parmesan, and steak rub. Sprinkle the mixture over the potatoes and toss once more.
9. Place the sheet pan on the main cooking grate for around 30 minutes until the potatoes are browned and tender.
10. While the fries cook, prepare the cheese sauce. In a skillet over moderately high heat, bring the cream to a simmer. Whisk in both kinds of cheese, followed by the hot sauce until melted and combined. Cover with a lid and keep warm.
11. Once the brisket has rested for half an hour and the fries are cooked, divide the fries between serving bowls. Top the fries with a portion of pulled brisket, and drizzle over some warm cheese sauce.
12. Serve with your choice of additional toppings.
13. Enjoy immediately.

Texas-style Beef Ribs

Servings: 4
Cooking Time: 6 Hours 3 Minutes
Ingredients:
· 2 tbsp. butter
· 1 C. white vinegar
· 1 C. yellow mustard

Bourbon Butter Smoked RibEyes

Preparation Time: 10 minutes
Servings: 4 servings per recipe
Ingredients:
• One tbsp minced chives or green onions
• Four (1 inch thick) rib-eye steaks
• ½ cup butter
• ½ tsp salt
• Two tbsp bourbon
• ½ tsp ground black pepper
• Two cloves of garlic
• Prime Rib Rub
• One tbsp minced parsley

Instructions:
• To make the Bourbon Butter, put the garlic, bourbon, butter, chives, parsley, pepper, and salt in a small bowl and toss with a wooden spoon. Butter can be made ahead of time and kept refrigerated until ready to use.
• Set the grill to 180°F and preheat for 15 minutes with the lid covered when you're ready to cook. If Super Smoke is available, use it for the best flavor.
• Season the steaks generously with the Prime Rib Rub.
• Place the steaks on the grate and smoke them for 1 hour.
• Transfer the steaks to a tray and preheat your grill to 500 degrees Fahrenheit.
• Transfer the steaks to the grill, flipping once, until they achieve a core temperature of 135°F for medium-rare, about Six to Eight minutes per side, while the grill is hot.
• Place the steaks on a serving plate and immediately top with a pat of bourbon butter.
• Allow 3 minutes for the meat to rest before serving.

· 2 tbsp. brown sugar
· 2 tbsp. Tabasco sauce
· 1 tsp. Worcestershire sauce
· 2 racks of beef ribs
· Salt and freshly ground black pepper, to taste

Directions:
1. For BBQ sauce: in a pan, melt butter over medium heat. Stir in vinegar, mustard, brown sugar, Tabasco and Worcestershire sauce and remove from heat.
2. Set aside to cool completely.

3.   Set the temperature of Grill to 225 degrees F and preheat with closed lid for 15 minutes.
4.   Season the rib racks with salt and black pepper evenly.
5.   Coat rib rack with cooled sauce evenly.
6.   Arrange the rib racks onto the grill and cook for about 5-6 hours, coating with sauce after every 2 hours.
ribs and serve.
Nutrition Info: Calories per serving: 504; Carbohydrates: 5.7g; Protein: 70.7g; Fat: 19.7g; Sugar: 3.6g; Sodium: 719mg; Fiber: 1.4g

Red Wine Braised Beef Ribs

(TOTAL COOK TIME 5 HOURS)
INGREDIENTS FOR 6-8 **SERVINGS**
THE MEAT
·   2 racks center-cut, beef back ribs, fat trimmed, membrane removed and patted dry
THE INGREDIENTS
·   Steak seasoning, as needed
·   Extra-virgin olive oil, as needed
·   Balsamic vinegar – 2-4 tablespoons
·   Cabernet Sauvignon – ½ cup
THE WOOD PELLET GRILL
·   Prepare your wood pellet grill for smoking to 250°F (121°C)
·   Use your favorite wood pellets
METHOD
1.   Coat the ribs with a film of olive oil and scatter over a light coating of steak seasoning. Set aside to rest for 10-15 minutes to allow the seasoning to penetrate the meat.
2.   Lay the ribs on the upper second shelf of the pellet grill, meat side facing up, and cook for 3 hours until a dark mahogany color.
3.   Remove from the heat while you prepare the braise.
4.   Increase the heat to 350°F (177°C).
5.   Place the ribs in the center of 2 sheets of foil. Pour the balsamic vinegar and red wine over the ribs, and wrap tightly to enclose the meat in the braise.
6.   Return the ribs to the upper shelf, meat side facing down, and cook for around 60 minutes or until your preferred texture is

7.   Remove the rib racks from grill and place onto a cutting board for about 10-15 minutes before slicing.
8.   With a sharp knife, cut the rib racks into equal-sized individual

reached. The meat should register an internal temperature of 212°F (100°C) before shredding.
7.   Rest the ribs while covered for 15-30 minutes.
8.   Shred, serve, and enjoy.

Smoked Beef with Smoked Garlic Mayo Dip

Preparation Time: 15 minutes
Cooking Time: 8 hours
Servings: 10
Ingredients:
·   5 pounds beef tenderloin
·   ¼ cup minced garlic
·   2 teaspoons black pepper
·   2 teaspoons salt
·   1 ½ teaspoons olive oil
·   5 cloves garlic
·   ½ cup mayonnaise
·   ¼ cup water
·   2 tablespoons red wine vinegar
·   2 tablespoons chives
Directions:
1.   Preheat the smoker to 250°F (121°C). Soak the hickory wood chips for about an hour before using.
2.   Combine minced garlic, black pepper, salt, and olive oil then stir until mixed.
3.   Rub the beef tenderloin with the spice mixture then place in the smoker.
4.   Wrap the garlic cloves with aluminum foil then place next to the beef tenderloin.
5.   Smoke the beef tenderloin and garlic for about 8 hours or until the internal temperature of the beef tenderloin reaches 145°F (63°C).

6. Remove the smoked beef tenderloin and garlic from the smoker then cut the smoked beef tenderloin into slices. Set aside.

7. Place mayonnaise and chives in a blender then pour water and red wine vinegar over mayonnaise.

8. Add the smoked garlic to the blender then blend until smooth.

9. Transfer the garlic and mayonnaise dip to a small bowl then place next to the smoked beef tenderloin.

10. Serve and enjoy.

Nutrition: Calories: 205 Carbs: 4g Fat: 12g Protein: 19g

Three Ingredient Beef Brisket

(TOTAL COOK TIME 6 HOUR 30 MINUTES)
INGREDIENTS FOR 10 SERVINGS
THE MEAT
· 1 whole beef brisket (15-lbs, 6.8-kgs)
· Yellow mustard – ½ cup
· Beef seasoning, any brand – ¼ cup
THE WOOD PELLET GRILL
· With the lid closed, prepare your wood pellet grill for smoking at 275-300°F (135-149°C)
· Cherry or oak wood pellets are good choices for this recipe
METHOD
1. First, trim the meat until only 0.25-ins (0.6-cms) of fat remains across the fat cap on the brisket's top. Remove and discard any silverskin and trim away the hard white fat between the muscle and the flat. Pat the beef, dry.
2. Cover the brisket on all sides with mustard.
3. For a height of 12-ins (30.5 -cms), scatter the beef seasoning over the meat, and using clean hands, pat it onto the meat gently.
4. Cook the meat for approximately 3 hours or until the thickest part registers 160-170°F (71-77°C).
5. Wrap the brisket tightly in aluminum foil. Return it to the heat and cook at 275°F (135°C) until cooked through. This step will take around 2 hours. You will need to check the meat for tenderness by sliding your thermometer into the thickest part. It is ready when it registers around 204°F (95°C) and is soft and tender.
6. Remove the brisket from the heat, cover with a clean tea towel, and set aside to rest for a minimum of 60 minutes.
7. Slice against the grain, serve and enjoy.

Chili Rib Eye Steaks

Preparation Time: 10 minutes
Cooking Time: 1 hour
Servings: 4
Ingredients:
• 4 rib-eye steaks, each about 12 ounces
• 1 tablespoon minced garlic
• 1 teaspoon salt
• 1 teaspoon brown sugar
• 2 tablespoons red chili powder
• 1 teaspoon ground cumin
• 2 tablespoons Worcestershire sauce
• 2 tablespoons olive oil
Directions:
1. Prepare the rub and for this, take a small bowl, place all of its ingredients in it and then stir until mixed.
2. Brush the paste on all sides of the steak, rub well, then place steaks into a plastic bag and let it marinate for a minimum of 4 hours.
3. Then return steaks to the grill grate and cook for 3 minutes per side until the internal temperature reaches 140 degrees F.
4. Transfer steaks to a dish, let rest for 5 minutes and then serve.
Nutrition: Calories: 293 Cal Fat: 0 g Protein: 32 g

Grilled Butter Basted Rib-Eye

Prep. Time: 5Mins
Cook Time: 15 Mins
Servings: 2
Ingredients

- Rib-Eye Steaks 2 (bone-in)
- Pepper
- Kosher Salt
- Unsalted Butter 4 tbsp

Instructions

1. Season the steaks on both sides with pepper and salt, then put aside for 20 mins at room temperature.

2. Preheat your to 500°F and leave the lid closed for approximately 15 mins. Preheat your grill grate by putting a pan large enough to hold this steak directly on top of it.

3. Put the steaks over the hottest part of your grill and cover for around 5 mins.

4. After 5 mins, remove the lid and add the butter to the pan; it should melt virtually instantaneously.

5. In the skillet, the grill side of the steaks should be facing up. Cook for 5-7 mins, brushing your steaks with butter every minute. Cook until the internal temperature reaches 125-130 degrees Fahrenheit.

6. Remove the steaks from the pan and lay them aside for 10 mins to rest. Drizzle the remaining butter over the steaks and serve.

Smoked Up Bulgogi

Preparation Time: 15 minutes
Cooking Time: 16 hours + 30 minutes
Serving: 8-10
Ingredients:

- 5 pound of Chuck Roast
- Everyday yellow mustard
- Foil pan

For Rub

- 1 tablespoon of salt
- 2 teaspoons of black pepper
- 1 teaspoon of cayenne pepper
- 1 teaspoon of oregano
- ½ a teaspoon of chili powder
- 2 teaspoons of garlic powder

For Bulgogi

- 2 pound (or more) of shaved chuck roast beef
- 4 cloves of garlic
- 1 inch of ginger
- 1 teaspoon of chili flakes
- 3 tablespoon of Korean hot sauce
- 4 tablespoon of red wine vinegar
- 6 tablespoon of soy sauce
- 6 tablespoon of sesame oil

Vegetables

- 1 green pepper
- 1 medium-sized onion
- 2 carrots
- Oil as needed

Directions:

1. Rinse meat thoroughly under cold water

2. Apply a nice coating of yellow mustard over the meat

3. Take a small bowl and mix all the ingredients listed under the rub

4. Sprinkle/massage the rub all over the sides of your meat

5. Take your drip pan and add water; cover with aluminum foil. Preheat your Smoker to 235 degrees F

6. Use water fill water pan halfway through and place it over drip pan. Add wood chips to the side tray

7. Gently place your meat onto the smoker grate

8. Smoke them for about 8-12 hours until the thickest part of the beef gives an internal temperature of 195 degrees Fahrenheit

9. Once the temperature is reached, wrap it up and let it rest for about 1 hour

10. It is now ready to be used for the Bulgogi

11. Slice up about 2-3 pound of meat off your chuck roast

12. Take a food processor and add garlic and ginger; process them until a fine paste forms

13. Take a bowl and add pepper flakes, garlic/ginger paste, brown sugar, Korean hot sauce, Soy sauce, rice wine vinegar, and sesame oil

14. Mix them well to prepare the marinade

15. Take a hot pan and add the beef slices alongside the marinade and simmer them until fully cooked

19. Add the meat followed by the vegetables, according to your preference

20. Let it rest for about 2 minutes and serve!

Nutrition: Calories: 948 Fats: 54g Carbs: 41g Fiber: 6g

Beef Tenderloin

Preparation Time: 10 minutes
Cooking Time: 1 hour 19 minutes
Servings: 12
Ingredients:
* 1 (5-pound) beef tenderloin, trimmed
* Kosher salt, as required
* ¼ cup olive oil
* Freshly ground black pepper, as required

Directions:
1. With kitchen strings, tie the tenderloin at 7-8 places.
2. Season tenderloin with kosher salt generously.
3. With a plastic wrap, cover the tenderloin and keep aside at room temperature for about 1 hour.
4. Preheat the Z Grills Wood Pellet Grill Smoker Grill & Smoker on grill setting to 225-250 degrees F.
5. Now, coat tenderloin with oil evenly and season with black pepper.
6. Arrange tenderloin onto the grill and cook for about 55-65 minutes.
7. Now, place cooking grate directly over hot coals and sear tenderloin for about 2 minutes per side.
8. Remove the tenderloin from the grill and place onto a cutting board for about 10-15 minutes before serving.
9. With a sharp knife, cut the tenderloin into desired-sized slices and serve.

Nutrition: Calories 425 Total Fat 21.5 g Saturated Fat 7.2 g Cholesterol 174 mg Sodium 123 mg Total Carbs 0 g Fiber 0 g Sugar 0 g Protein 54.7 g

Grilled Tomahawk Steak

Prep. Time: 5Mins
Cook Time: 1 Hr
Servings: 4
Ingredients
* Tomahawk Steaks 2
* Black Pepper Grounded 2 tbsp
* Kosher Salt 2 tbsp

* Paprika 1 tbsp
* Onion Powder ½ tbsp
* Garlic Powder ½ tbsp
* Brown Sugar ½ tbsp
* Cayenne Pepper ¼ tsp
* Ground Mustard 1 tsp

Instructions
1. In a small mixing bowl, combine both rub ingredients. When the grill is hot, season the steaks thoroughly with the rub and set them aside.
2. Preheat the to 225° F for 15 mins with the lid closed. Use Super Smoke if it's available for the finest flavor.
3. Place your steaks directly on the grill grate and cook for 45 to 60 mins, or until the internal temperature reaches 120° F.
4. Remove the steaks from the grill and set them aside to rest on a cutting board
5. Preheat your grill to 450 degrees Fahrenheit.
6. Cook the stakes directly over the grill grate for 7-10 mins on each side, or until the core temperature reaches 130° F.
7. Take the steaks from the grill and set them aside for 5 mins to rest before serving.

Cowboy Cut Steak

Preparation Time: 10 minutes
Cooking Time: 1 hour and 15 minutes
Servings: 4
Ingredients:
* 2 cowboy cut steak, each about 2 ½ pounds
* Salt as needed
* Beef rub as needed
* For the Gremolata:
* 2 tablespoons chopped mint
* 1 bunch of parsley, leaves separated
* 1 lemon, juiced
* 1 tablespoon lemon zest
* ½ teaspoon minced garlic
* ¼ teaspoon salt
* 1/8 teaspoon ground black pepper
* 1/4 cup olive oil

Directions:

1. Switch on the Wood Pellet Grill Smoker grill, fill the grill hopper with mesquite flavored Wood Pellet Grill Smokers, power the grill on by using the control panel, select 'smoke' on the temperature dial, or set the temperature to 225 degrees F and let it preheat for a minimum of 5 minutes.

2. When done, transfer steaks to a dish, let rest for 15 minutes, and meanwhile, change the smoking temperature of the grill to 450 degrees F and let it preheat for a minimum of 10 minutes.

3. Then return steaks to the grill grate and cook for 7 minutes per side until the internal temperature reaches 130 degrees F.

Nutrition: Calories: 361 Cal Fat: 31 g Carbs: 1 g Protein: 19 g Fiber: 0.2 g

Smoked Rib-Eyes with Bourbon Butter

Prep. Time: 10Mins
Cook Time: 1 Hr
Servings: 4
Ingredients

- Butter ½ c
- Bourbon 2 tbsp
- Minced Garlic 2 clove
- Green Onions 1 tbsp
- Salt ½ tsp
- Minced Parsley 1 tbsp
- Black Pepper ½ tsp (Grounded)
- Prime-Rib Scrub
- Rib-Eye Steaks 4 (1" Thick)

Instructions

1. To prepare the Bourbon Butter, whisk together the salt, parsley, garlic, butter, chives, pepper and bourbon in a large mixing bowl. Make the butter ahead of time and keep it refrigerated until ready to use.

2. Preheat the to 180° F for 15 mins with the top closed. Use Super Smoke if it's available for the finest flavor.

3. Season the steaks with a large amount of Prime-Rib Rub.

4. Place the steaks on the grill grate and cook for 1 hour.

5. Arrange your steaks on a tray and prepare your to 500 degrees F.

6. When the grill is still hot, return these steaks to the grill, turning one time only, until they reach a core temperature of 135° F for moderate-rare, around 6-8 mins on each side.

7. Arrange the steaks on a serving plate and top with a pat of bourbon butter very away.

8. Let the meat sit for 3 mins before eating.

Wood Pellet Grill Smoker Smoked Rib-eye Steaks

Preparation Time: 15 minutes
Cooking Time: 35 minutes
Servings: 1
Ingredients:

- 2-inch thick rib-eye steaks
- Steak rub of choice

Direction:

1. Preheat your Wood Pellet Grill Smoker grill to low smoke.

2. Sprinkle the steak with your favorite steak rub and place it on the grill. Let it smoke for 25 minutes.

3. Remove the steak from the grill and set the temperature to 400°F.

4. Return the steak to the grill and sear it for 5 minutes on each side.

5. Cook until the desired temperature is achieved; 125°F-rare, 145°F-Medium, and 165°F.-Well done.

6. Wrap the steak with foil and let rest for 10 minutes before serving. Enjoy.

Nutrition: Calories 225, Total fat 10.4g, Protein 32.5g, Sugar 0g, Fiber 0g, Sodium: 63mg,

Wood Pellet Grill Smoker Grill Deli-Style Roast Beef

Preparation Time: 15 minutes
Cooking Time: 4 hours
Servings: 2

Ingredients:
- 4lb round-bottomed roast
- 1 Tablespoon coconut oil
- 1/4 Tablespoon garlic powder
- 1/4 Tablespoon onion powder
- 1/4 Tablespoon thyme
- 1/4 Tablespoon oregano
- 1/2 Tablespoon paprika
- 1/2 Tablespoon salt
- 1/2 Tablespoon black pepper

Direction:

1. Combine all the dry hubs to get a dry rub.

2. Roll the roast in oil then coat with the rub.

3. Set your grill to 185°F and place the roast on the grill.

4. Smoke for 4 hours or until the internal temperature reaches 140°F.

5. Remove the roast from the grill and let rest for 10 minutes.

6. Slice thinly and serve.

Nutrition: Calories 90, Total fat 3g, Protein 14g, Sugar 0g, Fiber 0g, Sodium: 420mg

Beef Satay

Prep. Time: 10Mins

Cook Time: 10 Mins

Servings: 6

Ingredients
- Iron Steak Black Flat 2 lb
- Carne of Choice Asada Marinade 1 bottle
- Garlic 2 clove (Minced)
- Scallions 2 (Chopped)
- Peanut Sauce
- Crushed Peanuts ¼ c
- Limes 2

Instructions

1. Using a sharp knife, cut your steak into 1/3-inch slices on the sharp diagonal. Place the mixture in a large mixing bowl or a resealable plastic container. After pouring the Carne Asada marinade over the meat, stir in the garlic and scallions. 1 hour in the freezer

2. Remove the steak from the marinade and discard any remaining onion or garlic. The bamboo skewer should be threaded with each piece.

3. Preheat the on High for around 15 mins with the lid closed when you're ready to cook.

4. Grill satays for 3-4 mins on each side, flipping once.

5. Meanwhile, on one side of a tray or dish lay a small dish of peanut sauce. Place the satays on top of the chopped avocado on this serving plate. Serve with lime wedges on the side.

Beef Brisket

(TOTAL COOK TIME 6 HOURS 25 MINUTES)

INGREDIENTS FOR 10-12 SERVINGS

THE MEAT
- 1 beef brisket (15-lbs, 6.75-kgs)

THE BASTE
- Beef stock – ¼ cup

THE RUB
- Onion powder – 2 tablespoons
- Garlic powder – 2 tablespoons
- Paprika – 2 tablespoons
- Chili powder – 2 tablespoons
- Sea salt – 1 tablespoon
- Black pepper – 2 tablespoons
- Brown sugar – 1 tablespoon

THE WOOD PELLET GRILL
- With the lid closed, prepare your wood pellet grill for grilling at 225°F (107°C)
- Add your choice of wood pellets. Cherry or pecan are both good choices for this recipe

METHOD

1. First, in a bowl, prepared the rub: Combine the onion powder, garlic powder, paprika, chili powder, sea salt, black pepper, and brown sugar. Rub the mixture all over the beef brisket.

2. Lay the meat, fat side facing downwards, on the grill grate.

3. Cook the brisket for 3-4 hours or until it registers an internal temperature of 160°F (71°C). Remove from the grill.

4. Wrap the brisket in two layers of foil, and pour the beef stock into the foil parcel.

5. Return to the grill grate and cook for approximately 3 hours more, or until it registers an internal temperature of 205°F (96°C).

6.   Remove the meat from the grill, remove the foil, and set aside for 12-15 minutes to rest.
7.   Slice the meat against the grain and enjoy.

Mushroom Cream Sauce on Peppercorn Steaks

Preparation Time: 1 hour
Servings: 4 servings per recipe
Ingredients:
Sauce
- ½ cup white wine
- ½ cup heavy cream
- Salt
- ½ cup chicken stock
- Pepper
- One tbsp olive oil
- Sixteen ounces cremini mushrooms sliced thinly
- One clove of garlic, minced

Main
- 1½ tbsp Worcestershire sauce
- Kosher salt
- Ground black and green peppercorns
- ½ cup Dijon mustard
- Two cloves of garlic. Turned into a paste
- 4 Whole beef steaks
- 2 tbsp bourbon

Instructions:
- Combine the garlic, bourbon, mustard, and Worcestershire sauce in a small bowl. To combine the ingredients, whisk them together.
- Place the tenderloins on a wide piece of wrap and pour the sauce all over them. Wrap the plastic wrap tightly around the tenderloin on both sides. Allow 60 minutes for the mixture to come to room temperature.
- Remove the plastic wrap from the tenderloin and season generously on all surfaces with salt and peppercorns. Rub the peppercorns into the meat with your hands.
- Set the grill to 180°F and preheat for 15 minutes with the lid covered when you're ready to cook. If Super Smoke is available, use it for the best flavor.
- Smoke the steaks for 60 minutes by placing them directly on the grill grate. Then, take the steaks from the grill and set them aside.
- Preheat the grill to 500°F and cook for 15 minutes with the cover closed.
- Transfer the steaks to the grill when the grill is hot and cook until a thermometer reads 130°F, about Twenty to Thirty minutes depending on the size of the steak. Don't overcook the food.
- Now For the Mushroom Cream Sauce, combine the following ingredients in a mixing bowl. In a large pan, heat the oil over medium heat.
- Sauté the sliced mushrooms until softened and gently browned, being cautious not to overload the pan. Add the garlic and cook for another minute. Bring the white wine and chicken stock to a boil with the mushrooms.
- Reduce the heat to low and mix in the cream after 5 - 6 minutes of simmering. Season with pepper and salt to taste. Remove the pan from the heat and set it aside.
- Cover steaks with foil and place them on a tray. Remove the foil and let the meat rest for ten minutes before slicing it into thin slices.
- Spoon the sauce immediately onto the steaks to serve.

Beef Tenderloin with Tomato Vinaigrette

Prep. Time: 10Mins
Cook Time: 40Mins
Servings: 6
Ingredients
- Whole Beef 1
- Prime-Rib Scrub 1
- Tenderloin Steaks
- Olive Oil Extra-Virgin 2/3 c
- Fresh Thyme 1 tsp
- Salt and Pepper
- Tomatoes Plum 6
- Balsamic Vinegar 2 tbsp
- Thyme 1 tsp (Minced)

Instructions

1. Preheat the oven to 450°F and bake for 10-15 mins with the lid closed.

2. Tuck the narrow end of the tenderloin underneath the roast and secure it with the butcher's string. After rubbing the beef with olive oil, season it with Prime Rib Scrub or salt and pepper. Place your meat on the shelf in the small roasting pan.

3. Roast for around 20 mins in a hot grill. Preheat the oven to 350 degrees Fahrenheit (180 degrees Celsius). Cook for another 20 mins, or until the desired doneness is achieved.

4. Allow for a 5-minute rest period before slicing thinly. Serve with thyme sprigs as a garnish.

5. To make the vinaigrette, purée the tomatoes, olive oil, balsamic vinegar, and thyme leaves in a food processor or blender container until smooth. Season to taste with salt and pepper or Prime-Rib Scrub.

6. In a gravy boat, serve the tenderloin with the sauce.

Tin Foil Dinner

Preparation Time: 10 minutes
Servings: 4 servings per recipe
Ingredients:

- One small red onion, chopped
- Four sprigs thyme
- Eight tbsp butter, cut into cubes
- One pound stew meat
- One tsp fish sauce
- Two green bell peppers, chopped
- One clove of garlic, minced
- Salt
- Two russet potatoes, peeled and cubed
- Pepper
- One tbsp Veggie Rub
- One tbsp Worcestershire sauce

Instructions:

- Once ready to cook, heat the grill to 350°F with the lid shut for fifteen minutes.
- In a medium mixing bowl, place the stew meat. Combine the fish and Worcestershire sauce in a large mixing bowl. Salt, pepper, and Veggie Rub to taste. Re-mix to ensure an equitable distribution
- Four pieces of foil, torn and spread out on a flat surface Distribute the potatoes evenly among the four sheets of foil, then add the bell pepper, potato onion, garlic, and stew meat, finishing with thyme. 2 tablespoons butter on top of each packet
- Fold the foil in half and tightly wrap it around the object.
- Transfer the packets to a sheet tray and cook them. Cook for forty-five minutes to 1 hour, or until potatoes are soft and stew meat is cooked through.
- Remove the packet from the grill, open it, and sprinkle with fresh herbs if preferred.

Juicy Smoked Beef Brisket in Coke Marinade

(COOKING TIME 8 HOURS 10 MINUTES)
INGREDIENTS FOR 10 SERVINGS

- Beef brisket (4-lbs., 1.8-kg.)

THE MARINADE

- Coca-Cola - 4 cups
- Salt - 1 teaspoon
- Black pepper - 1 teaspoon

THE RUB

- Paprika - 1 ½ tablespoon
- Garlic powder - 1 ½ tablespoon
- Onion powder - 1 ½ tablespoon
- Dry mustard - 1 ½ tablespoon
- Salt - 1 teaspoon
- Chili powder - 1 ½ teaspoon
- Black pepper - 1 tablespoon
- Brown sugar - 3 tablespoons

THE SPRAY

- Beer - 2 cups
- Apple cider vinegar - ¼ cup
- Worcestershire sauce - 2 tablespoons

THE HEAT

- Classic blend wood pellet

METHOD

1.   Pour Coca-Cola and olive oil into a container then season it with salt and black pepper.

2.   Score the beef brisket at several places and put it into the cola mixture.

3.   Marinate the beef brisket for at 4 hours and store it in the fridge to keep the beef brisket fresh.

4.   After 4 hours, take the beef brisket out of the fridge and thaw it at room temperature.

5.   Next, plug the wood pellet smoker then fill the hopper with the wood pellet. Turn the switch on and set the wood pellet smoker for indirect heat.

6.   Adjust the temperature to 225°F (107°C) and let the wood pellet smoker reaches the desired temperature.

7.   In the meantime, combine paprika, garlic powder, onion powder, dry mustard, salt, chili powder, black pepper, and brown sugar. Mix well.

8.   Apply the rub mixture over the beef brisket and set aside.

9.   Place the seasoned beef brisket in the wood pellet smoker and smoke it for 8 hours.

10.   Pour the beer, apple juice, and Worcestershire sauce into a spray bottle. Shake to combine.

11.   Spray the beer mixture over the beef brisket and repeat it once every hour during the smoking time.

12.   Regularly check the internal temperature of the smoked beef brisket and once it reaches 205°F (96°C), remove it from the wood pellet smoker.

13.   Wrap the smoked beef brisket with a sheet of aluminum foil and let it rest for approximately an hour.

14.   After an hour, unwrap the smoked beef brisket and cut it into thin slices.

15.   Transfer the smoked beef brisket to a serving dish and enjoy!

Reverse Seared Rib-Eye Caps

Prep. Time: 5Mins
Cook Time: 70 mins

Servings: 4
Ingredients
- Rib-Eye Cap 1-½ lb
- Coffee Scrub 2 tbsp
- Beef Scrub 2 tbsp

Instructions

1. Remove any excess silver skin and fat from the rib-eye hat if necessary. Roll the cap into steaks by slicing it into four sections. Tie it with butcher's string to keep it tight.

2. In a small dish, combine all of the rubs. Brush the steaks generously with the rub mixture while the grill heats up.

3. Preheat the to 225°F for approximately 15 mins with the lid closed. Use Super Smoke if it's available for the finest flavor.

4. Place your steaks directly on the grill grate and smoke for 30 to 45 mins, or until they reach a core temperature of 120 degrees F.

5. Take the steaks from the grill and place them on a plate to cool.

6. Preheat the grill to 450 degrees Fahrenheit.

7. Cook the stakes over the grill grate for 3-4 mins on each side or until the core temperature reaches 130°F.

8. Take the steaks from the grill and set them aside for 5 mins to rest before serving.

Wood Pellet Grill Smoker Grill Prime Rib Roast

Preparation Time: 5 minutes
Cooking Time: 4 hours
Servings: 10
Ingredients:
- 7 lb bone prime rib roast
- Wood Pellet Grill Smoker prime rib rub

Direction:

1.   Coat the roast generously with the rub then wrap in a plastic wrap. let sit in the fridge for 24 hours to marinate.

2.   Set the temperatures to 500°F.to to preheat with the lid closed for 15 minutes.

3.   Place the rib directly on the grill fat side up and cook for 30 minutes.

4.   Reduce the temperature to 300°F and cook for 4 hours or until the internal temperature is 120°F- rare, 130°F-medium rare, 140°F-medium and 150°F-well done.

5.   Remove from the grill and let rest for 30 minutes then serve and enjoy.

Nutrition: Calories 290, Total fat 23g, Protein 19g, Sugar 0g, Fiber 0g, Sodium: 54mg,

Cocoa Crusted Grilled Flank Steak

Prep. Time: 15Mins
Cook Time: 6 Mins
Servings: 6
Ingredients

- Cocoa Powder 1 tbsp
- Chili Powder Chipotle 1 tsp
- Chili Powder 2 tsp
- Garlic Powder ½ tsp
- Brown Sugar 1-½ tbsp
- Onion Powder ½ tsp
- Kosher Salt 1 tbsp
- Cumin 1 tbsp
- Black Pepper ½ tsp
- Olive Oil
- Smoked Paprika 1 tbsp

Instructions

1. In a mixing bowl, add smoked paprika, cocoa powder, cumin, chipotle, chili powder, black pepper, kosher salt, garlic powder, onion powder and brown sugar to form the cocoa rub.

2. Brush both sides of a flank steak with cocoa rub after sprinkling it using olive oil.

3. Preheat the oven to its highest setting for approximately 15 mins with the lid covered until ready to cook.

4. Cook your flank steak for 3-5 mins each side over the grill grate, or until an instant thermometer reads 130° F.

5. Allow the flank steak to rest for approximately 10-15 mins after taking it from the grill to allow the juices to return to the meat.

6. Slice the meat against the grain on a sharp diagonal to serve. It is something to be proud of.

Sticky Ginger Smoked Beef Short Ribs With Cajun Seasoning

(COOKING TIME 6 HOURS 10 MINUTES)
INGREDIENTS FOR 10 SERVINGS
- Beef short ribs (5-lb., 2.3-kg.)
THE RUB
- Garlic powder - 2 tablespoons
- Onion powder - 2 tablespoons
- Cajun seasoning - 2 tablespoons
- Brown sugar - ¼ cup
- Chili powder - 2 teaspoons
- Kosher salt - ½ teaspoon
- Paprika - 2 teaspoons
- Oregano - 1 tablespoon
- Olive oil - 3 tablespoons
THE GLAZE
- Soy sauce - 1 cup
- Canola oil - 3 tablespoons
- Rice wine vinegar - 1 tablespoon
- Beef broth - 1 cup
- Brown sugar - ¾ cup
- Garlic powder - 1 tablespoon
- Ginger powder - 1 teaspoon
- Black pepper - ½ teaspoon
- Cayenne pepper - ½ teaspoon
THE HEAT
- Cherry wood pellet
METHOD

1.   Plug the wood pellet smoker then fill the hopper with the wood pellet. Turn the switch on and set the wood pellet smoker for indirect heat.

2.   Adjust the temperature to 225°F (107°C) and let the wood pellet smoker reaches the desired temperature.

3.   Combine garlic powder with onion powder, Cajun seasoning, brown sugar, chili powder, salt, paprika, and oregano.

4.   Pour olive oil into the seasoning mixture and mix until becoming a paste.

5.	Rub the beef short ribs with the seasoning mixture and set aside.
6.	Wait until the wood pellet smoker reaches the desired temperature and insert the seasoned beef short ribs into it.
7.	Smoke the beef short ribs for 2 hours and flip it. Continue smoking for another 2 hours.
8.	After 4 hours of smoking, take the smoked beef short ribs out of the wood pellet smoker and place it on a sheet of aluminum foil.
9.	Wrap the beef short ribs with the aluminum foil tightly, but let the other side open.
10.	Combine the glaze ingredients--soy sauce, canola oil, beef broth, and rice wine vinegar. Stir until combined.
11.	Season the glaze mixture with brown sugar, garlic powder, ginger powder, black pepper, and cayenne pepper. Mix well.
12.	Pour the glaze mixture into the aluminum foil with smoked beef short ribs and wrap it tightly. You can also use a disposable aluminum pan and cover it with a sheet of aluminum foil.
13.	Return the wrapped beef short ribs to the wood pellet smoker and smoke again for 2 hours.
14.	Check the internal temperature of the smoked beef short ribs and once it reaches 200°F (93°C), remove it from the wood pellet smoker.
15.	Carefully open the aluminum foil and take the smoked beef short ribs. It will be very hot.
16.	Place the smoked beef short ribs on a serving dish and pour the remaining liquid over it.
17.	Serve and enjoy!
18.	Return the wrapped beef back ribs to the wood pellet smoker and continue smoking it until the internal temperature reaches 190°F (88°C). It will take approximately an hour or two.
19.	Once it is done, take the wrapped beef back ribs out of the wood pellet smoker and let it rest for 30 minutes.
20.	Unwrap the smoked beef back ribs and transfer it to a serving dish.
21.	Cut the smoked beef back ribs into individual slices and serve.
22.	Enjoy!

BBQ Brisket with Coffee Rub

Prep. Time: 15Mins
Cook Time: 9 Hrs
Servings: 8
Ingredients
- Packer Brisket 15 lb
- Water 1-½ cup
- Coffee Scrub 2 tbsp
- Salt 2 tbsp

Instructions
1. Trim away any excess fat from the brisket, leaving a 1/4-inch cap largely on the base.
2. In a small basin, whisk together the water, coffee rub, and salt until the salt is practically dissolved. Per square inch, inject a coffee rub mixture into the brisket. On the exterior, season the brisket with the remaining rub and salt.
3. Preheat the to about 250° F for approximately 15 mins with the lid closed when ready to cook.
4. Put the brisket directly on the grill grate and cook for 6 hours, or until the internal temperature reaches 160 degrees F.
5. Wrap your brisket in two layers of aluminum foil and pour in half a cup of water. Tie the tin foil tightly to keep the liquid confined. Raise the temperature of the grill to 275 degrees Fahrenheit. Cook for a further 3 hours, or until the internal temperature reaches 204°F.
6. Carve the brisket into thin slices after removing it from the grill.

Cilantro Chili Smoked Beef Tenderloin With Savory Garlic Rub

(COOKING TIME 3 HOURS 10 MINUTES)

INGREDIENTS FOR 10 SERVINGS
• Beef tenderloin (4-lbs., 1.8-kg.)
THE MARINADE
• Vegetable oil - 1 cup
• White wine vinegar - ½ cup
• Honey - 1 ½ tablespoon
• Lemon juice - 2 teaspoons
• Minced garlic - 2 tablespoons
• Kosher salt - 1 teaspoon
• Dried parsley - 1 teaspoon
• Dried basil - 1 teaspoon
• Dried oregano - ¼ teaspoon
• Black pepper - ½ teaspoon
• Diced cilantro - 2 tablespoons
• Chili powder - 1 tablespoon
THE RUB
• Diced fresh thyme - 1 tablespoon
• Sweet paprika - 3 tablespoons
• Minced garlic - ¼ cup
• Ground red pepper - ½ teaspoon
THE HEAT
• Hickory wood pellet
METHOD
1. Pour vegetable oil, white wine vinegar, honey, and lemon juice into a container.
2. Add minced garlic, kosher salt, dried parsley, dried basil, dried oregano, black pepper, cilantro, and chili powder. Stir until combined.
3. Score the beef tenderloin at several places and put it into the marinade mixture.
4. Marinate the beef tenderloin for at least 4 hours and store it in the fridge to keep the beef tenderloin fresh.
5. After 4 hours, take the marinated beef tenderloin out of the fridge and thaw it at room temperature.
6. Next, plug the wood pellet smoker then fill the hopper with the wood pellet. Turn the switch on and set the wood pellet smoker for indirect heat.
7. Adjust the temperature to 225°F (107°C) and let the wood pellet smoker reaches the desired temperature.
8. In the meantime, combine minced garlic with fresh thyme, sweet paprika, and red pepper. Mix well.
9. Rub the garlic mixture over the marinated beef tenderloin and place it in the wood pellet smoker.

10. Smoke the beef tenderloin for 3 hours or until the internal temperature reaches 140°F (60°C).
11. Once it is done, remove the smoked beef tenderloin from the wood pellet smoker and transfer it to a serving dish.
12. Cut the smoked beef tenderloin into thick slices and serve.
13. Enjoy!

Smoked Tri-Tip

Prep. Time: 5Mins
Cook Time: 1 Hr
Servings: 6
Ingredients
• Pepper 1/8 c
• Salt 1/8 c
• Tri-Tip 1 3-5 lb
Instructions
1. Preheat the to 225° F with the lid closed for approximately 15 mins when ready to roast. Use Super Smoke if it's available for the finest flavor.
2. Season with salt and pepper. Season the meat with a good quantity of the pepper and salt mixture on both sides.
3. Place the tri-tip on the grill grate and cook for 60-90 mins, or until the internal temperature reaches 130° F.
4. When the tri-tip reaches 130° F, remove it from the grill and wrap it in foil.
5. Preheat the to 500 degrees Fahrenheit and cook for 15 mins with the lid closed.
6. Preheat the to 500 degrees Fahrenheit and cook for 15 mins with the lid closed. Remove the foil from the tri-tip and sear for 4 mins on each side until the grill reaches temperature.
7. Remove the meat from the grill and set it aside for 10-15 mins to rest. To serve, cut the meat against the grain.

Wood Pellet Grill Smoker Beef Short Rib Lollipop

Preparation Time: 15 minutes
Cooking Time: 3 hours
Servings: 4
Ingredients:
- 4 beef short rib lollipops
- BBQ Rub
- BBQ Sauce

Directions:
1. Preheat your Wood Pellet Grill Smoker to 2750F.
2. Season the short ribs with BBQ rub and place them on the grill.
3. Cook for 4 hours while turning occasionally until the meat is tender.
4. Apply the sauce on the meat in the last 30 minutes of cooking.
5. Serve and enjoy.

Nutrition: Calories 265, Total fat 19g, Saturated fat 9g, Total carbs 1g, Net carbs 0g Protein 22g, Sugars 1g, Fiber 0g, Sodium 60mmg

Garlic Parmesan Grilled Filet Mignon

Prep. Time: 15Mins
Cook Time: 10 Mins
Servings: 2
Ingredients
- Mignon Steaks Filet 4
- Black Pepper 1 tsp
- Salt 1 tsp
- Garlic Salt 1 tsp
- Garlic 4
- Parmesan Cheese 1 c
- Dijon Mustard 1 tbsp

Instructions
1. Preheat the grill on high for approximately 15 mins with the lid covered when ready to roast.
2. As your grill heats up, season your fillets with salt, garlic salt, and pepper. Mince the garlic and finely slice the Parmesan in a separate container, then combine the two.
3. Once the grill has achieved temperature, place the fillets on it and cook for approximately 4 mins on both sides.
4. Brush the fillets with Dijon mustard after 8 mins, then plunge them in the Parmesan cheese and minced garlic mixture before bringing them to the grill for another 1-2 mins, or until the melting of cheese.
5. Remove from the oven and set aside for 5 mins before serving.

Grill Beef Recipes

1. Simple Smoked Pulled Beef
Preparation Time: 15 minutes
Cooking Time: 9 hours
Servings: 10
Ingredients:
- 1 6-pound chuck roast
- 2 ½ tablespoons salt
- 2 ½ tablespoons black pepper
- 2 ½ tablespoons garlic powder
- ½ cup chopped onion
- 3 cups beef broth

Directions:
1. Preheat the smoker to 225°F (107°C). Let the lid closed and wait for 15 minutes.
2. Mix garlic powder with black pepper and salt until combined.
3. Rub the chuck roast with the spice mixture then using your hand massage the roast until it is thoroughly seasoned.
4. Place the seasoned roast on the grill then cook the roast for 3 hours. Spray the roast with beef broth once every hour.
5. After 3 hours, sprinkle chopped onion on the bottom of a pan then pours the remaining beef broth over the onion—about 2 cups.
6. Transfer the cooked roast to the pan then place the pan on the grill.
7. Increase the smoker's temperature to 250°F (121°C) then cooks for 3 hours more.
8. After 3 hours, cover the pan with aluminum foil then lower the temperature to 165°F (74°C).

9. Cook the roast for another 3 hours until done.

10. Once it is done, transfer the smoked beef to a flat surface and let it cool.

11. Once it is cold, using a fork shred the beef then place on a serving dish.

12. Serve and enjoy!

Nutrition: Calories: 104 Carbs: 6g Fat: 2g Protein: 16g

Three Ingredient Pot Roast

Prep. Time: 10Mins

Cook Time: 3 Hrs

Servings: 4

Ingredients

- Chuck Roast 4 lb
- Kosher Salt 2 tsp
- Yellow Onions 2
- Black Pepper Grounded
- Olive Oil ¼ c (Extra-Virgin)

Instructions

1. Preheat the to 400 degrees Fahrenheit for 15 mins with the lid covered until ready to roast. Place half of the chuck roast in a 3 to 4-quart Dutch oven.

2. Half of the onions are added, along with salt, pepper, and olive oil. The bulk of the elements have a representative.

3. Cover a Dutch oven with a tight cover and set it on your grill. Cook for approximately 2-3 hours, or until the chuck roast is easily shredded with a fork. Reduce the grill temperature to 350° F if the roast chuck is heating instead of simmering.

4. Remove the cover, then the Dutch oven off the grill. Allow your meat to cool completely before scraping the fat off the top.

5. Allow the meat to settle before refrigerating overnight and skimming the fat cap the following day before reheating. It will last nearly two days in the fridge.

Wood Pellet Grill Smoker Stuffed Peppers

Preparation Time: 20 minutes

Cooking Time: 5 hours

Servings: 6

Ingredients:

- 3 bell peppers, sliced in halves
- 1 lb ground beef, lean
- 1 onion, chopped
- 1/2 tbsp red pepper flakes
- 1/2 tbsp salt
- 1/4 tbsp pepper
- 1/2 tbsp garlic powder
- 1/2 tbsp onion powder
- 1/2 cup white rice
- 15 oz stewed tomatoes
- 8 oz tomato sauce
- o cups cabbage, shredded
- 1-1/2 cup water
- 2 cups cheddar cheese

Directions:

1. Arrange the pepper halves on a baking tray and set aside.

2. Preheat your grill to 3250F.

3. Brown the meat in a large skillet. Add onions, pepper flakes, salt, pepper garlic, and onion and cook until the meat is well cooked.

4. Add rice, stewed tomatoes, tomato sauce, cabbage, and water. Cover and simmer until the rice is well cooked, the cabbage is tender and there is no water in the rice.

5. Place the cooked beef mixture in the pepper halves and top with cheese.

6. Place in the grill and cook for 30 minutes.

7. Serve immediately and enjoy it.

Nutrition: Calories 422, Total fat 22g, Saturated fat 11g, Total carbs 24g, Net carbs 19g Protein 34g, Sugars 11g, Fiber 5g, Sodium 855mg

BBQ Beef Ribs

Prep. Time: 10 mins

Cook Time: 8 Hrs

Servings: 4

Ingredients

- Three-Bone of Beef Ribs 2 Rack (5-7 Lb)
- Beef Broth 2 c
- Cow meat BBQ Rub ¾ c

Instructions

1. About 15 mins before you're ready to cook, preheat the to 275° F.

2. Remove the membrane off the back of a rack of ribs, then flip the ribs meat-side down. Using a paper towel to capture and remove the membrane is one option.

3. Cover the surface with a thick coating of Meat Church. 'Holy Cow' BBQ Rep with the second rack, rubbing the steak mainly on all sides and fully covering it. Allow 10 mins for the rub to take effect. Repeat the procedure on the other side of a rack of ribs.

4. Place the ribs on the with the meat on top. Spritz the ribs with either beef broth or water every hour to keep them moist.

5. Keep smoking the ribs until they are soft to the touch. Temperatures in the core often exceed 210 degrees Fahrenheit. To make the process easier, cover your ribs shortly after the meat has reached a core temperature of nearly 160 degrees Fahrenheit.

6. Remove the ribs from the grill and lay them aside for 15-20 mins to rest and cool while nicely tented in aluminum foil. Remove your ribs into two long pieces, serve them fresh, or cut the meat off the bones and cube it for additional indulgence.

Simple Smoked Beef Brisket with Mocha Sauce

Preparation Time: 15 minutes
Cooking Time: 1 hour
Servings: 10
Ingredients:

- 5 pounds beef brisket
- 1 ½ tablespoons garlic powder
- 1 ½ tablespoons onion powder
- 4 tablespoons salt
- 4 tablespoons pepper
- 2 ½ tablespoons olive oil
- 1 cup chopped onion
- 2 teaspoons salt
- ¼ cup chopped chocolate dark
- ¼ cup sugar –
- ½ cup beer –
- 2 shots espresso

Directions:

1. Rub the beef brisket with garlic powder, onion powder, salt, and black pepper.

2. Wrap the seasoned beef brisket with a sheet of plastic wrap then store in the refrigerator overnight.

3. In the morning, remove the beef brisket from the refrigerator and thaw for about an hour.

4. Preheat the smoker to 250°F (121°C) with charcoal and hickory chips—using indirect heat. Place the beef brisket in the smoker and smoke for 8 hours.

5. Keep the temperature remain at 250°F (121°C) and add some more charcoal and hickory chips if it is necessary.

6. Meanwhile, preheat a saucepan over medium heat then pour olive oil into the saucepan.

7. Once the oil is hot, stir in chopped onion then sauté until wilted and aromatic.

8. Reduce the heat to low then add the remaining sauce ingredients to the saucepan. Mix well then bring to a simmer.

9. Remove the sauce from heat then set aside.

10. When the smoked beef brisket is ready, or the internal temperature has reached 190°F (88°C), remove from the smoker then transfer to a serving dish.

11. Drizzle the mocha sauce over the smoked beef brisket then serve.

12. Enjoy warm.

Nutrition: Calories: 210 Carbs: 1g Fat: 13g Protein: 19g

Short Ribs Braised with Creamy grits

Preparation Time: 30 minutes
Servings: 2 servings per recipe
Ingredients:

Grits:
* Half cup whole milk
* 2-2/3 tbsp butter
* 2/3 cup grits
* 1/8 cup heavy cream
* 2/3 cup water

Ribs:
* 2/3 diced stalk of celery
* 2-2/3 sprigs parsley flat-leaf
* Salt and pepper
* Four beef short ribs
* Two tbsp olive oil
* 2-2/3 cup red wine
* Four cups beef broth
* 2/3 diced medium onion
* 2/3 diced medium carrot
* 1-1/3 whole bay leaves
* 1-1/3 tbsp balsamic vinegar
* Four cloves of garlic
* 2-2/3 sprigs of thyme

Instructions:
* Set the temperature to 500°F and warm for 15 minutes with the lid covered when ready to cook.
* Season short ribs generously with pepper and salt. Place on the grill and cook for 5 minutes on each side, or until golden brown.
* Take off from the grill and turn down the heat to 350°F.
* In a big oven, heat oil. Combine the onion, garlic, carrot, celery, bay leaves and thyme sprigs in a large mixing bowl. Cook, stirring occasionally, for eight to ten minutes, or until the veggies start to caramelize. Combine the wine and balsamic vinegar in a mixing bowl.
* Evaporate the liquid to half and raise the temperature to 500°F. Bring the stock to a boil, then remove from the heat. In and around the meat, place the short ribs and parsley sprigs. Aluminum foil or a lid should be used to cover the dish tightly.
* Reduce the heat to 350 degrees Fahrenheit, lay the Dutch oven on top, and braise for about 3 hours, or until the meat is extremely soft. Allow the ribs to rest in their juices for 10 minutes before removing them from the pot.
* Strain the soup, pushing down with a spoon to get all of the juices from the veggies.

Remove the solids and throw them away. Reduce the sauce over moderate flame until it has thickened somewhat. Season with salt and pepper to taste.
* Return the short ribs to the sauce and keep heated until serving time.
* To make the Grits: In a medium saucepan over medium heat, bring the water, milk, cream, butter, and salt to a simmer.
* In a separate bowl, mix together the grits and keep mixing to remove any clumps. Bring to a gentle boil, then lower to medium-low heat until the grits are just bubbling. Cooking for 10 to 15 minutes, or until the grits are al dente and the moisture has been absorbed. If necessary, add extra water until the grits are fully cooked. To taste, season with salt and pepper.
* To serve, place the short ribs on a surface of grits and drizzle with the remaining braising liquid. Have fun!

Grilled Beef Steaks with Beer-Honey Sauce

Preparation Time: 15 minutes
Cooking Time: 55 minutes
Servings: 4
Ingredients
* 4 beef steaks
* Salt and pepper to taste
* 1 cup of beer
* 1 teaspoon thyme
* 1 tablespoon of honey
* 1 lemon juice
* 2 tablespoon olive oil

Directions:
1. Season beef steaks with salt and pepper.
2. In a bowl, combine beer, thyme, honey, lemon juice and olive oil.
3. Rub the beef steaks generously with beer mixture.
4. Start your Wood Pellet Grill Smoker grill, set the temperature on High and preheat, lid closed, for 10 to 15 minutes.

5.   As a general rule, you should grill steaks on high heat (450-500°F).

6.   Grill about 7-10 minutes per side at high temperatures or 15 minutes per side at the lower temperatures, or to your preference for doneness.

7.   Remove meat from the grill and let cool for 10 minutes.

8.   Serve.

Nutrition: Calories 355.77 Fat 12.57g Carbohydrates 7.68g Fiber 0.18g Protein 49.74g

Italian Meatballs Braised

Preparation Time: 30 minutes
Servings: 6 servings per recipe
Ingredients:
- One tsp dried oregano
- Extra virgin olive oil
- ½ cup basil leaves
- One-pound ground beef
- One pound ground pork
- One cup whole milk-ricotta
- ½ cup milk
- Two tsp kosher salt
- Two tsp fennel seed
- Three whole eggs whisked
- One whole (28 ounces) crushed tomatoes
- Four ounces Prosciutto
- One cup fresh white breadcrumb

Instructions:
- Preheat the oven to 375°F for 15 minutes when ready to cook. Mix the ground pork, beef, prosciutto, bread crumbs, Two teaspoons of salt, fennel seed, and oregano in a large mixing basin.
- Incorporate the milk, ricotta, and eggs in a separate mixing dish and whisk to combine.
- Blend the meats, bread crumbs, salt, and herbs in a mixing bowl with freshly cleansed hands until the mixture is evenly blended and the herbs are evenly mixed.
- Pour the mixture the liquid mixture over the meat, mixing it up with your hands.

Even when thoroughly blended, the mix will be sticky. Allow for a 10-minute rest period. Form 1 2-inch patty and cook in a small sauté pan until cooked thoroughly, about 2 minutes per side, to verify the seasoning of the mixture before cooking the full batch. Taste the meat mixture and adjust the seasoning as needed.

- Using parchment or butcher paper, line a large baking sheet. Alternatively, lightly oil a baking sheet and shape meatballs the size of golf balls with clean hands or an ice cream scoop. Place them on the baking sheet with some space between them, so they don't contact. About 48 meatballs should be made from this mixture.
- Set the baking sheet flat on the grill and cook for 20 minutes, flipping once, until the meatballs are cooked through when split in half. Remove from the grill, repeat with the second batch if necessary.
- Reduce the heat to 300°F on the grill.
- Place all of the meatballs in a large roasting pan after they have cooled enough to handle. Over the top, pour the crushed tomatoes. Drizzle 3 tbsp olive oil over the top and season with an additional teaspoon of salt.
- Aluminum foil should be tightly wrapped around the pan. Put on the grill and cook, tented, for 60-90 minutes, or until the meatballs are fork tender and the tomatoes have absorbed some of the meatballs' flavor.
- Remove the meatballs off the grill and top with basil leaves. The meatballs can also be cooked, cooled, refrigerated up to a day ahead of time, then brought to room temp and simmered in tomato sauce before serving. *Cook times will differ based on the temperature of the oven and the ambient temperature.

Spiced Smoked Beef with Oregano

Preparation Time: 10 minutes
Cooking Time: 8 hours
Servings: 10
Ingredients:

- 1 8-pounduntrimmed brisket
- 6 tablespoons paprika
- ¼ cup salt
- 3 tablespoons garlic powder
- 2 tablespoons onion powder
- 1 ½ tablespoons black pepper
- 1 ½ tablespoons dried parsley
- 2 ½ teaspoons cayenne pepper
- 2 ½ teaspoons cumin
- 1 ½ teaspoons coriander
- 2 teaspoons oregano
- ½ teaspoon hot chili powder
- Preheat the smoker prior to smoking.
- Add woodchips during the smoking time.

Directions:
1. Cook the brisket for 6 hours.
2. After 6 hours, usually the smoker temperature decreases to 170°F (77°C).
3. Take the brisket out from the smoker then wrap with aluminum foil.
4. Return the brisket to the smoker then cooks again for 2 hours—this will increase the tenderness of the smoked beef.
5. Once it is done, remove the smoked beef from the smoker then place in a serving dish.
6. Cut the smoked beef into slices then enjoy!

Nutrition: Calories: 267 Carbs: 0g Fat: 21g Protein: 20g

Grilled Steak Bulgogi Bowls

Preparation Time: 20 minutes
Servings: 4 servings per recipe
Ingredients:
Pickled Carrots
- Two tbsp sugar
- ¼ cup rice wine vinegar
- ¼ tsp red pepper flakes
- ½ tbsp kosher salt
- Two large carrots shaved thinly

Marinade
- One-inch fresh ginger, peeled
- One tbsp brown sugar
- One tbsp sesame oil
- ½ pear, peeled
- ¼ cup soy sauce
- One tbsp gochujang
- Two cloves of garlic

Main
- ½ cup thinly sliced cucumber
- Sesame seeds
- Thinly sliced green onion for garnishing
- Two pounds trimmed skirt steak
- Two cups cooked rice
- Four whole fried eggs
- One cup kimchi

Instructions:
- In a blender, purée all of the marinade ingredients until smooth.
- Pour the marinade over the steak in a resealable or vacuum-sealed bag. Seal the bag after squeezing out as much air as possible. Refrigerate for at least an hour or up to four hours, depending on how long you want to marinate.
- In a small bowl, combine all of the ingredients for the pickled carrots and set them aside to ferment for at least 1 hour (can store for up to a week).
- When ready to cook, preheat the grill to 450°F and cook for 15 minutes with the lid closed.
- Withdraw the steak from the marinade and set it straight on the grill grate in the center of the grill, where it will be the hottest. Cook for 20 minutes until caramelized and cooked through, flipping halfway through. Remove the steaks from the grill and set them aside to rest.
- Distribute the rice, kimchi, cucumbers, and carrots into four bowls to make the bowls. Sprinkle the bowls with thinly sliced skirt steak cut against the grain. Add a fried egg to each bowl and top with sesame and scallions.

Braised Mediterranean Beef Brisket

Preparation Time: 1 day
Servings: 4 servings per recipe
Ingredients:

- ½ tbsp dried oregano
- Four pounds beef brisket
- ½ cup beef stock
- 1½ tbsp dried rosemary
- One tbsp ground cumin seeds
- One tsp ground cinnamon
- ¼ tsp salt
- One tbsp dried coriander

Instructions:

- Plan on 8 to 12 hours of cooking time for a 6 to 8-pound brisket, or 90 minutes per pound. For brisket, a remote probed thermometer is essential.
- Combine all of the seasonings and thoroughly cover the brisket. Cover in plastic wrap and set aside. Allow the wrapped brisket to chill for 12 to 24 hours. Then, give yourself plenty of time to prepare the meal.
- Once ready to cook, preheat the grill to 180°F with the lid covered for 15 minutes.
- Place the brisket on the grill grate fat side down, insert the thermometer probe, and smoke for four hours.
- Preheat the grill to 250 degrees Fahrenheit after 4 hours.
- Remove the brisket from the grill and drape it in foil with beef stock when the internal temperature reaches 160°F. DO NOT remove the thermometer probe.
- Return the foiled brisket to the grill.
- Remove the brisket from the oven and let it rest for at least thirty min in the foil before slicing.

Blackened Steak

Preparation Time: 10 minutes
Cooking Time: 60 minutes
Servings: 4
Ingredients:

- 2 steaks, each about 40 ounces
- 4 tablespoons blackened rub
- 4 tablespoons butter, unsalted

Directions:

1. Switch on the Wood Pellet Grill Smoker grill, fill the grill hopper with hickory flavored Wood Pellet Grill Smokers, power the grill on by using the control panel, select 'smoke' on the temperature dial, or set the temperature to 225 degrees F and let it preheat for a minimum of 15 minutes.
2. Transfer steaks to a dish and then repeat with the remaining steak.
3. Let seared steaks rest for 10 minutes, then slice each steak across the grain and serve.

Nutrition: Calories: 184.4 Cal Fat: 8.8 g Carbs: 0 g Protein: 23.5 g

Beef Short Ribs Braised

Preparation Time: 20 minutes
Servings: 4 servings per recipe
Ingredients:

- Two Whole Carrots
- One Tablespoon brown sugar
- Six cups beef stock
- Four teaspoon salt
- Six rack beef short ribs (bone-in)
- Three whole garlic
- Two tbsp tomato paste
- 1½ cups onion
- Four cup celery
- 25.4 ounces red wine
- One tsp pepper
- One bunch of fennel, cleaned
- One whole leek, only white part
- Rosemary sprigs
- Thyme sprigs
- Quarter cup extra-virgin olive oil

Instructions:

- Preheat the oven to 400 degrees Fahrenheit and leave the lid covered for 15 minutes when ready to cook.
- Meanwhile, in a cast iron pan on the stovetop, heat the olive oil and add the fennel, leeks, onion, celery, and carrots; simmer for 20 minutes, turning regularly. Sauté for another 2 minutes after adding the garlic. Combine the wine and tomato paste in a mixing bowl.
- Bring it to a boil and simmer over high heat for 10 minutes, or until the liquid has reduced by half. One teaspoon salt and one teaspoon pepper Add the thyme and rosemary

to the skillet after tying them together using kitchen twine.

• In a Dutch oven, put the barbecued ribs on top of the veggies and mix the beef stock and brown sugar. Bring to a boil over high heat, then reduce to low heat. Tent the Dutch oven with foil and bake for 2 hours in the grill, just until the meat is extremely soft.

• Retrieve the ribs from the oven with care and set them aside. Remove the herbs and throw them away. Simmer the vegetables and sauce on a moderate flame for another 20 minutes, or until the sauce has reduced.

• Return the ribs to the pot.

• Cook until hot. Serve with vegetables and sauce on the side.

Blue Cheese Butter

• ¼ cup crumbled blue cheese
• Pepper
• Eight tbsp butter softened
• One tsp Worcestershire sauce
• One scallion minced

Main

• Beef Rub
• One (two pounds) London broil steak

Marinade

• Two tbsp vegetable oil or extra-virgin olive oil
• One tsp freshly ground black pepper
• One tsp sugar
• ¼ cup soy sauce
• ¼ cup water
• One tbsp ketchup
• One tsp Worcestershire sauce
• One clove of garlic, minced
• 2 tbsp red wine vinegar
• One small onion, chopped

Instructions:

• To make the marinade, mix the water, soy sauce, onion, garlic, oil, ketchup, Worcestershire sauce, red wine vinegar, pepper, and sugar in a small mixing bowl.

• Put the meat in a big resealable plastic bag and cover it with the marinade. Refrigerate for a minimum of 6 hours and up to 24 hours.

• Take the steak out of the fridge and set it aside to come to room temp.

• To make the blue cheese butter, combine the following ingredients in a small mixing bowl. Mix the butter, blue cheese, scallion, Worcestershire sauce, and pepper in a small bowl. Using a wooden spoon, mix the ingredients. If not using right away, cover and chill.

• Remove the steak from the marinade and pat it dry with paper towels after it has reached room temperature.

• Season with Beef Rub on all sides.

• Set the grill to 180°F and preheat for 15 minutes with the lid covered when you're ready to cook.

• Smoke the steak for 60 minutes by placing it directly on the grill grate.

• Place the meat on a serving plate. Preheat the grill to 500 degrees Fahrenheit with the lid covered.

• Return the steak to the grill when it's hot and cook for 15 to 20 minutes, or until the desired core temperature is attained, 130°F for medium-rare.

• Allow the meat to rest for three minutes before slicing thinly on a diagonal. Serve with a dollop of Blue Cheese Butter on top.

Coffee Rub Barbeque Brisket

Preparation Time: 15 minutes
Servings: 4 servings per recipe
Ingredients:

• 1 cup water
• 4½-pounds brisket
• 6 tbsp salt
• 6 tbsp Coffee Rub

Instructions:

• Remove any excess fat from the brisket and leave a 1/4" inch capping on the bottom.

• In a small dish, combine two tablespoons coffee rub, one cup water, and Two tablespoons salt, stirring until the salt is almost dissolved. Infuse the coffee rub into the brisket each square inch or so. Season the brisket on the outside with the remaining rub and salt.

• Once ready to cook, heat the grill to 250°F for 15 minutes with the lid closed.

• Place the brisket straight on the grill grate.

• Cook for 6 hours, or until the core temperature hits 160 degrees Fahrenheit.

• Cover the brisket in 2 layers of aluminum foil and pour half a cup of water over it. To keep the liquid contained, wrap the tin foil tightly. Return to the grill and raise the temperature to 275°F. Cook for 3 hours more, or until the internal temperature reaches 204°F.

• Remove the brisket off the grill and cut it into thin slices

Thai Beef Salad

Preparation Time: 10 minutes
Cooking Time: 10 minutes
Servings: 4
Ingredients:
• 1 ½ pound skirt steak
• 1 ½ teaspoon salt
• 1 teaspoon ground white pepper
• 4 jalapeño peppers, minced
• ½ teaspoon minced garlic
• 4 tablespoons Thai fish sauce
• 4 tablespoons lime juice
• 1 tablespoon brown sugar
• 1 small red onion, peeled, thinly sliced
• 6 cherry tomatoes, halved
• 2 green onions, ¼-inch diced
• 1 cucumber, deseeded, thinly sliced
• 1 heart of romaine lettuce, chopped
• ½ cup chopped mint
• 2 tablespoons cilantro
• ½ teaspoon red pepper flakes
• 1 tablespoon lime juice
• 2 tablespoons fish sauce

Directions:
1. Switch on the Wood Pellet Grill Smoker grill, fill the grill hopper with cherry flavored Wood Pellet Grill Smokers, power the grill on by using the control panel, select 'smoke' on the temperature dial, or set the temperature to 450 degrees F and let it preheat for a minimum of 15 minutes.

2. Take a large salad, place all the ingredients for the salad in it, drizzle with dressing and toss until well coated and mixed.

3. When done, transfer steak to a cutting board, let it rest for 10 minutes and then cut it into slices.

4. Add steak slices into the salad, toss until mixed, and then serve.

Nutrition: Calories: 128 Cal Fat: 6 g Carbs: 6 g Protein: 12 g Fiber: 1 g

Wood Pellet Grill Smoker Smoked Beef Roast

Preparation Time: 10 minutes
Cooking Time: 6 hours
Servings: 6
Ingredients:
• 1-3/4 lb beef sirloin tip roast
• 1/2 cup bbq rub
• 2 bottles amber beer
• 1 bottle BBQ sauce

Directions:
1. Turn the Wood Pellet Grill Smoker onto the smoke setting.

2. Rub the beef with bbq rub until well coated then place on the grill. Let smoke for 4 hours while flipping every 1 hour.

3. Transfer the beef to a pan and add the beer. The beef should be 1/2 way covered.

4. Braise the beef until fork tender. It will take 3 hours on the stovetop and 60 minutes on the instant pot.

5. Remove the beef from the ban and reserve 1 cup of the cooking liquid.

6. Use 2 forks to shred the beef into small pieces then return to the pan with the reserved braising liquid.

7. Add BBQ sauce and stir well then keep warm until serving. You can also reheat if it gets cold.

Nutrition: Calories 829, Total fat 46g, Saturated fat 18g, Total carbs 4g, Net carbs 4g Protein 86g, Sugars 0g, Fiber 0g, Sodium 181mmg

Bacon-Wrapped Beef Tenderloin

Preparation Time: 10 minutes
Servings: 4 servings per recipe
Ingredients:
* 8 Strips bacon
* 4 Pound Beef, Loins
* 4 Ounce Coffee Rub
* 4 Ounce Beef Rub

Instructions:
* Once you're ready to cook, fire up the grill as per the manufacturer's directions. Preheat the oven to 275 degrees Fahrenheit and bake for Ten to Fifteen minutes with the lid covered.
* Wrap the tenderloin in bacon after lightly seasoning it with the beef rub. Re-season with a second coating of coffee rub.
* Cook the tenderloin for 30 minutes on the grill. Check the inside temperature; 120 degrees F is the ideal temperature. If the required temperature has not been attained, continue cooking, checking every five minutes until it is.
* Remove the tenderloin from the grill and raise the temperature to 450°F. Bring tenderloin to grill after 10 minutes and caramelize for 5 minutes. Check the core temperature once more; it should be 135 ° F at this point.
* If the tenderloin has not reached the desired temperature, flip it and sear for another 5 minutes, or until it reaches 135 degrees F.
* Before slicing and serving, remove the tenderloin from the grill and set it aside to rest for 10 minutes.

Pastrami Short Ribs

Preparation Time: 15 minutes
Servings: 4 servings per recipe
Ingredients:
* Rub
* Three tbsp cracked black peppercorns
* Three tbsp coriander seeds
* Two tsp yellow mustard seeds
* Brine
* ¼ cup brown sugar
* Four tbsp pickling spices
* Two quarts of cold water
* 1/3 salt
* Four cloves of garlic
* One tsp pink curing salt
* Main
* One-liter Ginger Ale
* Two tbsp extra-virgin olive oil
* Short Ribs

Instructions:
* To make the brine, merge 2 quarts of cold water, salt, pink salt, and brown sugar in a large mixing dish. Stir until all of the sugar and salt crystals are gone. Add the short ribs after stirring in the garlic and pickling spices.
* Cover and chill for two days, stirring to redistribute spices twice a day.
* Drain the ribs, removing any particles, and pat it dry on paper towels when ready to cook.
* In a small resealable bag, coarsely crush coriander seeds, peppercorns, and mustard seeds.
* Drizzle olive oil on all surfaces of the ribs and coat lightly. Apply the rub on the meaty sides of the ribs and gently massage the spices in.
* Set the grill to 165°F and heat for 15 minutes with the lid closed when ready to cook.
* Place the short ribs directly on the barbecue grate, bone-side down, and smoke for 2 hours.
* Place the ribs in a roasting pan and set them aside. Fill the bottom of the pan with enough ginger ale to come slightly over the upper edge of the bones. Wrap the foil around the dish tightly.

- Raise the temperature to 300°F and cook the ribs for another 1 to 1-1/2 hours, or until they are tender. Then, remove from the oven, chill, and enjoy!

Grilled Beef Eye Fillet with Herb Rubs

Preparation Time: 15 minutes
Cooking Time: 1 hour
Servings: 6
Ingredients
- 2 lbs. beef eye fillet
- Salt and pepper to taste
- 2 tablespoon Olive oil
- 1/4 cup parsley, fresh and chopped
- 1/4 cup oregano leaves, fresh and chopped
- 2 tablespoon basil, fresh and chopped
- 2 tablespoon rosemary leaves, fresh and chopped
- 3 cloves garlic, crushed

Directions:
1. Season beef roast with salt and pepper and place in a shallow dish.
2. In a medium bowl, combine olive oil, chopped parsley, basil, oregano, rosemary, garlic, and oil. Rub the meat with the herb mixture from both sides
3. Bring the meat to room temperature 30 minutes before you put it on the grill.
4. Start your Wood Pellet Grill Smoker grill, set the temperature on High and preheat, lid closed, for 10 to 15 minutes.
5. As a general rule, you should grill steaks on high heat (450-500°F).
6. Grill about 7-10 minutes per side at high temperatures or 15-20 minutes per side at the lower temperatures, or to your preference for doneness.
7. When ready, let meat rest for 10 minutes, slice and serve.

Nutrition: Calories 427.93 cal Fat 31.8g Carbohydrates 3.78g Fiber 2.17g Protein 30.8g

Braised Five Alarm Chili

Preparation Time: 30 minutes
Servings: 4 servings per recipe
Ingredients:
- 1 Can plum tomatoes
- 1 tbsp tomato paste
- 1/4 Whole Bar of Chocolate
- 2 Pound beef
- salt
- 1 Can Chopped Tomatoes
- 1 Can crushed tomatoes
- 1 Can Black Beans
- 1 Can Kidney Beans
- 1 Can Small Can Chipotle Peppers
- 1/4 cup chili powder
- 1/2 red bell pepper diced and seeded
- 1/2 green bell pepper diced and seeded
- 1/8 Cup cumin
- 1/8 cup dried oregano
- 1 Whole Jalapeño, diced and seeded
- 1/2 Whole Poblano Pepper, diced and seeded
- 1/2 Tablespoon ground cinnamon
- 1 Bottle Stout Beer
- black pepper
- 1 1/2 tbsp olive oil
- 3 Clove garlic, minced
- 1 Small onion, diced
- 1/2 small red onion, diced

Instructions:
- Preheat the grill to 325 degrees Fahrenheit whenever ready to cook.
- Heat a Dutch oven on the stovetop beforehand. Season meat liberally with pepper and salt on all sides.
- In a Dutch oven, heat the olive oil and brown the beef on all surfaces, using two batches to avoid crowding the pan.
- After the meat has been browned, pour the beer into the Dutch oven and lid until it begins to boil.
- Add olive oil, onion, and garlic to a separate stovetop skillet and cook until golden brown and transparent. Cook for about ten minutes or until the peppers begin to soften.
- Combine the onions and peppers with the meat and beer. The beans, chipotle peppers, tomatoes and spices are then added. Cover with a cover and bring to a low simmer.

•   Transfer the Dutch to the grill and cook for three hours at 325°F, uncovered, just until the beef is very tender.
•   Stir in the tomato paste. If necessary, season with salt and pepper.
•   Cut the chocolate bar finely and stir it into the chili right before serving. Serve immediately.

Grilled Veal with Mustard Lemony Crust

Preparation Time: 15 minutes
Cooking Time: 2 hours and 45 minutes
Servings: 8
Ingredients
•   1 lb boneless veal leg round roast
•   1 tablespoon Dijon-style mustard
•   1 tablespoon lemon juice
•   1 teaspoon dried thyme, crushed
•   1 teaspoon dried basil, crushed
•   2 tablespoon water
•   1/2 teaspoon coarsely salt and ground pepper
•   1/4 cup breadcrumbs
Directions:
1.   Place meat on a rack in a shallow roasting pan.
2.   In a small mixing bowl stir together bread crumbs, water, mustard, lemon juice, basil, thyme, and pepper. Spread the mixture over surface of the meat.
3.   Start your Wood Pellet Grill Smoker grill, set the temperature on High and preheat, lid closed, for 10 to 15 minutes.
4.   As a general rule, you should grill steaks on high heat (450-500°F).
5.   Grill about 7-10 minutes per side at high temperatures or 15-20 minutes per side at the lower temperatures, or to your preference for doneness.
6.   Remove veal meat from the grill and let cool for 10 minutes.
Nutrition: Calories 172 cal Fat 3g Carbohydrates 4g Fiber 0g Protein 30g

Chef's Brisket

Preparation Time: 10 minutes
Servings: 4 servings per recipe
Ingredients:
•   One tbsp garlic paste
•   1/8 cup black pepper
•   1/2 beef brisket (whole packer), fat trimmed to a quarter inch
•   One tbsp onion powder
•   1/8 cup salt
Instructions:
•   The day before you want to prepare the brisket, season it. In a small bowl, combine the salt, garlic, onion powder, and pepper. Season the meat well with salt and pepper. Place in the refrigerator for at least eight hours or overnight.
•   Once ready to cook, preheat the grill to 225°F with the lid shut for fifteen minutes. If Super Smoke is available, use it for the best flavor.
•   Place the brisket fat side down on the grill grate in the grill's center. Smoke the brisket for Four to Five hours or till an interior temperature of 160°F to 165°F is reached.
•   Wrap the brisket in foil after removing it from the grill. Continue smoking at 225°F for another 3 to 4 hours, or until the brisket achieves a core temperature of 203°F, for a total of 8–10 hours smoking and cooking time.
•   Allow for one hour of resting time after removing the foil-wrapped brisket from the grill.
•   Cut the brisket against with the grain in ¼ inch thick pieces and serve after it has rested.

Brandy Beef Tenderloin

Preparation Time: 15 minutes
Cooking Time: 2 hours 2 minutes
Servings: 6
Ingredients:
For Brandy Butter:
•   ½ cup butter
•   1 ounce brandy
For Brandy Sauce:

- 2 ounces brandy
- 8 garlic cloves, minced
- ¼ cup mixed fresh herbs (parsley, rosemary and thyme), chopped
- 2 teaspoons honey
- 2 teaspoons hot English mustard

For Tenderloin:
- 1 (2-pound) center-cut beef tenderloin
- Salt and cracked black peppercorns, as required

Directions:
1. Preheat the Z Grills Wood Pellet Grill Smoker Grill & Smoker on grill setting to 230 degrees F.
2. For brandy butter: in a pan, melt butter over medium-low heat.
3. Stir in brandy and remove from heat.
4. Set aside, covered to keep warm.
5. For brandy sauce: in a bowl, add all ingredients and mix until well combined.
6. Season the tenderloin with salt and black peppercorns generously.
7. Coat tenderloin with brandy sauce evenly.
8. With a baster-injector, inject tenderloin with brandy butter.
9. Place the tenderloin onto the grill and cook for about ½-2 hours, injecting with brandy butter occasionally.
10. Remove the tenderloin from grill and place onto a cutting board for about 10-15 minutes before serving.
11. With a sharp knife, cut the tenderloin into desired-sized slices and serve.

Nutrition: Calories 496 Total Fat 29.3 g Saturated Fat 15 g Cholesterol 180 mg Sodium 240 mg Total Carbs 4.4 g Fiber 0.7 g Sugar 2 g Protein 44.4 g

Roasted Herb and Garlic Prime Rib

Preparation Time: 30 minutes
Servings: 4 servings per recipe
Ingredients:
- ½ tbsp fresh rosemary
- Salt
- 6 cups beef broth
- Pepper
- ½ (six pounds) prime rib roast, boneless
- 2½ cloves of garlic, chopped
- ¼ cup olive or vegetable oil
- Prime Rib Rub
- One tbsp red wine vinegar
- ¼ cup fresh parsley

Instructions:
- Butcher's twine should be used to tie the roast at Two-inch intervals.
- Blend the garlic, parsley, red wine vinegar, and rosemary in a blender jar or small food processor. Pulse in a few teaspoons of oil to finely cut the garlic and herbs. In a tiny stream, drizzle in the remaining oil until the batter is thoroughly combined.
- Place the roast in a large ziplock bag and dump the herb mixture over it, making sure it is covered on all sides.
- Place the roast in the fridge for two hours to marinade.
- Take the roast out of the plastic bag and toss out the marinade. Allow the roast to come to room temperature before liberally seasoning it with Rib Rub on all sides.
- In a roasting pan, place the roast fat side up on a V-shaped rack. In the bottom of the pan, pour 4 cups beef broth.
- Set the grill to 400°F and heat for fifteen minutes beforehand with the lid covered once you're ready to cook.
- Place the pan on the grill grate with the prime rib and cook for 30 minutes.
- Reduce the temperature to 225°F after 30 minutes and cook for another 2 to 3 hours, or until the core temperature of the meat reaches 130°F for medium-rare.
- Move the roast to a work surface and set aside for 20 minutes, loosely covered with foil.
- To make the juice, combine the following ingredients in a mixing bowl. Deglaze the roasting pan with Two cups of beef stock over medium heat. Scrape all the brown fragments from the pan with a wooden spoon.
- Remove the solids from the juice and skim whatever fat that rises to the top into a small saucepan. Taste and adjust the heat to medium if necessary (if the juice tastes a little

weak, the reduction will concentrate the flavor). Season the juice to taste with pepper and salt as needed. Before serving, reheat the dish.

• Chop the roast into thick pieces and serve with beef au jus on the side.

Spicy Chuck Roast

Preparation Time: 10 minutes
Cooking Time: 4½ hours
Servings: 8
Ingredients:
• 2 tablespoons onion powder
• 2 tablespoons garlic powder
• 1 tablespoon red chili powder
• 1 tablespoon cayenne pepper
• Salt and ground black pepper, as required
• 1 (3 pound) beef chuck roast
• 16 fluid ounces warm beef broth
Directions:
1. Preheat the Z Grills Wood Pellet Grill Smoker Grill & Smoker on grill setting to 250 degrees F.
2. In a bowl, mix together spices, salt and black pepper.
3. Rub the chuck roast with spice mixture evenly.
4. Place the rump roast onto the grill and cook for about 1½ hours per side.
5. Now, arrange chuck roast in a steaming pan with beef broth.
6. With a piece of foil, cover the pan and cook for about 2-3 hours.
7. Remove the chuck roast from grill and place onto a cutting board for about 20 minutes before slicing.
8. With a sharp knife, cut the chuck roast into desired-sized slices and serve.
Nutrition: Calories 645 Total Fat 48 g Saturated Fat 19 g Cholesterol 175 mg Sodium 329 mg Total Carbs 4.2 g Fiber 1 g Sugar 1.4 g Protein 46.4 g

Beef Stuffed Bell Peppers

Preparation Time: 20 minutes
Cooking Time: 1 hour
Servings: 6
Ingredients:
• 6 large bell peppers
• 1 pound ground beef
• 1 small onion, chopped
• 2 garlic cloves, minced
• 2 cups cooked rice
• 1 cup frozen corn, thawed
• 1 cup cooked black beans
• 2/3 cup salsa
• 2 tablespoons Cajun rub
• 1½ cups Monterey Jack cheese, grated
Directions:
1. Cut each bell pepper in half lengthwise through the stem.
2. Carefully, remove the seeds and ribs.
3. For stuffing: heat a large frying pan and cook the beef for about 6-7 minutes or until browned completely.
4. Add onion and garlic and cook for about 2-3 minutes.
5. Stir in remaining ingredients except cheese and cook for about 5 minutes.
6. Remove from the heat and set aside to cool slightly.
7. Preheat the Z Grills Wood Pellet Grill Smoker Grill & Smoker on grill setting to 350 degrees F.
8. Stuff each bell pepper half with stuffing mixture evenly.
9. Arrange the peppers onto grill, stuffing side up and cook for about 40 minutes.
10. Sprinkle each bell pepper half with cheese and cook for about 5 minutes more.
11. Remove the bell peppers from grill and serve hot.
Nutrition: Calories 675 Total Fat 14.8 g Saturated Fat 7.5 g Cholesterol 93 mg Sodium 1167 mg Total Carbs 90.7 g Fiber 8.7 g Sugar 9.1 g Protein 43.9 g

Smoked Bacon

Preparation Time: 20 minutes
Cooking Time: 3 hours
Servings: 12
Ingredients:
· Pork belly, fat trimmed – 2 pounds
· Salt – ½ cup
· Brown sugar – ½ cup
· Ground black pepper – 1 tablespoon
Directions:
1. Before preheating the grill, cure the pork and for this, stir together all of the ingredients for it and then rub it well on the pork belly.
2. Place pork belly into a large plastic bag, seal it, and let it rest for 8 days in the refrigerator.
3. Then remove pork belly from the refrigerator, rinse well and pat dry.

4. When the grill has preheated, place the pork belly on the grilling rack and let smoke for 3 hours or until the control panel

shows the internal temperature of 150 degrees F, turning halfway.
5. Check the fire after one hour of smoking and add more wood pallets if required.
6. When done, remove pork from the grill, wrap it in plastic wrap, and rest for 1 hour in the freezer until pork is firm and nearly frozen.
7. When ready to eat, cut pork into slices and then serve.
Nutrition: Calories per serving: 688; Protein: 58.9g; Carbs: 2.7g; Fat: 47.3g Sugar: 0.2g

Bacon Smoked Brisket Flat

Prep Time: 10 mins
Cook Time: 1 hrs
Servings: 2
Ingredients:
· 1/2 lbs bacon
· 4 lbs brisket flat, trimmed
· Tt grill lonestar brisket rub
Instructions:
1. Smoked brisket is no exception to the rule that anything tastes better with bacon.
2. Start your grill in smoke mode and let it run for 10 minutes with the lid open.
3. Double the temperature of your barbecue to 250°f. Set up a gas or charcoal grill for low, indirect fire.
4. Place the brisket in an aluminum pan lined with foil. Season the fat side of the brisket with grill lonestar brisket rub before flipping and seasoning the meat side.
5. Place the brisket on the grill for 1 hour to smoke.
6. Toss the brisket with tongs such that the fat side is up, then drape half of the bacon slices over the brisket. After 2 hours, cut the browned bacon and set aside.
7. Continue cooking until the fresh bacon strips are browned and the internal temperature of the brisket reads 202°f, which will usually take a further 3 to 4 hours.
8. Remove the brisket from the grill and let it rest for 1 hour before slicing thinly. Serve hot.
Difficulty: 5
Nutrition: Per Serving: 56 calories; protein 2g; carbohydrates 5.3g; fat 2.1g; sodium 654.3mg.

Bacon Stuffed Smoked Pork Loin

Prep Time: 1 hour 20 mins

Serving: **Serves** 4
Ingredients
*   Bacon Grease
*   1 tbsp. fresh oregano
*   3 Pound Pork Loin, Butterflied
*   1/3 Cup grated Parmesan cheese
*   1/3 Cup Craisins
*   6 Pieces asparagus
*   Pork & Poultry Rub
*   1 tbsp. fresh thyme
*   1/4 Cup chopped walnuts
*   6 Slices sliced bacon

Instructions

*   On your worktable, lay out two large pieces of butcher's twine. Place pork loin butterflied perpendicular to twine.
*   Use the Pork and Poultry rub to season the inside of the pork loin.
*   Layer all the ingredients in a line on one end of the loin, starting with the craisins, thyme, asparagus, chopped walnuts, and oregano.
*   Add the bacon and parmesan cheese on top.
*   Carefully roll up the pork loin, starting at the end with all of the fillings and securing both ends with butcher's twine.
*   Roll the pork loin in the bacon fat and season with additional Pork and Poultry. Shake on the outside.
*   Set the temperature to 180°F and preheat for 15 minutes with the lid covered when ready to cook. Smoke the filled pork loin for 1 hour directly on the grill grate.
*   Remove the pork loin and preheat the oven to 350 degrees Fahrenheit.
*   Place the loin back on the and cook for another 30 to 45 minutes, or until an instant-read thermometer registers 135°F.

Place the pork loin on a platter and cover it with aluminum foil to keep it warm. Allow for 15 minutes of resting time before slicing and serving. Enjoy!

Scalloped Potatoes With Ham, Corn & Bacon

Prep Time: 10 mins
Cook Time: 45 mins
Servings: 2
Ingredients:
·   1 1/2 cups cooked bacon, chopped
·   1 tablespoon butter
·   1 1/2 cup cooked ham, cubed
·   5-6 large potatoes, red
·   Salt and pepper
·   1 cup whole kernel corn
·   Milk

Instructions:

1.   Set your grill grill to smoke mode, allow the fire to catch, and then preheat to 350 degrees' f (177 degrees c).
2.   Spread softened butter evenly over the bottom of a baking bowl. Slice the potatoes as evenly as possible.
3.   Fill the pan with enough potatoes to reach the rim. Cover the potatoes with some of the bacon, sausage, and corn. Repeat until you've made a few layers and used all of the rice, ham, beans, and bacon.
4.   Cover with cream, nearly fully filling the mixture, after adding 1 tablespoon of butter. Season with salt and pepper to taste.
5.   Cook for 1 hour on the barbecue, then serve!

Difficulty: 3
Nutrition: Per Serving: 68 calories; protein 2.9g; carbohydrates 4.5g; fat 2.2g; sodium 621.6mg.

Roasted Green Beans with Bacon

Preparation Time: 15 minutes
Cooking Time: 20 minutes
Servings: 6
Ingredients:
*   1-pound green beans
*   4 strips bacon, cut into small pieces
*   4 tablespoons extra virgin olive oil
*   2 cloves garlic, minced
*   1 teaspoon salt

Directions:

1. Fire the Wood Pellet Grill Smoker Grill to 4000F. Use desired wood pellets when cooking. Keep lid unopened and let it preheat for at most 15 minutes

2. Toss all ingredients on a sheet tray and spread out evenly.

3. Place the tray on the grill grate and roast for 20 minutes.

Nutrition: Calories: 65 Cal Fat: 5.3 g Carbohydrates: 3 g Protein: 1.3 g Fiber: 0 g

Applewood Smoked Bacon

Prep Time: 2 hours 10 mins
Serving: **Serves** 8
Ingredients
- 1/2 Cup brown sugar
- 2 Pound pork belly (skin removed)
- 1/2 Cup kosher salt
- 1 tbsp. black pepper

Instructions
- In a bowl, combine the salt, brown sugar, and black pepper.
- Cover the pork belly with the bacon cure mixture. Remove as much air as possible and place it in a plastic bag.
- Refrigerate for at least 8 days. Flip the pork belly over every two days to ensure that the juices are evenly distributed on both sides of the meat.
- Remove the pork belly from the fridge after 8 days. Rinse the pork belly thoroughly, ensuring that all of the cure is removed, then pat dry.
- Set the to 180°F and preheat for 15 minutes with the lid covered when you're ready to cook. If Super Smoke is available, use it for the best flavor.
- In a jelly roll pan, pour a layer of ice, then arrange a rack on top of the ice, followed by the pork belly. The ice will keep the pork belly from becoming too hot while it is being smoked.
- Place the ice pan and the pork rack immediately on the grill grate. Smoke the pork for two to three hours, or until it reaches a temperature of about 150°F on the inside.

- Wrap the bacon in plastic wrap after smoking the pig and set it in the freezer for 30 to 60 minutes, or until the bacon is nearly frozen and the meat is firm. It makes cutting a lot easier.
- The bacon should be cut to the proper thickness. Use alone or in your favorite recipes. Enjoy!
- Set the temperature to 400°F and preheat for 15 minutes with the lid covered when ready to cook.
- Place bacon slices directly on the grill grate and cook for 8 to 10 minutes, flipping once or twice, until desired crispness is achieved.
- To maintain the crispiness, transfer to a platter lined with paper towels

Hot Bacon Explosion

Prep Time: 15 mins
Cooking Time: 30 mins
Servings: 2
Ingredients
- 1 package cream cheese
- 1 package of Italian sausage or brats
- ¼ C Fromaggio blend cheese (Asiago, Parmesan, Romano)
- 2 packages thick cut bacon
- ½ bottle BBQ Sauce
- 3 to 6 jalapeños depending on size

Instructions:
1. Jalapenos should be washed, capped, and cored. Using a gadget like the "Pepper Whipper" makes this procedure go much faster. The Pepper Whipper is the transparent plastic gadget on the chopping board if you've never seen one before. They're cheap, simple, and straightforward to use, and you'll need one if you do a lot of A.B.T.s.

2. To make mixing simpler, place cream cheese in a bowl and either microwave for a few seconds to soften it or let it out on the counter for 20 to 30 minutes. In a stand mixer on the low speed, combine 14 cup of mixed cheese, 1.5 tablespoons AP Rub, and 3 tablespoons Smokin Sauce with cream cheese.

3. Transfer the cheese mixture to a zip-top plastic bag. Remove one corner of the bag from the cheese mixture and pipe it into the jalapenos. Make sure the cheese reaches the very bottom of each jalapeo.

4. To make a bacon weaving, lay the bacon out on a cutting board.

5. Remove the casings from the brats, combine the meat, and spread evenly over the bacon weave. Drizzle Smokin' Sauce over the sausage.

6. Cut one jalapeno's tip off. Place it in the center of the weave/sausage canvas, with a jalapeno on either side. This will result in a very long jalapeno.

7. Form a roll by wrapping the weave and sausage around the jalapenos. Add additional AP Rub to the mix.

8. Smoke on a 250°F Pitboss until the interior temperature reaches at least 145°F, or until the firmness and color you choose. To ensure that the bacon is thoroughly cooked, aim for more direct heat or cooking on the side of the pit with the highest heat. Brush with Smokin' Sauce during the last 15 minutes of cooking and again right before removing from the pit.

9. Allow for at least 25 minutes of cooling time before slicing to allow the cream cheese to resolidify. Then relax and enjoy yourself.

Difficulty: 5

Nutrition: Per Serving: 55 calories; protein 5.8g; carbohydrates 8.2g; fat 5.7g; sodium 568.0mg.

Bacon-Swiss Cheesesteak Meatloaf

Preparation Time: 15 minutes
Cooking Time: 2 hours
Servings: 8-10
Ingredients:
- 1 tablespoon canola oil
- 2 garlic cloves, finely chopped
- 1 medium onion, finely chopped
- 1 poblano chile, stemmed, seeded, and finely chopped
- 2 pounds extra-lean ground beef
- 2 tablespoons Montreal steak seasoning
- 1 tablespoon A.1. Steak Sauce
- ½ pound bacon, cooked and crumbled
- 2 cups shredded Swiss cheese
- 1 egg, beaten
- 2 cups breadcrumbs
- ½ cup Tiger Sauce

Directions:

1. On your stove top, heat the canola oil in a medium sauté pan over medium-high heat. Add the garlic, onion, and poblano, and sauté for 3 to 5 minutes, or until the onion is just barely translucent.

2. Supply your smoker with wood pellets and follow the manufacturer's specific start-up procedure. Preheat, with the lid closed, to 225°F.

3. In a large bowl, combine the sautéed vegetables, ground beef, steak seasoning, steak sauce, bacon, Swiss cheese, egg, and breadcrumbs. Mix with your hands until well incorporated, then shape into a loaf.

Smoked Turketta (Bacon Wrapped Turkey Breast)

Prep Time: 10 mins
Cook Time: 1 hr
Servings: 2
Ingredients:
· 1 shady turketta

Instructions:

1. It doesn't get any better than this for thanksgiving turkey! Treat your family to a delectable turketta roast.

2. A turketta is a boneless turkey breast covered in bacon and seasoned with savory seasoning. It can be smoked, fried, grilled, or roasted.

3. Set your grill pellet grill to smoke mode and leave the lid open for 10 minutes before preheating to 250°f. Set up a gas or charcoal grill for low, indirect fire.

4. Place the turketta directly on the grill grate and smoke for 212 to 3 hours, or until the internal temperature reaches 165°f.

Difficulty: 2

Nutrition: Per Serving: 77 calories; protein 4.2g; carbohydrates 6.4g; fat 5.7g; sodium 648.6mg.

. Put the meatloaf in a cast iron skillet and place it on the grill. Insert meat thermometer inserted in the loaf reads 165°F.

5. Top with the meatloaf with the Tiger Sauce, remove from the grill, and let rest for about 10 minutes before serving.

Nutrition: Calories: 120 Cal Fat: 2 g Carbohydrates: 0 g Protein: 23 gFiber: 0 g

Bacon-Wrapped Pork Tenderloin

Preparation Time: 15 minutes
Cooking Time: 40 minutes
Servings: 4
Ingredients:

- 1 pork tenderloin.
- 4 strips of bacon.
- Rub:
- 8 tablespoons of brown sugar.
- 3 tablespoons of kosher salt to taste.
- 1 tablespoon of chili powder.
- 1 teaspoon of black pepper to taste.
- 1 teaspoon of onion powder.
- 1 teaspoon of garlic powder.

Directions:

1. Using a small mixing bowl, add sugar, chili powder, onion powder, garlic powder, salt, and pepper to taste, mix properly to combine, and set aside. Use a sharp knife to trim off fats present on the pork, then coat with 1/4 of the prepared rub. Make sure you coat all sides.

2. Roll each pork tenderloin with a piece of bacon, lay the meat on a cutting board, then pound with a meat mallet to give an even thickness, secure the ends of the bacon with toothpicks to hold still. Coat the meat again with just a little more of the rub spice, then set aside.

3. Preheat a Wood Pellet Grill Smoker smoker and Grill to 350 degrees F, place the pork tenderloin on the grill, and grill for about fifteen minutes. Increase the temperature of the grill to 400 degrees F and cook for another fifteen minutes until it is cooked through and reads an internal temperature of 145 degrees F.

4. Once cooked, let the pork rest for a few minutes, slice, and serve.

Nutrition: Calories 236 Fat 8g Carbohydrates 10g Protein 29g

Buffalo Candied Bacon

Prep Time: 30 mins
Cook Time: 20 mins
Servings: 2
Ingredients

- 1 lb thick-sliced bacon
- 1/4 cup Frank's hot wing sauce
- 1/2 cup brown sugar
- 1/4 tsp cayenne pepper

Instructions:

1. So, I've got a pound of thick-sliced bacon, and I'm going to show you what it looks like here. I usually use pepper bacon, but I didn't have any on hand, and I'm not going out in the snow.

2. A quarter cup of Frank's spicy wing sauce, half a cup of brown sugar, and a quarter teaspoon of cayenne pepper have been combined.

3. I mixed it up and brushed it on with the back of a spoon because it's really thick on both sides of this bacon, put it on a sheet pan with foil because it's very messy, and I'm going to put it on the Pitboss that looks like it's heated up to about 350 for about 15 minutes, then flip it over for another 15 minutes, and just watch it closely because it'll candy up really nice.

4. For my buffalo bacon candy, I cooked it for approximately 15 minutes on each side at 375 degrees on the Pitboss. It's a fantastic tailgate accessory. I'm going to bring this in, let it cool for about 10 minutes so it can solidify

up and get crispy, and then we'll eat it. Have fun!
Difficulty: 2
Nutrition: Per Serving: 185 calories; protein 88.6g; carbohydrates 70g; fat 28.3g; sodium 545.3mg.

Bacon Wrapped with Asparagus

Preparation Time: 15 minutes
Cooking Time: 25-30 minutes
Servings: 4-6
Recommended pellet: Optional
Ingredients:
•   1-pound fresh thick asparagus (15-20 spears)
•   Extra virgin olive oil
•   5 sliced bacon
•   1 teaspoon of Western Love or salted pepper
Directions:
1. Cut off the wooden ends of the asparagus and make them all the same length.
2. Divide the asparagus into a bundle of three spears and split with olive oil. Wrap each bundle with a piece of bacon, then dust with seasonings or salt pepper for seasoning.
3. Set the wood pellet smoker grill for indirect cooking and place a Teflon coated fiberglass mat on the grate (to prevent asparagus from sticking to the grate grate). Preheat to 400 degrees Fahrenheit using all types of pellets. The grill can be preheated during asparagus Preparation Guide.
4. Bake the asparagus wrapped in bacon for 25-30 minutes until the asparagus is soft and the bacon is cooked and crispy.
Nutrition: Calories 77, Total fat 1g, Saturated fat 1g, Total carbs 17g, Net carbs 15g, Protein 3g, Sugars 6g, Fiber 2g, Sodium 14mg, Potassium 243mg

Hearty Pig Candies

Preparation Time: 20 minutes

Cooking Time: 2 hours
Servings: 10
Ingredients:
•   Nonstick cooking spray
•   2 pound of bacon slices
•   1 cup of firmly packed brown sugar
•   2-3 teaspoon of cayenne pepper
•   ½ a cup of maple syrup
Directions:
1.   Take your drip pan and add water; cover with aluminum foil. Pre-heat your smoker to 225 degrees F
2.   Use water fill water pan halfway through and place it over drip pan. Add wood chips to the side tray
3.   Remove the grill rack from your smoker and cover with aluminum foil; spray the foils with cooking spay
4.   Lay the bacon in a single layer, making sure to leave a bit of space in between
5.   Take a small bowl and add brown sugar, cayenne, and mix
6.   Baste the bacon with ¼ cup of maple syrup
7.   Sprinkle half of the rub on top of the bacon
8.   Transfer the rack to the smoker alongside the bacon and smoke for 1 hour
9.   Flip the bacon and baste with another ¼ cup of maple syrup, sprinkle more rub, and a smoker for 1 hour more
10.   Once the bacon is brown and firm, it's ready to be served!
Nutrition: Calories: 152 Fats: 10g Carbs: 13g Fiber: 2g

Bacon Wrapped Chicken Breasts

Preparation Time: 0 minute
Cooking Time: 3 hours
Servings: 6
Ingredients:
For Brine:
•   ¼ cup brown sugar
•   ¼ cup kosher salt
•   4 cups water
For Chicken:

- 6 skinless, boneless chicken breasts
- ¼ cup chicken rub
- 18 bacon slices
- 1½ cups BBQ sauce

Directions:

1. For brine: in a large pitcher, dissolve sugar and salt in water.
2. Place the chicken breasts in brine and refrigerate for about 2 hours, flipping once in the middle way.
3. Preheat the Wood Pellet Grill Smoker grill & Smoker on grill setting to 230 degrees F.
4. Remove chicken breasts from brine and rinse under cold running water.
5. Season chicken breasts with rub generously.
6. Arrange 3 bacon strips of bacon onto a cutting board, against each other.
7. Place 1 chicken breast across the bacon, leaving enough bacon on the left side to wrap it over just a little.
8. Wrap the bacon strips around chicken breast and secure with toothpicks.
9. Repeat with remaining breasts and bacon slices.
10. Arrange the chicken breasts into Wood Pellet Grill Smoker grill and cook for about 2½ hours.
11. Coat the breasts with BBQ sauce and cook for about 30 minutes more.
12. Serve immediately.

Nutrition: Calories 481 Total Fat 12.3 g Saturated Fat 4.2 g Cholesterol 41 mg Sodium 3000 mg
Total Carbs 32 g Fiber 0.4g Sugar 22.2 g Protein 55.9 g

Explosive Smoky Bacon

Preparation Time: 20 Minutes
Cooking Time: 2 Hours and 10 Minutes
Servings: 10
Ingredients:

- 1 pound thick-cut bacon
- One tablespoon BBQ spice rub
- 2 pounds bulk pork sausage
- 1 cup cheddar cheese, shredded
- Four garlic cloves, minced
- 18 ounces BBQ sauce

Directions:

1. Take your drip pan and add water; cover with aluminum foil.
2. Pre-heat your smoker to 225 degrees F
3. Use water fill water pan halfway through and place it over drip pan.
4. Add wood chips to the side tray
5. Reserve about ½ a pound of your bacon for cooking later on
6. Lay 2 strips of your remaining bacon on a clean surface in an X formation
7. Alternate the horizontal and vertical bacon strips by waving them tightly in an over and under to create a lattice-like pattern
8. Sprinkle one teaspoon of BBQ rub over the woven bacon
9. Arrange ½ a pound of your bacon in a large-sized skillet and cook them for 10 minutes over medium-high heat
10. Drain the cooked slices on a kitchen towel and crumble them
11. Place your sausages in a large-sized re-sealable bag
12. While the sausages are still in the bag, roll them out to a square that has the same sized as the woven bacon
13. Cut off the bag from the sausage and arrange them sausage over the woven bacon
14. Toss away the bag
15. Sprinkle some crumbled bacon, green onions, cheddar cheese, and garlic over the rolled sausages
16. Pour about ¾ bottle of your BBQ sauce over the sausage and season with some more BBQ rub
17. Roll up the woven bacon tightly all around the sausage, forming a loaf
18. Cook the bacon-sausage loaf in your smoker for about one and a ½ hour
19. Brush up the woven bacon with remaining BBQ sauce and keep smoking for about 30 minutes until the center of the loaf is no longer pink
20. Use an instant thermometer to check if the internal temperature is at least 165 degrees Fahrenheit

21.   If yes, then take it out and let it rest for 30 minutes
22.   Slice and serve!
Nutrition: Calories: 507 Fats: 36g Carbs: 20g Fiber: 2g

Apple Bacon Smoked Ham With Glazed Carrots

Prep Time: 10 mins
Cook Time: 1 hour 30 mins
Servings: 2
Ingredients:
·   1 1/2 cup apple cider
·   3 tablespoon apple cider vinegar
·   2 apples
·   1 lb. Bacon
·   2 tablespoon butter, unsalted
·   2 tablespoon cornstarch
·   3 tablespoon Dijon mustard
·   grill smoke infused Applewood bacon rub
·   1/2 cup pure maple syrup
·   1 large bone in spiral cut smoked ham
·   2 tablespoons yellow mustard
Instructions:
1.   For a really delicious, sweet Easter Sunday treat, this twice-smoked ham blends excellent apple and bacon tastes. Because the spiral cut ham has already been pre-cut, it is one of the fastest cuts of meat to smoke, taking only two hours on your grill pellet barbecue.
2.   Turn your grill on to smoke mode, wait for the fire to catch, and then reduce the temperature to 250 degrees Fahrenheit (121 degrees c).
3.   Cook the bacon for 25 minutes on the grill, flipping after 15 minutes. Thinly slice the apples while the bacon is melting. Reduce the temperature to 225 degrees F after the bacon is done (107 degrees c).
4.   Place the spiral-sliced ham in an aluminum foil-lined roasting pan. Begin by placing an apple in the first slice, then each subsequent slice. Bacon strips should be used to fill the remaining pieces. Smoke from the grill To season the meat, use an applewood bacon rub. To add flavor, pour any remaining apple cider into the bottom of the pan.
5.   Cook the ham for 60 minutes on the burner.
6.   In a separate saucepan, whisk together apple juice, maple syrup, apple cider vinegar, Dijon mustard, yellow mustard, cornstarch, and grill smoke infused Applewood bacon rub. Bring the water to a rolling boil. Reduce the heat to low and whisk often until the sauce has thickened and decreased (approximately 15-20 minutes). Stir in the butter until it is completely melted. As the glaze sits, it should thicken.
7.   After 60 minutes, add the carrots to the roasting pan and coat the entire ham. Glaze every 30 minutes till the dish is finished.
8.   Before serving, remove the ham from the grill and cover it with foil for 20 minutes.
9.   Serve with any leftover warmed-up sauce if desired.
Difficulty: 7
Nutrition: Calories: 347kcal | Carbohydrates: 65 | Protein: 55g | Fat 30g | Saturated fat 21g | Fiber: 8g | Sugar: 11

Ham, Bacon, Corn, And Potato Bake

(TOTAL COOK TIME 1 HOUR 30 MINUTES)
INGREDIENTS FOR 4 SERVINGS
THE MEAT
·   Ham, cooked and cubed – 1 ½ cups
·   Bacon, cooked, and chopped – 1½ cups
THE INGREDIENTS
·   Butter, softened, and divided– 1 tablespoon + 1 teaspoon
·   6 large red potatoes, uniformly sliced
·   Whole kernel corn – 1 cup
·   Whole milk, as needed
·   Salt and freshly ground black pepper
THE WOOD PELLET GRILL
·   Prepare your wood pellet grill for smoking to 350°F (177°C)
·   Use your favorite wood pellets
METHOD

1.   Grease the bottom of a baking dish with 1 teaspoon of softened butter.

2.   Lay enough potato slices in the bottom of the baking dish to cover.

3.   Top with ham, bacon, and corn. Repeat this layering process until you have made a few layers and used all of the ingredients. The final layer should be potato.

4.   Add 1 tablespoon of butter to the final layer and pour over enough milk to almost cover. Season with salt and black pepper.

5.   Grill for 60 minutes.

6.   Remove from the grill, allow to cool slightly for a few minutes, and serve.

Bacon Cordon Blue

Preparation Time: 30 minutes
Cooking Time: 2 to 2.5 hours
Servings: 6
Ingredients:

- 24 bacon slices
- 3 large boneless, skinless chicken breasts, butterfly
- 3 extra virgin olive oils with roasted garlic flavor
- 3 Yang original dry lab or poultry seasonings
- 12 slice black forest ham
- 12-slice provolone cheese

Directions:

1.   Using apple or cherry pellets, configure a wood pellet smoker grill for indirect cooking and preheat (180 ° F to 200 ° F) for smoking.

2.   Inhale bacon cordon blue for 1 hour.

3.   After smoking for 1 hour, raise the pit temperature to 350 ° F.

4.   Bacon cordon blue occurs when the internal temperature reaches 165 ° F and the bacon becomes crispy.

5.   Rest for 15 minutes under a loose foil tent before serving.

Nutrition: Calories 956, Total fat 47g, Saturated fat 13g, Total carbs 1g, Net carbs 1g Protein 124g, Sugars 0g, Fiber 0g, Sodium 1750mg

Bacon Salad with Roasted Beet

Prep. Time: 15 Mins
Cook Time: 45 Mins
Servings: 4
Ingredients

- Spinach
- Raw Beets 2 (Thinly sliced and peeled)
- Champagne Vinaigrette ¼ Cup
- Avocados 2 (Diced)
- Ripe Pears 2 (Sliced)
- Red Leaf Lettuce 1 Head
- Raw Pecans ¼ Cup
- Bacon 8 Slices

Instructions

1. Preheat the to 400°F and keep the lid covered until ready to cook for 15 mins.

2. Arrange beets on a foil-lined (baking sheet) and top with bacon. Cook for 25 mins on a baking sheet directly on the grill grate.

3. Coat the beets with the bacon grease that has been condensed.

4. Cook for a further 15 mins, or until the beets are tender and the bacon is crispy, dividing it out evenly.

5. Add the walnuts or pecans and continue to roast for another 5 mins. Using a spoon, remove the nuts and place them on paper towels to cool and drain.

6. Once the bacon has cooled to the touch, roughly chop it into medium pieces.

7. Toss the avocado, almonds, bacon, beets, lettuce and peas together in a large salad dish. Toss with a spray of champagne vinaigrette before serving. Enjoy.

Bacon Cheddar Slider

Preparation Time: 30 minutes
Cooking Time: 15 minutes
Servings: 6-10 (1-2 sliders each as an appetizer)
Recommended pellet: Optional
Ingredients:

- 1-pound ground beef (80% lean)
- 1/2 teaspoon of garlic salt
- 1/2 teaspoon salt
- 1/2 teaspoon of garlic

* 1/2 teaspoon onion
* 1/2 teaspoon black pepper
o bacon slices, cut in half
* ½Cup mayonnaise
* 2 teaspoons of creamy wasabi (optional)
o (1 oz) sliced sharp cheddar cheese, cut in half (optional)
* Sliced red onion
* ½Cup sliced kosher dill pickles
* 12 mini breads sliced horizontally
* Ketchup

Directions:
1. Place ground beef, garlic salt, seasoned salt, garlic powder, onion powder and black hupe pepper in a medium bowl.
2. Divide the meat mixture into 12 equal parts, shape into small thin round patties (about 2 ounces each) and save.
3. Cook the bacon on medium heat over medium heat for 5-8 minutes until crunchy. Set aside.
4. To make the sauce, mix the mayonnaise and horseradish in a small bowl, if used.
5. Set up a wood pellet smoker grill for direct cooking to use griddle accessories. Contact the manufacturer to see if there is a griddle accessory that works with the wooden pellet smoker grill.
6. Spray a cooking spray on the griddle cooking surface for best non-stick results.
7. Preheat wood pellet smoker grill to 350 ° F using selected pellets. Griddle surface should be approximately 400 ° F.
8. Grill the putty for 3-4 minutes each until the internal temperature reaches 160 ° F.
9. If necessary, place a sharp cheddar cheese slice on each patty while the patty is on the griddle or after the patty is removed from the griddle. Place a small amount of mayonnaise mixture, a slice of red onion, and a hamburger pate in the lower half of each roll. Pickled slices, bacon, and ketchup.

Nutrition: Calories 77, Total fat 1g, Saturated fat 1g, Total carbs 17g, Net carbs 15g, Protein 3g, Sugars 6g, Fiber 2g, Sodium 14mg, Potassium 243mg

Bacon Onion Ring

Prep. Time: 10 Mins
Cook Time: 1 Hr
Servings: 6
Ingredients
* Bacon 16 Slices
* Vidalia Onion 2 (sliced)
* Chili Garlic Sauce 1 tbsp
* Yellow Mustard 1 tbsp
* Honey 1 tsp

Instructions
1. Wrap a piece of bacon around each onion ring until it is completely covered with bacon. Because some onion slices are thicker than others, forming a ring with two pieces of bacon is required.
2. Poke a skewer through the bacon-folded onion slice to prevent the bacon from unraveling during cooking.
3. Preheat the oven to 400 degrees Fahrenheit and cook for 10 to 15 mins with the lid covered when ready to cook.
4. Combine the yellow mustard, chile spicy garlic sauce, and yellow mustard in a shallow bowl; stir in the honey.
Cook the fillets for 90 mins on a grill, flipping halfway through. Have fun with it.

Onion Bacon Ring

Preparation Time: 10 Minutes
Cooking Time: 1 Hour and 30 Minutes
Servings: 6 to 8
Ingredients:
* 2 large Onions, cut into ½ inch slices
* 1 Package of Bacon
* 1 tsp. of Honey
* 1 tbsp. Mustard, yellow
* 1 tbsp. Garlic chili sauce

Direction:
1. Wrap Bacon around onion rings. Wrap until you out of bacon. Place on skewers.
2. Preheat the grill to 400F with closed lid.
3. In the meantime, on a bowl combine the mustard and garlic chili sauce. Add honey and stir well.

4. Grill the onion bacon rings for 1 h and 30 minutes. Flip once.
5. Serve with the sauce and enjoy!
Nutrition: Calories: 90 Protein: 2g Carbs: 9g Fat: 7g

Spicy Bacon Wrapped Grilled Chicken Skewers

Prep. Time: 3 Hrs
Cooking Time: 20 Mins
Servings: 6
Ingredients
- Ranch Half c
- Garlic Powder Half tsp
- Chili Sauce Half tbsp
- Dried Oregano Half tsp
- Chicken Breast Cubed
- Whole Red Onion 1 (Sliced)
- Strips Bacon 8 (Sliced)
- Green Bell Peppers 1 (Sliced)

Instructions

1. In a large mixing cup, combine ranch dressing, chili sauce, garlic powder, and oregano. Toss in the cubed chicken and toss well to coat. Allow the chicken to rest in the refrigerator for 1 to 3 hours.
2. Preheat the oven to high for 20 mins with the top closed.
3. Assemble the skewers by topping them with onion wedges, a piece of bacon, tomato, and chicken. Before weaving the bacon around the chicken parts, alternate the bacon and chicken.
4. Finish each skewer with a pepper and onion wedge. Do not clog the skewer to promote quicker and more equal cooking. Replace the skewers and repeat with the remaining skewers.
5. Place the skewers on the grill plate with a piece of foil below the skewers' ends to prevent them from burning.
6. Cook for 5 mins on each side, flipping once for a total cooking time of 20 mins. Take the skewers out of the mix. Have fun with it.

Bacon-Wrapped Asparagus

Preparation Time:15 MIN
Cooking Time:25 – 30 MIN
Servings:6
Ingredients:
- 15 - 20 spears of fresh asparagus (1 pound)
- Olive oil (extra virgin)
o slices bacon (thinly sliced)
- 1 teaspoon salt and pepper (or your preferred rub)

Directions:
1. Break off the ends of the asparagus, then trim it all so they're down to the same length.
2. Separate the asparagus into bundles—3 spears per bundle. Then spritz them with some olive oil.
3. Use a piece of bacon to wrap up each bundle. When you're done, lightly dust the wrapped bundle with some salt and pepper to taste, or your preferred rub.
4. Set up your wood pellet smoker grill so that it's ready for indirect cooking.
5. Put some fiberglass mats on your grates. Make sure they're the fiberglass kind. This will keep your asparagus from getting stuck on your grill gates.
6. Preheat your grill to 400°F, with whatever pellets you prefer. You can do this as you prep your asparagus.
7. Grill the wraps for 25 minutes to 30 minutes, tops. The goal is to get your asparagus looking nice and tender, and the bacon deliciously crispy.
Nutrition: Calories: 71 Fat: 3g Carbs: 1g Protein: 6g Intolerances: Gluten-Free, Egg-Free, Lactose-Free

Bacon lattice turkey

Prep. Time: 30 mins
Cook Time: 180 mins
Servings: 7
Ingredients
- Apples 2
- Celery stick 2 (herb mix)
- Bacon
- Onion 1 sliced

- grills champion chicken seasoning
- Pepper
- Brined turkey 1

Instructions

1. Preheat the grill to 300 degrees Fahrenheit.
2. Ensure that the giblets and innards of the turkey have been removed.
3. A paper towel can be used to clean and dry the turkey's exterior and internal sections.
4. Fruit and vegetables may be placed inside the turkey after being sliced into large pieces.
5. Use a large amount of chicken spice to coat the whole turkey.
6. set bacon in a lattice pattern on a versatile cutting board. Encompass the breasts with the turkey's top.
7. To taste, season with black pepper and champion chicken.
8. Allow the turkey to rest for 30 mins.

Bacon BBQ Bites

Preparation Time: 10 Minutes
Cooking Time: 30 Minutes
Servings: 4
Ingredients:

- 1 tbsp. Fennel, ground
- ½ cup of Brown Sugar
- 1 lb. Slab Bacon, cut into cubes (1 inch)
- 1 tsp. Black pepper
- Salt

Directions:

1. Take an aluminum foil and then fold in half. Once you do that, then turn the edges so that a rim is made. With a fork make small holes on the bottom. In this way, the excess fat will escape and will make the bites crispy.
2. Preheat the grill to 350F with closed lid.
3. In a bowl combine the black pepper, salt, fennel, and sugar. Stir.
4. Place the pork in the seasoning mixture. Toss to coat. Transfer on the foil.
5. Place the foil on the grill. Bake for 25 minutes, or until crispy and bubbly.
6. Serve and enjoy!

Nutrition: Calories: 300 Protein: 27g Carbs: 4g Fat: 36g

Jam Bacon

Prep. Time: 10 mins
Cook Time: 30 mins
Servings: 8
Ingredients

- Smoked, Chopped middle bacon 10 rashers.
- Water ⅔ cup
- Chopped shallots 4
- Bourbon ⅔ cup
- Balsamic vinegar ¼ cup
- Brown sugar ⅔ cup
- Chili flakes
- Smoked paprika 2 tbsp
- Tabasco sauce 2 tbsp

Instructions

1. Set your grill for cooking.
2. Place the casserole dish on the grill to preheat it for grilling (without the lid).
3. After the BBQ has heated up, adjust the flame control to medium. Cook, occasionally stirring, for 10 mins, or until the shallots are soft.
4. In the casserole dish, combine the remaining ingredients. Cook on low heat for 25 mins.

Bacon Jalapeno Wraps

Preparation Time: 5 minutes
Cooking Time: 10 minutes
Servings: 4
Ingredients:

- 1 package bacon, uncured and nitrate free
- fresh jalapeno peppers, halved lengthwise and seeded
- 1 (8 ounce) package cream cheese

Directions:

1. Preheat your Wood Pellet Grill Smoker grill smoker for high heat.
2. Fill jalapeno halves with cream cheese.
3. Wrap each with bacon. Secure with a toothpick.
4. Place on the grill, and cook until bacon is crispy, about 5 to 7 minutes per side.

5.   Remove to a platter to cool and serve warm.

Nutrition Energy (calories): 460 kcalProtein: 14.16 g Fat: 43.86 g Carbohydrates: 2.29 g Calcium, Ca7 mg Magnesium, Mg17 mg Phosphorus, P206 mg Iron, Fe0.52 mg

Bacon-Onion Jam and Strip Steak

Preparation Time: 10 minutes
Servings: 4 servings per recipe
Ingredients:
- ½ cup brown sugar
- One tbsp balsamic vinegar
- Extra-virgin olive oil
- Four New York strip steaks
- Prime Rib Rub
- Six tbsp strong coffee, freshly brewed
- ½ cup apple juice
- One-pound bacon, cut into small pieces
- Two small sweet onions

Instructions:
- Refrigerate the steaks for 30 minutes before cooking to allow them to come to ambient temperature Rib Rub should be used on all sides of the steaks.
- When you're ready to cook, warm your grill at 350 degrees F for 15 minutes with the lid closed.
- Place the chopped bacon on the heated grill grate in a cast iron pan. Cook for 15 minutes, just until the fat has drained from the bacon.
- Drain all except One tbsp of the bacon fat from the pan after removing the bacon.
- Cook the onions in the cast iron pan for about ten minutes on the grill or until they have softened. After that, add the brown sugar and cook for another 15 to 20 minutes to caramelize onions.
- Cook, stirring regularly until the onions are thick and "jammy," about 20 minutes more after adding the apple juice, coffee or water, and cooked bacon.
- Mix in the balsamic vinegar and transfer to a bowl to cool. (Refrigerate any leftover bacon-onion jam; this bacon-onion jam tastes best at room temp, so allow it to come to room temperature before serving.)
- Preheat the grill on high for 15 minutes, with the lid, shut
- Drizzle the steaks lightly with olive oil and cook for four to five minutes on each side on the grill for medium-rare until it's done to your liking.
- Retrieve them from the grill once they've finished cooking and let them rest for about ten min before slicing.
- Add the bacon-onion jam to each steak, and you've got yourself some serious cash.

Heavenly Rabbit Smoke

Preparation Time: 10 minutes
Cooking Time: Nil
Serving: 5
Ingredients
- 1 teaspoon dried thyme
- 1 teaspoon dried parsley
- 2 teaspoons dried oregano
- ½ teaspoon dried marjoram
- ½ teaspoon ground nutmeg
- ½ teaspoon ground cinnamon
- 1 teaspoon chicken bouillon granules
- 1 and ½ teaspoons garlic powder
- 1 teaspoon cracked pepper
- ½ teaspoon salt
- 1 and ½ teaspoon onion powder

Directions:

1.   Mix the ingredients mentioned above to prepare the seasoning and use it as needed.
Nutrition: Calories: 20 Carbs: 5g Protein: 1g

Smoked Rabbit

Preparation Time: 15 minutes
Cooking Time: 3 hours
Servings: 4
Ingredients:
- 1 (3 pounds) whole rabbit
- 1 tbsp dried rosemary
- 1/3 cup olive oil
- 1 tbsp dried thyme
- 1 tbsp cracked black pepper
- 1 tsp sea salt
- One-half cup dry white wine
- 1 cup apple juice
- 1 tbsp dried oregano
- 1 tbsp freshly grated lemon zest

Directions:
1.   Rinse and pat dry the rabbit. Cover it with the dried rosemary, olive oil, thyme, black pepper and sea salt, making sure the entire rabbit is coated.
2.   Cover the rabbit with plastic wrap and place it in the refrigerator.
3.   Consume within two to three days. Thaw overnight and refrigerate for 8 hours. Season the rabbit with the white wine, apple juice, oregano and lemon zest.
4.   Cover with a layer of plastic wrap and refrigerate overnight. Heat up your barbecue/smoking machine to medium heat. Place the rabbit on the smoker. Smoke it for three hours, or until the liquid in the pan reduces by three quarters.
5.   Check every hour to baste the rabbit with the reduced liquid. When finished, remove from smoker and let the rabbit cool down. Slice to serve.
Nutrition Energy (calories): 301 kcal Protein: 6.85 g Fat: 24.64 g Carbohydrates: 14.3 g Calcium, Ca225 mg Magnesium, Mg22 mg Phosphorus, P161 mg Iron, Fe0.54 mg Fiber0.7 g

Spicy and Hot Smoked Rabbit Barbecue

Preparation time: 20 minutes
Smoking time: 3 hours 10 minutes
Temperature: 200ºF
Portion: 10
Recommended Pellet: Mesquite
Ingredients:
- Rabbit (6-lb., 2.7-kg.)
The Brine:
- 2 tbsp. kosher salt
- ½ cup white vinegar
- 1 quart water
The Rub:
- 2 tbsp. garlic powder
- 1 tbsp. cayenne pepper
- 1 tbsp. Kosher salt

• 1 tbsp. black pepper
The Glaze:
• 2 tbsp. Garlic powder
• 2 tsp. Diced jalapeno pepper
• 1 tsp. Cayenne pepper
• 2 tbsp. Olive oil
• 2 cups Ketchup
• 1 cup Brown sugar
• 1 cup Apple cider vinegar
• ½ cup Apple juice
• ½ cup Honey
• 1 tbsp. Worcestershire sauce
• 1 tsp. Kosher salt
• 1 tsp. Black pepper
The Heat:
• Use charcoal and Hickory wood chunks for indirect smokes.
The Water Pan:
• 2 cups apple juice

Directions:

1.Pour water into a container, then stir in kosher salt and white vinegar.

2.Score the rabbit at several places, then put the rabbit into the brine. Soak the rabbit for at least an hour.

3.After an hour, take the rabbit out of the brine, then wash and rinse it. Pat the rabbit dry.

4.Prepare the grill and set it for indirect heat.

5.Place charcoal and starters in a grill, then ignite the starters. Put the burning charcoal on one side of the grill.

6.Place a heavy-duty aluminum pan, then place it on the other side of the grill.

7.Pour apple juice into the aluminum pan, then place wood chunks on top of the burning charcoal. Set the grill grate.

8.Cover the grill with the lid and set the temperature to 200°F (93°C).

9.Combine the rub ingredients—garlic powder, cayenne pepper, kosher salt, and black pepper in a bowl, then mix well.

10.Rub the rabbit with the spice mixture, then place it on the grate inside the grill. Smoke the seasoned rabbit for 3 hours.

11.Maintain the heat and control the temperature. Add more charcoal and wood chunks if it is needed.

12.Next, pour olive oil, ketchup, apple juice, apple cider vinegar, and honey into a bowl, then season with garlic powder, diced jalapeno pepper, cayenne pepper, brown sugar, Worcestershire sauce, salt, and pepper, then stir until incorporated.

13.After 15 minutes of smoking, baste the rabbit with the glaze mixture and repeat once every 30 minutes.

14.Once the smoked rabbit is tender, and the smoked rabbit's internal temperature has reached 170°F (77°C), remove it from the grill.

15.Place the smoked rabbit on a serving dish and serve. Enjoy!

Nutrition:
Amount per 155 g
= 1 serving(s)
Energy (calories): 247 kcal
Protein: 1.47 g
Fat: 2.99 g
Carbohydrates: 57.38 g

Smoked Rabbit

Preparation Time: 15 minutes + 60 minutes marinate time
Smoking Time: 2 hours
Temperature: 200-325°F
Portion: 5
Recommended Pellets: Alder
Ingredients:
• One cottontail skinned and gutted
• 2 tbsp. salt
• ½ cup white vinegar
• Water as needed
For Rub
• 1 tbsp. garlic powder
• 1 tbsp. cayenne pepper
• 1 tbsp. salt
• One bottle BBQ sauce

Directions:

1.Take a bowl and add in your kosher salt alongside the white vinegar to make your brine

2.Pour the brine over your rabbit using a shallow dish and add just enough water to cover up the whole of your rabbit

3.Let it sit for an hour

4.Pre-heat your smoker to a temperature of 200 degree

5.Take a bowl and whisk in the garlic powder, salt, pepper, and cayenne pepper to make the rubbing
6.Season the rabbit nicely
7.Toss your rabbit in your smoker and add the hickory wood to your wood chamber
8.Let it smoke for two hours and keep adding wood pellets after every 15 minutes
9.Remove the rabbit from your smoker and serve hot
Nutrition:
Calories: 824
Fats: 42g
Carbs: 35g
Fiber: 3g

Rabbit Stew

Preparation Time: 15 minutes
Cooking Time: 2 hours and 30 minutes
Servings: 4
Ingredients:
· 1 (3 pounds) rabbit (cut into bite sizes)
· One-fourth cup olive oil
· 1 medium onion (chopped)
· 1 carrot (diced)
· 1 stalk celery (diced)
· 2 roman tomato (sliced)
· 1 red bell pepper (sliced)
· 2 garlic cloves (minced)
· 1 cup red wine
· 4 cups chicken broth
· 2 bay leaves
· 2 tbsp flour
· 1 tsp dried thyme
· 1 tsp salt
· 1 tsp ground black pepper
Directions:
1. Prepare your grilling machine.
2. In a large pot over medium heat, add in olive oil and heat. Sauté onion, celery, carrot, red bell pepper, and garlic for 2 minutes, stirring constantly.
3. Add in rabbit pieces, red wine, dried thyme, bay leaves, salt, & ground black pepper. Stir to coat rabbit. Add in enough broth so that rabbit is submerged, then cover.

4. Bring to a boil then turn heat to low. Simmer for at least 2 hours. Check occasionally to make sure rabbit is submerged and that there is adequate liquid.
5. Mix together 4 tbsp flour and 1 cup of broth. Slowly stir into rabbit. Continue cooking on low heat uncovered for 30 minutes until rabbit is tender.
Nutrition Energy (calories): 1112 kcal Protein: 54.24 g Fat: 45.03 g Carbohydrates: 116.63 g Calcium, Ca58 mg Magnesium, Mg62 mg Phosphorus, P373 mg Iron, Fe3.72 mg Fiber2.1 g

White Wine Smoked Rabbit Garlic

Preparation Time: 15 minutes
Smoking Time: 2 hours 10 minutes
Temperature: 165-275ºF
Portion: 5
Recommended pellets: apple
Ingredients
•Rabbit (6-lb., 2.7-kg.)
The Marinade
•Olive oil - 1 cup
•Red wine vinegar - 2 tablespoons
•Minced garlic - ¼ cup
•Kosher salt - 2 tablespoons
•Pepper - 1 ½ teaspoon
•Bay leaves - 2
•Fresh rosemary leaves - 2 sprigs
•Lemon juice - 3 tablespoons
•White wine - ¼ cup
Directions:
1.Combine the entire marinade ingredients-- olive oil, red wine vinegar, minced garlic, kosher salt, pepper, bay leaves, fresh rosemary, lemon juice, and white wine. Mix well.
2.Rub the spice mixture over the rabbit and place it in a disposable aluminum pan.
3.Cover the rabbit with plastic wrap then marinate it for at least 2 hours. Store the rabbit in the refrigerator to keep it fresh.
4.After 2 hours, take the rabbit out of the refrigerator and thaw it at room temperature.

5.Plug the wood pellet smoker and place the wood pellet inside the hopper. Turn the switch on.

6.Set the temperature to 275°F (135°C) and prepare the wood pellet smoker for indirect heat. Wait until the wood pellet smoker is ready.

7.Insert the aluminum pan with the rabbit into the wood pellet smoker and smoke it for 2 hours.

8.Once the internal temperature of the smoked rabbit reaches 165°F (74°C), remove it from the wood pellet smoker and transfer it to a serving dish.

Nutrition:

Calories: 157,

Fat: 10g,

Carbohydrates: 10g,

Dietary Fiber: 1.3 g,

Protein: 11.1g

Braised Rabbit and Red Wine Stew

Preparation Time: 30 minutes
Cooking Time: 2 hours
Servings: 4-6 servings
Ingredients:

· 1 skinless rabbit, chopped into pieces (3-lb, 1.4-kgs)
· Olive oil – 1 tablespoon
· Salted butter – 2 tablespoons
· 1 yellow onion, peeled and chopped
· 1 celery stalk, peeled and chopped
· 1 carrot, peeled and chopped
· 2 garlic cloves, peeled and minced
· Flour – 2 tablespoons
· Chicken broth – 4 cups
· Dry red wine – 1 cup
· 1 thyme sprig
· 2 bay leaves
· Salt and black pepper – to taste
· Crusty baguette – to serve

Directions:

1. Warm the olive oil in a Dutch oven over moderately high heat. Add the rabbit pieces to the pot in batches and cook until browned and golden. Set the meat to one side.

2. Melt the butter in the same pot and add the onion, celery, and carrot. Sauté for10-12 minutes until soft. Add the garlic and sauté for another 60 seconds.

3. Sprinkle over the flour and stir well to combine, cook for 60 more seconds.

4. Next, pour in the chicken broth and red wine. Return the meat to the pot along with the thyme and bay leaves and bring to a simmer.

5. Cover the Wood Pellet Grill Smoker oven with a lid and place on the grill. Cook for approximately 2 hours until the rabbit is cooked through and tender. Season with salt and pepper to taste.

6. Serve with crusty bread.

Nutrition Energy (calories): 407 kcal Protein: 42.07 g Fat: 21.69 g Carbohydrates: 6.56 g Calcium, Ca40 mg

Magnesium, Mg40 mg Phosphorus, P288 mg Iron, Fe2.48 mg Fiber0.8 g

Heavenly Rabbit Smoke

Preparation Time: 10 minutes
Cooking Time: Nil
Serving: 5
Ingredients

· 1 teaspoon dried thyme
· 1 teaspoon dried parsley
· 2 teaspoons dried oregano
· ½ teaspoon dried marjoram
· ½ teaspoon ground nutmeg
· ½ teaspoon ground cinnamon
· 1 teaspoon chicken bouillon granules
· 1 and ½ teaspoons garlic powder
· 1 teaspoon cracked pepper
· ½ teaspoon salt
· 1 and ½ teaspoon onion powder

Directions:

1. Mix the ingredients mentioned above to prepare the seasoning and use it as needed.

Nutrition:

Calories: 20

Carbs: 5g

Protein: 1g

Grilled Rabbit with Wine and Rosemary Marinade

Preparation Time: 10 minutes
Cooking Time: 40 minutes
Servings: 6
Ingredients:
· 1 rabbit cut into pieces
· For marinade
· 3 cloves of garlic, mashed
· 1 1/2 tsp rosemary
· 1 cup of white wine, dry
· 1/2 cup olive oil
· 1 tbsp white vinegar
· 1 tsp mustard
· 1/2 tsp cumin
· Salt and ground pepper to taste
Directions:
1. Whisk all marinade ingredients from the list.
2. Place the rabbit meat in marinade and toss to combine well.
3. Cover with plastic wrap and refrigerate for several hours (preferably overnight).
4. Remove meat from marinade and pat dry on a paper towel.
5. Set the Smoke Temperature to High.
6. Place the rabbit pieces directly on grill rack.
7. Grill for about 12 to 15 minutes per side.
8. The rabbit meat is ready when no longer pink inside and the juices run clear.
9. Serve hot.
Nutrition Energy (calories): 269 kcal Protein: 15.45 Fat: 22.29 g Carbohydrates: 1.4 g Calcium, Ca17 mg Magnesium, Mg14 mg Phosphorus, P121 mg Iron, Fe1.55 mg Fiber0.2 g

Grilled Wild Rabbit with Rosemary and Garlic

Preparation Time: 15 minutes
Cooking Time: 1 hour
Servings: 4
Ingredients:
· 1 - 2 wild rabbits (about 2 pounds)
· 2 cloves of garlic, melted
· 2 tbsp of rosemary dried, crushed
· Juice from 1 lemon
· 1/4 cup olive oil
· Salt and freshly ground pepper
Directions:
1. If we use a whole rabbit, cut up a rabbit by removing the front legs, which are not attached to the body by bone.
2. Slide your knife up from underneath, along the ribs, and slice through. Cut the trunk into slices of 4-5 cm thick.
3. In a bowl, mix the dry ingredients and lemon juice.
4. Brush the rabbit pieces with the garlic-rosemary mixtures.
5. Start the pellet grill to pre-heat to 300 degrees.
6. Lay the rabbit pieces onto grill rack.
7. Grill for about 12 - 15 minutes per side.
8. Serve.
Nutrition Energy (calories): 733 kcal Protein: 25.22 g Fat: 15.42 g Carbohydrates: 128.9 g Calcium, Ca42 mg Magnesium, Mg303 mg Phosphorus, P740 mg Iron, Fe3.5 mg Fiber10.7 g Sugars, total4.57 g

Grilled Rabbit

Prep Time: 5 minutes| **Cooking Time**: 40 minutes| **Temperature:** 500F & 425F|
Servings: 8
Ingredients:
o 1 whole rabbit fryer
o 1 cup spicy plum sauce
For grilling:
o Assorted veggies
Directions:
1. Preheat the grill to 500F.

2.   In the meantime, cut the rabbit rib cage pressing down flat.
3.   Spread half of the sauce on the rabbit inside, then lay the rabbit on the grill with marinade side down.
4.   Lower the heat to 425F. Cover and cook for 15 to 20 minutes.
5.   Then coat the rabbit's top side with the remaining sauce and flip the rabbit, then coat with the sauce.
6.   Add assorted veggies and cover the grill. Cook for 15 to 20 minutes more or until the internal temperature reads 160F and all juices run clear.
7.   Remove and rest for 10 minutes.
8.   Chop and serve.

NUTRITION:

Calories: 115|Fat: 4.6g| Carb: 1g| Protein: 16.5g

Cajun-Style Smoked Turkey

(TOTAL COOK TIME 18 HOURS)
INGREDIENTS FOR 10 SERVINGS
THE MEAT
· 1 fresh whole turkey (12-lbs, 5.4-kgs)
THE RUB
· Kosher salt – 3 tablespoons
· Light brown sugar – 3 tablespoons
· Paprika – 2 teaspoons
· Dried oregano – 2 teaspoons
· Cayenne pepper – 2 teaspoons
· Garlic powder – 1 teaspoon
· Unsalted butter, softened – ½ cup
THE WOOD PELLET GRILL
· With the lid closed, preheat your smoker to 225°F (107°C) for 15-20 minutes
· Hickory wood pellets are recommended for this recipe
METHOD

1. First, prepare the rub. In a bowl, combine the salt with brown sugar, paprika, oregano, cayenne, and garlic powder. Put to one side.
2. Remove and discard the giblets from the turkey. Pat the bird dry with kitchen paper.
3. Rub 1 tablespoon of the rub from Step 1 into the turkey's cavity. Set 1 tablespoon of the rub aside. Scatter the remaining rub over the surface of the bird and rub into its skin. Transfer the prepared bird to the fridge, uncovered for 12-24 hours.
4. Stir the butter with the 1 tablespoon of rub set aside earlier. Loosen the skin from the bird's breast and spread the butter mixture under the skin. Replace the skin, and secure it in place with toothpicks. Tie the ends of the turkey's leg together with butcher twine, tuck the wing tips underneath, and set aside at room temperature for 30 minutes.
5. Remove the bird from the fridge and smoke, breast side facing upwards for 5-6 hours, or until it registers an internal temperature of 155°F (68°C).
6. Remove the turkey from your pellet grill and loosely cover with foil. Allow the bird to rest for 25 minutes before carving.

Cured Turkey Drumstick

Preparation Time: 20 minutes
Cooking Time: 2.5 hours to 3 hours
Servings: 3
Ingredients:
· 3 fresh or thawed frozen turkey drumsticks
· 3 tablespoons extra virgin olive oil
· Brine component
· 4 cups of filtered water
· ¼ Cup kosher salt
· ¼ cup brown sugar
· 1 teaspoon garlic powder
· Poultry seasoning 1 teaspoon
· 1/2 teaspoon red pepper flakes
· 1 teaspoon pink hardened salt
Directions:
1. Put the salt water ingredients in a 1 gallon sealable bag. Add the turkey drumstick to the salt water and refrigerate for 12 hours.
2. After 12 hours, remove the drumstick from the saline, rinse with cold water, and pat dry with a paper towel.
3. Air dry the drumstick in the refrigerator without a cover for 2 hours.
4. Remove the drumsticks from the refrigerator and rub a tablespoon of extra virgin olive oil under and over each drumstick.
5. Set the Wood Pellet Grill Smoker or grill for indirect cooking and preheat to 250 degrees Fahrenheit using hickory or maple Wood Pellet Grill Smokers.
6. Place the drumstick on the grill and smoke at 250 ° F for 2 hours.
7. After 2 hours, increase grill temperature to 325 ° F.
8. Cook the turkey drumstick at 325 ° F until the internal temperature of the thickest part of

each drumstick is 180 ° F with an instant reading digital thermometer.

9.	Place a smoked turkey drumstick under a loose foil tent for 15 minutes before eating.

Nutrition: Calories: 278 Carbs: 0g Fat: 13g Protein: 37g

Smoked Bone In-Turkey Breast

Preparation Time: 20 minutes
Cooking Time: 3-4 hours
Servings: 6-8
Ingredients:

·	1 (8-10 pounds) boned turkey breast
o	tablespoons extra virgin olive oil
·	5 Yang original dry lab or poultry seasonings

Directions:

1.	Configure a wood pellet smoker grill for indirect cooking and preheat to 225 ° F using hickory or pecan pellets.

2.	Smoke the boned turkey breast directly in a V rack or grill at 225 ° F for 2 hours.

3.	After 2 hours of hickory smoke, raise the pit temperature to 325 ° F. Roast until the thickest part of the turkey breast reaches an internal temperature of 170 ° F and the juice is clear.

4.	Place the hickory smoked turkey breast under a loose foil tent for 20 minutes, then scrape the grain.

Nutrition: Calories 956, Total fat 47g, Saturated fat 13g, Total carbs 1g, Net carbs 1g Protein 124g, Sugars 0g, Fiber 0g, Sodium 1750mg

Roast Turkey Orange

Preparation Time: 30 Minutes
Cooking Time: 2 hours 30 minutes
Servings:
Ingredients:

·	1 Frozen Long Island turkey
·	3 tablespoons west
·	1 large orange, cut into wedges

·	Three celery stems chopped into large chunks
·	Half a small red onion, a quarter
·	Orange sauce:
·	2 orange cups
·	2 tablespoons soy sauce
·	2 tablespoons orange marmalade
·	2 tablespoons honey
·	3 teaspoons grated raw

Directions:

1.	Remove the nibble from the turkey's cavity and neck and retain or discard for another use. Wash the duck and pat some dry paper towel.

2.	Remove excess fat from tail, neck and cavity. Use a sharp scalpel knife tip to pierce the turkey's skin entirely, so that it does not penetrate the duck's meat, to help dissolve the fat layer beneath the skin.

3.	Add the seasoning inside the cavity with one cup of rub or seasoning.

4.	Season the outside of the turkey with the remaining friction or seasoning.

5.	Fill the cavity with orange wedges, celery and onion. Duck legs are tied with butcher twine to make filling easier. Place the turkey's breast up on a small rack of shallow roast bread.

6.	To make the sauce, mix the ingredients in the saucepan over low heat and cook until the sauce is thick and syrupy. Set aside and let cool.

7.	Set the Wood Pellet Grill Smoker smoker grill for indirect cooking and use the Wood Pellet Grill Smokers to preheat to 350 ° F.

8.	Roast the turkey at 350 ° F for 2 hours.

9.	After 2 hours, brush the turkey freely with orange sauce.

10. Roast the orange glass turkey for another 30 minutes, making sure that the inside temperature of the thickest part of the leg reaches 165 ° F.

11. Place turkey under loose foil tent for 20 minutes before serving.

12. Discard the orange wedge, celery and onion. Serve with a quarter of turkey with poultry scissors.

Nutrition: Calories: 216 Carbs: 2g Fat: 11g Protein: 34g

Apple Aroma Smoked Whole Turkey with Dry Rub

(Cooking Time 5 hours 10 minutes)
Ingredients for 10 servings
· Whole turkey (7-lb., 3.2-kg.)
The Brine
· Apple juice - 3 quarts
· Orange juice - 1 quart
· Kosher salt - ½ cup
· Brown sugar - ½ cup
· Cloves - 3
· Ground nutmeg - 1 teaspoon
· Ground cinnamon - 1 teaspoon
The Rub
· Brown sugar - ¼ cup
· Black pepper - 1 teaspoon
· Smoked paprika - 1 tablespoon
· Garlic powder - 1 teaspoon
· Kosher salt - ½ teaspoon
The Heat
· Hickory wood pellet
Method
1. Pour apple juice and orange juice into a container. Stir a bit.
2. Season the liquid mixture with salt, brown sugar, cloves, nutmeg, and cinnamon. Mix well.
3. Dip the turkey into the brine mixture and soak it for at least 4 hours to overnight. Store it in the fridge to keep the turkey fresh.
4. On the next day, remove the turkey from the fridge and take it out of the brine mixture. Thaw it at room temperature.
5. Wash and rinse the turkey then pat it dray.
6. Next, combine the rub ingredients--brown sugar, black pepper, smoked paprika, garlic powder, and kosher salt. Mix until combined.
7. Rub it over the turkey including the cavity and set it aside.
8. After that, plug the wood pellet smoker then fill the hopper with the wood pellet. Turn the switch on and set the wood pellet smoker for indirect heat.
9. Adjust the temperature to 275°F (135°C) and let the wood pellet smoker reaches the desired temperature.
10. Place the seasoned turkey on the grill grate inside the wood pellet smoker and smoke it for 5 hours.
11. Regularly check the internal temperature of the smoked turkey and once it reaches 165°F (74°C), remove the smoked turkey from the wood pellet smoker.
12. Place the smoked turkey on a serving dish and serve.
13. Enjoy!

Smoked Beer-Can Turkey Recipe

Preparation Time: 30 minutes
Cooking Time: 2-3 hours
Servings: 8
Ingredients
For the brine
· 2 quarts apple juice
· 1 cup kosher salt
· 1/2 cup brown sugar
· 1/4 cup molasses
· 3 quarts ice cold water
· One whole natural turkey, 12 to 14 pounds
For the rub
· 1 tbsp. paprika
· 1 tsp. kosher salt
· 1 tsp. chili powder
· 1 tsp. garlic powder
· 1 tsp. freshly ground black pepper
· 1/2 teaspoon onion powder
· 1/2 teaspoon dried thyme
· 1/2 teaspoon dried oregano
· 1/4 teaspoon ground cumin
· 1/4 teaspoon cayenne pepper
One medium chunk of applewood or other light smoking wood
· 1 (24 ounces) tall can of beer
Type of fire: indirect
Grill heat: medium
Directions
To make the brine:
1. Whisk together the apple juice, salt, brown sugar and molasses in a large container until the salt and sugar have dissolved. Mix 3 liters of ice cold water. Dip the turkey, breast side down, into the brine. Put the container in the refrigerator and salt for 12 hours. To help make the rub: In a little bowl, combine paprika, salt, chili powder, garlic powder,

black pepper, onion powder, thyme, oregano, cumin, and cayenne pepper. Reserve.

2. Remove the turkey from the brine. Dry inside and outside with paper towels. I use fingers to gently separate the skin from the flesh under the breasts and around the thighs. Spread about 1 1/2 tablespoons of rubbing under your chest and thighs. Sprinkle remaining friction around the turkey inside and out.

3. Turn up smoker or grill to 325degrees F, adding smoking wood chunks when at temperature. When the wood is ignited and generating smoke, drink or empty 1/3 of beer and place the smokers can. Carefully lower turkey onto beer can, legs down. Adjust turkey legs, so it stands vertical stably. Cover and smoke until an instant-read thermometer register 160degrees F in the breast's thickest portion, about 2-3 hours.

4. Take away the turkey from the smoker and invite to rest, uncovered, for 20 to 30 minutes. Remove beer can carve and serve.

Nutrition: Energy (calories): 325 kcal Protein: 9.61 g Fat: 21.98 g Carbohydrates: 22.51 g

Hickory Smoke Patchcock Turkey

Preparation Time: 20 minutes
Cooking Time: 3-4 hours
Servings: 8-10
Ingredients:
·   1 (14 lb.) fresh or thawed frozen young turkey
·   ¼ Extra virgin olive oil with cup roasted garlic flavor
o   poultry seasonings or original dry lab in January

Directions:
1. Configure a wood pellet smoking grill for indirect cooking and preheat to 225 ° F using hickory pellets.
2. Place the turkey skin down on a non-stick grill mat made of Teflon-coated fiberglass.
3. Suck the turkey at 225 ° F for 2 hours.

4. After 2 hours, raise the pit temperature to 350 ° F.

5. Roast turkey until the thickest part of the chest reaches an internal temperature of 170 ° F and the juice is clear.

6. Place the Hickory smoked roast turkey under a loose foil tent for 20 minutes before engraving.

Nutrition: Calories 956, Total fat 47g, Saturated fat 13g, Total carbs 1g, Net carbs 1g Protein 124g, Sugars 0g, Fiber 0g, Sodium 1750mg

Smoked Turkey with Fig BBQ Sauce

Preparation Time: 4 hours
Cooking Time: 2 hours
Servings: 4
Ingredients
·   `1 Gallon water
·   `1/2 Cup sugar
·   `2 dried bay leaves
·   `2 large thyme sprigs
·   `6 peppercorns
·   `1/2 Cup salt
·   `6 Turkey Thighs
·   `1/2 Cup Ras El Hanout
·   `6 Tablespoon extra-virgin olive oil
·   `1 Cup Wood Pellet Grill Smoker Apricot BBQ Sauce
·   `4 Figs, fresh

Directions:
1. In a large pot, bring the water and sugar to a boil. Add the peppercorns, thyme, bay leaves, salt, and stir to dissolve the salt. Mix in the turkey thighs and place a lid on top, weight it down if possible. Simmer over medium-low heat for one hour. Remove the lid and let cool. Remove the turkey thighs from the pot and refrigerate until cool enough to handle.

2. Increase the heat to a medium-high and reduce the syrup by half, about 40 minutes. Strain through a fine sieve into a small bowl. Discard the solids. Return the syrup to low heat and add the Wood Pellet Grill Smoker Apricot BBQ Sauce and Ras El Hanout. Stir

well and cook an additional 5 minutes, remove from heat.

3.   Preheat Wood Pellet Grill Smoker to 275F and place the turkey thighs back in the pot for 30 minutes to crisp up slightly. Remove and towel dry with paper towels. Slice the figs in half, quarter the thighs, and assemble each plate with a thigh, a fig, and 2 tablespoons of sauce. Serve immediately.

Nutrition Energy (calories): 2102 kcal Protein: 14.55 g Fat: 205.81 g Carbohydrates: 57.98 g Calcium, Ca215 mg Magnesium, Mg65 mg Phosphorus, P303 mg Iron, Fe6.64 mg

Mix Herbs Smoked Turkey Wings

(Cooking Time 2 hours 10 minutes)
Ingredients for 10 servings
·   Turkey wings (4-lbs., 1.8-kg.)
The Brine
·   Cold water - 1 quart
·   Lemon juice - 3 tablespoons
·   Kosher salt - 3 tablespoons
·   Brown sugar - ¼ cup
·   Black pepper - ½ teaspoon
·   Minced garlic - 2 tablespoons
·   Dried rosemary - 1 tablespoon
·   Dried thyme - 1 tablespoon
·   Dried sage - 1 tablespoon
·   Dried marjoram - 1 teaspoons
·   Oregano - 1 tablespoon
The Heat
·   Alder wood pellet
Method
1.   Add lemon juice, kosher salt, brown sugar, black pepper, minced garlic, dried rosemary, thyme, sage, marjoram, and oregano to the cold water. Stir until dissolved.

2.   Put the turkey wings into the brine mixture and soak them for at least 4 hours or overnight. Store them in the fridge to keep the turkey wings fresh.

3.   On the next day, remove the turkey wings from the fridge and take them out of the brine.

4.   Wash and rinse the turkey wings then pat them dry.

5.   Next, plug the wood pellet smoker then fill the hopper with the wood pellet. Turn the switch on and set the wood pellet smoker for indirect heat.

6.   Adjust the temperature to 275°F (135°C) and let the wood pellet smoker reaches the desired temperature.

7.   Wait until the wood pellet smoker is ready and arrange the seasoned turkey wings on the grill grate inside the wood pellet smoker and smoke them for 2 hours.

8.   Once the internal temperature of the smoked turkey wings reaches 165°F (74°C), remove the smoked turkey wings from the wood pellet smoker.

9.   Transfer the smoked turkey wings to a serving dish and serve.

10. Enjoy!

Turkey Jerky

Preparation Time: 30 mins.
Cooking Time: 2 hrs. 30 mins.
Servings: 8
Ingredients:
·   One T. Asian chili-garlic paste
·   One T. curing salt
·   ½ c. soy sauce
·   ¼ c. water
·   Two T. honey
·   Two T. lime juice
·   Two pounds boneless, skinless turkey breast
Directions:
1.   Mix together the salt, water, lime juice, chili-garlic paste, honey, and soy sauce.

2.   Slice the turkey into thin strips. Lay the slices into a large zip-top baggie. If there is more meat that can fit into one bag, use as many as you need. Pour marinade over the turkey.

3.   Seal the bag and shake it around so that each slice gets coated with the marinade. Place the bag into the refrigerator overnight.

4.   Add wood pellets to your smoker and follow your cooker's startup procedure.

Preheat your smoker, with your lid closed, until it reaches 350.

5.   Take the sliced turkey out of the bags. Use paper towels to pat them dry. Place them evenly over the grill into one layer. Smoke the turkey for two hours. The jerky should feel dry but still chewable when done.

6.   Place into the zip-top bag to keep fresh until ready to eat.

Nutrition: Calories: 80 Protein: 13g Carbs: 5.1g Fat: 0.8g

Smoked Bourbon & Orange Brined Turkey

Preparation Time: 30 minutes
Cooking Time: 1 hour 30 minutes
Servings: 2-4
Ingredients:
·   Wood Pellet Grill Smoker Orange Brine (From Kit)
·   Wood Pellet Grill Smoker Turkey Rub (From Kit)
·   1.25-2.5 Gallons Cold Water
·   1 Cup Bourbon
·   1 Tbsp. Butter, Melted
Directions:
1. Mix Wood Pellet Grill Smoker Orange Brine seasoning (from Orange Brine & Turkey Rub Kit) with one quart of water. Boil for 5 minutes. Remove from heat, add 1 gallon of cold water and bourbon.
2. Place turkey breast side down in a large container. Pour cooled brine mix over bird. Add cold water until bird is submerged. Refrigerate for 24 hours.
3. Remove turkey and disregard brine. Blot turkey dry with paper towels. Combine butter and Grand Marnier and coat outside of turkey.
4. Season outside of turkey with Wood Pellet Grill Smoker Turkey Rub (from Orange Brine & Turkey Rub Kit).
5. When ready to cook, set temperature to 225 F and preheat, lid closed for 15 minutes.
Nutrition: Calories 956, Total fat 47g, Saturated fat 13g, Total carbs 1g, Net carbs 1g

Protein 124g, Sugars 0g, Fiber 0g, Sodium 1750mg

Smoked Turkey Legs Rub

Preparation Time: 5 minutes
Cooking Time: 0 minutes
Servings: 1
Ingredients:
·   3 tbsp. Onion powder
·   2 tbsp. Paprika
·   1 tbsp. Garlic powder
·   1 tsp. ground Pepper
·   1 tsp. ground Cumin
·   3 tbsp. Vegetable oil
Directions:
1.   Simply place all ingredients into an airtight jar, stir well to combine then close.
2.   Use within six months.
Nutrition: Calories: 10 Sugar: 1g Protein: 2g

Maple Bourbon Smoked Turkey Leg

(Cooking Time 3 hours 10 minutes)
Ingredients for 10 servings
·   Turkey legs (4-lbs., 1.8-kg.)
The Marinade
·   Maple syrup - ½ cup
·   Bourbon - ¼ cup
·   Apple juice - 2 tablespoon
·   Brown sugar - ½ cup
·   Kosher salt - 1 teaspoon
·   Pepper - ½ teaspoon
The Rub
·   Maple syrup - ½ cup
·   Ketchup - ¾ cup
·   Red wine vinegar - 3 tablespoons
·   Worcestershire sauce - 1 tablespoon
·   Ground mustard - 2 teaspoons
·   Paprika - 2 teaspoons
·   Salt - ¼ teaspoon
·   Black pepper - ¼ teaspoon
·   Brown sugar - 2 tablespoons
The Heat

· Apple wood pellet
Method
1. Combine the marinade ingredients--maple syrup, bourbon, apple juice, brown sugar, kosher salt, and pepper. Mix well.
2. Rub the mixture over the turkey legs and set aside.
3. Next, plug the wood pellet smoker then fill the hopper with the wood pellet. Turn the switch on and set the wood pellet smoker for indirect heat.
4. Adjust the temperature to 275°F (135°C) and let the wood pellet smoker reaches the desired temperature.
5. Arrange the turkey legs on the grill grate inside the wood pellet smoker and smoke them for an hour.
6. In the meantime, combine the glaze ingredients--maple syrup, ketchup, red wine vinegar, Worcestershire sauce, ground mustard, paprika, salt, black pepper, and brown sugar. Mix well.
7. After an hour of smoking, baste half the glaze mixture over the turkey legs and continue smoking for another 2 hours. Repeat it once every 30 minutes.
8. Once the internal temperature of the smoked turkey legs reaches 165°F (74°C), remove them from the wood pellet smoker and transfer them to a serving dish.
9. Baste the remaining glaze mixture over the smoked turkey legs and serve.
10. Enjoy!

Buttered Turkey

Preparation Time: 15 minutes
Cooking Time: 4 hours
Servings: 16
Ingredients:
· ½ pound butter, softened
· 2 tablespoons fresh thyme, chopped
· 2 fresh rosemary, chopped
· 6 garlic cloves, crushed
· 1 (20-pound) whole turkey, neck and giblets removed
· Salt and ground black pepper, as required

Directions:
1. Preheat the Wood Pellet Grill Smoker grill & Smoker on smoke setting to 300 degrees F, using charcoal.
2. In a bowl, place butter, fresh herbs, garlic, salt and black pepper and mix well.
3. With your fingers, separate the turkey skin from breast to create a pocket.
4. Stuff the breast pocket with ¼-inch thick layer of butter mixture.
5. Season the turkey with salt and black pepper evenly.
6. Arrange the turkey onto the grill and cook for 3-4 hours.
7. Remove turkey from pallet grill and place onto a cutting board for about 15-20 minutes before carving.
8. With a sharp knife, cut the turkey into desired-sized pieces and serve.
Nutrition: Calories 965 Total Fat 52 g Saturated Fat 19.9 g Cholesterol 385 mg Sodium 1916 mg Total Carbs 0.6 g Fiber 0.2 g Sugar 0 g Protein 106.5 g

Traditional Thanksgiving Turkey

Preparation Time: 30 minutes
Cooking Time: 1 hour 30 minutes
Servings: 2-4
Ingredients:
· 1 (18-20lb) Turkey
· 1/2 Lb. Butter, Softened
· 8 Sprigs Thyme
· 6 Cloves Garlic, Minced
· 1 Sprig Rosemary, Rough Chop
Directions:
1. In a small bowl, combine butter with the minced garlic, thyme leaves, chopped rosemary, black pepper and kosher salt.
2. Prepare the turkey by separating the skin from the breast creating a pocket to stuff the butter-herb mixture in.
3. Cover the entire breast with 1/4" thickness of butter mixture.
4. Season the whole turkey with kosher salt and black pepper. As an option, you can also

stuff the turkey cavity with Traditional Stuffing.

5. When ready to cook, set the temperature to 300 F and preheat, lid closed for 15 minutes.

Nutrition: Calories 956, Total fat 47g, Saturated fat 13g, Total carbs 1g, Net carbs 1g Protein 124g, Sugars 0g, Fiber 0g, Sodium 1750mg

Thanksgiving Turkey Brine

Preparation Time: 15 Minutes
Cooking Time: 0 Minutes
Servings: ¼ Cup
Ingredients:
- 2 gallons water
- 2 cups coarse kosher salt
- 2 cups packed light brown sugar

Directions:

1. In a clean 5-gallon bucket, stir together the water, salt, and brown sugar until the salt and sugar dissolve completely.

Nutrition: Calories: 10 Carbs: 6g Protein: 1g

Roasted Spatchcock Turkey

Preparation Time: 30 minutes
Cooking Time: 3-4 hours
Servings: 4
Ingredients:
- 1 (18-20 Lb.) Whole Turkey
- 4 tbsps. Turkey Rub
- 1 tbsp. Jacobsen Sea Salt
- 4 Cloves Garlic, Minced
- 3 tbsps. Parsley, Chopped
- 1 tbsp. Rosemary, Chopped
- 2 tbsps. Thyme Leaves, Chopped
- 2 Scallions, Chopped
- 3 tbsps. Olive Oil

Directions:

1. When ready to cook, turn temperature to High and preheat, lid closed for 15 minutes.

2. On a cutting board, mix the garlic, parsley, thyme, rosemary and green onions. Chop the mixture until it turns into a paste. Set aside.

3. Spatchcock the turkey: With a large knife or shears, cut the bird open along the backbone on both sides, through the ribs, and remove the backbone.

4. Once the bird is open, split the breastbone to spread the bird flat, allowing it to roast evenly.

5. With the bird's breast facing up, season the outside with half of the Turkey Rub, then follow 2/3 of the herb mixture by rubbing it into the bird. Drizzle with olive oil.

6. Roll over the bird and then season generously with the remaining Turkey Rub.

7. Place the turkey exactly on the grill grate and cook for 30 minutes.

8. Turn to low temperature on the grill to 300 degrees F and continue to cook for 3-4 hours or until the internal temperature reaches 160 degrees F in the breast.

9. The finished inside temperature should reach 165 degrees F, but it will continue to rise after the bird is totally removed it from the grill.

10. Prepare the bird and let it rest 20-25 minutes before carving. Enjoy!

Nutrition: Energy (calories): 25 kcal Protein: 0.7 g Fat: 1.53 g Carbohydrates: 2.59 g

Hot Turkey And Bacon Dip

(TOTAL COOK TIME 35 MINUTES)
INGREDIENTS FOR 2 SERVINGS
THE MEAT
- Turkey, cooked and diced (6-ozs, 170-gms)
THE SAUCE
- Cream cheese, room temperature (16-ozs, 453.6-gms)
- Sour cream – 1 cup
- Mature white Cheddar cheese, shredded and divided (12-ozs, 340-gms)
- Romano cheese – ¼ cup
- Fresh parsley, chopped and divided– ¼ cup
- Garlic, peeled and minced – 1 tablespoon
- Paprika – ½ teaspoon
- Dried mustard – ½ teaspoon
- Bourbon molasses – 1 tablespoon

- 6 slices bacon, cooked and chopped
- 2 fresh Roma tomatoes, diced

THE WOOD PELLET GRILL
- Preheat your wood pellet grill to 400°F (204°C)
- Choose your favorite wood pellets for this recipe

METHOD
1. To prepare the sauce, in a bowl, combine the cream cheese with sour cream, half of the shredded white Cheddar, Romano cheese, cooked turkey, half of the parsley, garlic, paprika, mustard, and molasses. Mix thoroughly to incorporate.
2. Add the sauce to a large skillet, top with the remaining half of shredded Cheddar followed by the chopped bacon and diced tomatoes.
3. Transfer the skillet to the grill and cook for 5-10 minutes, until the cheese is melted and golden.
4. Remove the pan from the grill and enjoy.

Please add 4 cups of chicken stock and then sprinkle with salt and pepper.
3. Put the prepped turkey on the rack into the roasting pan and place it in the wood pellet grill.
4. Cook for 3-4 hours or until the breast reaches 160 degrees F. When you remove from the grill, the turkey will continue to cook and reach a finished internal temperature of 165degrees F.
5. Rinse the drippings into a saucepan and simmer on low.
6. In a larger saucepan, combine butter and flour with a whisk stirring until golden tan. It takes about 8 minutes, stirring constantly.
7. Next, whisk the drippings into the roux and cook until it comes to a boil. Season with salt and pepper and serve hot. Enjoy!

Nutrition: Energy (calories): 621 kcal Protein: 99.57 g 182% Fat: 13.18 g Carbohydrates: 19.82 g

Home Turkey Gravy

Preparation Time: 30 minutes
Cooking Time: 3-4 hours
Servings: 8
Ingredients:
- 4 cups Homemade Chicken Stock
- 2 Large Onions Cut Into 8th
- 4 Carrots, Rough Chop
- 4 Celery Stalks
- 8 Sprigs Thyme
- 8 Cloves Garlic, Peeled and Smashed
- 1 Turkey Neck
- 1 cup Flour
- 1 Stick Butter, Cut into About 8 Pieces
- 1 tsp. Kosher Salt
- 1 tsp. Cracked Black Pepper

Directions:
1. When all are prepared ready to cook, set the temperature to 350 degrees and preheat with the lid closed for 15 minutes.
2. In a large pan, place turkey neck, plus onion, celery, also carrot, garlic, and thyme.

Turkey

(TOTAL COOK TIME 28 HOURS)
INGREDIENTS FOR 8-10 SERVINGS
THE MEAT
- 1 whole turkey, rinsed and patted dry (14-16-lbs, 6.35- 7.25-kgs)
- 2 cans diced tomatoes (14-ozs, 397-gms) each
- 2 red onions, peeled and thinly sliced

THE STUFFING
- Chorizo sausage, casing removed (9-ozs,
- White onion, peeled and chopped – 1 cup
- 2 garlic cloves, peeled and minced
- 2 stalks celery, trimmed and chopped
- 1 Granny Smith apple, cored and diced
- Pecans, chopped – ½ cup
- Dried marjoram – ¼ tablespoon
- Dried thyme – ¼ tablespoons
- Salt – ¼ tablespoon
- Chicken stock – ¾ cup
- Cornbread, cubed – 4 cups

THE MARINADE
- 6 garlic cloves, peeled
- Adobo sauce – 3 tablespoons

- Tomato paste – 3 tablespoons
- Chicken broth – 4 cups
- Freshly squeezed juice of 2 orange
- Freshly squeezed juice of 1 lime
- Freshly squeezed juice of 1 lemon
- Pork rub, to season

THE WOOD PELLET GRILL

- For the studding and the turkey, prepare your wood pellet grill with the lid closed, and preheat to 450°F (232°C)
- Choose your favorite wood chips for this recipe

METHOD

1. To prepare the chorizo, apple, pecan, and cornbread stuffing, place a skillet on your preheated wood pellet grill.

2. Sauté the chorizo meat in the skillet while frequently stirring for 5 minutes. You will need to break the meat up as it cooks using the back of a wooden spoon.

3. Add the onion and garlic to the pan and cook until softened, for 2-3 minutes.

4. Next, add the celery, apple, pecans, marjoram, thyme, and salt and sauté for an additional 5 minutes.

5. Pour in the chicken stock, remove the skillet from the heat and fold in the cornbread cubes.

6. Return the stuffing to the grill and cook until the surface is light brown and toasted.

7. Stuff the bird as directed.

8. For the marinade, in a food processor or blender, combine the garlic cloves with the Adobo sauce, tomato paste, chicken broth, fresh orange juice, lime juice, lemon juice, and pork rub. Process the ingredients on high to create a silky smooth sauce and put to one side.

9. Add the turkey to a large ziplock bag, and pour the marinade over the turkey. Seal and massage to coat the bird in the marinade. Transfer the turkey to a roasting sheet and place in the fridge for 24-48 hours. You will need to turn the bird every 8 hours.

10. When you are ready to begin cooking, spread the tomatoes and sliced onion evenly over a roasting pan.

11. Place the turkey, breast side upward on the bed of veggies.

12. Stuff the bird with the homemade stuffing from Steps 1-7, close the cavity, and tie with kitchen twine. Pour any remaining marinade over the turkey.

13. Roast the turkey for 30 minutes on the preheated grill. When half an hour has elapsed, open the grill and cover the bird with foil. You will need to crimp the foil around its edges. Turn the grill heat down to 350°F (177°C), and cook for another 2½ hours.

14. Remove the bird from the heat, and baste with its pan juices. Uncovered, return the turkey to the grill and increase the heat to 400°F (204°C). Continue to cook for 15 minutes until the turkey skin is crisp and golden and the internal temperature of the meat registers 165°F (74°C).

15. Remove the cooked turkey from the wood pellet grill and set aside to rest for 30 minutes before serving.

Roasted Autumn Brined Turkey Breast

Preparation Time: 40 minutes
Cooking Time: 3-4 hours
Servings: 6
Ingredients:
o Cups Apple Cider
- 2 Cloves Garlic, Smashed
- 1/3 Cup Brown Sugar
- 1 tbsp. Allspice
- 1/3 cup Kosher Salt
- 3 Bay Leaves
- 4 Cups Ice Water
- 1 Turkey Breast
- 1/2 Cup Plus Two Tbsps. Unsalted Butter, Softened
- Pork and Poultry Rub

Directions:
For the Brine:

1. In a large pot or saucepan, Mix 4 cups of apple cider, the garlic cloves, brown sugar, allspice, salt and bay leaves. Simmer on the stovetop for 5 minutes, stirring often.

2. Take off the stovetop and add in the ice water.

3.   Put turkey in the brine and add water as needed until the turkey is fully submerged. Cover and refrigerate overnight.

For the Cider Glaze:

1.   Let the remaining 2 cups of apple cider in a saucepan until reduced to 1/4 cup, about 30-45 minutes. Whisk in butter and cool completely.

2.   After the turkey has brined overnight, drain the turkey and rinse.

3.   Using your fingers, take two tablespoons of the softened butter and smear it under the breast's skin. Season the breast of the turkey with Pork & Poultry Rub.

4.   When ready to cook, turn the temperature to 325 degrees F and preheat, lid closed for 15 minutes.

5.   Cook turkey until it reaches an inside temperature of 160 degrees F, about 3-4 hrs. After the first 20 minutes of cooking, rub turkey with the cider glaze.

6.   When the breast starts to get too dark you should cover it with foil. Let stand 30 minutes before carving. Enjoy!

Nutrition: Energy (calories): 680 kcal Protein: 62.27 g Fat: 32.92 g Carbohydrates: 30.71 g

Texas-style turkey

Prep. Time: 15 mins
Cook Time: 240 mins
Servings: 6
Ingredients
·   Coarse black pepper ½ c
·   Butter 1 lb
·   kosher salt ½ c
·   Turkey 1 (brined)
Instructions
1. Preheat the grill to 300 degrees Fahrenheit.
2. Liberally season the turkey with kosher salt and black pepper.
3. Grill till the internal temperature reaches 145° F or until the skin has browned to your liking.
4. Put one pound of sliced butter in the roasting pan and coat the turkey.

5. Return the breast and thigh to the grill and cook till the internal temperature reaches 165° F.

6. Allow 30 mins for the meat to rest before cutting and serving.

Smoked Wild Turkey Jerky

Preparation Time: 30 minutes
Cooking Time: 20 minutes
Servings: 12
Ingredients:
·   3 Lb. Turkey Breast, Thinly Sliced
·   2 Cups Soy Sauce
·   1 cup Brown Sugar
o Garlic Cloves, Chopped
·   2 tbsps. Fresh Ginger, Chopped
·   1 tbsp. Ground Black Pepper
·   3 tbsps. Honey
Directions:
1.   Make all ingredients and combine in a large zip-top bag then mix. Place the zip-top bag in a container and place in the refrigerator for 12 to 24 hours.
2.   Prepare and ready to cook, turn temperature up to 180 degrees F and preheat, lid closed for 15 minutes.
3.   Rinse the marinade and place the turkey strips on the grill.
4.   Leave to smoke for 4 hours or until the jerky is dry. Enjoy!

Nutrition: Energy (calories): 1085 kcal Protein: 127.1 g Fat: 47.44 g Carbohydrates: 29.32 g

Teriyaki Turkey

Preparation Time: 30 Minutes
Cooking Time: 4 Hours
Servings: 10
Ingredients:
Glaze
·   1/4 cup melted butter
·   1/2 cup apple cider

- Two cloves garlic, minced
- 1/2 teaspoon ground ginger
- Two tablespoons soy sauce
- Two tablespoons honey

Turkey
- Two tablespoons chicken seasoning
- One whole turkey

Thickener
- One tablespoon cold water
- One teaspoon cornstarch

Directions:
1. Add the glaze ingredients to a pan over medium heat.
2. Bring to a boil and then simmer for 5 minutes.
3. Reserve 5 tablespoons of the mixture.
4. Add the remaining to a marinade injection.
5. Place the turkey in a baking pan.
6. Season with the chicken seasoning.
7. Turn on the wood pellet grill.
8. Set it to 300 degrees F.
9. Add the turkey to the grill.
10. Cook for 3 hours.
11. Add the thickener to the reserved mixture.
12. Brush the turkey with this sauce.
13. Cook for another 1 hour.

Nutrition: Calories 935 Total fat 53g Saturated fat 15g Protein 107g Sodium 320mg

Roasted cider brined turkey breast

Prep. Time: 20 mins
Cook Time: 4 hrs
Servings: 6

Ingredients
- Apple cider 6 c
- Brown sugar 0.3 c
- Smashed garlic cloves 2
- Allspice 1 tbsp
- Three Bay leaves
- Kosher salt 0.3 c
- Turkey's breast 1
- Softened unsalted butter 1/2 c and 2 tbsp
- Unsalted butter 5/8 c
- Poultry rub and pork

Instructions
1. In a large jar, combine bay leaves, salt, apple cider, allspice, garlic cloves, and brown sugar to make the brine. Cook for 5 mins on the stovetop, stirring often.
2. Remove the pan from the heat and whisk in the ice water until it is completely cool. If necessary, add more water to the brine before the turkey is fully immersed. Cover and refrigerate overnight.
3. Reduce the leftover apple cider to a saucepan for 30-45 mins to make the cider glaze. Allow cooling completely after whisking in the butter.
4. Reduce the leftover apple cider in the pot over 30-45 mins to produce the cider glaze. Allow cooling completely after whisking in the butter.
5. After the turkey has brined overnight, drain and clean it. 2 tbsp softened butter, rubbed with your hands beneath the surface of the breast
6. Lightly coat the turkey breast with poultry and pork rub.
7. Preheat the to 325°F for approximately 15 mins with the top closed.
8. Cook the turkey for 3 to 4 hours, or until the internal temperature reaches 160 degrees Fahrenheit.
9. For the first 20 mins of preparation and every 45 mins after that, rub the turkey exclusively with cider glaze. If the breast grows too dark, cover it with foil.
10. Allow 30 mins for the meat to rest before cutting.

Texas Turkey

Preparation Time: 30 Minutes
Cooking Time: 4 Hours and 30 Minutes
Servings: 8
Ingredients:
- One pre-brined turkey
- Salt and pepper to taste
- 1 lb. butter

Directions:

1.   Preheat your wood pellet grill to 300 degrees F.
2.   Season the turkey with salt and pepper.
3.   Grill for 3 hours.
4.   Add the turkey to a roasting pan.
5.   Cover the turkey with the butter.
6.   Cover with foil.
7.   Add to the grill and cook for another 1 hour.
8.   Let rest for 20 minutes before carving and serving.

Nutrition: Calories 935 Total fat 53g Saturated fat 15g Protein 107g Sodium 320mg

Roasted stuffed turkey breast

Prep. Time: 20mins
Cook time: 40 mins
Servings: 6
Ingredients

· Turkey breast 1 (boneless)
· Assorted mushrooms 0.75 c
· Chopped bacon slices 5 (thick-cut)
· Chopped scallions 1 bunch
· Panko breadcrumbs 3 tbsp
· White wine 0.1 c
· Salt
· Black pepper

Instructions

1. Preheat the to 375 degrees Fahrenheit and cook for 15 mins with the lid closed.

2. Cut each turkey breast horizontally, do not cut all the way through. Place the breasts flat on the table, open.

3. Cook bacon in a skillet over medium heat until crispy. Take the bacon from the pan and place it on a plate to cool. Before browning the mushrooms, sauté them in bacon oil. After adding the scallions, cook for another 2 mins. Cook the white wine until it is completely gone. After combining the breadcrumbs and bacon, season with pepper and salt.

4. Allow the filling to chill in the refrigerator for 15-20 mins. After the turkey breast has been cool down, pour the stuffing over it and carefully press it in to ensure it sticks. Roll the turkey breasts tightly and tie them together using butcher's twine at 1" intervals. Tuck the ends of the turkey breasts under and tie them together lengthwise with twine.

5. Season the outside of the turkey breast with salt and pepper. On the grill, cook for around 40 mins. Check your core temperature; it should be 165 degrees Fahrenheit. As soon as the turkey reaches the desired temperature, remove it from the grill and set it aside to rest for approximately 10 mins. Serve by cutting into slices.

Buttery Apple Smoked Turkey

Serving: 30 minutes
Cooking Time: 6 Hours
Servings: 1
Ingredients:

· Whole Turkey - 1 (10-lbs., 4.5-kgs)
· The Rub
· Minced garlic – 2 tablespoons
· Salt – 2 ½ tablespoons
· The Filling
· Garlic powder – 1 ½ tablespoons
· Black pepper – 1 ½ tablespoons
· Butter – 1 cup
· Unsweetened apple juice – 1 cup
· Fresh apples – 2
· Chopped onion – 1 cup
· The Fire
·   Preheat the smoker an hour prior to smoking.
·   Use charcoal and hickory wood chips for smoking.

Directions:

1.   Preheat a smoker to 225°F (107°C) with charcoal and hickory wood chips.

2.   Rub the turkey with salt and minced garlic then set aside.

3.   After that, cut the apples into cubes then combine with garlic powder, black pepper, butter, and chopped onion.

4.   Pour the unsweetened apple juice over the filling mixture then mix well.

5.   Fill the turkey's cavity with the filling mixture then cover the turkey with aluminum foil.

6. Place in the smoker once the smoker is ready and smoke it for 10 hours or until the internal temperature has reached 180°F (82°C). Don't forget to check the smoke and add more wood chips if it is necessary.

7. When the turkey is done, remove from the smoker then let it sit for a few minutes.

8. Unwrap the turkey then place on a flat surface.

9. Cut the turkey into pieces or slices then serve.

10. Enjoy.

Nutrition: Carbohydrates: 37 g Protein: 9 g Sodium: 565 mg Cholesterol: 49 mg

Injected drunken smoked turkey legs

Prep. Time: 15 mins
Cook Time: 30 mins
Servings: 4
Ingredients
· Frank's red-hot sauce 1 bottle
· Butter Half c
· Brown sugar 1 c
· Bourbon or whiskey Half c
· garlic cloves 3 (Minced)
· Cajun seasoning 1tsp
· Chicken stock 1/2 c
· Turkey's legs 6

Instructions

1. Except for the turkey legs, combine all of the ingredients in a large pot. Bring the pot to a low boil, then reduce to low heat. Allow the marinade to cool before putting the turkey legs in a resealable bag. Allow for almost 24 hours of marinating time in the fridge.

2. Remove the turkey legs from the bag and save the marinade.

3. Bring half of the marinade to a boil, then set aside the other half to use as a basting sauce.

4. With chicken reserve, dilute half of the marinade. Fill a meat injector midway with the chicken stock/marinade mixture and inject it into the turkey leg's meaty areas several times. Before the turkey legs puff up, inject the marinade inside them.

5. Preheat the to 250 degrees Fahrenheit and cook for about 15 mins with the lid closed. If you have access to super smoke, use it for the best flavor.

6. Place the turkey legs on the grill grate and cook for 1-1/2 to 3 hours, depending on the size of the turkey legs, or until an instant-read thermometer registers 165°F. Baste the legs with the boiled, refrigerated marinade every 45 mins.

Smoked Turkey in Beer Brine

Preparation time: 30 minutes
Cooking Time: 6 Hours
Servings: 1
Ingredients:
· Whole Turkey - 1 (10-lbs., 4.5-kgs)
· The Brine
· Water – 1 liter
· Salt – 2 cups
· Brown sugar – 1 sugar
· Bay leaves – 3 leaves
· Thyme – 1 cup
· Chopped onion – 1 cup
· Cold beer – 1 gallon
· The Fire
· Preheat the smoker an hour prior to smoking.
· Use charcoal and hickory wood chips for smoking.

Directions:

1. Pour water into a pot then add salt, brown sugar, bay leaves, thyme, and chopped onion. Bring to boil.

2. Once it is boiled, remove from heat and let it cool. Usually, it will take approximately 30 minutes.

3. When the brine is cool, transfer to a container then pour cold beer into it. Mix until incorporated.

4. Add turkey to the container then refrigerate for 24 hours until the turkey is completely seasoned.

5. After 24 hours, remove from the refrigerator and dry using a paper towel. Set aside.

6. Preheat a smoker to 225°F (107°C) with charcoal and hickory wood chips.

7. Place the turkey in the smoker then smoke for 6 hours or until the internal temperature has reached 160°F (71°C).

8. Remove the smoked turkey from the smoker then let it warm.

9. Cut the smoked turkey into pieces or slices then arrange on a serving dish.

10. Serve and enjoy.

Nutrition: Carbohydrates: 37 g Protein: 9 g Sodium: 565 mg Cholesterol: 49 mg

Smoked turkey jerky

Prep. Time: 8 hrs
Cook Time: 4 hrs
Servings: 6
Ingredients
· Soy sauce 1/2 c
· Honey 2 tbsp
· Water 0.25 c
· Asian garlic chili sauce 2 tbsp
· Morton 1 tbsp
· Turkey breast 4 lb (boneless)

Instructions

1. In a mixing bowl, mix the soy sauce, curing salt, lime juice, water, chili, garlic paste, and honey. With a tiny knife, cut the turkey along the grain, which will help it stay together tighter as it dries. It is necessary to remove any superfluous fat, connective tissue, and membrane.

2. Place half of the turkey slices in a large resealable plastic bag. Toss the turkey slices in the marinating mixture and massage the bag to ensure that all of the slices are coated. After closing the container, chill it for several hours or overnight.

3. Preheat oven to 180°F and pre-heat for 15 mins with lid closed.

4. Remove the turkey from the marinade and toss it. Dry each turkey slice with a paper towel. Arrange the veggies on the grill grate on a single sheet.

5. Smoke for 2-4 hours, or until jerky is crispy when bent in half but still malleable and chewy.

6. Transfer the jerky to a plastic container while it is still soft. Allow one hour for the jerky to rest at room temperature. Refrigerate the jerky after squeezing the air out of the wrapper. It would keep in the fridge for a few weeks. Make the most of it.

Lightly Spiced Smoked Turkey

Preparation time: 30 minutes
Cooking Time: 6 Hours
Servings: 10
Ingredients:
· Whole Turkey - 1 (10-lbs., 4.5-kgs)
· Vegetable oil – ¼ cup
· The Injection
· Beer – ¾ cup, at room temperature
· Butter – ½ cup, melted
· Garlic – 6 cloves
· Worcestershire sauce – 2 ½ tablespoons
· Creole seasoning – 1 ½ tablespoons
· Hot sauce – 1 ½ tablespoons
· Salt – 1 ½ tablespoons
· Cayenne pepper – ½ teaspoon
· The Rub
· Paprika – 1 ½ teaspoons
· Garlic powder – 1 teaspoon
· Onion powder – 1 teaspoon
· Thyme – ¾ teaspoon
· Oregano – ¼ teaspoon
· Cumin – ¼ teaspoon
· Salt – ½ teaspoon
· Black pepper – 1 teaspoon
· The Fire
· Preheat the smoker an hour prior to smoking.
· Use charcoal and hickory wood chips for smoking.

Directions:

1. Preheat a smoker to 225°F (107°C) with charcoal and hickory wood chips. Wait until the smoker is ready.

2. Place garlic, Worcestershire sauce, Creole seasoning, hot sauce, salt, and cayenne pepper in a blender.

3. Pour beer and melted butter into the blender then blend until smooth.

4. Inject all sides of the turkey—give space about 1-inch. Set aside.

5. After that, make the rub by combining paprika with garlic powder, onion powder, thyme, oregano, cumin, salt, and black pepper. Mix well.

6. Rub the turkey with the spice mixture then lightly brush with vegetable oil.

7. When the smoker is ready, place the seasoned turkey in the smoker.

8. Smoke the turkey for 6 hours or until the internal temperature has reached 160°F (71°C).

9. Remove the turkey from the smoker then let it sit for a few minutes.

10. Carve the smoked turkey then serve.

11. Enjoy!

Nutrition: Carbohydrates: 27 g Protein: 19 g Sodium: 65 mg Cholesterol: 49 mg

BBQ dry rubbed turkey drumsticks

Prep. Time: 10 mins
Cook Time: 120 mins
Servings: 6
Ingredients
· Black pepper ½ tbsp
· Cayenne pepper ½ tsp
· Brown sugar 1 tbsp
· Coriander ground ½ tbsp
· Honeysuckle White turkey drumsticks 1 pack
· Granulated garlic ½ tbsp
· Olive oil 2 tbsp
· Kosher salt 1 tbsp
Instructions
1. Preheat your grill to 225°F by setting it on to smoke mode and leaving the lid open for approximately 10 mins. If you're using a gas or charcoal grill, make sure it's set to medium-low, indirect heat.

2. On a sheet pan, season turkey legs with granulated garlic, brown sugar, salt, cayenne, pepper, and ground coriander. Drizzle with olive oil.

3. Smoke the turkey legs for 12 hours, checking the core temperature every 1 hour.

4. Increase the oven temperature to 325°F and cook the turkey legs for another 25-30 mins, or until the internal temperature reaches 170°F.

5. Take the turkey drumsticks from the grill and let them rest for about 10 mins before serving.

Tempting Tarragon Turkey Breasts

Preparation Time: 20 Minutes (Marinating Time: Overnight)
Cooking Time: 3½ to 4 hours
Servings: 4 to 5
Ingredients:
For the marinade
· ¾ cup heavy (whipping) cream
· ¼ cup Dijon mustard
· ¼ cup dry white wine
· 2 tablespoons olive oil
· ½ cup chopped scallions, both white and green parts, divided
· 3 tablespoons fresh tarragon, finely chopped
· 6 garlic cloves, coarsely chopped
· 1 teaspoon salt
· 1 teaspoon freshly ground black pepper
For the turkey:
· (6- to 7-pound) bone-in turkey breast
· ¼ cup (½ stick) unsalted butter, melted
Directions:
1. To make the marinade
2. In a large bowl, whisk together the cream, mustard, wine, and olive oil until blended.
3. Stir in ¼ cup of scallions and the tarragon, garlic, salt, and pepper.
4. Rub the marinade all over the turkey breast and under the skin. Cover and refrigerate overnight.
5. To make the turkey

6. Following the manufacturer's specific start-up procedure, preheat the smoker to 250°F, and add apple or mesquite wood.

7. Remove the turkey from the refrigerator and place it directly on the smoker rack. Do not rinse it.

8. Smoke the turkey for 3½ to 4 hours (about 30 minutes per pound), basting it with the butter twice during smoking, until the skin is browned and the internal temperature registers 165°F.

9. Remove the turkey from the heat and let it rest for 10 minutes.

10. Sprinkle with the remaining scallions before serving.

Nutrition: Calories: 165 cal Fat: 14g Carbohydrates: 0.5g Fiber: 0 g Protein: 15.2g

Jalapeno Injection Turkey

Preparation Time: 15 minutes
Cooking Time: 4 hours and 10 minutes
Servings: 6
Ingredients:

·   15 pounds whole turkey, giblet removed
·   ½ of medium red onion, peeled and minced
·   8 jalapeño peppers
·   2 tablespoons minced garlic
·   4 tablespoons garlic powder
·   6 tablespoons Italian seasoning
·   1 cup butter, softened, unsalted
·   ¼ cup olive oil
·   1 cup chicken broth

Directions:

1. Open hopper of the smoker, add dry pallets, make sure ash-can is in place, then open the ash damper, power on the smoker and close the ash damper.

2. Set the temperature of the smoker to 200 degrees F, let preheat for 30 minutes or until the green light on the dial blinks that indicate smoker has reached to set temperature.

3. Meanwhile, place a large saucepan over medium-high heat, add oil and butter and when the butter melts, add onion, garlic, and peppers and cook for 3 to 5 minutes or until nicely golden brown.

4. Pour in broth, stir well, let the mixture boil for 5 minutes, then remove pan from the heat and strain the mixture to get just liquid.

5. Inject turkey generously with prepared liquid, then spray the outside of turkey with butter spray and season well with garlic and Italian seasoning.

6. Place turkey on the smoker grill, shut with lid, smoke for 30 minutes, then increase the temperature to 325 degrees F and continue smoking the turkey for 3 hours or until the internal temperature of turkey reach to 165 degrees F.

7. When done, transfer turkey to a cutting board, let rest for 5 minutes, then carve into slices and serve.

Nutrition: Calories: 131 cal Fat: 7 g Protein: 13 g Carbohydrates: 3 g Fiber: 0.7 g

Maple Turkey Breast

Preparation Time: 4 hours and 30 minutes
Cooking Time: 2 hours
Servings: 4
Ingredients:

·   3 tablespoons olive oil
·   3 tablespoons dark brown sugar
·   3 tablespoons garlic, minced
·   2 tablespoons Cajun seasoning
·   2 tablespoons Worcestershire sauce
·   6 lb. turkey breast fillets

Directions:

1. Combine olive oil, sugar, garlic, Cajun seasoning and Worcestershire sauce in a bowl.

2. Soak the turkey breast fillets in the marinade.

3. Cover and marinate for 4 hours.

4. Grill the turkey at 180 degrees F for 2 hours.

Serving Suggestion: Let rest for 15 minutes before serving.

Preparation / Cooking Tips: You can also sprinkle dry rub on the turkey before grilling.

Nutrition: Calories: 416 Cal Fat: 13.3 g Carbs: 0 g Protein: 69.8 g Fiber: 0 g

Homemade Turkey Gravy

Preparation Time: 20 minutes
Cooking Time: 3 hours 20 minutes
Servings: 8-12
Ingredients:

- 1 turkey, neck
- 2 large Onion, eight
- 4 celeries, stalks
- 4 large carrots, fresh
- 8 clove garlic, smashed
- 8 thyme sprigs
- 4 cup chicken broth
- 1 teaspoon chicken broth
- 1 teaspoon salt
- 1 teaspoon cracked black pepper
- 1 butter, sticks
- 1 cup all-purpose flour

Directions:

1. When ready to cook, set the temperature to 350F and preheat the Wood Pellet Grill Smoker grill with the lid closed, for 15 minutes.

2. Place turkey neck, celery, carrot (roughly chopped), garlic, onion and thyme on a roasting pan. Add four cups of chicken stock then season with salt and pepper.

3. Move the prepped turkey on the rack into the roasting pan and place in the Wood Pellet Grill Smoker grill.

4. Cook for about 3-4 hours until the breast reaches 160F. The turkey will continue to cook and it will reach a finished internal temperature of 165F.

5. Strain the drippings into a saucepan and simmer on low.

6. In a saucepan, mix butter (cut into 8 pieces) and flour with a whisk stirring until golden tan. This takes about 8 minutes, stirrings constantly.

7. Whisk the drippings into the roux then cook until it comes to a boil. Season with salt and pepper.

Nutrition: Calories 160kcal Carbohydrate 27g Protein 55g Fat 23g Saturated Fat 6.1g

Boneless stuffed turkey breast

Prep. Time: 10 mins
Cook time: 90 mins
Servings: 6
Ingredients

- Bay leaf 1
- Butter divided 3 tbsp
- Black pepper 1/2 tsp
- Celery rib 1 (minced)
- Cremini mushrooms 4 Oz
- Black pepper
- Dried cranberries ½ c
- Honeysuckle White turkey breast (boneless) 1 pack
- Garlic cloves 2 (minced)
- Marsala wine ½ c
- Rosemary sprigs1
- Olive oil 1 tbsp
- Rubbed sage 1/2 tsp
- Sea salt To taste
- Salt 1/2 tsp
- Stuffing mix 6 oz
- Yellow onion 1 (chopped)
- Turkey stock divided 1.25 c

Instructions

1. Preheat your pitmaster grill to 325°F by activating the smoke mode and leaving the lid open for around 10 mins. Whether you're using a charcoal barbecue or a gas grill, set the temperature to medium-low.

2. Melt butter and olive oil in a large pan over medium heat. Cook, stirring regularly, for 3 mins, or until the onions and celery are soft.

3. After combining the garlic and mushrooms, cook for approximately 5 mins or until the mushrooms are gently browned.

4. Deglaze with Marsala liquid, scraping some browned bits from the pan's bottom with a wooden spoon.

5. Remove the heat after adding the sage, black pepper, dried cranberries, and salt, and simmer for approximately 2 mins.

6. Fold the stuffing into the vegetable mixture, then gently drizzle in the turkey stock, frequently stirring until the stuffing is well absorbed.

7. Place the skin-side down turkey breasts on a large cutting board and butterfly them. Season

with pepper and salt, then pour a spoonful of filling over the top, leaving a 1" gap.

8. Begin rolling the turkey breast with the lowest amount of skin on the side. Use butcher's string to truss your turkey breast and safeguard the stuffing. Season with pepper and salt and cook in the remaining butter in a skillet.

9. Sprinkle a little rosemary on top, then pour the remaining 14 cups of stock and 1 bay leaf all over the turkey. Place on the grill.

10. Cook the turkey for 1-1 1/2 hours, or until the internal temperature reaches 165° F.

11. Remove the stuffed turkey breast from the grill and set it aside to rest for approximately 15 mins before slicing and serving with the remaining stuffing.

6. Wash the brine off the legs with cold water, then dry thoroughly with paper towels.

7. When ready to cook, start the Wood Pellet Grill Smoker grill according to grill instructions. Set the heat to 250F and preheat, lid closed for 10 to 15 minutes.

8. Place turkey legs directly on the grill grate.

9. After 2 ½ hours, wrap a piece of bacon around each leg then finish cooking them for 30 to 40 minutes of smoking.

10. The total smoking time for the legs will be 3 hours or until the internal temperature reaches 165F on an instant-read meat thermometer. Serve, Enjoy!

Nutrition: Calories 390kcal Total Fat 14g Saturated Fat 0g Cholesterol 64mg Sodium 738mg Carbohydrates 44g

Bacon Wrapped Turkey Legs

Preparation Time: 10 minutes
Cooking Time: 3 hours
Servings: 4-6
Ingredients:
- Gallon water
- To taste Wood Pellet Grill Smoker rub
- ½ cup pink curing salt
- ½ cup brown sugar
- 6 whole peppercorns
- 2 whole dried bay leaves
- ½ gallon ice water
- 8 whole turkey legs
- 16 sliced bacon

Directions:
1. In a large stockpot, mix one gallon of water, the rub, curing salt, brown sugar, peppercorns and bay leaves.

2. Boil it to over high heat to dissolve the salt and sugar granules. Take off the heat then add in ½ gallon of ice and water.

3. The brine must be at least to room temperature, if not colder.

4. Place the turkey legs, completely submerged in the brine.

5. After 24 hours, drain the turkey legs then remove the brine.

Smoked Turkey Patties

Preparation Time: 20 minutes
Cooking Time: 40 minutes
Servings: 6
Ingredients:
- 2 lbs. turkey minced meat
- 1/2 cup of parsley finely chopped
- 2/3 cup of onion finely chopped
- 1 red bell pepper finely chopped
- 1 large egg at room temperature
- Salt and pepper to taste
- 1/2 tsp dry oregano
- 1/2 tsp dry thyme

Directions:
1. In a bowl, combine well all ingredients.

2. Make from the mixture patties.

3. Start Wood Pellet Grill Smoker grill on (recommended apple or oak Wood Pellet Grill Smoker) lid open, until the fire is established (4-5 minutes). Increase the temperature to 350F and allow to pre-heat, lid closed, for 10 - 15 minutes.

4. Place patties on the grill racks and cook with lid covered for 30 to 40 minutes.

5. Your turkey patties are ready when you reach a temperature of 130F

6. Serve hot.

Nutrition: Calories: 251 Carbohydrates: 3.4g Fat: 12.5 Fiber: 0.9g Protein: 31.2g

Thanksgiving Dinner Turkey

Preparation Time: 15 minutes
Cooking Time: 4 hours
Servings: 16
Ingredients:
- ½ lb. butter, softened
- 2 tbsp. fresh thyme, chopped
- 2 tbsp. fresh rosemary, chopped
- 6 garlic cloves, crushed
- 1 (20-lb.) whole turkey, neck and giblets removed
- Salt and ground black pepper

Directions:
1. Set the temperature of Grill to 300 degrees F and preheat with closed lid for 15 mins, using charcoal.
2. In a bowl, place butter, fresh herbs, garlic, salt and black pepper and mix well.
3. Separate the turkey skin from breast to create a pocket.
4. Stuff the breast pocket with ¼-inch thick layer of butter mixture.
5. Season turkey with salt and black pepper.
6. Arrange the turkey onto the grill and cook for 3-4 hours.
7. Remove the turkey from grill and place onto a cutting board for about 15-20 mins before carving.
8. Cut the turkey into desired-sized pieces and serve.

Nutrition: Calories per serving: 965 Carbohydrates: 0.6; Protein: 106.5g Fat: 52g Sugar: 0g Sodium: 1916mg Fiber: 0.2g

Savory-Sweet Turkey Legs

Preparation Time: 10 minutes
Cooking Time: 5 hours

Servings: 4
Ingredients:
- 1 gallon hot water
- 1 cup curing salt (such as Morton Tender Quick)
- ¼ cup packed light brown sugar
- 1 teaspoon freshly ground black pepper
- 1 teaspoon ground cloves
- 1 bay leaf
- 2 teaspoons liquid smoke
- 4 turkey legs
- Mandarin Glaze, for serving

Directions:
1. In a huge container with a lid, stir together the water, curing salt, brown sugar, pepper, cloves, bay leaf, and liquid smoke until the salt and sugar are dissolved; let come to room temperature.
2. Submerge the turkey legs in the seasoned brine, cover, and refrigerate overnight.
3. When ready to smoke, remove the turkey legs from the brine and rinse them; discard the brine.
4. Supply your smoker with Wood Pellet Grill Smoker and follow the manufacturer's specific start-up procedure. Preheat, with the lid closed, to 225°F.
5. Arrange the turkey legs on the grill, close the lid, and smoke for 4 to 5 hours, or until dark brown and a meat thermometer inserted in the thickest part of the meat reads 165°F.
6. Serve with Mandarin Glaze on the side or drizzled over the turkey legs.

Nutrition: Calories: 190 Carbs: 1g Fat: 9g Protein: 24g

Hoisin Turkey Wings

Preparation Time: 15 minutes
Cooking Time: 1 hour
Servings: 8
Ingredients:
- 2 pounds turkey wings
- ½ cup hoisin sauce
- 1 tablespoon honey
- 2 teaspoons soy sauce

- 2 garlic cloves (minced)
- 1 teaspoons freshly grated ginger
- 2 teaspoons sesame oil
- 1 teaspoons pepper or to taste
- 1 teaspoons salt or to taste
- ¼ cup pineapple juice
- 1 tablespoon chopped green onions
- 1 tablespoon sesame seeds
- 1 lemon (cut into wedges)

Directions:

1. In a huge container, combine the honey, garlic, ginger, soy, hoisin sauce, sesame oil, pepper and salt. Put all the mixture into a zip lock bag and add the wings. Refrigerate for 2 hours.

2. Remove turkey from the marinade and reserve the marinade. Let the turkey rest for a few minutes, until it is at room temperature.

3. Preheat your grill to 300°F with the lid closed for 15 minutes.

4. Arrange the wings into a grilling basket and place the basket on the grill.

5. Grill for 1 hour or until the internal temperature of the wings reaches 165°F.

6. Meanwhile, pour the reserved marinade into a saucepan over medium-high heat. Stir in the pineapple juice.

7. Wait to boil then reduce heat and simmer for until the sauce thickens.

8. Brush the wings with sauce and cook for 6 minutes more. Remove the wings from heat.

9. Serve and garnish it with green onions, sesame seeds and lemon wedges.

Nutrition: Calories: 115 Fat: 4.8g Carbs: 11.9g Protein 6.8g

Whole Turkey

Preparation Time: 10 Minutes
Cooking Time: 7 Hours And 30 Minutes
Servings: 10
Ingredients:

- 1 frozen whole turkey, giblets removed, thawed
- 2 tablespoons orange zest
- 2 tablespoons chopped fresh parsley
- 1 teaspoon salt
- 2 tablespoons chopped fresh rosemary
- 1 teaspoon ground black pepper
- 2 tablespoons chopped fresh sage
- 1 cup butter, unsalted, softened, divided
- 2 tablespoons chopped fresh thyme
- ½ cup water
- 14.5-ounce chicken broth

Directions:

1. Open hopper of the smoker, add dry pallets, make sure ash-can is in place, then open the ash damper, power on the smoker and close the ash damper.

2. Set the temperature of the smoker to 180 degrees F, let preheat for 30 minutes or until the green light on the dial blinks that indicate smoker has reached to set temperature.

3. Meanwhile, prepare the turkey and for this, tuck its wings under it by using kitchen twine.

4. Place ½ cup butter in a bowl, add thyme, parsley, and sage, orange zest, and rosemary, stir well until combined and then brush this mixture generously on the inside and outside of the turkey and season the external of turkey with salt and black pepper.

5. Place turkey on a roasting pan, breast side up, pour in broth and water, add the remaining butter in the pan, then place the pan on the smoker grill and shut with lid.

6. Smoke the turkey for 3 hours, then increase the temperature to 350 degrees F and continue smoking the turkey for 4 hours or until thoroughly cooked and the internal temperature of the turkey reaches to 165 degrees F, basting turkey with the dripping every 30 minutes, but not in the last hour.

7. When you are done, take off the roasting pan from the smoker and let the turkey rest for 20 minutes.

8. Carve turkey into pieces and serve.

Nutrition: Calories: 146 Fat: 8 g Protein: 18 g Carbs: 1 g

Smoked Turkey Mayo with Green Apple

Preparation Time: 20 minutes
Cooking Time: 4 hours 10 minutes
Servings: 10
Ingredients:
· Whole turkey (4-lbs., 1.8-kg.)
· The Rub
· Mayonnaise – ½ cup
· Salt – ¾ teaspoon
· Brown sugar – ¼ cup
· Ground mustard – 2 tablespoons
· Black pepper – 1 teaspoon
· Onion powder – 1 ½ tablespoons
· Ground cumin – 1 ½ tablespoons
· Chili powder – 2 tablespoons
· Cayenne pepper – ½ tablespoon
· Old Bay Seasoning – ½ teaspoon
· The Filling
· Sliced green apples – 3 cups

Directions:

1. Place salt, brown sugar, brown mustard, black pepper, onion powder, ground cumin, chili powder, cayenne pepper, and old bay seasoning in a bowl then mix well. Set aside.
2. Next, fill the turkey cavity with sliced green apples then baste mayonnaise over the turkey skin.
3. Sprinkle the dry spice mixture over the turkey then wrap with aluminum foil.
4. Marinate the turkey for at least 4 hours or overnight and store in the fridge to keep it fresh.
5. On the next day, remove the turkey from the fridge and thaw at room temperature.
6. Meanwhile, plug the Wood Pellet Grill Smoker smoker then fill the hopper with the Wood Pellet Grill Smoker. Turn the switch on.
7. Set the Wood Pellet Grill Smoker smoker for indirect heat then adjust the temperature to 275°F (135°C).
8. Unwrap the turkey and place in the Wood Pellet Grill Smoker smoker.
9. Smoke the turkey for 4 hours or until the internal temperature has reached 170°F (77°C).
10. Remove the smoked turkey from the Wood Pellet Grill Smoker smoker and serve.

Nutrition: Calories: 340 Carbs: 40g Fat: 10g Protein: 21g

Barbecue Chili Smoked Turkey Breast

Preparation Time: 15 minutes
Cooking Time: 4 hours 20 minutes
Servings: 8
Ingredients:
· Turkey breast (3-lb., 1.4-kg.)
· The Rub
· Salt – ¾ teaspoon
· Pepper – ½ teaspoon
· The Glaze
· Olive oil – 1 tablespoon
· Ketchup – ¾ cup
· White vinegar – 3 tablespoons
· Brown sugar – 3 tablespoons
· Smoked paprika – 1 tablespoons
· Chili powder – ¾ teaspoon
· Cayenne powder – ¼ teaspoon

Directions:

1. Score the turkey breast at several places then sprinkle salt and pepper over it.
2. Let the seasoned turkey breast rest for approximately 10 minutes.
3. In the meantime, plug the Wood Pellet Grill Smoker smoker then fill the hopper with the Wood Pellet Grill Smoker. Turn the switch on.
4. Set the Wood Pellet Grill Smoker smoker for indirect heat then adjust the temperature to 275°F (135°C).
5. Place the seasoned turkey breast in the Wood Pellet Grill Smoker smoker and smoke for 2 hours.
6. In the meantime, combine olive oil, ketchup, white vinegar, brown sugar, smoked paprika; chili powder, garlic powder, and cayenne pepper in a saucepan then stir until incorporated. Wait to simmer then remove from heat.
7. After 2 hours of smoking, baste the sauce over the turkey breast and continue smoking for another 2 hours.

8.   Once the internal temperature of the smoked turkey breast has reached 170°F (77°C) remove from the Wood Pellet Grill Smoker smoker and wrap with aluminum foil.

9.   Let the smoked turkey breast rest for approximately 15 minutes to 30 minutes then unwrap it.

10. Cut the smoked turkey breast into thick slices then serve.

Nutrition: Calories: 290 Carbs: 2g Fat: 3g Protein: 63g

CHAPTER 11: VEGETABLES RECIPES

6. Pour in the vegetable broth, and using an immersion blender, blend until smooth.

7. Add cream and enjoy.

Grilled Butternut Squash Soup

(TOTAL COOK TIME 1 HOUR 5 MINUTES)
INGREDIENTS FOR 4 SERVINGS
THE VEGETABLES
· 2 large butternut squash, halved and seeded
THE INGREDIENTS
· Olive oil, divided – 2 tablespoons
· Salt and black pepper
· 1 large shallot bulb, chopped
· Salt, divided – 2 teaspoons
· 8 garlic cloves, peeled and minced
· Pure maple syrup – 2 teaspoons
· Ground nutmeg – ½ teaspoon
· Vegetable broth – 3 cups
· Heavy cream – ½ cup
THE WOOD PELLET GRILL
· You will be preparing this recipe over an open flame

METHOD
1. Brush the cut side of the squash with olive oil and season generously with salt and black pepper.
2. With the hood open, place the squash facing downwards and cook until charred.

3. Continue to cook the squash until fork-tender and cooked through, for approximately 45-50 minutes. Put aside to cool for around 10 minutes. Using a spoon, scoop out the cooled squash flesh, discard the skin, and transfer the flesh to a bowl.
4. In the meantime, in a frying pan, over moderate heat, warm 1 tablespoon of olive oil. Add the shallot and 1 teaspoon of salt. Cook while frequently stirring for 3-4 minutes. Next, add the garlic and cook, while frequently stirring until fragrant, for around 60 seconds.
5. Finally, add the butternut squash set aside earlier, maple syrup, nutmeg, and a dash of black pepper.

Wood Pellet Grill Smoker Grilled Vegetables

Preparation Time: 5 Minutes
Cooking Time: 15 Minutes
Servings: 12
Ingredients:
· One veggie tray
· 1/4 cup vegetable oil
· 1-2 tbsp Wood Pellet Grill Smoker veggie seasoning
Directions:
1. Preheat your Wood Pellet Grill Smoker to 375oF.
2. Meanwhile, toss the veggies in oil placed on a sheet pan, large, then splash with the seasoning.
3. Place on the Wood Pellet Grill Smoker and grill for about 10-15 minutes.
4. Remove, serve, and enjoy.
Nutrition: Calories 44 Total fat 5g Total carbs 10.8g Protein 0g Sugars 0g Fiber 0g, Sodium 36mg Potassium 116mg

Lemon Herbs Smoked Asparagus

(Cooking Time 1 Hour)
Ingredients for 10 servings
· Asparagus (2-lbs., 0.9-kg.)
The Rub
· Minced garlic - 2 tablespoons
· Grated lemon zest - 1 teaspoon
· Diced parsley - 1 teaspoon
· Diced fresh chives - 1 teaspoon
· Diced fresh rosemary - 1 teaspoon
· Salt - ¼ teaspoon
· Black pepper - ¼ teaspoon
· Olive oil - 2 tablespoons
· Lemon juice - 2 tablespoons

The Heat
· Apple wood pellet
Method
1. Cut and trim the asparagus. Set aside.
2. Mix minced garlic with lemon zest, parsley, chives, rosemary, salt, and black pepper.
3. Drizzle olive oil and lemon juice over the spice mixture. Stir until becoming a paste.
4. Rub the asparagus with the seasoning paste and spread the asparagus in a disposable aluminum pan.
5. Next, plug the wood pellet smoker then fill the hopper with the wood pellet. Turn the switch on and set the wood pellet smoker for indirect heat.
6. Adjust the temperature to 225°F (107°C) and let the wood pellet smoker reaches the desired temperature.
7. Insert the aluminum pan with asparagus into the wood pellet smoker and smoke it for an hour or until tender.
8. Once it is done, remove the smoked asparagus from the wood pellet smoker and transfer it to a serving dish.
9. Serve and enjoy!

Roasted Sherry Root Vegetables

Prep. Time: 20 Mins
Cook Time: 1 Hr
Servings: 8
Ingredients
· Red Onion 1
· Whole Fennel Bulb 1
· Whole Turnips 2 (Cut and peeled Into Chunks)
· Olive Oil 3 Tbsp (Extra-Virgin)
· Small Red-Skin Potatoes 4
· Dry Sherry ¼ Cup
· Garlic 1 Head
· Whole Golden Beets 2 Tsp (Diced and trimmed Large)
· Veggie Rub 2 Tsp
· Carrots 2 Cup (cut and peeled)
· Small Yukon Gold Potatoes 4
· Thyme Leaves 1 Tbsp (Fresh)
· Whole Parsnips 2

Instructions
1. Arrange the chopped veggies on a large sheet tray.
2. Using a serrated knife, cut roughly half an inch off the top of the garlic head to show the clove tops, leaving the garlic skin intact around each clove.
3. Place the garlic cloves on the aluminum foil square, drizzle with 1 tablespoon olive oil, and wrap the foil all around the garlic loosely. On a sheet plate, combine the remaining veggies.
4. Drizzle the remaining olive oil over the veggies. In a mixing dish, mix the dry sherry, two tablespoons Veggie Rub, and the thyme. To combine, whisk everything together.
5. Preheat the to 500°F with the lid covered for at least 15 mins when ready to cook.
6. Cook for 60 to 90 mins, occasionally stirring, until the veggies are soft and beginning to brown.
7. Squeeze the garlic cloves over the veggies while stirring to combine. Remove the papery garlic husks and discard them. Serve immediately. Enjoy.

Easy Smoked Vegetables

Preparation Time: 15 minutes
Cooking Time: 1 ½ hour
Servings: 6
Ingredients:
· 1 cup of pecan wood chips
· 1 ear fresh corn, silk strands removed, and husks, cut corn into 1-inch pieces
· 1 medium yellow squash, 1/2-inch slices
· 1 small red onion, thin wedges
· 1 small green bell pepper, 1-inch strips
· 1 small red bell pepper, 1-inch strips
· 1 small yellow bell pepper, 1-inch strips
· 1 cup mushrooms, halved
· 2 tbsp vegetable oil
· Vegetable seasonings
Directions:
1. Take a large bowl and toss all the vegetables together in it.
2. Sprinkle it with seasoning and coat all the vegetables well with it.

3.   Place the wood chips and a bowl of water in the smoker.

4.   Preheat the smoker at 100°F or ten minutes.

5.   Put the vegetables in a pan and add to the middle rack of the electric smoker.

6.   Smoke for thirty minutes until the vegetable becomes tender.

7.   When done, serve, and enjoy.

Nutrition: Calories: 97 Cal Fat: 5 g Carbohydrates: 11 g Protein: 2 g Fiber: 3 g

Fall Vegetables (Roasted)

Prep. Time: 5 Mins
Cook Time: 30 Mins
Servings: 6
Ingredients
·   Pound Potatoes
·   Salt and Pepper
·   Olive Oil 2 Tbsp
·   Pound Butternut Squash 2 Tbsp Chopped
·   Mushrooms 1 Pint (Cut)
·   Brussels Sprouts ½ lb (Fresh)

Instructions

1. When ready to cook, preheat the grill according to the manufacturer's recommendations. Preheat oven to 400°F and bake for 10 to 15 mins with the lid covered.

2. Spread out the potatoes and squash on the sheet pan and toss with salt, olive oil, and pepper. Place directly on the grate and cook for 15 mins. Toss in the brussels sprouts and mushrooms to coat.

3. Grill for another 15 to 20 mins, or until the vegetables are lightly browned and cooked through. As needed, adjust the seasoning. Enjoy.

Smoked Potatoes

Preparation Time: 30 minutes
Cooking Time: 2 hours
Servings: 4
Ingredients:

• 1.5 lb. potatoes (gemstone)
• Fresh parsley (chopped)
• 1/4 cup Parmesan (grated)
Marinade **ingredients**:
• 6 cloves garlic (minced)
• 2 tablespoons olive oil
• 1/2 teaspoon dried dill
• 1/2 teaspoon basil (dried)
• 1/2 teaspoon oregano (dried)
• 1/2 teaspoon Italian seasoning (dried)
• 1/4 teaspoon fresh pepper (ground)
• 1/2 teaspoon kosher salt

Directions:

1. Initial step is rinsing the potatoes with water. When done, place the potatoes in a large zip lock bag.

2. In a mixing bowl, add and combine the minced garlic cloves, dill, Italian seasoning, basil and ground pepper. Add this mixture in the zip lock bag together with the potatoes.

3. Coat the potatoes by shaking the zip lock bag and refrigerate for 2 hours.

4. Once ready to cook, preheat your smoker to 225F.

5. Use aluminum foil to make a foil packet and place in the potatoes.

6. Pour in two tablespoons of water in the foil and fold it in half on its edges.

7. Put the foil packet on the smoker rack and smoke for 2 hours.

8. Remove from the smoker and top with the grated parmesan and parsley.

Nutrition: Calories- 210| Fat- 8.9g| Saturated fat- 2.1g| Carbohydrates- 28.9g| Fiber-4.3g| Sugars- 2.1g| Protein- 5.5g| Sodium- 368mg| Cholesterol- 5mg|

Roasted Baby Rainbow Carrots

(TOTAL COOK TIME 20 MINUTES)
INGREDIENTS FOR 6-8 SERVINGS
THE VEGETABLES
·   Baby rainbow carrots, rinsed, cleaned, and patted dry (1.5-lbs, 0.7-kgs)
THE INGREDIENTS
·   Extra-virgin olive oil – 2 tablespoon
·   Sea salt – ½ teaspoon

· Freshly ground black pepper – ¼ teaspoon
THE WOOD PELLET GRILL
· With the lid closed, preheat your wood pellet grill to 450°F (232°C)
METHOD
1. In an aluminum pan, toss the carrots with olive oil, salt, and black pepper.
2. When the grill is at the correct temperature, open the lid, and roast the carrots until fork-tender for 15-20 minutes.
3. Serve and enjoy.

Grilled Asparagus

Preparation Time: 5 minutes
Cooking Time: 20 minutes
Servings: 4
Ingredients:
· 3 cups of vegetables sliced
· 2 tbsp. of olive oil
· 2 tbsp. of garlic & herb seasoning
Directions:
1. Preheat your Wood Pellet Grill Smoker grill to a temperature of about 350°F
2. While your Wood Pellet Grill Smoker is heating, slice the vegetables. Cut the spears from the Broccoli and the Zucchini; then wash the outsides and slice into spears; cut the peppers into wide strips. You can also grill carrots, corn, asparagus, and potatoes -grill at a temperature of about 350°F for about 20 minutes. Serve and enjoy!
Nutrition Calories: 47, Fat: 3g, Carbohydrates: 1g, Dietary Fiber: 1g, Protein: 2.2g

Smoked Artichokes

Preparation Time: 15 minutes
Cooking Time: 2 hours
Servings: 3
Ingredients:
THE VEGETABLE
• Whole artichoke hearts, canned – 15
THE SEASONING

• Cajun seasoning – 1 tablespoon
• Cayenne pepper – 1 tablespoon
Directions:
1. In the meantime, prepare artichoke hearts.
2. For this, cut each artichoke heart into halve.
3. Stir together ingredients for seasoning and sprinkle generously all over artichoke hearts.
4. When ready to smoke, place a prepared pouch of woodchips over charcoal and when start to smoke, brush the smoking grate with oil generously, place seasoned artichoke hearts on the grate above the drip pan.
5. Set lid on smoker and monitor temperature through temperature gauge or temperature probes and maintain it.
6. Close down the lower air vent if the temperature is above 250 degrees or open up the lower air vent if the temperature drops below 255 degrees F and add few more hot coals.
7. Check every hour if more water needs to add in the drip pan and add more hot coals using tongs along with another pouch of wood chips to keep the smoke going.
8. Let smoke for 2 hours or until artichoke hearts are cooked through and tender.
9. Serve with herb mayonnaise and pork steaks.

Jalapeño Poppers (Roasted)

Prep. Time: 15 Mins
Cook Time: 30 Mins
Servings: 2
Ingredients
· Bacon 8 Slices (Middle Cut)
· Cheddar Cheese 2 Oz (Sharp)
· Cream Cheese 2 Cup
· Chopped Green Onions ½ Cup
· Seeded Sliced Tomato 4 Tbsp
· Juice of lime 2 Tsp
· Chopped Cilantro 4 Tbsp
· Garlic Clove 2 (Minced Tiny)
· Kosher Salt ½ Tsp
Instructions
1. Preheat the oven to 350°F for 10 to 15 mins after it's ready to cook. Cook for 10 to 15 mins,

flipping halfway through until cooked through and crispy. Remove yourself from the grill, but leave it turned on. Thinly slice the bacon and set it aside after it has cooled enough to handle.

2. Mix cream cheese, cheddar cheese, green onions, garlic, salt, cilantro, lime juice, tomatoes, and chopped bacon together in a stand mixer bowl. With the aid of a paddle, blend everything on medium speed. Fill a bag halfway with the mixture.

3. Remove the seeds and ribs from jalapenos by cutting off the tops and using a small knife to remove the seeds and ribs (paring). Fill each pepper with the filling, ensuring that it rises a quarter-inch beyond the pepper's surface. Replace each pepper's top.

4. Roll out the rest of the bacon pieces with a rolling pin until they are 1/8 inch thick. Halve all of the pieces. Using a toothpick, attach half of a bacon slice over each pepper.

5. Fill a Jalapeno Popper Tray halfway with the peppers. Cook for 30 to 40 mins, until the peppers are soft, the bacon is crispy, and the cheese is melted. Enjoy.

Smoked Cabbage Garlic with Canola Oil

(Cooking Time 3 Hours)
Ingredients for 10 servings
·   Whole cabbages (3-lb., 1.4-kg.)
The Spices
·   Butter - ¼ cup
·   Canola oil - 2 tablespoons
·   Garlic powder - 1 teaspoon
·   Ground ginger - ½ teaspoon
·   Salt - ¼ teaspoon
·   Chili powder - ¼ teaspoon
·   Ground turmeric - ¼ teaspoon
The Heat
·   Maple wood pellet
Method
1. Melt butter and mix with canola oil.
2.   Add garlic powder, ginger, salt, chili powder, and ground turmeric. Mix well.

3. Cut the cabbages into thick slices and baste the mixture over them.

4. Next, plug the wood pellet smoker then fill the hopper with the wood pellet. Turn the switch on and

5. set the wood pellet smoker for indirect heat.

6. Adjust the temperature to 275°F (135°C) and let the wood pellet smoker reaches the desired temperature.

7. Arrange the seasoned cabbage wedges in the wood pellet smoker and smoke them for 3 hours or until tender.

8. Once it is done, take the smoked cabbages out of the wood pellet smoker and transfer them to a serving dish.

9. Serve and enjoy.

Beer-Braised Corned Beef and Irish Vegetables

Prep. Time: 5 Mins
Cook Time: 7 Hrs
Servings: 6
Ingredients
·   Beef brisket Corned 4 lb
·   Brown Sugar 1 tbsp
·   Pickling Spice 1 tbsp
·   Medium Onion half (Chopped)
·   Garlic clove 4 (Smashed or Minced)
·   Guinness Beer 12 Oz
·   Carrots 4 (Peeled and Sliced In ¾-Inch Slices)
·   Red Potatoes 1 lb (Halved)
·   Cabbage Head half (sliced Into Wedges)
·   Fresh Thyme 1 tsp
·   Slice Parsley

Instructions

1. Preheat the to 180° F, then cook for 15 mins with the lid closed until ready. Use Super Smoke if it's available for the finest flavor.

2. Put the barbecued beef brisket (fat-side-up) on the grill and cook for 3 hours.

3. After 3 hours, increase the temperature to 250° F and warm for approximately 15 mins.

4. Combine the garlic cloves, corned meat, brown sugar, pickling spice, and onion in an oven or large saucepan.

5. Fill the bottle with Guinness. Securely cover the pan and cook for 4-5 hours, or until the meat is cooked. Flip the brisket halfway through the cooking period.

6. Simmer the broccoli, sliced carrots, thyme and potatoes for approximately an hour, or until the brisket is done, then cover and cook for another 30 mins, or until the vegetables are fork-tender.

7. Rest the meat for roughly 10 mins before slicing and serving.

Roasted Fall Vegetables

Preparation Time: 10 minutes
Cooking Time: 35 minutes
Servings: 8
Ingredients:
· Potatoes – ½ pound
· Brussels sprouts, halved – ½ pound
· Butternut squash, dice – ½ pound
· Cremini mushrooms, halved – 1 pint
· Salt – 1 tablespoon
· Ground black pepper – ¾ tablespoon
· Olive oil – 2 tablespoons

Directions:
1. In the meantime, take a large bowl, place potatoes in it, add salt and black pepper, drizzle with oil and then toss until coated.
2. Take a sheet tray and then spread seasoned potatoes on it.
3. When the grill has preheated, place sheet pan containing potatoes on the grilling rack and then grill for 15 minutes.
4. Then add mushrooms and sprouts into the pan, toss to coat and then continue grilling for 20 minutes until all the vegetables have turned nicely browned and thoroughly cooked.
5. Serve immediately.

Nutrition: Calories: 80 Carbs: 7g Fat: 6g Protein: 1g

Smoked Hummus with Roasted Vegetables

Prep Time: 55 mins
Serving: **Serves** 4
Ingredients
· 2 Cup cauliflower,
· salt
· 1 tbsp. minced garlic,
· 6 Tablespoon extra-virgin olive oil
· 1 tsp. salt
· 4 tbsp. lemon juice
· 1 1/2 Cup chickpeas
· 2 Cup fresh Brussels sprouts
· 1 sliced red onion,
· 1/3 Cup tahini
· 2 Whole portobello mushroom
· black pepper
· 2 Cup butternut squash

Instructions
· Drain and rinse the chickpeas before spreading them out on a sheet tray to make the hummus. Place tray on the grill grate and smoke for 15-20 minutes, or until the desired level of smoke is achieved.
· Combine smoked chickpeas, lemon juice, garlic, tahini, salt, and olive oil in the food processor or blender and process until fully combined but not entirely smooth. Place in a bowl and set aside.
· Raise the grill's temperature to a maximum and heat it.
· Drizzle the vegetables with olive oil and put them out on a sheet tray. Roast the vegetables on a sheet tray in the grill for 15-20 minutes, or until gently browned and cooked through.
· Place the hummus in a serving bowl or plate and top with the roasted vegetables to serve.
· Serve with pita bread and a drizzle of olive oil. Enjoy!

Smoked Cauliflower Curry with Chili

(Cooking Time 2 Hours)
Ingredients for 10 servings
· Whole cabbages (3-lb., 1.4-kg.)

The Spices
· Vegetable oil - 2 tablespoons
· Greek yogurt - 1 cup
· Lemon juice - 2 tablespoons
· Grated lemon zest - 1 teaspoon
· Chili powder - ½ teaspoon
· Ground cumin - 1 teaspoon
· Garlic powder - 1 tablespoon
· Curry powder - 1 tablespoon
· Kosher salt - ½ teaspoon
· Black pepper - ½ teaspoon
The Heat
· Apple wood pellet
Method
1. Combine Greek yogurt with vegetable oil with lemon juice.
2. Season the liquid mixture with grated lemon zest, chili powder, cumin, garlic powder, curry powder, salt, and black pepper. Stir until incorporated.
3. Rub the seasoning mixture over the cabbage and wrap it with aluminum foil.
4. Next, plug the wood pellet smoker then fill the hopper with the wood pellet. Turn the switch on and set the wood pellet smoker for indirect heat.
5. Adjust the temperature to 275°F (135°C) and let the wood pellet smoker reaches the desired temperature.
6. Place the wrapped cauliflower in the wood pellet smoker and smoke it for 2 hours.
7. Once it is done, remove the smoked cauliflower from the wood pellet smoker and let it rest for 15 minutes.
8. Unwrap the smoked cauliflower and serve.
9. Enjoy!

Grilled Corn With Honey Butter and Smoked Salt

Prep Time: 25 mins
Serving: **Serves** 4
Ingredients
· 1/2 Cup honey
· 2 tbsp. olive oil
· 1 tsp. black pepper
· 6 Pieces husked corn
· 1 tbsp. Smoked Salt
· 1/2 Cup butter
Instructions
· Set the temperature to Maximum and warm for 15 minutes with the lid covered when ready to cook.
· Brush the corn with oil and grill it, flipping it once in a while. Cook the corn thoroughly and slightly browned on the outside after about 10 minutes.
· Whisk the butter and honey together for 1 minute in the bowl of a stand mixer until light and fluffy.
· Brush warm corn over the top after removing it from the bowl. Season with pepper and smoked salt before serving.

Roasted Pumpkin Seeds

Preparation Time: 10 minutes
Cooking Time: 40 minutes
Servings: 8
Ingredients:
· Pumpkin seeds – 1 pound
· Salt – 1 tablespoon
· Olive oil – 1 tablespoon
Directions:
1. In the meantime, take a baking sheet, grease it with oil, spread pumpkin seeds on it and then stir until coated.
2. When the grill has preheated, place baking sheet containing pumpkin sees on the grilling rack and let grill for 20 minutes.
3. Season pumpkin seeds with salt, switch temperature of the grill to 325 degrees F, and continue grilling for 20 minutes until roasted.
4. When done, let pumpkin seeds cool slightly and then serve.
Nutrition: Calories: 130 Carbs: 13g Fat: 5g Protein 8g

Grilled Peach Salsa

Prep Time: 30 mins
Serving: **Serves** 6

Ingredients
· 1 minced jalapeño
· 4 heirloom tomato
· 4 tbsp. extra-virgin olive oil
· 1 Bunch minced cilantro leaves
· 2 Clove minced garlic,
· 4 peaches (halved)
· salt
· 2 lemons (juiced)
Instructions
· When set to cook, preheat the grill to 500 degrees Fahrenheit with the lid covered for 15 minutes.
· Season the sliced side of the peaches with salt and drizzle with olive oil. Place the peaches cut side down around the grill's perimeter. Cook for around 20 minutes until grill marks appear. It's ideal to choose peaches that aren't too ripe and are still firm.
· When the peaches are cool enough to handle, remove them from the grill and dice them. Combine diced minced cilantro, garlic, jalapeno, olive oil, tomatoes, and lime juice in a large mixing basin. Season with salt and pepper to taste. If necessary, add more lime juice.
· Serve with chips or a variety of other meals. Enjoy!

Smoked Vegetables

Preparation Time: 15 minutes
Cooking Time: 45 minutes
Servings: 4
Ingredients:
· Summer squash (sliced)
· Olive oil
· Balsamic vinegar
· Red onion
· Zucchini (sliced)
· Red pepper
· Black pepper
· Garlic (sliced)
· Sea salt
Directions:
1. Add all ingredients in a mixing bowl and combine.

2. Preheat smoker to 350F.
3. Smoked for 30 to 45 minutes or till well cooked through.
Nutrition: Calories- 120 Fat- 7g Sat fat- 1g Carbohydrates- 12g Protein- 2g Potassium- 514mg Sodium- 595mg Fiber- 2g Sugar- 7g Vitamin C- 67.3mg Vitamin A- 1225IU

Sweet Potato Fries

Preparation Time: 30 Minutes
Cooking Time: 40 Minutes
Servings: 4
Ingredients:
· Three sweet potatoes, sliced into strips
· Four tablespoons olive oil
· Two tablespoons fresh rosemary, chopped
· Salt and pepper to taste
Directions:
1. Set the Wood Pellet Grill Smoker wood pellet grill to 450 degrees F.
2. Preheat it for 10 minutes.
3. Spread the sweet potato strips in the baking pan.
4. Toss in olive oil and sprinkle with rosemary, salt, and pepper.
5. Cook for 15 minutes.
6. Flip and cook for another 15 minutes.
7. Flip and cook for ten more minutes.
Nutrition: Calories 118 Total fat 7.6g Total carbs 10.8g Protein 5.4g Sugars 3.7g Fiber 2.5g, Sodium 3500mg Potassium 536mg

Sweet Potato Steak Fries

Prep Time: 50 mins
Serving: **Serves** 4
Ingredients
· 4 Tablespoon extra-virgin olive oil
· salt and pepper
· 3 Whole sweet potatoes
· 2 tbsp. fresh chopped rosemary
Instructions
· Set the to 450°F and preheat for 15 minutes with the lid covered when you're ready to cook.

· Toss sweet potatoes with rosemary, pepper, salt and olive oil before serving. Place on a baking sheet lined with parchment paper and grill. Cook for 15 minutes, then flip and cook for another 40 to 45 minutes, or until gently browned and cooked through.
· Serve with a dipping sauce of your choice. Enjoy!

Wood Pellet Grill Smoker Grilled Zucchini

Preparation Time: 30 Minutes
Cooking Time: 10 Minutes
Servings: 4
Ingredients:
· Four zucchinis, sliced into strips
· One tablespoon sherry vinegar
· Two tablespoons olive oil
· Salt and pepper to taste
· Two fresh thyme, chopped

Directions:
1. Place the zucchini strips in a bowl.
2. Mix the remaining fixings and pour them into the zucchini.
3. Coat evenly.
4. Set the Wood Pellet Grill Smoker wood pellet grill to 350 degrees F.
5. Preheat for 15 minutes while the lid is closed.
6. Place the zucchini on the grill.
7. Cook for 3 minutes per side.

Nutrition: Calories 118 Total fat 7.6g Total carbs 10.8g Protein 5.4g Sugars 3.7g Fiber 2.5g, Sodium 3500mg Potassium 536mg

Grilled Asparagus and Honey Glazed Carrots

Prep Time: 50 mins
Serving: **Serves** 4
Ingredients
· 2 tbsp. honey
· 1 Bunch asparagus
· 2 tbsp. olive oil
· sea salt
· lemon zest
· 1 Pound carrot

Instructions
· All vegetables should be rinsed in cold water. Drizzle olive oil over asparagus and season generously with sea salt. Drizzle honey over the carrots and season with a pinch of salt.
· Preheat the to 350°F for 15 minutes with the lid closed when ready to cook.
· Cook the carrots first for 10-15 minutes on the grill, then add the asparagus and cook again for the next 15 to 20 minutes, or until they're cooked to your preference.
· Serve the asparagus with a sprinkling of fresh lemon zest. Enjoy!

Baked Parmesan Mushrooms

Preparation Time: 15 Minutes
Cooking Time: 15 Minutes
Servings: 8
Ingredients:
· Eight mushroom caps
· 1/2 cup Parmesan cheese, grated
· 1/2 teaspoon garlic salt
· 1/4 cup mayonnaise
· Pinch paprika
· Hot sauce

Directions:
1. Place mushroom caps in a baking pan.
2. Mix the remaining ingredients in a bowl.
3. Scoop the mixture onto the mushroom.
4. Place the baking pan on the grill.
5. Cook in the Wood Pellet Grill Smoker wood pellet grill at 350 degrees F for 15 minutes while the lid is closed.

Nutrition: Calories 118 Total fat 7.6g Total carbs 10.8g Protein 5.4g Sugars 3.7g Fiber 2.5g, Sodium 3500mg Potassium 536mg

Grilled Broccoli Rabe

Prep Time: 25 mins

Serving: **Serves** 4
Ingredients
· 4 tbsp. extra-virgin olive oil
· 1 lemon, halved
· kosher salt
· 4 Bunch broccoli rabe or broccolini
Instructions
· Set the to 450°F and preheat for 15 minutes with the lid covered when you're ready to cook.
· Spray the olive oil over the broccoli rabe on a dish or in a mixing bowl. Mix thoroughly with your hands, evenly coating the vegetables in oil. Season with a pinch of salt.
· Arrange the broccoli rabe in a single layer on the bottom grill grate. Cook for 5 to 15 minutes with the lid closed. On the first side, you want some color and a little char. Cook for a few minutes more on the other side.
· Move the broccoli rabe to a serving tray and drizzle half a lemon juice over the top.
· On the side, serve with extra lemon wedges. Enjoy!

Wood Pellet Grill Smoker Smoked Vegetables

Preparation Time: 5 Minutes
Cooking Time: 20 Minutes
Servings: 4
Ingredients
· 1 head of broccoli
· 4 carrots
· 16 oz snow peas
· 1 tbsp olive oil
· 1 cup mushrooms, chopped
· 1-1/2 tbsp pepper
· 1 tbsp garlic powder
Directions:
1. Cut broccoli and carrots into bite-size pieces. Add snow peas and combine.
2. Toss the veggies with oil and seasoning.
3. Now cover a pan, sheet, with parchment paper. Place veggies on top.
4. Meanwhile, set your wood pellet smoker to 180oF.
5. Place the pan into the smoker. Smoke for about 5 minutes.

6. Adjust smoker temperature to 400oF and continue cooking for another 10-15 minutes until slightly brown broccoli tips.
7. Remove, Serve, and enjoy.
Nutrition: Calories 111, Total fat 4g, Saturated fat 1g, Total Carbs 15g, Net Carbs 9g, Protein 5g, Sugars 7g, Fiber 6g, Sodium 0mg, Potassium 109mg

Grilled Street Corn

Prep Time: 20 mins
Serving: **Serves** 6
Ingredients
· 1 tbsp. chile powder
· 1 lime (zested and juiced)
· salt
· 1 finely chopped cilantro
· 6 ears corn, husked
· 1/2 cup chopped cilantro
· 1/4 cup mayonnaise
· 1/2 cup cotija cheese
· 1 As Needed extra-virgin olive oil
Instructions
· Set the to 450°F and heat for 15 minutes with the lid covered when you're ready to cook.
· Brush the corn with oil and lay it on the grill, flipping it once in a while.
· In a mixing dish, combine mayonnaise, chile powder, cilantro, lime juice, and zest while the corn grills. Season with salt and pepper.
· Cook the corn through and slightly brown on the outside for about 10 minutes. Remove the grill from the heat.
· Coat the corn with chile mayonnaise, then top with Cotija cheese and cilantro. Enjoy!

Roasted Vegetables

Preparation Time: 20 Minutes
Cooking Time: 20 to 40 Minutes
Servings: 4
Ingredients:
· 1 cup cauliflower floret

- 1 cup small mushroom, half
- One medium zucchini, sliced in half
- One medium yellow squash, sliced in half
- One medium-sized red pepper, chopped to 1.5-2 inches
- One small red onion, chopped to 1½-2 inch
o ounces small baby carrot
- Six mid-stem asparagus spears, cut into 1-inch pieces
- 1 cup cherry or grape tomato
- ¼ Extra virgin olive oil with cup roasted garlic flavor
- 2 tbsp. of balsamic vinegar
- Three garlic, chopped
- 1 tsp. dry time
- 1 tsp. dried oregano
- One teaspoon of garlic salt
- ½ teaspoon black pepper

Directions:

1. Put cauliflower florets, mushrooms, zucchini, yellow pumpkin, red peppers, red onions, carrots, asparagus, and tomatoes in a large bowl.
2. Add olive oil, balsamic vinegar, garlic, thyme, oregano, garlic salt, and black hu to add to the vegetables.
3. Gently throw the vegetables by hand until completely covered with olive oil, herbs, and spices.
4. Spread the seasoned vegetables evenly on a non-stick grill tray/bread/basket (about 15 x 12 inches).
5. Set the wood pellet smoker and grill for indirect cooking and preheat to 425 degrees Fahrenheit using all wood pellets.
6. Transfer the grill tray to a preheated smoker and grill and roast the vegetables for 20-40 minutes or until the vegetables are perfectly cooked. Please put it out immediately.

Nutrition: Calories: 114 Carbs: 17g Fat: 4g Protein: 3g

Grilled Chili-Lime Corn

Prep Time: 50 mins
Serving: **Serves** 8

Ingredients
- 1 tsp. Rub
- 1 tbsp. lime zest
- 12 ears corn
- 1/2 tsp. onion powder
- 2 tbsp. lemon juice
- 1 tsp. chili powder

Instructions

- Soak the corn ears in water for 4 to 8 hours, still in their husks.
- When prepared to cook, preheat the oven to 350°F with the lid covered for 15 minutes.
- Corn should be placed immediately on the barbecue grates. Cook for 45 minutes total, turning the corn every 15 minutes.
- In an oven-safe dish, combine lime zest, butter, lime juice, onion powder, Summer Shandy rub, and chili powder. Grill for 10 minutes. Remove the butter and corn from the grill.
- Pull back the corn husk but do not remove it, and remove the corn silk. Rub the corn with the melted chili-lime butter, using the corn husk as a handle. Enjoy!

Smoked Vegetables with Vinaigrette

Preparation Time: 15 minutes
Cooking Time: 4 hours
Servings: 4
Ingredients:
- Zucchini (thickly Sliced)
- Red potatoes (small in size & chopped)
- Red onions (chopped)
- Yellow medium squash (thickly sliced)
- Red pepper (chopped)

Vinaigrette **ingredients:**
- 1/3 cup olive oil
- 1/4 cup vinegar (balsamic)
- 2 teaspoons Dijon mustard
- Pepper
- Salt

Directions:

1. Add and combine balsamic vinegar, olive oil, Mustard, pepper and salt in a bowl.

2. In a casserole dish, add all the vegetables and combine. Coat the vegetables with the balsamic vinaigrette by tossing.

3. Preheat your smoker to 225F.

4. Put the dish with the vegetables in the smoker and smoke for 4 hours.

Nutrition: Calories- 225| Fat- 17.2g| Saturated fat- 2.5g| Carbohydrates- 16.8g| Protein- 2.8g| Sodium- 196mg| Cholesterol- 0mg| Calcium- 35mg| Potassium- 483mg| Iron- 1mg|

Roasted Sheet Pan Vegetables

Preparation Time: 15 minutes
Cooking Time: 30 minutes
Serving: 4
Ingredients

· 1 small purple cauliflower, cut into florets
· 1 small yellow cauliflower, cut into florets
· 4 cups butternut squash
· 2 cups mushroom, fresh
· 3 tablespoons extra virgin olive oil
· 2 teaspoons salt
· 2 teaspoons black pepper

Direction

1. Start making a fire to 3500F for 15 minutes. Use the best wood pellets when cooking.

2. Place the vegetables in a baking tray and season with olive oil, salt, and pepper. Toss to coat all vegetables.

3. Place in the grill and cook for 20 minutes. Make sure to shake the tray halfway through the cooking time for even cooking.

Nutrition Energy (calories): 151 kcal Protein: 5.62 g Fat: 5.22 g Carbohydrates: 25.44 g Calcium, Ca105 mg Magnesium, Mg75 mg Phosphorus, P150 mg Iron, Fe1.93 mg Fiber6.3 g Sugars, total6.57 g

Roasted Okra

(TOTAL COOK TIME 10 MINUTES)
INGREDIENTS FOR 4 SERVINGS
THE VEGETABLES

· Okra, stems trimmed and removed (1-lb, 0.45-kgs)

THE INGREDIENTS

· Chicken seasoning – 1 tablespoon
· Olive oil – 1 tablespoon
· Freshly squeezed juice of ½ lemon

THE WOOD PELLET GRILL

· Preheat your wood pellet grill to 450°F (232°C)
· Choose your favorite wood chips for this recipe

METHOD

1. In a bowl, combine the okra with chicken seasoning and olive oil, toss to combine, and transfer to a grill basket.

2. Place the basket on the middle of the hot grill and cook for 5 minutes, using tongs to shake the basket occasionally. Cook until the okra is charred and blistered in spots.

3. Remove from the grill and squeeze over the fresh lemon juice.

4. Serve.

CHAPTER 12: GAME RECIPES

6. Cook the birds until they reach an internal temperature of 160°F (71°C).

7. Serve and enjoy.

Mandarin Orange-Glazed Game Hens

(TOTAL COOK TIME 55 MINUTES)
INGREDIENTS FOR 4 SERVINGS
THE GAME
· 4 whole Cornish hens, giblets removed and patted dry
THE INGREDIENTS
· Onion powder – 2 tablespoons
· Granulated garlic – 1 tablespoon
· Sea salt – 1 tablespoon
· Ground ginger – 1 tablespoon
· 12-15 fresh thyme sprigs
· 2 large size mandarin oranges, quartered and seeded
· Olive oil – 2 tablespoons
· 1 bottle mandarin orange sauce, store-bought (12-ozs, 340-gms)
THE WOOD PELLET GRILL
· With the lid closed, set your pellet grill to 375°F (190°C) for 12-15 minutes

· Mesquite wood pellets are a good choice for this recipe
METHOD
1. First, in a small bowl, combine the onion powder with garlic, sea salt, and ground ginger.

2. Place 4-5 sprigs of fresh thyme into each of the bird's cavities and add 1 wedge of mandarin orange to each cavity.

3. Season each Cornish hen with the onion powder spice mix, and then rub all over with olive oil. Using kitchen twine, tie the bird's legs together.

4. Cook the game hens on the pellet grill for 20 minutes.

5. When 20 minutes have elapsed, brush each Cornish hen with the mandarin orange sauce.

Wild Elk Tenderloin Kabobs

Prep Time: 15 minutes | **Cooking Time**: 15 minutes | **Temperature:** 500F | **Servings**: 8
Ingredients:
o 3 lb. elk tenderloin, cut into 2-inch chunks
o 3 tbsp balsamic vinegar
o 3 tbsp olive oil
o 3 yellow squash, whole
o 3 zucchinis, whole
o 12 sweet peppers, small
o 12 cherry tomatoes
o 2 tbsp prime rib rub
Directions:
1. Drizzle elk tenderloin chunks with vinegar and oil, and then let sit in a bowl.
2. Meanwhile, chop squash and zucchini into ¾-inch thick coins.
3. Now cut ends off from the peppers and remove seeds.
4. Place peppers, tomatoes, zucchini, and squash coins in the bowl with tenderloin, then toss them. Add more vinegar and oil until everything is lightly coated.
5. Now generously add rib rub and continue tossing.
6. Stack meat and vegetables, alternating them onto the skewer.
7. In the meantime, preheat the grill to 500F with the lid closed for 15 minutes.
8. Place the kabobs on the grate directly and grill for 15 minutes.
9. Serve.
NUTRITION:
Calories: 349 | Fat: 9.7g | Carb: 20.7g | Protein: 46g

Chili-Rubbed Smoked Goat Shoulder

(TOTAL COOK TIME 30 HOURS 15 MINUTES)

INGREDIENTS FOR 4 SERVINGS

THE GAME

· 1 bone-in goat (5-lbs, 2.25-kgs)

THE RUB

· 4 Anaheim red chilies, chopped
· 2 fresh Thai bird chilies, chopped
· 8 garlic cloves, peeled and crushed
· A thumb of fresh ginger, peeled and chopped 3-ins (7.6-cms)
· A bunch of flat-leaf parsley leaves
· Sea salt – 2 tablespoons
· Extra-virgin olive oil – ¼ cup

THE WOOD PELLET GRILL

· Preheat your wood pellet grill for indirect smoking to 225-250°F (107-121°C)
· Choose your favorite wood pellets for this recipe

METHOD

1. Prepare the goat the day before you intend to serve.
2. Using a pestle and mortar, pound the Anaheim and Thai bird chilies along with the ginger, garlic, parsley leaves, and sea salt to form a coarse paste consistency. You will need to pound each ingredient before you add the next. Finally, add the oil, pounding to create a smooth paste.
3. Rub the mixture all over the meat, cover, and transfer to the fridge for 24 hours to marinate.
4. The following day, remove the meat from the fridge and keep any leftover rub to use as a baste during smoking.
5. Place the meat in the wood pellet grill and smoke for around 3 hours. Occasionally baste the meat with any leftover rub.
6. When 3 hours have elapsed, jiggle the leg to check for tenderness. If it feels as it could pull away easily from the joint, it is good to go. If not, continue to cook for another 3-4 hours. As a guide, the total cooking time is around 6-8 hours but will depend on the appliance's ability to maintain the temperature.
7. Serve and enjoy.

Grilled Quail, South Carolina Style

Prep Time: 20 minutes | **Cooking Time**: 20 minutes | **Temperature:** 400F | Servings: 4

Ingredients:

o 4 tbsp butter
o 1/2 grated onion
o 3-4 tbsp vegetable oil
o 1/2 cup yellow mustard
o 1/2 cup sugar, brown
o 1/2 cup cider vinegar
o 1 tbsp dry mustard
o 1 tbsp cayenne
o Salt to taste
o 8-16 quails

Directions:

1. Melt butter in a pan and sauté onions for 4 minutes.
2. Add all other ingredients except quails and simmer for 20 minutes. Simmer slowly.
3. Buzz in a blender to make a smooth sauce.
4. Flatten and remove quail's backbone by cutting along the side using kitchen shears. Place the quails on a cutting board with the breast side up, then press them to flatten.
5. Meanwhile, preheat the grill to 400F and place the quails with the breast side up.
6. Grill the quails with the lid closed for about 5 minutes. Rub the breast side using your sauce as it cooks.
7. Turn over the quails and grill for another 2 minutes with the lid open.
8. Turn over again and rub with sauce once more, cover your grill and cook for 2 to 4 minutes.
9. Remove quails from the grill and rub with sauce once more.

NUTRITION:

Calories: 673 | Fat: 40g | Carb: 9g | Protein: 45g

Game Day Chicken Drumsticks

Preparation Time: 15 minutes
Cooking Time: 1 hour
Servings: 8
Ingredients:
For Brine:

- ½ C. brown sugar
- ½ C. kosher salt
- 5 C. water
- 2 (12-oz.) bottles beer
- 8 chicken drumsticks
- For Coating:
- ¼ C. olive oil
- ½ C. BBQ rub
- 1 tbsp. fresh parsley, minced
- 1 tbsp. fresh chives, minced
- ¾ C. BBQ sauce
- ¼ C. beer

Directions:
1. For brine: in a bucket, dissolve brown sugar and kosher salt in water and beer.
2. Place the chicken drumsticks in brine and refrigerate, covered for about 3 hours.
3. Set the temperature of Grill to 275 degrees F and preheat with closed lid for 15 mins.
4. Remove chicken drumsticks from brine and rinse under cold running water.
5. With paper towels, pat dry chicken drumsticks.
6. Coat drumsticks with olive oil and rub with BBQ rub evenly.
7. Sprinkle the drumsticks with parsley and chives.
8. Arrange the chicken drumsticks onto the grill and cook for about 45 mins.
9. Meanwhile, in a bowl, mix together BBQ sauce and beer.
10. Remove from grill and coat the drumsticks with BBQ sauce evenly.
11. Cook for about 15 mins more.
12. Serve immediately.

Nutrition: Calories per serving: 448 Carbohydrates: 20.5g Protein: 47.2g Fat: 16.1g Sugar: 14.9g Sodium: 9700mg Fiber: 0.2g

Smoked Pheasant

Prep Time: 15 minutes | **Cooking Time**: 1 hour 45 minutes| **Temperature**: 275F| **Servings**: 3

Ingredients:
o 3 whole pheasant
o 3 tbsp smoky rooster booster rub
o Saskatchewan rub as needed
o 1 quartered red bell pepper, whole, and core removed
o 1 white onion, whole and sliced into thin sections
o 4 tbsp olive oil
o Pepper to taste
o Salt to taste
o 1 whole box rice pilaf

Directions:
1. Preheat the grill to 275F while the lid closed for about 10 to 15 minutes.
2. Clean pheasant thighs and breasts, then rinse and place in a zip lock bag.
3. Add rooster booster rub and a generous amount of Saskatchewan rub. Shake well and set aside.
4. Brush pepper and onions lightly using oil, then splash with pepper and salt. Place them on a tin foil and to one side of the grill.
5. Smoke the veggies for about 1 hour, then place your pheasant on the grill.
6. Cook for 30 to 45 minutes.
7. Remove and serve with rice pilaf.

NUTRITION:
Calories: 926|Fat: 24.9g| Carb: 4.8g| Protein: 161g

Smoked Gator Ribs

(TOTAL COOK TIME 10 HOURS 45 MINUTES)
INGREDIENTS FOR 6-8 SERVINGS
THE GAME
- 10-12 small alligator ribs (5-lbs, 2.25-kgs)

THE DRY RUB
- Smoked paprika – 2 tablespoons
- Garlic powder – 1 tablespoon
- Onion powder – 1 tablespoon
- Dried oregano – 1 teaspoon
- Kosher salt – 2 teaspoons
- Freshly ground black pepper – ½ teaspoon
- Cayenne pepper – ½ teaspoon

THE INGREDIENTS
- Buttermilk – 2 cups
- Louisiana hot sauce, any brand – ½ tablespoon

- Yellow mustard – ¼ cup
- BBQ sauce, of choice – 2 cups

THE WOOD PELLET GRILL
- Preheat your wood pellet grill for indirect cooking to 250°F (121°C)
- Use your favorite wood pellets for this recipe

METHOD
1. In a small bowl, combine the rub ingredients (smoked paprika, garlic powder, onion powder, dried oregano, kosher salt, black pepper, and cayenne).
2. Combine the buttermilk with the hot sauce and 1 tablespoon of the rub from Step 1, until fully incorporated. Store the remaining dry rub until needed.
3. Divide the ribs between 2 ziplock bags, and cover with the buttermilk mixture. Seal the ziplock bags and place in the fridge overnight.
4. The following day, remove the ribs from the buttermilk mixture, rinse and pat dry. Next, cover the ribs with yellow mustard and season with the remaining dry rub.
5. Cook the ribs, covered for around 2 ½ hours, until tender.
6. Brush all over with BBQ sauce, and return to the heat for 10 minutes until the sauce is sticky.
7. Remove, set aside to rest for 4-6 minutes before serving.

Smoked Moose Roast with Cranberry-Mint Sauce

Prep Time: 2 hours | **Cooking Time**: 1 hour 15 minutes | **Temperature**: 275F|
Servings: 6
Ingredients:
o 2-1/2 lbs. moose loin roast
o Salt to taste, kosher
o 2 tbsp olive oil
o Favorite rub
o 1 can, 14-oz, cranberry sauce, whole berry
o 1/4 tbsp cardamom, ground
o 1 tbsp chopped mint, fresh and packed
o Cracked pepper to taste, fresh

Directions:
1. Tie moose roast using kitchen wire and season with salt, then let it sit for 2 hours at room temperature. Then pat dry using paper towels.
2. Preheat the grill to 275F.
3. Meanwhile, heat oil in a pan until it smokes.
4. Now sear your meat until a golden crust on all sides.
5. Remove meat from the pan and splash with rub generously.
6. Smoke the meat in your grill for 1 hour until the internal temperature reads 125F.
7. Remove meat and loosely wrap in foil, then allow your meat to carry over until 135F for medium-rare.
8. In the meantime, combine cranberry sauce, cardamom, mint, pepper, and salt. Heat on low, occasionally stirring until warmed through.
9. Rest for 15 minutes.
10. Slice and serve with sauce.

NUTRITION:
Calories: 850 |Fat: 12.4g| Carb: 6.3g| Protein: 132.4g

Venison Meatloaf

(TOTAL COOK TIME 1 HOUR 35 MINUTES)
INGREDIENTS FOR 4 SERVINGS
THE GAME
- Ground venison (2-lbs, 0.9-kgs)
- Nonstick cooking spray

THE INGREDIENTS
- 1 whole onion, peeled and diced
- 1 egg, beaten
- Salt and black pepper
- Breadcrumbs - 1 cup
- Milk – 1 cup
- Worcestershire sauce – 1 tablespoon
- Onion soup mix (1-oz, 28-gms)

THE GLAZE
- Ketchup – ¼ cup
- Brown sugar – ¼ cup
- Apple cider vinegar – ¼ cuop

THE WOOD PELLET GRILL

· With the lid closed, preheat your wood pellet grill to 350°F (177°C)
· Use your choice of big game wood pellets
METHOD
1. Spritz a loaf pan with nonstick cooking spray.
2. In a bowl, using your hands, combine the ground venison with the onion, beaten egg, salt, black pepper, breadcrumbs, milk, Worcestershire sauce, and onion soup mix. Take care not to overwork the mixture.
3. In a small bowl, for the glaze, combine the ketchup with brown sugar and apple cider vinegar.
4. Spread approximately half of the ketchup glaze on the bottom and up the sides of the loaf pan.
5. Add the venison meatloaf mixture to the pan and spread the remaining glaze evenly over the top.
6. Place directly on the grill grate and bake for 75 minutes or until the meatloaf registers 165°F (74°C).
7. Remove the meatloaf from the pellet grill and allow to cool for 2-3 minutes before slicing and serving.

Baked venison Meatloaf

Prep Time: 10 minutes | **Cooking Time**: 1 hour 30 minutes | **Temperature**: 500F|
Servings: 6
Ingredients:
- 2 pounds venison, ground
- 1-pound pork, ground
- 1 cup breadcrumbs
- 1 cup milk
- 2 tbsp. onion, diced
- 3 tbsp. salt
- 1 tbsp. black pepper
- ½ tbsp. thyme
- 1 ½ pounds parsnips, chopped
- 1 ½ pounds russet potatoes, chopped
- ¼ cup butter

Directions:
1. Fire the grill to 500F. Close the lid and preheat for 15 minutes.

2. Combine all ingredients in a bowl, place the mixture in a greased loaf pan.
3. Place in the grill and cook for 1 hour and 30 minutes or until the internal temperature reads at 160F.
NUTRITION:
Calories: 668|Fat: 22g| Carb: 45.7g| Protein: 70.4g

Game Day Sausage Snacks

Prep time: 15 mins
Cook time: 5 mins
Servings: 15
Ingredients
· 12 ounces ground pork sausage
· 12 ounces spicy ground pork sausage
· 1 (16 ounce) jar processed cheese sauce
· 1 (1 pound) loaf sliced pumpernickel party bread
Instructions
1. Preheat the oven to broil.
2. In a big, deep pan, combine the ground pork sausage and the spicy ground pork sausage. Cook until uniformly browned over medium-high heat. Sausage should be drained. Add the processed cheese sauce to the mix. On a medium baking sheet, arrange pumpernickel party bread pieces in a single layer. Evenly distribute the sausage mixture on each piece.
3. Broil the bread pieces for 3 to 5 minutes, until toasted, checking often.
Difficulty: 2
Nutrition: Calories: 685kcal | Carbohydrates: 33 | Protein: 35g | Fat 20g | Saturated fat 29g | Fiber: 6g | Sugar: 5

Hickory Smoked Cornish Game Hen Recipe

Preparation Time: 10 minutes
Cooking Time: 1 hour
Servings: 4
Ingredients

· 1 tbsp. Neely's dry rub
· 1 tbsp. kosher salt, plus more for seasonings
· 1 tsp. freshly ground black pepper, plus more for seasonings
· 4 (1 1/2 to 2 lbs.) Cornish game hens, washed and dried well
· 2 tbsp. butter
· One shallot, finely chopped
· 1 cup chicken broth
· 3/4 cup freshly squeezed orange juice
· 2 tbsp. apple cider vinegar
· hot sauce dash

Directions

1. Whisk together the dry mixture, salt and pepper in a small mixing bowl. Then season the washed and dried game hens with the rub and place them on a baking sheet. Close with plastic wrap and refrigerate for 1 hour.

2. Meanwhile, in a little saucepan over medium heat, add butter to melt. When melted, add the shallots and sauté until tender—season with salt and pepper, to taste. Then add the chicken broth and orange juice. Boil and reduce down to 1/2 cup, about ten minutes. It will quickly coat the trunk of a spoon and become slightly syrupy. When it reduced, add the apple cider vinegar and hot sauce—taste for seasoning.

3. Prepare your grill/smoker for indirect heat with charcoal and hickory chips. Sustain your temperature at 275 degrees F.

4. Arrange the overall game hens on the grill and cover—smoke for 40 minutes. Open the cover and brush the hens with the glaze, making sure to find yourself in all of the nooks and crannies. Then cover the grill and smoke for an additional 15 minutes. Take away the hens from the grill to a serving platter and let rest, covered with foil for a quarter-hour before serving.

Nutrition: Energy (calories): 177 kcal Protein: 13.43 g Fat: 9.98 g Carbohydrates: 8.04 g

Grilled Venison Kabob

Prep Time: 10 minutes | **Cooking Time**: 15 minutes | **Temperature:** 500F| **Servings**: 6

Ingredients:

• 1 venison, blackstrap steaks cut into large cubes
• 2 whole red onion, quartered
• 2 whole green bell pepper, sliced into big squares
• Oil as needs
• Salt and pepper to taste

Directions:

1. Place all ingredients in a bowl.
2. Toss to coat the meat and vegetables with oil and seasoning.
3. Thread the meat and vegetables into the metal skewers in an alternating manner.
4. Fire the grill to 500F.
5. Close the lid and preheat for 15 minutes.
6. Place the kabobs on the grill grate and cook for 15 minutes.
7. Turn once halfway through the cooking time.
8. Serve.

NUTRITION:

Calories: 267|Fat: 10.4| Carb: 10.1g| Protein: 32.4g

Grilled Game Hens with Rosemary sprig

Preparation Time: 20 minutes
Smoking Time: 60minutes
Temperature: 165⁰F
Portion: 4
Recommended pellets: Hardwood Lumber pellets, Hickory Pellets
Ingredients:
The Meat:
•4 Game hens, giblets removed
The Rub:
•4 tbsp. melted butter, unsalted
•4 tsp. chicken rub
•Other **Ingredients:**
•4 rosemary sprig
•The Fire:

•According to the user manual, fill the grill's hopper with 2 pounds of wood pellets, any flavor, and set the grill.

•Switch on the grill, select the "smoke" setting, shut with the lid, and use the control panel to set the temperature to 375 degrees F.

•Wait for 10 to 15 minutes or until the fire starts in the grill and it reaches the set temperature.

Directions:

1.In the meantime, prepare hens and for this, rinse well, pat dry, then tuck their wings and tie their legs by using a kitchen string.

2.Then rub melted butter outside of hens, sprinkle with chicken rub, and then place a sprig of rosemary into the cavity of each hen.

3.When the grill has preheated, place hens on the grilling rack and grill for 1 hour or until the control panel shows 165 degrees F's internal temperature, turning halfway.

4.When done, remove hens from the grill and let them rest for 5 minutes.

5.Serve immediately.

Nutrition: Amount per 143 g = 1 serving(s) Energy (calories): 276 kcal Protein: 30.09 g Fat: 16.66 g Carbohydrates: 0.05 g

Grill-Roasted Venison

Prep Time: 6 minutes | **Cooking Time**: 35 minutes | **Temperature**: 375F| **Servings**: 8

Ingredients:

o 2 Pounds of Venison Roast, about 8 rib

o 1 tbsp. of extra-virgin olive oil

o As needed of Prime Rib Rub

Directions:

1.   Se the grill to 375F and preheat with the lid closed for 15 minutes.

2.   Rub the olive oil on top of the roast and coat well. Season the venison with rib rub.

3.   Put the roast on top of the grill grate with bone side down.

4.   Cook for 20 to 25 minutes or until the internal temperature reaches about 125F at the thickcst part of the meat.

5.   Remove the meat from the grill and rest for 10 minutes.

6.   Serve.

NUTRITION:

Calories: 292.9|Fat: 2.3g| Carb: 3g| Protein: 29.4g

Teriyaki Marinade

(TOTAL COOK TIME 10 MINUTES)
INGREDIENTS FOR 2 CUPS
THE INGREDIENTS

·   Soy sauce – 1 cup
·   Brown sugar – ¾ cup
·   Water – ½ cup
·   Vegetable oil – 1 tablespoon
·   White vinegar – 1 tablespoon
·   4 garlic cloves, peeled and minced
·   3 green onions, thinly sliced

METHOD

1.   Add all the ingredients (soy sauce, brown sugar, water, vegetable, vinegar, garlic, and green onions) to a bowl and stir to combine until the sugar dissolves.

2.   Add your choice of meat or seafood to the marinade, toss to combine, and chill* until ready to cook.

*For fish marinate for 1 hour, poultry marinate for 2-10 hours, red meat marinate for 4-24 hours.

Spatchcocked Quail with Smoked Fruit

Prep Time: 20 minutes| **Cooking Time**: 1 hour | **Temperature**: 225F| **Servings**: 4

Ingredients:

•   4 quail, spatchcocked
•   2 tsp. salt
•   2 tsp. ground black pepper
•   2 tsp. garlic powder
•   4 ripe peaches or pears
•   4 tbsp. (½ stick) salted butter, softened
•   1 tbsp. sugar
•   1 tsp. ground cinnamon

Directions:

1.	Preheat the grill to 225F with the lid closed.
2.	Season, the quail with salt, pepper, and garlic powder.
3.	Cut the pears in half and remove the pits.
4.	In a bowl, combine the butter, sugar, and cinnamon. Set aside.
5.	Arrange the quail on the grill grate and close the lid.

nu:
Calories: 452|Fat: 25g| Carb: 37g| Protein: 22.6g

Cornish Game Hen

Preparation time: 30 minutes
Smoking time: 2-3 hours
Temperature: 275⁰F
Portion: 4
Recommended Pellet: Alder
Ingredients:
• 2 Cornish Game Hens
• Salt as needed
• Fresh ground pepper as needed
• 1 cup quick-cooking seasoned browned rice
• 1 small onion, chopped
• ½ cup orange juice, squeezed
• ½ cup apricot jelly
Directions:
1.Pre-heat your smoker to 275 degrees Fahrenheit
2.Season the birds with pepper and salt
3.Take a small saucepan over low heat and add two tablespoons of butter, melt the butter and stir in rice and onion
4.Stuff the hens with the rice mix and secure the legs with twine
5.Rinse the saucepan and put it back to low heat
6.Melt remaining two tablespoons of butter and stir in orange juice alongside apricot jelly
7.Whisk until smooth
8.Baste the hen with the jelly glaze
9.Transfer the birds to your smoker and smoke for 2-3 hours until the internal temperature reaches 170 degrees Fahrenheit
10.Brush with more jelly, and enjoy it!

Nutrition:
Amount per 201 g
Energy (calories): 232 kcal
Protein: 30.07 g
Fat: 4.96 g
Carbohydrates: 16.47 g

Big Game Day BBQ Ribs

Prep time: 25 min
Cook time: 3 hours
Serving: 6
Pellets any blend
Difficulty: hard
Ingredients
2 Rack St. Louis-Style Ribs
1/4 cup Big Game Rub
1 cup BBQ apricot sauce
1 cup nectarine nectar
Instructions
• Ribs should be washed and dried. Remove the membrane from the rear of the ribs.
• When ready to cook, warm the Wood pellet to 275°F with the lid covered for 15 minutes.
• Apply a thin layer of rub to the back and sides of the ribs. Allow 5 minutes for resting. Turn the ribs over, apply a thick layer of rub to the top, and set aside for 15 minutes to "sweat."
• Place the ribs directly on the barbecue grate, bone side down, and cook for 2 to 2-1/2 hours. Check for doneness; the meat should be pulling away from the bones, and the internal temperature should be 160°F.
• Remove the ribs from the grill and place them on top of a piece of foil, meat side down. Wrap foil firmly over the ribs to form a package and pour 1/2 cup peach nectar over them.
• Return the ribs to the grill, bone side up, for another 30 to 45 minutes, or until cooked but not falling-apart tender.
• Remove the ribs from the grill and coat the front and back with sauce. Return the ribs to the Wood pellet for 15 minutes to let the sauce solidify.

- Remove from the oven, set aside for 15 minutes to cool before slicing and serving. Enjoy!

Nutritional facts
- Fat 88 g
- Calories 1590 kcal
- Carbs 143 g
- Protein 62 g

Smoked Whole Duck

Preparation time: 15 minutes
Smoking time: 2 hours 30 minutes
Temperature: 300°F
Portion: 4
Recommended Pellet: hickory wood
Ingredients:
- 2 tbsp. of baking soda
- 1 tbsp. of Chinese five spices
- 1 thawed duck
- 1 Granny smith cored and diced apple
- 1 quartered sliced orange
- 2 tbsp. of chicken seasoning, divided

Directions:
1.Start by washing the duck under cool running water from the inside and out; then pat the meat dry with clean paper towels
2.Combine the Chicken seasoning and the Chinese Five spice; then combine with the baking soda for extra crispy skin
3.Season the duck from the inside and out
4.Tuck the apple and the orange and apple slices into the cavity.
5.Turn your Wood Pellet Smoker Grill to smoke model; then let the fire catch and set it to about 300°F to preheat
6.Place the duck on the grill grate or in a pan. Roast for about 2 ½ hours at a temperature of about 160°F
7.Place the foil loosely on top of the duck and let rest for about 15 minutes.
8.Serve and enjoy your delicious dish!
Nutrition:
Amount per 184 g
= 1 serving(s)
Energy (calories): 310 kcal
Protein: 23.8 g

Fat: 20.62 g
Carbohydrates: 5.92 g

Wild Game Chili

Preparation Time: 50 minutes
Cooking Time: 6 hours
Servings: 8-12 servings
Ingredients:
- 3 slices of bacon, chopped
- Venison or wild hog, ground into small cubes (3-lb, 1.4-kgs)
- 1 large onion, peeled, finely chopped
- Beer
- Canned chopped green chilies
- Cumin seeds, crushed – 1 tablespoon
- Chili seasoning mix, of choice 2/3 cup
- Tomato juice
- Hot pepper sauce – 1 tablespoon
- White cornmeal – ½ cup

Directions:
1. In a frying pan, sauté the bacon with the onions, until the bacon is just browned.
2. Add the game and sear all over.
3. In a pan, add 1½ cups of beer along with the green chilies, cumin, and chili mix, simmering until it is a gravy-like consistency.
4. Add the remaining beer followed by the tomato juice and hot pepper sauce.
5. Pour the mixture into a pan and transfer to the smoker.
6. Smoke-cook for between 4-6 hours.
7. Before serving, add the cornmeal and stir to thicken and combine.
8. Simmer for 20 minutes and serve with flour tortillas.
Nutrition Energy (calories): 557 kcal Protein: 21.69 g Fat: 6.34 g Carbohydrates: 107.3 g Calcium, Ca43 mg
Magnesium, Mg238 mg Phosphorus, P589 mg Iron, Fe3.73 mg Fiber10 g

Braised Wild Game Shredded Tacos

Prep time: 20 min
Cook time: 9 hr.
Serving: 8-12
Pellets any blend
Difficulty: medium

Ingredients:

- Three garlic cloves (fresh)
- 4-pound big wild game neck chops
- Four tbsp. butter (from grass-fed cows)
- Bone broth, 3/4 cup
- 2 tsp. coffee rub
- Two tbsp. rub for prime rib
- Four jalapeno peppers
- 2 tbsp. Sriracha BBQ Glaze by Sugar Lips
- a dozen tortillas
- Three sliced avocados
- Two bunches of chopped cilantros

Instructions:

- Set your grill to 250 degrees Fahrenheit and preheat for 15 minutes with the lid covered until you're ready to cook.
- Place a large Dutch oven on the burner with the grass-fed butter and garlic. Sear the game meat on both sides in the Dutch oven.
- Remove from the grill and season with the Wood pellet Prime Rib and Coffee rubs.
- Cover the saucepan and add the bone broth. Wrap foil around the lids' seams firmly.
- Cook for 8 hours without looking by placing the pot on the barbecue grate. Cooking times will vary based on the temperature of the set and the ambient temperature.
- Remove the cover and use a fork to twist the meat. Drizzle Sriracha Sugar Lips on top and cover with the lid if the meat readily rips. If the meat is still not falling apart, cover and simmer for another hour or until tender.
- Reduce the temperature of the grill to 180 degrees. Place the jalapenos on the grill grate for 20 minutes to smoke.
- Wrap a stack of tortillas in foil and place them on the grill to warm up with 10 minutes left.
- Remove the meat from the Dutch oven and shred with two big forks. Cover saucepan with another sprinkle of Sriracha Sugar Lips.
- Remove the jalapenos and tortillas from the grill and slice them.
- Shredded meat, jalapenos, and avocados go well together in tacos. Serve with cilantro as a garnish. Enjoy!

Nutritional facts

- Fats16.5 g
- Calories403.3
- Carbs27.6 g
- Protein43.7 g

Yogurt Marinade Smoked Quails with Peanut Chili Sauce

(Cooking Time 2 hours 10 minutes)
Ingredients for 10 servings

- Quails (3-lb., 1.4-kg.)

The Marinade

- Greek yogurt - 1 ½ cup
- Lemon juice - 3 tablespoons
- Grated ginger - 1 teaspoon
- Paprika - 1 tablespoon
- Ground coriander - 1 tablespoon
- Ground cumin - 1 teaspoon
- Ground turmeric - ½ teaspoon
- Chopped cilantro - 3 tablespoons
- Kosher salt - ½ teaspoon

The Sauce

- Peanut butter - ¼ cup
- Roasted peanut - ¼ cup
- Chopped cilantro - 2 tablespoons
- Green chili flakes - 1 teaspoon
- Lemon juice - 1 tablespoon
- Soy sauce - 1 teaspoon
- Brown sugar - 1 teaspoon
- Ginger powder - ¼ teaspoon
- Garlic powder - ¼ teaspoon
- Sesame oil - 1 teaspoon

The Heat

- Hickory wood pellet

Method

1. Pour yogurt into a container together with lemon juice.
2. Season the liquid mixture with grated ginger, paprika, coriander, cumin, turmeric, cilantro, and salt. Mix well.

3. Rub the quails with the yogurt mixture and marinate them for at least 4 hours. Store them in the fridge to keep the quails fresh.

4. After 4 hours, take the quails out of the fridge and thaw them at room temperature.

5. Next, plug the wood pellet smoker then fill the hopper with the wood pellet. Turn the switch on and set the wood pellet smoker for indirect heat.

6. Adjust the temperature to 250°F (121°C) and let the wood pellet smoker reaches the desired temperature.

7. Arrange the marinated quails on the grill grate inside the wood pellet smoker and smoke them for 2 hours.

8. In the meantime, place the entire sauce ingredients--peanut butter, roasted peanuts, chopped cilantro, chili flakes, lemon juice, soy sauce, brown sugar, ginger powder, garlic powder, and sesame oil in a food processor. Process until smooth.

9. Check the internal temperature of the smoked quails and once it reaches 165°F (74°C), remove the smoked quails from the wood pellet smoker.

10. Transfer the smoked quails to a serving dish and serve.

11. Enjoy!

Smoked and Braised Duck Legs

Prep time: 30 min
Cook time: 2 hr.
Serving: 4
Pellets any blend
Difficulty: medium
Ingredients
- Two tbsp. cayenne pepper
- 6 Large Duck Legs
- 2 Tablespoon Salt 1
- 1 Tablespoon of Brown Sugar
- 2 tbsp. Canola Oil
- one bunch of fresh thyme
- 2 halved large carrots
- 2 halved medium onions
- Four garlic cloves
- Two celery stalks
- Rosemary, one sprig
- Two bay leaves, whole
- 3 quarts of your favourite stock
- 2 Cups Rose Wein

Instructions
- Combine the salt, pepper, sugar, and thyme the night before you intend to cook. Dry the duck legs and massage them with the mixture. Place duck legs in a pan on a cooling rack and refrigerate overnight.
- Remove the duck legs from the refrigerator and rinse them with cold water before patting them dry with paper towels.
- When ready to cook, preheat the Wood pellet to 450°F with the lid covered for 15 minutes.
- Preheat the grill for 15 to 20 minutes with a big cast iron pan on top. Pour in enough oil to coat the bottom of the pan.
- Cook for 10 to 15 minutes, or until skin is crisp and mahogany brown, with duck legs skin-side down in the pan.
- Cook for another 5 minutes on the other side. Flip the duck legs over so the flat side is facing up.
- Combine all of the aromatics, the red wine, and enough stock to cover the duck 3/4 of the way.
- Reduce the temperature of the Wood Palette to 350°F and braise the duck legs for 2 hours, or until extremely delicate. Reduce the temperature of the Wood Palette to 180°F for the final 20 minutes of cooking to infuse the legs with an additional smoky flavour.
- Transfer the duck legs to a plate and cover with foil to keep warm.
- Strain the braising liquid into a saucepan and simmer until slightly thickened to create the sauce.
- To taste, season with salt and pepper. Serve the duck legs with a sauce and veggies that have been cooked. Enjoy!

Nutritional facts
- Fat 10.4g
- Calories 309.7
- Carbs 0g
- Protein 50.6g

Seared Duck Breasts

Prep time: 5 min
Cook time: 10 min
Serving: 4
Pellets any blend
Difficulty: easy
Ingredients
- 3 Ounce Chicken Rub
- 3 Breasts of Duck

Instructions
- When ready to cook, preheat the Wood pellet to 500°F with the lid covered for 15 minutes.
- Wood pellet Chicken Rub is used to season the bottoms of duck breasts.
- Allow 10 minutes for the duck breasts to rest.
- Cook for 4 minutes with the skin side down on the grill. Grill for a further 4 minutes on the opposite side.
- When the breasts have reached an internal temperature of 130°F, remove them from the Wood pellet (for medium-rare). The duck will continue to cook until it reaches a final internal temperature of 135 degrees Fahrenheit.
- Allow 10 minutes to settle before slicing. Enjoy!

Nutritional facts
- Fat 4.4g
- Calories 243.6
- Carbs 0g
- Protein 48g

Smoked Duck Breast Bacon

Prep time: 30 min
Cook time: 30 min
Serving: 6
Pellets any blend
Difficulty: easy
Ingredients
- 2 Cups Strong Coffee, Freshly Brewed
- 2 1/2 Tablespoon Curing Salt
- 4 cup water
- 1 cup Kosher salt
- a half-cup of dark brown sugar
- Molasses, 1/4 cup
- Duck Breasts, 3 Pounds (Skin-On)
- 3 quarts ice

Instructions
- In a jar with a cover, combine 4 cups of water, coffee, kosher salt, brown sugar, and curing salt. Mix until the solids are completely dissolved. Stir in the molasses until it's fully dissolved. Stir, 3 cups ice, until the remedy is cold
- Add the duck breasts to the cure and keep them immersed by weighing them down with a big plate. Refrigerate for at least 6 hours in a covered container.
- Remove the duck breasts from the brine and discard the brine. Duck breasts should be rinsed under cold running water and patted dry.
- When ready to cook, warm the Wood pellet to 165°F with the lid covered for 15 minutes. If Super Smoke is available, use it for the best taste.
- Smoke the duck breasts for 2 hours on the grill grate.
- Cool the duck fully before wrapping it in plastic wrap and storing it in the fridge until ready to use.
- To cook, finely slice the breast and fry it in a skillet like pig bacon. Alternatively, thinly slice the breast, put on a wood plank heated to 350°F, and cook for 10 minutes on each side. Enjoy!

Nutritional facts
- Fat 7g
- Calories 110
- Carbs 1g
- Protein 3g

Pan-Roasted Game Birds

Prep time: 10 minutes | **Cook time**: 1 hour | **Serves** 6
4 pounds (1.8 kg) game birds
4 tablespoons melted butter, divided
Salt and black pepper, to taste
2 whole lemons, halved
1 bunch fresh thyme
1 bunch fresh parsley
1 bunch fresh rosemary

1. When ready to cook, set grill temperature to high and preheat, lid closed for 15 minutes. Put a large cast iron skillet on the grill while preheating.

2. Rub 2 tablespoons of butter all over the game birds and season the inside and outside with salt and pepper.

3. Stuff the cavity of each bird of half a lemon, a sprig of parsley, thyme, and rosemary. Truss the birds by simply tying the legs together with string.

4. Add the remaining 2 tablespoons of butter to the cast iron skillet on the grill. Place the birds in the hot cast iron skillet and roast for 45 to 60 minutes, or until the internal temperature reaches 165°F (74°C).

5. Rest for 10 minutes before serving.

Per Serving

Calories: 416 | Fat: 12g | Carbs: 3g | Protein: 70g | Sugar: 1g | Sodium: 268mg

Celery and Apple Stuffed Smoked Cornish Hen with Cinnamon Rub

(Cooking Time 2 hours 10 minutes)

Ingredients for 10 servings

· Cornish hens (6-lb., 2.7-kg.)

The Rub

· Brown sugar - ¾ cup
· Smoked paprika - ½ cup
· Kosher salt - 1 ½ teaspoon
· Chili powder - 1 tablespoon
· Garlic powder - 1 tablespoon
· Onion powder - 2 teaspoons
· Black pepper - ½ teaspoon
· Ground cinnamon - ½ teaspoon
· Cayenne pepper - 1 teaspoon

The Stuff

· Fresh lemons - 2
· Fresh apples - 2
· Chopped leek - 2 tablespoons
· Chopped celery stalks - 2 tablespoons

The Heat

· Cherry wood pellet

Method

1. Combine the rub ingredients--brown sugar, smoked paprika, kosher salt, chili powder, garlic powder, onion powder, black pepper, cinnamon, and cayenne pepper. Mix well.

2. Rub the spice mixture over the Cornish hens, including the cavity, and set aside.

3. Next, cut lemon and apples into slices.

4. Combine the sliced lemon and apple with chopped leek and celery stalks. Mix well.

5. Fill the cavity with the stuff mixture and set aside.

6. After that, plug the wood pellet smoker then fill the hopper with the wood pellet. Turn the switch on and set the wood pellet smoker for indirect heat.

7. Adjust the temperature to 250°F (121°C) and let the wood pellet smoker reaches the desired temperature.

8. Place the stuffed Cornish hens on the grill grate inside the wood pellet smoker and smoke them for 2 hours.

9. Once the internal temperature of the smoked Cornish hens reaches 165°F (74°C), remove them from the wood pellet smoker.

10. Transfer the smoked Cornish hens to a serving dish and serve.

11. Enjoy!

Buffalo & Pork Stuffed Poblano Peppers

Prep time: 15 min
Cook time: 45 min
Serving: 4
Pellets any blend
Difficulty: medium

Ingredients

• One teaspoon minced garlic
• 6 Poblano Peppers, Medium
• 1/4 cup parsley (fresh)
• 2 tsp. extra-virgin olive oil
• 2 Oil from Vegetables
• 1 Diced Medium Yellow Onion
• Ground Pork (1/2 pound)
• Ground Buffalo, 1/2 pound
• a quarter teaspoon of salt
• Flakes of red pepper

- a half-teaspoon of black pepper
- Tomato Sauce (8 oz.)
- 2 Cups Cooked Rice

Instructions
- Set the Wood pellet to High and warm for 15 minutes with the lid covered when you're ready to cook.
- Drizzle olive oil over all but one of the poblano peppers and season with salt and pepper. Toss to coat completely.
- Roast peppers for 10 minutes, or until the skin is browned and blistered, directly on the grill grate. Remove them from the grill and put them aside to cool.
- Preheat a cast-iron pan on the grill for 20 minutes with the lid covered.
- Garlic should be minced, and parsley, onion, and the remaining poblano pepper should be chopped.
- Peppers should be cut in half lengthwise. With a spoon, scrape out the ribs and seeds.
- The onions and diced poblano pepper are added next, followed by the oil. Cook for 3 minutes or until soft. Pork, buffalo, garlic, parsley, salt, black pepper, and pepper flakes are added to the pan.
- Cook, stirring with a heavy wooden spoon to break up the lumps until the meat is browned, approximately 6 minutes. Stir in the rice and tomato sauce well.
- Remove from the fire and season with salt and pepper to taste. Reduce the grill's temperature to 350 degrees F.
- Place the peppers on a baking pan and stuff them with the rice mixture. Place pan on grill and cook peppers for 25 to 30 minutes, or until very tender and filling is cooked through.
- Before serving, remove the steak from the grill and set it aside to rest for 10 minutes. Enjoy!

Nutritional facts
- Fat 29g
- Calories 596
- Carbs 34g
- Protein 53g

Smoked Whole Duck

Preparation Time: 15 minutes
Cooking Time: 2 hours
Servings: 4
Ingredients:
- 2 tbsp. baking soda
- 1 tbsp. Chinese five spices
- 1 Thawed duck
- 1 Granny smith cored and diced apple
- 1 Quartered sliced orange
- 2 tbsp. chicken seasoning, divided

Directions:
1. Start by washing the duck under cool running water from the inside and out; then pat the meat dry with clean paper towels
2. Combine the Chicken seasoning and the Chinese Five spice together; then combine with the baking soda for extra crispy skin
3. Season the duck from the inside and out
4. Tuck the apple and the orange and apple slices into the cavity.
5. Turn your Smoker Grill to smoke model; then let the fire catch and set it to about 300°F to preheat
6. Place the duck on the grill grate or in a pan; then roast for about 2 ½ hours at a temperature of about 160°F
7. Place the foil loosely on top of the duck and let rest for about 15 minutes.
8. Serve and enjoy your delicious dish!

Nutrition:
- Calories: 157
- Fat: 10g
- Carbs: 10g
- Fiber: 1.3 g
- Protein: 11.1g

Bison Tomahawk Steak

Prep time: 5 min
Cook time: 15 min
Serving: 2
Pellets any blend
Difficulty: easy
Ingredients
- 2 tsp. salt (smoked)
- 2 1/2 lb. Buffalo Rib-Eye Steak, Bone-In

• 1 1/2 teaspoon pepper
Instructions
• Preheat the oven to 450 degrees F and leave the lid covered for 10 to 15 minutes when ready to cook.
• Season the meat with salt and pepper and coat evenly. Directly on the grill grate, place the steak.
• Grill for 6 minutes on one side, then turn and cook for another 6 minutes or until the internal temperature reaches 140 degrees for medium-rare and 145 degrees for medium. Enjoy!
Nutritional facts
• Fat: 12g
• Calories: 208
• Carbs: 0g
• Protein: 25g

Wild Game Chili

Preparation Time: 50 minutes
Cooking Time: 6 hours
Servings: 8-12 servings
Ingredients:
·   3 slices of bacon, chopped
·   Venison or wild hog, ground into small cubes (3-lb, 1.4-kgs)
·   1 large onion, peeled, finely chopped
·   Beer
·   Canned chopped green chilies
·   Cumin seeds, crushed – 1 tablespoon
·   Chili seasoning mix, of choice 2/3 cup
·   Tomato juice
·   Hot pepper sauce – 1 tablespoon
·   White cornmeal – ½ cup
Directions:
1.   In a frying pan, sauté the bacon with the onions, until the bacon is just browned.
2.   Add the game and sear all over.
3.   In a pan, add 1½ cups of beer along with the green chilies, cumin, and chili mix, simmering until it is a gravy-like consistency.
4.   Add the remaining beer followed by the tomato juice and hot pepper sauce.
5.   Pour the mixture into a pan and transfer to the smoker.

6.   Smoke-cook for between 4-6 hours.
7.   Before serving, add the cornmeal and stir to thicken and combine.
8.   Simmer for 20 minutes and serve with flour tortillas.
Nutrition Energy (calories): 557 kcal Protein: 21.69 g Fat: 6.34 g Carbohydrates: 107.3 g Calcium, Ca43 mg
Magnesium, Mg238 mg Phosphorus, P589 mg Iron, Fe3.73 mg Fiber10 g

Spiced Smoked Venison Tender

Preparation time: 20 minutes
Cooking time: 7 hours and 10 minutes
Servings: 10
Ingredients
·   5 lbs. (2.3 kg.) venison
For the rub:
·   3 tbsps. black pepper
·   2 tbsps. paprika
·   1 ½ tbsp. kosher salt
·   1 tbsp. garlic powder
·   1 tbsp. onion powder
·   ¾ tbsp. cayenne pepper
·   ¾ tbsp. coriander
·   ½ tbsp. dill
For the heat:
·   Use charcoal and alder wood chunks for indirect smokes.
For the water pan:
·   2 cups beef broth
·   ½ tsp. ginger
·   1 lemongrass
Directions
1.   Rub the venison with black pepper, paprika, kosher salt, garlic powder, onion powder, cayenne pepper, coriander, and dill.
2.   Prepare the grill and set it for indirect heat.
3.   Place charcoal and starters in a grill, then ignite the starters. Put the burning charcoal on one side of the grill.
4.   Place a heavy-duty aluminum pan, then place it on the other side of the grill.
5.   Pour beef broth into the aluminum pan, then add ginger and lemongrass to the broth.

6.   Place wood chunks on top of the burning charcoal, then set the grill grate.

7.   Cover the grill with the lid and set the temperature to 200°F (93°C).

8.   Wait until the grill reaches the desired temperature, then place the seasoned venison on the grate inside the grill.

9.   Maintain the heat and control the temperature. Add more charcoal and wood chunks if it is necessary.

10. Once the smoked venison's internal temperature has reached 160°F (71°C), remove it from the grill and transfer it to a serving dish. Serve and enjoy.

Nutrition

·   Calories: 30
·   Protein: 3.28 g.
·   Fat: 0.6 g.
·   Carbohydrates: 3.72 g.

All American BBQ Spare Ribs

Preparation Time: 15 minutes
Cooking Time: 2 hours
Servings: 8
Ingredients:

·   2 racks grill, 2.75 kg skinned pork ribs
·   2 to 3 tbsp. chicken seasoning
·   1 cup apple juice, cider, or beer
·   50 g barbecue sauce

Directions:

1.   Remove the silver skin part on the back of the ribs (Indian I butcher said not yet). Said would prevent the penetration of the herbs and smoke.

2.   Sprinkle the chicken seasoning on both sides of the ribs. When you are ready to cook, start the grill on SMOKE with the lid open until there is a good fire (4 to 5 minutes).

3.   Increase the temperature to 95 ° C and preheat with the lid closed for 10 to 15 minutes. Arrange the ribs on the racks or grid, with the bones down. Cook for 3 to 4 hours. After 1 hour, spray with call juice. Repeat said after every hour of cooking. After 3 to 4 hours of cooking, rub the ribs with the barbecue sauce. Grill for another 30 minutes to 1 hour,

cut into individual ribs and serve with extra barbecue sauce.

Nutrition:

·   Calories: 157
·   Fat: 10g
·   Carbs: 10g
·   Fiber: 1.3 g
·   Protein: 11.1g

Fried Poultry or Game with Garnish

Preparation Time: 10 minutes
Cooking Time: 2 hours
Servings: 4
Ingredients:

·   250 g chicken, or 250 g turkey, or ¼ pheasant, 2/3 hazel grouse, or gray partridge
·   6 g butter
·   25 g mayonnaise with gherkins
·   Lettuce leaves or parsley (for garnish) (optional)
·   150 g ready-made garnish of green lettuce leaves, pickled cucumbers, red cabbage, Provencal cabbage, pickled tomatoes, pickled apples, and pears
·   Salt

Directions:

1.   Chilled fried poultry is cut into portions. Hazel grouse and partridge are used whole or carcasses are cut in half (see the materials "Features of frying poultry and game" and "Refueling of poultry and game").

2.   Pieces of poultry or game are placed on a dish, garnished with bouquets of green lettuce, pickled cucumbers, red cabbage, Provencal cabbage, pickled tomatoes, as well as pickled pears and apples (see the recipe "Sauerkraut Salad (Provencal)").

3.   On top, the dish is additionally decorated with salad leaves or parsley sprigs. Separately, mayonnaise with gherkins is served in a gravy boat (see "Sauce mayonnaise with gherkins").

Recommendations:

Read about the properties of apples, butter, red cabbage, and white cabbage in the articles

"Apples", "Butter", "Red cabbage", "White cabbage (fresh)".
Nutrition:
· Calories: 176
· Fat: 10g
· Carbs: 10g
· Fiber: 1.3 g
· Protein: 11.1g

Cajun Crab Stuffed Shrimp and Jicama Corn Salad

Preparation time: 20 minutes
Cooking time: 3–5 minutes
Servings: 4
Ingredients
· Shrimp, stuffed
· lump crab meat
· red onion
· garlic seasoning, minced
· lime juice
· lime zest
· jalapeño
· ritz crackers
· bacon
· red onion and jalapeño, grilled
Directions
1.	Pick cartilage from the crab. Combine ingredients wrap with bacon. Grill till browned.
2.	Remoulade mayo, chili sauce, tiger sauce, creole mustard, lemon juice, lemon zest, scallions, parsley, minced celery, minced garlic, salt, capers chopped, salt, black pepper. Combine all ingredients and chill Jicama corn salad.
3.	We diced the corn on the cob, black beans, carrot, scallions, cilantro, basil, lime juice, lime zest, cumin red bell pepper, grill red peppercorn on the cob.
4.	Rinse black beans. Combine ingredients and chill.
Nutrition
· Calories: 94
· Protein: 13.51 g.
· Fat: 1.13 g.
· Carbohydrates: 7.48 g.

Quail on the Grill Marinated with Vinegar and Onions

Preparation Time: 15 minutes
Cooking Time: 1 ½ hour
Servings: 6
Ingredients:
· 4 pcs. quail
For the marinade:
· 2 pcs. onions
· 30 ml vinegar (9%)
· Salt to taste
· Ground black pepper, to taste
· 1 garlic clove
Directions:
1.	Wash quail carcasses under running cold water, dry on paper towels, and put on a cutting board with the backup.
2.	Using kitchen scissors, cut each quail along the back, unfold the ribs to the sides, and lay the carcass breast up. Beat the carcass lightly with a meat hammer (you can use the handle of a knife instead of a hammer).
3.	For the marinade, peel and cut onions into several pieces. Fold in a blender and puree with a clove of garlic.
4.	In a separate bowl, mix the vinegar with 50 ml of cold water.
5.	Place the quail carcasses in a suitable bowl or food container, shifting with onion and garlic gruel, sprinkle with salt and pepper to taste. Stir it well so that the meat is well covered with the onion mass on all sides.
6.	Pour diluted vinegar over the quail, stir, put a little oppression, and put in the refrigerator for at least 2-3 hours, or better overnight.
7.	Burn firewood in the grill to the "gray" coals. Grease the sieve with vegetable oil; lay the quail carcasses, laying them out, as shown in the photo. Remember to shake off all the onions from them.
8.	Bake over glowing coals, turning the wire rack from one side to the other from time to time. The quails on the wire rack are ready in about 20 minutes. Their readiness can be easily checked by piercing the breast with a knife: if clear juice flows out without impurities of blood, then the meat can be removed from the barbecue. Transfer the

finished quails to a dish, cover with foil and let them rest for another 20 minutes. Then you can serve it with fresh vegetables, herbs, and sauce to taste. Enjoy your meal!

Nutrition:

- Calories: 186
- Fat: 10g
- Carbs: 21g
- Fiber: 1.3 g
- Protein: 11.1g

Grilled Lamb Sandwiches

Servings: 6
Cooking Time: 50 Minutes
Ingredients:
- 1 (4 pounds) boneless lamb.
- 1 cup of raspberry vinegar.
- 2 tablespoons of olive oil.
- 1 tablespoon of chopped fresh thyme.
- 2 pressed garlic cloves.
- 1/4 teaspoon of salt to taste.
- 1/4 teaspoon of ground pepper.
- Sliced bread.

Directions:
1. Using a large mixing bowl, add in the raspberry vinegar, oil, and thyme then mix properly to combine. Add in the lamb, toss to combine then let it sit in the refrigerator for about eight hours or overnight. Next, discard the marinade the season the lamb with salt and pepper to taste. Preheat a
2. Wood Pellet Smoker and grill to 400-500 degrees F, add in the seasoned lamb and grill for about thirty to forty minutes until it attains a temperature of 150 degrees F. Once cooked, let the lamb cool for a few minutes, slice as desired then serve on the bread with your favorite topping.

Nutrition Info: Calories: 407 Cal Fat: 23 g Carbohydrates: 26 g Protein: 72 g Fiber: 2.3 g

Tuna Burgers

Preparation Time: 30 minutes
Cooking Time: 15 minutes
Servings: 4 - 6
Ingredients:
- 2 lbs. Tuna steak, ground
- 2 Eggs
- 1 Bell pepper, diced
- 1 teaspoon Worcestershire or soy sauce
- 1 Onion, Diced
- 1 tablespoon Salmon rub seasoning
- 1 tablespoon Saskatchewan Seasoning

Directions:
1. In a large bowl combine the salmon seasoning, Saskatchewan seasoning, bell pepper, onion, soy/Worcestershire sauce, eggs, and tuna. Mix well. Oil the hands, make patties.
2. Preheat the grill to high.
3. Grill the tuna patties for 10 - 15 min. Flip after 7 minutes.

Nutrition: Calories: 236 Protein: 18g Carbohydrates: 1g Fat: 5g Fiber: 0.7g

Smash Burger

Preparation Time: 10 minutes
Servings: 4 servings per recipe
Ingredients:
- Two thinly sliced medium white onions
- Two cups shredded iceberg lettuce
- Ketchup
- Mustard
- Sliced pickles
- One pound 80% ground beef
- One tsp salt
- Four slices of cheese American
- Four potato buns or white burger buns
- Beef Rub
- 1/2 tsp black pepper
- Butter melted

Instructions:
- Season ground beef with pepper and salt or beef-rub and shape into 3oz-4oz balls.
- Set the grill to 450°F and heat for 15 minutes with the lid covered when you're ready to cook. While the grill preheats, place a cast-iron skillet on the grate.
- Using fat or butter, grease the skillet. To begin caramelizing the onions, place them on the skillet's corner. Next, arrange burger balls on a heated skillet and squash them flat with a

spatula until they're thin and flat (about a half-inch).

· Cook until the burgers have a nice brown color.

· Flip the burger carefully, sprinkle some onions on top, then top with cheese. Next, butter the buns and cook them on the skillet.

· Remove the burgers and buns from the grill and assemble the burgers in the following order: bottom bun, chosen sauce, Lettuce, patty with caramelized onions and cheese, an additional layer of Lettuce, homemade pickles, a little extra sauce, and the top bun. Serve right away. Have fun!

BBQ pulled turkey sandwiches

Prep. Time: 15mins
Cook Time: 2 hrs
Servings: 6
Ingredients
· Turkey's thighs 6
· Chicken broth 1.5 c
· Poultry rub pork
· Kaiser buns 1 split
· BBQ sauce 1 c
Instructions
1. The turkey thighs may be seasoned on both sides with the poultry rub and pork.
2. Preheat the oven to 180°F and pre-heat for 15 mins with the lid closed.
3. Place the turkey thighs directly over the grill grate for around 30 mins to smoke.
4. Transfer the thighs to a roasting pan or aluminum foil. Pour the soup around the thighs. To maintain the heat in a pan, cover it with a lid or foil.
5. Preheat the grill to 325 degrees Fahrenheit with the lid closed. Grill the thighs until they reach an internal temperature of 180° F.
6. Take the pan off the stove but leave it turned on. Allow the turkey thighs to cool somewhat before proceeding with the treatment.
7. Collect the drippings in a jar and keep them away. Remove the skin and discard it
8. After shredding the turkey flesh with your fingers, return it to the roasting pan.

9. Pour in your favorite barbecue sauce, along with some of the drippings.
10. Following covering the sheet with foil, reheat the BBQ turkey over for 20-30 mins.
11. Serve with toasted buns if desired.
2. Maple smoked thanksgiving turkey
Prep. Time: 20 mins
Cook Time: 375 mins
Servings: 8
Ingredients
· Butter 1 c
· champion chicken seasoning 2 tbsp
· Maple syrup ½ c
· Turkey 1 (pre-brined)
Instructions
1. Preheat the oven to 250 degrees Fahrenheit.
2. Combine melted butter and maple syrup in a mixing bowl. Load the marinade compressor halfway with syrup and butter, then use the needle to pierce the meat while pushing the nozzle to inject the taste. The marinade may be injected into the thigh, wings and breasts' densest areas.
3. Spread the room-temperature butter and champion chicken powder all over the turkey, being careful to get it all the way under the skin.
4. Place the turkey in an aluminum pan on the grill to catch all of the drippings.
5. When the breast and thigh flesh reaches 165° F to 170° F, take the turkey from the grill and lay it aside to rest for 15 mins before carving.

Ultimate Lamb Burgers

Preparation Time: 20 minutes
Cooking Time: 30 minutes
Servings: 4
Ingredients:
Wood Pellet Grill Smokers: Apple
Burger:
· 2 lbs. ground lamb
· 1 jalapeño
· 6 scallions, diced
· 2 tablespoons mint
· 2 tablespoons dill, minced

- · 3 cloves garlic, minced
- · Salt and pepper
- · 4 brioche buns
- · 4 slices manchego cheese

Sauce:
- · 1 cup mayonnaise
- · 2 teaspoons lemon juice
- · 2 cloves garlic
- · 1 bell pepper, diced
- · salt and pepper

Directions

1. When ready to cook, turn your smoker to 400F and preheat.
2. Add the mint, scallions, salt, garlic, dill, jalapeño, lamb, and pepper to the mixing bowl.
3. Form the lamb mixture into eight patties.
4. Lay the pepper on the grill and cook for 20 minutes.
5. Take the pepper from the grill and place it in a bag, and seal. After ten minutes, remove pepper from the bag, remove seeds and peel the skin.
6. Add the garlic, lemon juice, mayo, roasted red pepper, salt, and pepper and process until smooth. Serve alongside the burger.
7. Lay the lamb burgers on the grill, and cook for five minutes per side, then place in the buns with a slice of cheese, and serve with the homemade sauce.

Nutrition: Calories: 50 Carbs: 4g Fiber: 2g Fat: 2.5g Protein: 2g

Grilled Cheesesteak Sandwich

Preparation Time: 5 minutes
Servings: 4 servings per recipe
Ingredients:
- • One (one and a half pounds) New York strip slices
- • Four hoagie rolls
- • Pepper
- • Four slices of provolone cheese
- • One sliced green bell pepper
- • Salt
- • One sliced red bell pepper
- • Beef Rub

- • One tbsp canola oil
- • One sliced yellow bell pepper
- • One yellow onion large, sliced into rounds

Instructions:
- • Set the grill to 500°F and heat for 15 minutes with the lid covered when you're ready to cook.
- • While the grill preheats, place a cast-iron skillet directly on the grate.
- • Sprinkle the peppers and onions with salt and pepper to taste. Beef Rub is used to season the strip steak slices.
- • One tablespoon canola oil lightly oiled cast iron griddle Season with salt and onions.
- • Five minutes until onions are transparent. Add the peppers and simmer for another 10 minutes, or until softened and cooked thoroughly.
- • Put the seasoned steak pieces directly on the grate next to the skillet and cook for three minutes per side, until nicely browned and cooked through, whilst peppers and onions are cooking.
- • To toast the buns, place them cut-side down on the top grill grate.
- • Transfer the steak to the skillet to assemble the sandwiches when it's done. Top each mound of steak with a heaping of peppers and onions, followed by a slice of provolone.
- • Allow the cheese to melt by closing the lid. Transfer each pile on the buns with two spatulas and serve immediately. Have fun!

Chicago-Style Turkey Dogs

(TOTAL COOK TIME 30 MINUTES)
INGREDIENTS FOR 8 SERVINGS
THE MEAT
- · 8 turkey hot dogs 12-ins (30.5-cms) long

THE INGREDIENTS
- · 8 hot dog buns 12-ins (30.5-cms) long
- · Yellow mustard, as needed
- · Sweet pickle relish – ¾ cup
- · White onion, peeled and diced – 1 cup
- · 2 large tomatoes, cored and cut into wedges
- · 8 dill pickled spears

· 16 pickled sport peppers in vinegar
THE WOOD PELLET GRILL
· With the lid closed, preheat your smoker to 375°f (190°c) for 15 minutes
· Pecan wood pellets are recommended for this recipe
METHOD
1. Add the hot dogs to the grill in a single layer, and cook for 10-15 minutes, turning every 5 minutes.
2. Place the hot dog buns on the grill for the final 3 minutes of cooking the hot dogs to warm through.
3. Remove the hot dogs and buns from the grill.
4. To assemble: Add a hot dog to the bottom half of each bun. Top with yellow mustard, sweet pickle relish, and onion. Arrange the slices of fresh tomato on one side of the hot dog, and the pickle spears on the other side, and the sport peppers down the center.
5. Add the top half of the bun to cover the filling, serve and enjoy.

Mini Portobello Burgers

Preparation Time: 15 minutes
Cooking Time: 15 minutes
Servings: 4
Ingredients:
· 4 portobello mushroom caps
· 4 slices mozzarella cheese
· 4 buns, like brioche
· For the marinade:
· 1/4 cup balsamic vinegar
· 2 tablespoons olive oil
· 1 teaspoon dried basil
· 1 teaspoon dried oregano
· 1 teaspoon garlic powder
· 1/4 teaspoon sea salt
· 1/4 teaspoon black pepper
Directions:
1. Whisk together marinade ingredients in a large mixing bowl. Add mushroom caps and toss to coat.
2. Fire up the grill for medium-high heat.

3. Place mushrooms on the grill; reserve marinade for basting.
4. Grill for 5 to 8 minutes on each side
5. Brush with marinade frequently.
6. Top with mozzarella cheese during the last 2 minutes of grilling.
7. Remove from grill and serve on brioche buns.
Nutrition Energy (calories): 372 kcal Protein: 3.18 g Fat: 24.08 g Carbohydrates: 35.24 g Calcium, Ca133 mg Magnesium, Mg14 mg Phosphorus, P93 mg Iron, Fe1.35 mg

BQ Pulled Pork Sandwiches

Preparation Time: 10 minutes
Cooking Time: 1 hour 30 minutes
Servings: 6
Ingredients:
· 8-10lbs of bone-in pork butt roast
· 12 Kaiser Rolls
· 1 cup of yellow mustard
· Coleslaw
· 1 bottle of BBQ sauce
· 5 oz. of sugar
Directions
1. Push the temperature to 225 degrees F and set your smoker to preheat
2. Now take out the pork roast from the packaging and keep it on a cookie sheet
3. Rub it thoroughly with yellow mustard
4. Now take a bowl and mix the BBQ sauce along with sugar in it
5. Use this mix to rub the roast thoroughly and give time for the rub to seep inside and melt in the meat
6. Now place this roast in the smoker and allow it to cook for 6 hours
7. When done, remove it from the smoker and
8. then wrap it in tin foil
9. Push the temperature to 250 degrees F and cook it for a couple of hours. The internal temperature should reach 200 degrees F
10. Let the pork butt rest in the foil for an hour before pulling it out
11. Now take the Kaiser roll and cut it into half

12. Mix the pulled pork with some BBQ sauce and pile on the top of each halved roll
13. Top it with coleslaw and serve
Nutrition: Calories: 426; Protein: 65.3g; Carbs: 20.4g; Fat: 8.4g Sugar: 17.8g

Pellet Smoked "Green" Beef Burgers

Preparation Time: 10 minutes
Cooking Time: 1 hour
Servings: 6
Ingredients
- 1 lb. ground beef
- 1 lb. frozen spinach, thawed and drained
- 1 onion finely diced
- 1 large egg at room temperature
- 3 Tbsp. of flour all-purposes
- 1 tsp of fresh basil, chopped
- 1 Tbsp. of fresh parsley chopped
- salt and ground pepper to taste

Directions
1. In a large bowl, add all ingredients from the list above.
2. Knead the mixture until all ingredients combined well.
3. Form the mixture into equal balls.
4. Flip the "ON" switch, to preheat, your smoker. Pellets (recommended Hickory or Pecan) from the hopper are automatically delivered to the fire-pot by an auger.
5. Put up the temperature to 225°F or to smoke. It takes 10 minutes.
6. Place the racks into the smoker, and place burgers onto racks.
7. Smoke your burgers for 60 to 90 minutes (check burgers on 45 minutes).
8. The internal temperature should be about 145°F for medium-rare or, if using commercial ground beef, cook it to at least medium, 160°F.
9. Allow burgers to rest for 10 minutes and serve.
Nutrition Calories: 238.78 Carbs: Fat: 17.1g Fiber: 3g Protein: 17.5g

Smoked Moink Burger

Preparation Time: 10 minutes
Servings: 4 servings per recipe
Ingredients:
- ¼ cup Worcestershire sauce
- Pepper
- One pound Ground Sirloin
- One tsp garlic, minced
- ½ pound ground pork
- Salt

Instructions:
- In a mixing dish, mix all of the ingredients and stir well. Make four patties out of the mixture.
- Preheat the grill to 350 degrees Fahrenheit and close the cover for 15 minutes when ready to cook.
- Cook till the burgers reach a temp of 160 degrees Fahrenheit on the inside.
- Top with your favorite cheese and serve with your preferred toppings a few mins before the burgers are done.

Sheer Spicy Hamburgers on Pellet Grill

Preparation Time: 5 minutes
Cooking Time: 1 hour and 45 minutes
Servings: 6
Ingredients
- 3 lb. of ground beef
- 1 large egg from free-range chicken
- 2 tsp of chili flakes
- 2 tsp of chili powder
- 2 Tbsp of panko bread crumbs
- Sea salt to taste
- 1 Lemon juice for serving

Directions
1. In a large bowl, combine and mix us all ingredients.
2. Form the meat mixture into 6 patties.
3. Start your pellet grill on SMOKE with the lid open until the fire is established). Set the temperature to 380°F and preheat, lid closed, for 10 to 15 minutes.

4.   Arrange your patties on a grill and smoke the burgers for 60 to 90 minutes (check burgers on 45 minutes)
5.   Your burgers are ready when the internal temperature is 145 °F for medium-rare.
6.   In the case that you use commercial ground beef, the internal temperature has to be at least medium, 160 °F.
7.   Sprinkle with lemon juice and serve immediately.
Nutrition Calories: 587 Carbs: 3g Fat: 48g Fiber: 0.5g Protein: 41.6g

Smoked Cheddar Burgers (Pellet Smoker)

Preparation Time: 10 minutes
Cooking Time: 1 hour and 40 minutes
Servings: 6
Ingredients
· 1 1/2 lb. of ground beef
· 1/4 lb. of ground pork
· slices of cheddar cheese
· 1 tbsp of onion powder
· 1 tbsp of garlic powder
· Salt and ground black pepper to taste
Directions
1.   Preheat your Pellet Smoker.
2.   Put up the temperature to 225°F or to smoke; it takes 10 minutes.
3.   In a bowl, mix all ingredients until combined well.
4.   Shape your mixture into 6 burgers.
5.   Smoke up the burgers for 60 to 90 minutes (check burgers on 45 minutes)
6.   Your burgers are ready when the internal temperature is 145 °F for medium-rare.
7.   In the case that you use commercial ground beef, the internal temperature has to be at least medium, 160 °F.
8.   Allow burgers to rest for 10 minutes and serve.
9.   Serve with buns and your favorite dressing, sauce, and potatoes.
Nutrition Calories: 576 Carbs: Fat: 47.6g Fiber: 0.32g Protein: 32g

Burgers Stuffed with Chorizo Cheese

Preparation Time: 20 minutes
Servings: 4 servings per recipe
Ingredients:
· 400 gr of lean minced meat
· 100 gr of chorizo (spiced beef)
· 50 gr of beef spices (Prime Rib Rub)
· 8 slices of cheddar cheese
· 2 tablespoons butter
· 1 sliced red onion
· 1 sliced lettuce
· whole hamburger buns
Instructions:
1.   In a bowl, combine the beef, chorizo and beef spices.
2.   Prepare 8 patties. To make the burger filling, place 1 patty then 1 slice of cheese and top with another patty. Press the ends together around the burger to adhere,
3.   Continue until all four patties are done.
4.   Preheat the oven to 160° with the lid covered for 15 minutes.
5.   Cook the burgers on the grill for fifteen minutes per side. Top each burger with a slice of cheese and melt if desired. Remove from grill and cover with aluminum foil and let rest for 10 minutes.
6.   Drizzle the buns with melted butter and grill for 45 seconds on the grill while the burgers rest.
7.   Remove the buns from the grill and form the burger with the meat, onion and lettuce. Enjoy.

Bunny Dogs with Sweet and Spicy Jalapenos Relish

Preparation Time: 20 minutes
Cooking Time: 35-40 minutes
Serving: 8
Ingredients
· 8 hot dog-size carrots, peeled
· One-fourth cup honey
· One-fourth cup yellow mustard
· Nonstick cooking spray or butter, for greasing

- Salt
- ground black pepper
- 8 hot dog buns
- Sweet spicy jalapenos relish

Direction

1. Prepare the carrots by removing the stems and slicing in half lengthwise.
2. In a small bowl, whisk together the honey and mustard.
3. Prepare the smoker grill.
4. Brush the carrots on both sides with the honey mustard and season with salt and pepper; put on the baking sheet.
5. Place the baking sheet on the grill grate, close the lid, and smoke for 35 to 40 minutes, or until tender and starting to brown.
6. To serve, lightly toast the hot dog buns on the grill and top each with two slices of carrot and some relish.

Nutrition Energy (calories): 951 kcal Protein: 14 g Fat: 5.31 g Carbohydrates: 242 g Calcium, Ca82 mg Magnesium, Mg179 mg Phosphorus, P375 mg Iron, Fe10.96 mg

Wood Pellet Grill Smoker BBQ simple Turkey Sandwiches

Preparation Time: 30 minutes
Cooking Time: 45 minutes
Servings: 10
Ingredients:

o Turkey Thighs, Skin-On
- 1 1/2 Cups Chicken or Turkey Broth
- Pork & Poultry Rub
- 1 Cup barbeque Sauce, Or More as Needed

o Buns or Kaiser Rolls, Split and Buttered

Directions:

1. Season turkey thighs on both sides with the Pork & Poultry rub.
2. When ready to cook, turn temperature to 180 degrees F and preheat, lid closed for 15 minutes.
3. Arrange the turkey thighs exactly on the grill grate and smoke for 30 minutes.
4. Transfer the thighs to sturdy disposable aluminum foil or baking tray. Pour the broth around the thighs and then cover the pan with foil or a lid.
5. Increase temperature to 325 degrees F and preheat, lid closed. Roast the thighs until it reaches an internal temperature of 180 degrees F.
6. Remove pan from the grill, but leave the grill on. Let the turkey thighs cool slightly up to they can be handled comfortably.
7. Let the drops drip off and keep. Remove skin and discard.
8. Pull out the shredded turkey meat with your fingers and return it to the roasting pan.
9. Add a cup or more of your favorite BBQ Sauce along with some of the drippings.
10. Recover the pan with foil and reheat the BBQ turkey on the grill for 20 to 30 minutes.
11. Serve with toasted buns if desired. Enjoy!

Nutrition: Energy (calories): 25 kcal Protein: 0.7 g Fat: 1.53 g Carbohydrates: 2.59 g

Cheeseburger

(TOTAL COOK TIME 25 MINUTES)
INGREDIENTS FOR 4 SERVINGS
THE MEAT
- Ground beef, fresh (2-lbs, 0.9-kgs)

THE INGREDIENTS
- 1 egg, beaten
- Evaporated milk – 3 tablespoons
- Worcestershire sauce – 2 tablespoons
- Dry breadcrumbs – 1 cup
- All-purpose rub, of choice – 1 tablespoon
- 4 slices Cheddar cheese
- 4 hamburger buns, split
- Sauce or dressing, to serve, optional

THE WOOD PELLET GRILL
- Prepare your wood pellet grill for grilling at 300°F (149°C)
- Add your choice of wood pellets

METHOD

1. First, in a bowl, combine the ground beef with the beaten egg, evaporated milk, Worcestershire sauce, breadcrumbs, and all-purpose rub. Using clean hands, combine the mixture and divide it into 4 equal portions.

Next, divide each portion in half. Flatten to yield 8 flat patties that you will later combine to create 4 patties.

2.   When the patties are flattened, add a slice of cheese to the middle of the 4 patties. Lay the remaining 4 patties on top, and pinch the sides tightly to seal in the filling. Be aware the patties will shrink during cooking.

3.   Grill the patties for 6-8 minutes on each side, depending on your preferred level of doneness.

4.   Remove from the grill, place each one inside a burger bun and top with your favorite sauce or dressing.

5.   Enjoy.

Prosciutto Pesto Hot Dog

Preparation Time: 15 minutes
Cooking Time: 15 minutes
Servings: 4
Ingredients:
·   4 smoked turkey hot dogs
·   4 large hot dog buns or split top hoagies
·   ounces fresh mozzarella cheese
·   1/3 cup pesto, divided
·   3 ounces prosciutto, sliced thinly
·   1/4 cup marinate artichoke hearts, chopped
·   Olive oil, for drizzling
·   Parmesan cheese, shaved for garnish

Direction

1.   Heat up the entire grill smoker to medium heat.

2.   Add hot dogs, to one side, and reduce that side's heat to low. Grill until cooked through; about 5 to 7 minutes; turning occasionally.

3.   Fry the sliced prosciutto until crispy on the other side of the grill; about 3 minutes. Drain on a paper towel lined plate; and set aside.

4.   Top the hot dogs with thin slices of the mozzarella cheese, and remove once the cheese is melted.

5.   Toast the buns on the grill for 2 minutes and remove.

6.   Spread pesto onto the toasted buns.

7.   Top with mozzarella covered hot dog.

8.   Top with all the remaining ingredients.

9.   Serve immediately!

Nutrition   Energy (calories): 267 kcal Protein: 19.76 g Fat: 17.13 g Carbohydrates: 10.22 g Calcium, Ca465 mg Magnesium, Mg41 mg Phosphorus, P376 mg Iron, Fe1.4 mg

Turkey Sandwich

Preparation Time: 5 Minutes
Cooking Time: 25 Minutes
Servings: 4
Ingredients:
·   Eight bread slices
·   1 cup gravy
·   2 cups turkey, cooked and shredded

Directions:
1.   Set your wood pellet grill to smoke.
2.   Preheat it to 400 degrees F.
3.   Place a grill mat on top of the grates.
4.   Add the turkey on top of the mat.
5.   Cook for 10 minutes.
6.   Toast the bread in the flame broiler.
7.   Top the bread with the gravy and shredded turkey.

Nutrition: Calories 935 Total fat 53g Saturated fat 15g Protein 107g Sodium 320mg

Pork Belly Sandwich

(TOTAL COOK TIME 2 HOURS 35 MINUTES)
INGREDIENTS FOR 6 SERVINGS
THE MEAT
·   Center-cut pork belly (2-lbs, 0.9-kgs)
THE INGREDIENTS
·   Salt and freshly ground black pepper to season
·   BBQ rub, of choice, as needed
·   6 star cross buns, split
·   Nonstick cooking spray oil
·   Mayonnaise – ½ cup
·   Smoked Cheddar cheese, shredded (8-ozs, 226.8-gms)

· Smoky BBQ sauce, store-bought, of choice – ½ cup
· Onion straws (6-ozs, 170-gms)
THE WOOD PELLET GRILL
· Preheat your wood pellet grill for smoking to 300°F (149°C)
· Use hickory wood pellets for this recipe
METHOD
1. Season the meat with salt, black pepper, and your choice of BBQ rub.
2. Place the pork belly, fat side facing down and smoke for around 2 ½ hours, or until the meat registers an internal temperature of 185-195°F (85-90°C).
3. Spritz the bottom of the buns with nonstick spray oil and toast until golden.
4. Spread mayonnaise on the bottom half of each bun. Top with cheese, pork belly, a dollop of BBQ sauce, and onion straws.
5. Enjoy.

Grilled Veggie Sandwich

Preparation time: 30 minutes
Cooking time: 30 minutes
Servings: 4-6
Ingredients:
· Pellet: hardwood, pecan
· Smoked hummus
· 1-1/2 cups chickpeas
· 1/3 cup tahini
· 1 tbsp. minced garlic
· 2 tbsps. olive oil
· 1 tsp. kosher salt
· 4 tbsps. lemon juice
· Grilled veggie sandwich
· One small eggplant, sliced into strips
· One small zucchini, cut into strips
· One small yellow squash, sliced into strips
· Two large Portobello mushrooms
· Olive oil
· Salt and pepper to taste
· Two heirloom tomatoes, sliced
· One bunch of basil leaves pulled
· Four ciabatta buns
· 1/2 cup ricotta
· Juice of 1 lemon

· One garlic clove minced
· Salt and pepper to taste
Directions:
1. Ready to cook, turn temperature to 180 degrees F and preheat, lid closed for 15 minutes.
2. In a prepared bowl of a food processor, combine the smoked chickpeas, tahini, garlic, olive oil, salt and lemon juice and blend until smooth but not completely smooth. Transfer to a bowl and reserve.
3. Increase grill temp to high (400-500 degrees F).
4. While the vegetables are cooking, mix the ricotta, the lemon juice, garlic, salt and some pepper.
5. Cut the ciabatta buns in half and then open them up—spread the hummus on one side and ricotta on the other. Stack the grilled veggies and top with tomatoes and basil. Enjoy!
Nutrition: Calories: 376 Carbs: 57g Fat: 16g Protein: 10g

Lamb Burgers

(TOTAL COOK TIME 20 MINUTES)
INGREDIENTS FOR 4 SERVINGS
THE MEAT
· Ground lamb (1.5-lbs, 0.7-kgs)
· 4 pita bread, to serve
THE INGREDIENTS
· 1 small onion, peeled and finely chopped
· 1 garlic clove, peeled and minced
· Fresh mint, chopped – 3 tablespoons
· Dried hot red pepper flakes – ½ teaspoon
· Ground cumin – ½ teaspoon
· Coarsely ground sea salt and black pepper
THE TOPPINGS
· 1 cucumber, peeled and finely sliced
· 1 fresh Roma tomato, thinly sliced
· 4 red onion rings
· Greek yogurt – ¾ cup
· Feta cheese, crumbled (4-ozs, 113-gms)
THE WOOD PELLET GRILL
· Preheat your pellet grill for direct grilling to high heat
· Brush the grill grate with oil

· Choose your favorite wood pellets for this recipe
METHOD
1. To prepare the burgers, add the lamb, onion, garlic, mint, hot pepper flakes, and cumin to a bowl, and using a wooden spoon, combine. With clean hands, form the mixture into 4 evenly-sized patties. Make a small indent in the middle of each burger.
2. Season the burgers with salt and black pepper on both sides and place them directly on the oiled grill grate. Grill for approximately 3 minutes until the bottoms are browned. Flip over and cook on the other side for 5-7 minutes, depending on your preferred level of doneness. For medium burgers, the internal temperature should register 160°F (71°C).
3. In the meantime, make a slit in the top of the pita and warm them on the grill.
4. Place the burgers inside the pita and top with cucumber, tomatoes, red onion, Greek yogurt, and crumbled feta cheese.
5. Enjoy.

Grilled Triple Cheeseburger

Preparation Time: 10 minutes
Servings: 4 servings per recipe
Ingredients:
· Two tsp sweet pickle relish
· ½ tsp distilled white vinegar
· Two tbsp mayonnaise
· ½ tsp sugar
· One tbsp ketchup
· Four Whole hamburger buns
· One Large white onion, sliced
· Butter lettuce
· Pickles
· Four pounds 80% lean ground beef
· One tbsp Beef Rub
· One large tomato, sliced
· Twelve Slices American cheese
Instructions:
· Divide the meat mixture into 12 five-ounce patties. Beef Rub should be thoroughly applied to both sides.

· For the Special Sauce, combine all sauce ingredients and leave aside until ready to use.
· Set the grill to 400°F and preheat for 15 minutes with the lid covered when you're ready to cook.
· Place burgers on the grill and heat for 4 minutes before flipping and cooking for another 2 minutes.
· Cook for an additional 2 minutes or until the cheese has melted.
· Position the buns on the grill to toast if preferred during the last minute of cooking.
· Remove everything from the grill and assemble burgers on the bun with special sauce, three burger patties, Lettuce, tomato, onions, and pickles.

Vegetable Sandwich

Preparation Time: 30 minutes
Cooking Time: 45 minutes
Servings: 4
Ingredients:
For the Smoked Hummus:
· 1 1/2 cups cooked chickpeas
· 1 tablespoon minced garlic
· 1 teaspoon salt
· 4 tablespoons lemon juice
· 2 tablespoon olive oil
· 1/3 cup tahini
For the Vegetables:
· 2 large portobello mushrooms
· 1 small eggplant, destemmed, sliced into strips
· 1 teaspoon salt
· 1 small zucchini, trimmed, sliced into strips
· ½ teaspoon ground black pepper
· 1 small yellow squash, peeled, sliced into strips
· ¼ cup olive oil
For the Cheese:
· 1 lemon, juiced
· ½ teaspoon minced garlic
· ¼ teaspoon ground black pepper
· ¼ teaspoon salt
· 1/2 cup ricotta cheese
To Assemble:

- 1 bunch basil, leaves chopped
- 2 heirloom tomatoes, sliced
- 4 ciabatta buns, halved

Directions:

1. Switch on the Wood Pellet Grill Smoker grill, fill the grill hopper with pecan flavored Wood Pellet Grill Smokers, power the grill on by using the control panel, select 'smoke' on the temperature dial, or set the temperature to 180 degrees F and let it preheat for a minimum of 15 minutes.

2. Meanwhile, prepare the hummus, and for this, take a sheet tray and spread chickpeas on it.

3. When the grill has preheated, open the lid, place sheet tray on the grill grate, shut the grill and smoke for 20 minutes.

4. When done, transfer chickpeas to a food processor, add remaining ingredients for the hummus in it, and pulse for 2 minutes until smooth, set aside until required.

5. Change the smoking temperature to 500 degrees F, shut with lid, and let it preheat for 10 minutes.

6. Meanwhile, prepare vegetables and for this, take a large bowl, place all the vegetables in it, add salt and black pepper, drizzle with oil and lemon juice and toss until coated.

7. Place vegetables on the grill grate, shut with lid and then smoke for eggplant, zucchini, and squash for 15 minutes and mushrooms for 25 minutes.

8. Meanwhile, prepare the cheese and for this, take a small bowl, place all of its ingredients in it and stir until well combined.

9. Assemble the sandwich for this, cut buns in half lengthwise, spread prepared hummus on one side, spread cheese on the other side, then stuff with grilled vegetables and top with tomatoes and basil.

10. Serve straight away.

Nutrition: Calories: 560 Cal Fat: 40 g Carbs: 45 g Protein: 8.3 g Fiber: 6.8 g

Smokey Burgers

Preparation Time: 15 minutes

Servings: 4 servings per recipe

Ingredients:

- Half tbsp Worcestershire sauce
- One-pound ground beef
- One tbsp Beef Rub

Instructions:

- Combine ground beef, Beef Rub, Worcestershire sauce in a mixing bowl.
- Make eight hamburger patties with the beef mixture.
- Set the grill to 180°F and preheat for 15 minutes with the lid covered when you're ready to cook. If Super Smoke is available, use it for the best flavor.
- Smoke for 2 hours by placing patties straight on the grill grate.
- Remove from the grill after 2 hours and served with your preferred toppings.

Chipotle Turkey Burgers

(TOTAL COOK TIME 55 MINUTES)
INGREDIENTS FOR 8 SERVINGS
THE MEAT

- Ground turkey (2-lbs, 0.9-kgs)

THE INGREDIENTS

- Onion, peeled, finely chopped – ½ cup
- Fresh cilantro, chopped – 3 tablespoons
- 2 chipotle chilies in adobo sauce
- Garlic powder – 2 teaspoons
- Onion powder – 2 teaspoon
- Beef rub, of choice – 3 tablespoons
- 8 Pepper Jack cheese slices
- 8 sesame seed hamburger buns, split

THE WOOD PELLET GRILL

- With the lid closed, preheat your smoker to 375°F (107°C) for 15-20 minutes
- Choose your favorite wood pellets for this recipe

METHOD

1. In a large bowl, combine the ground turkey with the onions, cilantro, chipotle chilies, garlic powder, onion powder, and beef rub. Using clean hands, form the mixture into 8 even size patties.

2. Cook the burgers in the preheated grill for approximately 45 minutes or until the meat

registers an internal temperature of 165°F (74°C).

3.   Just before you remove the burgers from the grill, top each one with a slice of cheese and serve inside a hamburger bun.

Grilled Wagu Burgers

Preparation Time: 5 minutes
Servings: 4 servings per recipe
Ingredients:
· 4 burger buns
· One heirloom tomato, sliced
· Two pounds wagyu ground beef
· Butter lettuce
· Salt
· Pepper
· One red onion, sliced
· Six slices of American cheese

Instructions:
· Set the grill to 500°F and heat for fifteen minutes with the lid covered once you're ready to cook.
· Season 4 burger patties generously with pepper and salt.
· Arrange burger patties straight on the grill grate. Cook for four minutes once the grill is hot.
· Cook for 4 minutes longer on the other side (for a medium burger, adjust the cooking time to your desired doneness), then top over cheese in the last intervals of cooking.
· Remove from the grill and set aside for 2 minutes to cool.
· Butter lettuce, heirloom tomato, and red onion, as well as any desired sauces, go into your burger.

Grilled Steak with American Cheese Sandwich

Preparation Time: 10 minutes
Cooking Time: 55 minutes
Servings: 4

Ingredients
· 1 pound of beef steak.
· 1/2 teaspoon of salt to taste.
· 1/2 teaspoon of pepper to taste.
· 1 tablespoon of Worcestershire sauce.
· 2 tablespoons of butter.
· 1 chopped onion.
· 1/2 chopped green bell pepper.
· Salt and pepper to taste.
· 8 slices of American Cheese.
· 8 slices of white bread.
· 4 tablespoons of butter.

Directions:
1.   Turn your Wood Pellet Grill Smoker Smoker and Grill to smoke and fire up for about four to five minutes. Set the temperature of the grill to 450 degrees F and let it preheat for about ten to fifteen minutes with its lid closed.
2.   Next, place a non-stick skillet on the griddle and preheat for about fifteen minutes until it becomes hot. Once hot, add in the butter and let melt. Once the butter melts, add in the onions and green bell pepper then cook for about five minutes until they become brown in color, set aside.
3.   Next, still using the same pan on the griddle, add in the steak, Worcestershire sauce, salt, and pepper to taste then cook for about five to six minutes until it is cooked through. Add in the cooked bell pepper mixture; stir to combine then heat for another three minutes, set aside.
4.   Use a sharp knife to slice the bread in half, butter each side then grill for about three to four minutes with its sides down. To assemble, add slices of cheese on each bread slice, top with the steak mixture then your favorite toppings, close the sandwich with another bread slice then serve.
Nutrition: Calories 589 cal Carbohydrates 28g Protein 24g Fat 41g Fiber 2g

Beef Burgers GrassFed

Preparation Time: 10 minutes
Servings: 4 servings per recipe

Ingredients:
· Four slices of provolone cheese
· Four slices tomato
· 2-pound grass-fed ground beef
· Four tsp kosher salt
· Burger toppings of your liking
· Four whole brioche burger buns

Instructions:
· Cut the ground meat into four equal parts. Remove the meat from the packaging and shape it into burger patties about Five inches across to avoid overworking it. The meat should not be kneaded.
· 1 tsp kosher salt, split in half on each side, on each burger
· Once ready to cook, preheat the grill to 415°F with the lid shut for fifteen minutes.
· On the grill grate, place the hamburgers. For medium-rare, cook for 12 minutes. The outside of the meat should be beautifully browned. Your thermometer should read 130°F when inserted into the center of the burger.
· Put provolone slices to the burgers in the last few cooking moments and toast the buns on the grill. Serve with a side of condiments.

Big Burgers With Homemade Bacon Jam

(TOTAL COOK TIME 45 MINUTES)
INGREDIENTS FOR 6 SERVINGS
THE MEAT
· Ground chuck (0.75-lbs, 0.34-kgs)
· Ground ribeye (0.75-lbs, 0.34-kgs)
THE JAM
· Bacon, sliced (1-lb, 0.45-kgs)
· Yellow onion, peeled and sliced (1-lb, 0.45-kgs)
· Asada seasoning mix – 1 tablespoon
· Minced garlic – 1 tablespoon
· Brown sugar – ½ cup
· Coffee – ½ cup
· Cider vinegar – ½ cup
· Maple syrup – ½ cup
· Dried thyme – ¼ teaspoon
THE BURGER

· Tri-tip seasoning blend, as needed
· 6 slices Havarti cheese
· Mayonnaise – 10 tablespoons
· Chipotle ketchup – 6 tablespoons
· 6 potato rolls, split and toasted
THE WOOD PELLET GRILL
· Prepare your wood pellet grill to 450°F (232°C)
· Set up for direct grilling
· Use your favorite wood pellets
METHOD
1. First, prepare the bacon jam. In a skillet over moderate heat, cook the bacon until lightly browned. Take the bacon out of the skillet using a slotted spoon and set aside on a plate covered with kitchen paper to drain.
2. Next, add the onion and Asada seasoning mix to the skillet and sauté for 5-10 minutes until translucent. Add the minced garlic and brown sugar, sauté for 60 seconds.
3. Stir the coffee, vinegar, maple syrup, and thyme into the mixture in the skillet and bring to a simmer. Return the bacon to the skillet.
4. Turn the heat down to low and cook until a syrup-like consistency.
5. Transfer to a food processor and pulse until jam-like. Allow to cool and transfer to Mason jars. Store in the refrigerator.
6. Next, make the burgers. Combine the ground chuck and ribeye in a bowl and season with the tri-tip blend. Form the mixture into 6 evenly-sized patties.
7. Place the patties on the grill, and when browned, flip and season. Cook for another 2 minutes until the bottoms begin to brown.
8. Arrange a slice of cheese on top of each patty and allow to melt a little.
9. Meanwhile, in a small bowl, combine the mayonnaise and chipotle ketchup. Spread the mixture inside the toasted buns.
10. Take the cheeseburgers off the grill and place them inside the buns. Top each burger with a spoonful of bacon jam.
11. Serve straight away.

Bacon-Wrapped Hotdogs

Preparation Time: 15 minutes
Servings: 6 servings per recipe
Ingredients:
·   Four ounces Jack cheese
·   Six hot dogs buns
·   Six sliced bacon
·   Six whole hot dogs
Instructions:
·   Make eight long strips out of the cheese. Cut the hot dogs longitudinally, keeping a "hinge" on a side, then stuff each with a piece of cheese.
·   Wrap a slice of bacon around each hot dog in a spiral and fasten with toothpicks.
·   Preheat the grill to 350°F for 15 minutes with the lid closed when ready to cook.
·   Cook the hot dogs on the grill for 20 to 30 minutes, until the bacon has browned up.
·   Place the hot dog inside the bun with a piece of cheese on top. Serve immediately with your favorite toppings on top of the buns.

Delicious BLT Sandwich

Preparation Time: 15 minutes
Cooking Time: 35 minutes
Servings: 4-6
Ingredients
·   8 slices of bacon
·   1/2 romaine heart
·   1sliced tomato
·   4 slices of sandwich bread
·   3 tablespoons of mayonnaise
·   Salted butter
·   Sea salt to taste
·   Pepper to taste
Directions:
1.   Preheat a Wood Pellet Grill Smoker Smoker and Grill to 350 degrees F for about fifteen minutes with its lid closed.
2.   Place the bacon slices on the preheated grill and cook for about fifteen to twenty minutes until they become crispy.
3.   Next, butter both sides of the bread, place a grill pan on the griddle of the Wood Pellet Grill Smoker, and toast the bread for a few minutes until they become brown on both sides, set aside.
4.   Using a small mixing bowl, add in the sliced tomatoes, season with salt and pepper to taste then mix to coat.
5.   Next, spread mayo on both sides of the toasted bread, top with the lettuce, tomato, and bacon then enjoy.
Nutrition: Calories 284 cal Protein 19g Fat 19g Carbohydrates 11g Fiber 2g

Hot Dogs of Barbeque Brisket

Preparation Time: 5 minutes
Servings: 4 servings per recipe
Ingredients:
·   4 whole hot dog buns
·   One onion, diced
·   Two whole jalapeños
·   4 whole hot dogs
·   ½ pound leftover beef brisket
·   ½ cup shredded cheddar cheese
·   ½ cup BBQ Sauce
Instructions:
·   Once you're ready to cook, fire up the grill as per the manufacturer's directions. Heat the grill to 450 degrees Fahrenheit for 15 minutes with the lid closed.
·   Arrange hot dogs flat on the grill grate and cook for ten minutes or until heated through and golden browned, rotating regularly.
·   To keep the brisket slices moist, wrap them in aluminum foil with a little BBQ sauce. Place next to the hot dogs on the grill grate and cook until heated for about six minutes.
·   Place a hot dog in the bun and top with brisket, additional cheddar cheese BBQ sauce, onion, and jalapenos to serve.

Cheeseburger Egg Rolls

(TOTAL COOK TIME 40 MINUTES)
INGREDIENTS FOR 18 SERVINGS
THE MEAT
·   Ground brisket (2-lbs, 0.9-kgs)

THE SPRING ROLLS
· Tri-tip seasoning, as needed
· 1 yellow onion, peeled and thinly sliced
· Spicy dill pickles – ½ cup
· Smoky mustard – ½ cup
· 18 egg roll wrappers
· 18 slices American cheese
· Vegetable oil for frying, divided – 8 cups
THE DIP
· Mango, peeled and chopped – ¼ cup
· Sriracha – 1 tablespoon
· Ketchup – 1 tablespoon
· Spicy dill pickles – 1 teaspoon
THE WOOD PELLET GRILL
· Prepare your wood pellet grill to high heat, and arrange a skillet on the grates to preheat
· Set up for direct grilling
· Use your favorite wood pellets
METHOD
1. Add the ground brisket to the preheated grill, season with tri-tip seasoning, and sauté until browned. Transfer the browned meat to a side bowl, but don't drain the fat from the grill.
2. Add the sliced onion to the grill, sprinkle over more seasoning, and sauté until the onions start to scorch. Reduce the heat to moderately low and continue cooking onions until they are softened and caramelized.
3. Transfer the onions to the bowl from Step 1 along and add the pickles and mustard. Stir to combine and season as needed.
4. Assemble the egg rolls. Lay one egg roll wrapper down on a clean worktop, so it is positioned like a diamond. Arrange a slice of cheese on the wrapper and top with a ¼ cup of the beef mixture. Fold the wrapper tip that is closest to you over the filling and roll. Wet the surface of the egg roll with a little water to seal. Repeat the process until all 18 egg rolls are assembled.
5. Heat half of the oil in a large Dutch oven on the grill's side burner until the oil reaches 375°F (190°C).
6. Fry the prepared egg rolls in batches. The egg rolls are cooked when they are evenly golden brown, which will take approximately 2-3 minutes.
7. In the meantime, prepare the dip. Combine the mango, Srirahca, ketchup, and dill pickles in a bowl. Serve the dip alongside the cooked spring rolls and enjoy.

Brisket Sandwich with Special Homemade Sauce

Preparation Time: 200 minutes
Servings: 8 servings per recipe
Ingredients:
· 6 lbs of beef breast
· Beef spices
· 8 sandwiches with Tuscan or ciabatta bread
· Pickles to taste
· Iceberg lettuce for stuffing
Sauce
· ¼ cup BBQ sauce of choice
· 1/8 cup chopped pickles
· 1/8 cup mustard
· 3/8 cup mayonnaise
· ¼ cup ketchup
Instructions:
· Plan on 8 to 12 hours of cooking time for a Six to Eight-pound brisket, or 90 minutes per pound. For brisket, the thermometer is essential.
· Using your choice rub, such as Beef Rub, Rib Rub, or pepper and salt, thoroughly coat the brisket.
· Cover using plastic wrap and set aside. Allow the brisket to sit in the refrigerator for twelve to twenty-four hours.
· Set the grill to 180°F and preheat for 15 minutes with the lid covered when you're ready to cook. If Super Smoke is available, use it for the best flavor.
· Place the brisket on the grill grate fat side down, insert the thermometer probe. Smoke for four hours.
· Increase the temperature of the grill to 250°F after 4 hours. Take the brisket from the grill and cover it in foil when the interior temperature reaches 160°F.
· Replace the probe. Return the foiled brisket to the grill and heat until it reaches a temperature of 204°F.
· Remove the brisket from the pan and let it rest for at least thirty min in the foil.

· To make the special sauce, combine ketchup, BBQ sauce, mustard, mayonnaise, and sliced pickles. Spread the sauce on the buns.

· After resting, slice the brisket and serve it on buns with extra pickles and iceberg lettuce.

Bacon, Egg, And Cheese Sandwich

Preparation Time: 15 minutes
Cooking Time: 20 minutes
Servings: 4
Ingredients
· 2 large eggs
· 2 tablespoons of milk or water
· A pinch of salt to taste
· A pinch of pepper to taste
· 3 teaspoons of butter
· 4 slices of white bread
· 2 slices of Jack cheese
· 4 slices of bacon

Directions:
1. Using a small mixing bowl, add in the eggs, milk, salt, and pepper to taste then mix properly to combine.
2. Preheat a Wood Pellet Grill Smoker Smoker and Grill to 400 degrees F for about ten to fifteen minutes with its lid closed.
3. Place the bacon slices on the preheated grill and grill for about eight to ten minutes, flipping once until it becomes crispy. Set the bacon aside on a paper-lined towel.
4. Decrease the temperature of the grill to 350 degrees F, place a grill pan on the grill, and let it heat for about ten minutes.
5. Spread two tablespoons of butter on the cut side of the bread, place the bread on the skillet pan and toast for about two minutes until brown in color.
6. Place the cheese on the toasted bread, close the lid of the grill then cook for about one minute until the cheese melts completely, set aside. Still using the same grill pan, add in the rest of the butter then let melt. Pour in the egg mixture and cook for a few minutes until it is cooked as desired.

7. Assemble the sandwich as desired then serve.
Nutrition: Calories 401 cal Fat 23g Carbohydrates 26g Fiber 3g Protein 23g

Greek Grilled Scallop Sandwiches

Preparation time: 30 minutes
Servings:4
Ingredients:
· Salt and black pepper
· 1 small black plum, thinly sliced
· Rice vinegar, 1 ½ tsp
· Olive oil
· Pinch of saffron threads
· 12 large sea scallops
· Greek-style whole-milk yogurt
· 36 pea tendrils, 1 cup
· 2 thin slices of prosciutto

Instructions:
· Preheat the grill. Prepare the wood pellet grill and lubricate it with oil. Mix the yogurt, saffron, and vinegar in a mixing dish and add salt and pepper.
· Spray the plum slices with oil and grill for 30 seconds per side over high heat until gently browned. Drizzle the scallops with oil, add salt and pepper, grill them over high heat for about 1 1/2 minutes per side, or until seared and just heated through.
· Each scallop should be halved crosswise. On the bottom half of each scallop lay a plum slice. Place the prosciutto strips atop the plums, top with two pea tendrils, and the scallop tops.
· Place 3 toothpicks on each dish and fix with toothpicks. 1 teaspoon of the yogurt sauce should be spread on each scallop sandwich, and the rest should be topped.

Pork Tenderloin Sandwiches

Preparation Time: 10 MINUTES
Cooking Time: 25 MINUTES
Servings: 6

Ingredients

- 2 (3/4-lb.) pork tenderloins
- 1 teaspoon garlic powder
- 1 teaspoon sea salt
- 1 teaspoon dry mustard
- 1/2 teaspoon coarsely ground pepper
- Olive oil, for brushing
- whole wheat hamburger buns
- tablespoons barbecue sauce

Direction

1. Stir the garlic, salt, pepper, and mustard together in a small mixing bowl.
2. Rub pork tenderloins evenly with olive oil, then seasoning mix.
3. Preheat grill to medium-high heat, and cook 10 to 12 minutes on each side or until a meat thermometer inserted into thickest portion registers 155°F.
4. Slice thin and evenly pile onto hamburger buns.
5. Drizzle each sandwich with barbecue sauce and serve.

Nutrition Energy (calories): 250 kcal Protein: 39.97 g Fat: 5.54 g Carbohydrates: 7.57 g Calcium, Ca18 mg Magnesium, Mg47 mg Phosphorus, P412 mg Iron, Fe1.92 mg Potassium, K686 mg

Funfetti Ice Cream Sandwich

Prep. Time: 1 min
Cook Time: 8 mins
Servings: 8

Ingredients

- Flour ½ Cup.
- Baking Soda ½ tsp
- Baking Powder 1 tsp
- Salt 2/3 tsp
- Butter 1 Cup
- Sugar 1 Cup
- Egg 1
- Vanilla 1 tsp
- Sprinkles 3/4 Cup (Multi-Colored)
- Milk 2 tbsp
- Ice Cream

Instructions

1. When ready to cook, pre-heat the to 350 °F with the lid covered for approximately 10 to 15 mins.
2. In a mixing bowl, combine the flour, milk, salt, and baking soda. Using an electric mixer, cream the sugar and butter together until light and fluffy. Stir together the egg and vanilla essence in a separate dish.
3. Add cup of flour mixture slowly until all of the flour has been added.
4. Place 2 tbsp dough on a prepared cookie sheet, spacing them 4" apart. Flatten the dough with the base of a sugar-dusted glass to keep it from sticking.
5. Place the cookie sheet on the grill and cook for 8 mins, or until nicely browned on both sides. Take the cookies from the grill and place them on a cooling rack.
6. Spread desired quantity of ice cream between two cookies, roll in sprinkles on the edges and devour right away. Have fun with it.

Garlic Parmesan Grilled Cheese Sandwiches

Preparation Time: 2 minutes
Cooking Time: 7 minutes
Servings: 1
Ingredients:

- 2 slices Italian bread, sliced thin
- 2 slices provolone cheese
- 2 tablespoons butter, softened
- Garlic powder, for dusting
- Dried parsley, for dusting
- Parmesan Cheese, shredded, for dusting

Directions:

1. Spread batter evenly across 2 slices of bread and sprinkle each buttered side with garlic and parsley.
2. Sprinkle a few tablespoons of Parmesan cheese over each buttered side of bread and gently press the cheese into the bread.
3. Preheat the grill to medium heat and place one slice of bread, buttered side down into the skillet.
4. Top with provolone slices and second slice of bread with the butter side up.

5. Cook, 3 minutes and flip to cook 3 minutes on the other side; cook until bread is golden and parmesan cheese is crispy.

6. Serve warm with your favorite sides!

Nutrition Energy (calories): 507 kcal Protein: 14.94 g Fat: 38.8 g Carbohydrates: 25.72 g Calcium, Ca447 mg Magnesium, Mg29 mg Phosphorus, P641 mg Iron, Fe1.67 m Potassium, K222 mg

Brie stuffed turkey burgers

Prep. Time: 15 mins
Cook time: 25 mins
Servings: 9
Ingredients
- Blueberry spread (jalapeno)
- Burger buns
- Bar brie cheese 7 Oz
- Sweet burger seasoning (onion) of
- Spinach
- Red Bell peppers 2
- Turkey ground 3 lb

Instructions

1. Brie should be cut into half-inch-wide by one-inch-high pieces.

2. 3 lbs ground turkey, generously seasoned with onion burger seasoning in a mixing bowl.

3. Start dividing the meat into third-pound balls after the spice has been mixed into the ground turkey. Half of the burger patty should go on the base of the burger press, with around three slices of cheese in the middle.

4. Place half of your burger patty on top of the cheese. Press the burger two times with the burger button, and you're done. Flipping the press to drop your burger.

5. Remove the burgers from the grill and begin creating your masterpiece. You can use any retain you want because the sweet & spicy jam adds a lot of spice to the burger.

CHAPTER 14: CHEESE AND BREAD RECIPES

Wood Pellet Grill Smoker Smoked Nut Mix

Preparation Time: 15 minutes
Cooking Time: 20 minutes
Servings: 8
Ingredients
· 3 cups mixed nuts (pecans, peanuts, almonds etc.)
· 1/2 tbsp brown sugar
1 tbsp thyme, dried
· 1/4 tbsp mustard powder
· 1 tbsp olive oil, extra-virgin
Directions:
1. Preheat your Wood Pellet Grill Smoker grill to 250oF with the lid closed for about 15 minutes.
2. Combine all ingredients in a bowl, large, then transfer into a cookie sheet lined with parchment paper.
3. Place the cookie sheet on a grill and grill for about 20 minutes.

4. Remove the nuts from the grill and let cool.
5. Serve and enjoy.
Nutrition: Calories 249, Total fat 21.5g, Saturated fat 3.5g, Total carbs 12.3g, Net carbs 10.1g, Protein 5.7g, Sugars 5.6g, Fiber 2.1g, Sodium 111mg, Potassium 205mg

Chicken Rolls With Speck And Scamorza Cheese

Prep Time: 20 minutes | **Cook Time**: 16 minutes | Difficult Level: Simple
Ingredients for 4 servings:
1 chicken breast of 14 oz
8 slices of speck
8 slices of smoked cheese
Salt and pepper to taste
Olive oil to taste
Directions:
Start by cleaning the chicken breasts of excessive fat or pieces of bone.
Wash and dry the chicken breast and then cut it horizontally to obtain the 4 slices and beat them with the meat tenderizer, wrapping them with baking paper.
Take a slice of chicken and stuff it first with 2 slices of cheese and then with two slices of speck, then roll the slice over itself.
Preheat the grill to 392°F for 10 minutes with the lid closed.
Place the rolls on the grill, well spaced to be able to turn them easily.
Cook for 4 minutes, then rotate them to 90°with the help of the barbecue tongs, and continue cooking for 4 minutes on each side, for a total of 16 minutes.
Remove from the heat and place on a serving dish.
Let the meat rest for a couple of minutes then serve.
Nutrition per 100g:
Calories 272 kcal | Protein: 23g | Carbs: 6g | Fat 14g

Butternut Squash Macaroni plus Cheese

Prep. Time: 5 Mins
Cook Time: 50 Mins
Serving: 2
Ingredients
· Medium Butternut Squash 1
· Small Yellow Onion 1
· Uncooked Macaroni 2 Cup
· Chicken Broth 1/2 Cup
· Pepper
· Milk 1 Cup
· Salt
· Cheese Grated 1 Cup
Instructions

1. When you're ready to cook, turn on the grill, set the temperature to 225 degrees Fahrenheit, and shut the lid for 10 to 15 mins to warm.

2. Poke the butternut squash with a fork several times before placing it on the grill grate. Cook for 40-60 mins, or until the veggies are soft. After the meat has been cooked, scoop it out and throw the seeds.

3. Prepare elbow macaroni according to the package directions. Drain and set aside the water.

4. In a medium pan, sauté the chopped onion until aromatic and golden. Combine broth, salt, milk, butternut squash and onions in a food processor. Puree the ingredients until it is creamy and thick Season with pepper and salt to taste.

5. Boil the pasta and toss it with the pureed sauce and grated cheese. Whisk to melt the cheese, and gradually add milk until you get the desired consistency. Before serving, reheat the dish. Have fun with it.

Chilli Cheese Quesadillas

Prep Time: 10 minutes | **Cooking Time**: 30 minutes | **Servings**: 2

Ingredients:

225g / 8oz chopped cheddar
2 red chillies seeded and finely chopped
4 tomatoes skinned seeded and diced
2 shallots finely chopped
1 clove garlic crushed or finely chopped
50g pine nuts toasted
4 tablespoons chopped fresh coriander
12 x 20cm flour tortillas

Directions:

Combine all of the Ingredients in a mixing dish and leave aside for 10 minutes to enable the flavors to blend. Fill each tortilla wrap with a little quantity of the mixture.

Before the cheese starts to melt, roll the wraps up and place them on the grill. With just enough time for the onion and garlic to melt, you should be able to produce the most amazing chili cheese wrap.

Keep a few to the side so no one notices them, since these tiny fellas may depart your barbeque so rapidly that there will be nothing left for you...always it's a good idea to have a backup plan!

Nutrition per 100g:

Calories 251 kcal | Protein: 18g | Carbs: 10g | Fat 12g

Grilled Homemade Croutons

Preparation Time: 10 minutes
Cooking Time: 30 minutes
Servings: 6
Ingredients
·   2 tbsp Mediterranean Blend Seasoning
·   1/4 cup olive oil
·   6 cups cubed bread
Directions:
1.   Preheat your Wood Pellet Grill Smoker grill to 250oF.
2.   Combine seasoning and oil in a bowl then drizzle the mixture over the bread cubes. Toss to evenly coat.
3.   Layer the bread cubes on a cookie sheet, large, and place on the grill.
4.   Bake for about 30 minutes. Stir at intervals of 5 minutes for browning evenly.
5.   Once dried out and golden brown, remove from the grill.
6.   Serve and enjoy!
Nutrition: Calories 188, Total fat 10g, Saturated fat 2g, Total carbs 20g, Net carbs 19g, Protein 4g, Sugars 2g, Fiber 1g, Sodium 1716mg, Potassium 875mg

Vegan Grilled Cheese (Classic & Bacon)

Prep Time: 15 mins, Serving: 1, Difficulty: Easy
Ingredients
·   2 slices sandwich bread
·   1 tablespoon vegan butter
·   4 slices bacon

· 1/3 cup vegan cheese

Instruction

· Prepare a cast iron pan on moderate flame.

· In a heated skillet, melt 1 tablespoon of vegan butter. Heat until the sandwiches appear lightly browned and crusty. Flip the sandwich with a spatula as you just want to inspect its development.

· Put an additional 1 tbsp of butter into the skillet and delicately turn the sandwich with a spatula.

· Finish with a small sprinkling of vegan cheese shreds on the toasted side.

· Cook till the bottom is lightly browned. Turn the sandwich swiftly once again, frying only long enough for the cheese on the exterior to get cooked and crunchy.

Cold Smoked Cheese

Prep. Time: 5 Mins
Cook Time: 2 Hrs
Serving: 8
Ingredients

· Favored Kind of Block Cheese: Cheddar, Provol 1, Mozzarella

Instructions

1. Pre-heat the to 165°F and close the lid for 15 mins till ready to cook.

2. Transfer the contents of the half-size pan to the full-size pan. Fill a half-size pan halfway with ice until it reaches the tip.

3. In a half-size pan, place the cheese on toothpicks or a cooling rack to allow air to flow and prevent sticking. To cook, put the pan on the grill.

4. Smoke the cheese for an hour. On the grill, turn the cheese over. After adding additional ice to the melting water surrounding the pan, continue to smoke for the next hour.

5. Remove the cheese from the grill by wrapping it in parchment paper. Refrigerate for 2 to 3 days to let flavors come together. As a result, the smoke fragrance would be mellowed.

6. After 2 to 3 days, remove from the freezer, unfold, skin, and serve with the favorite cracker, pickled veggies, and wine. Have fun with it.

Smoked Mac and Cheese

Preparation Time: 2 minutes
Cooking Time: 1 hour
Servings: 2
Ingredients

· 1/2 cup butter, salted
· 1/3 cup flour
· 1/2 tbsp salt
· 6 cups whole milk
· Dash of Worcestershire
· 1/2 tbsp dry mustard
· 1 lb small cooked shells, al dente in well-salted water
· 2 cups white cheddar, smoked
· 2 cups cheddar jack cheese
· 1 cup crushed ritz

Directions:

1. Set your grill on "smoke" and run for about 5-10 minutes with the lid open until fire establishes. Now turn your grill to 325 oF then close the lid.

2. Melt butter in a saucepan, medium, over low--medium heat then whisk in flour.

3. Cook while whisking for about 5-6 minutes over low heat until light tan color.

4. Whisk in salt, milk, Worcestershire, and mustard over low-medium heat stirring frequently until a thickened sauce.

5. Stir noodles, small shells, white sauce, and 1 cup cheddar cheese in a large baking dish, 10x3" high-sided, coated with butter.

6. Top with 1 cup cheddar cheese and ritz.

7. Place on the grill and bake for about 25-30 minutes until a bubbly mixture and cheese melts.

8. Serve immediately. Enjoy!

Nutrition: Calories 628, Total fat 42g, Saturated fat 24g, Total carbs 38g, Net carbs 37g, Protein 25g, Sugars 11g, Fiber 1g, Sodium 807mg, Potassium 699mg

For Maggi Macaroni and Cheese

Method of preparation: Grilling
Preparation time: 30 minutes
Cooking time: 1 hour 30 minutes
Servings: 8
Ingredients:
¼ cup all-purpose flour
½ stick butter
Butter, for greasing
1-pound cooked elbow macaroni
1 cup grated Parmesan
8 ounces cream cheese
2 cup shredded Monterey Jack
3 tsp. garlic powder
2 tsp. salt
1 tsp. pepper
2 cups shredded Cheddar, divided
3 cups of milk
Directions:
Put the butter into the pot and melt. Mix in the flour. Stir constantly for a minute. Mix in the pepper, salt, garlic powder, and milk. Let it boil.
After lowering the heat, let it simmer for about 5 mins, or until it has thickened. Remove from the heat.
Mix in the cream cheese, parmesan, Monterey Jack, and 1½ cup of cheddar. Stir everything until melted. Fold in the pasta.
Add wood pellets to your smoker and follow your cooker's startup procedure. Preheat your smoker, with your lid closed, until it reaches 225.
Butter a 9" x 13" baking pan. Pour the macaroni mixture into the pan and lay on the grill. Cover and allow it to smoke for an hour, or until it has become bubbly. Top the macaroni with the rest of the cheddar during the last
Serve.
Nutrition:
Calories: 493 Protein: 19.29 g Carbs: 52.15 g Fat: 22.84 g

Wood Pellet Grill Smoker Grill Apple Crisp

Preparation Time: 20 minutes
Cooking Time: 1 hour
Servings: 15
Ingredients
· Apples
· 10 large apples
· 1/2 cup flour
1 cup sugar, dark brown
· 1/2 tbsp cinnamon
· 1/2 cup butter slices
· Crisp
3 cups oatmeal, old-fashioned
· 1-1/2 cups softened butter, salted
· 1-1/2 tbsp cinnamon
1 cups brown sugar
Directions:
1.   Preheat your grill to 350 oF.
2.   Wash, peel, core, and dice the apples into cubes, medium-size
3.   Mix together flour, dark brown sugar, and cinnamon then toss with your apple cubes.
4.   Spray a baking pan, 10x13", with cooking spray then place apples inside. Top with butter slices.
5.   Mix all crisp ingredients in a medium bowl until well combined. Place the mixture over the apples.
6.   Place on the grill and cook for about 1-hour checking after every 15-20 minutes to ensure cooking is even. Do not place it on the hottest grill part.
7.   Remove and let sit for about 20-25 minutes
8.   It's very warm.
Nutrition: Calories 528, Total fat 26g, Saturated fat 16g, Total carbs 75g, Net carbs 70g, Protein 4g, Sugars 51g, Fiber 5g, Sodium 209mg, Potassium 122mg

Fromage Macaroni and Cheese

Method of preparation: Grilling
Preparation time: 30 minutes
Cooking time: 1 hour
Servings: 8

Ingredients:
¼ cup all-purpose flour
½ stick butter
Butter, for greasing
1-pound cooked elbow macaroni
1 cup grated Parmesan
8 ounces cream cheese
2 cup shredded Monterey Jack
3 tsp. garlic powder
2 tsp. salt
1 tsp. pepper
2 cup shredded Cheddar, divided
3 cup of milk
Directions:
Add the butter to a pot and melt. Mix in the flour. Stir constantly for a minute. Mix in the pepper, salt, garlic powder, and milk. Let it boil.

After lowering the heat, let it simmer for about 5 mins, or until it has thickened. Remove from the heat.

Mix in the cream cheese, parmesan, Monterey Jack, and 1½ cup of cheddar. Stir everything until melted. Fold in the pasta.

Add wood pellets to your smoker and keep your cooker's startup procedure. Preheat your smoker, with your lid closed, until it reaches 225°F.

Butter a 9" x 13" baking pan. Pour the macaroni mixture into the pan and lay on the grill. Cover and allow it to smoke for an hour, or until it has become bubbly. Top the macaroni with the rest of the cheddar during the last

Serve.

Nutrition:
Calories: 180 Carbs: 19 g Fat: 8 g Protein: 8 g

Rosemary Cheese Bread

Preparation Time: 10 minutes
Cooking Time: 12 minutes
Servings: 30 Breadstick
Ingredients:
- 1½ cup sunflower seeds
- ½ tsp sea salt
- 1egg
- 1tsp fresh rosemary (finely chopped)
- 2tsp xanthan gum
- 2tbsp cream cheese
- 2cups grated mozzarella

Directions:
1. Preheat the grill to 400°F with the lid closed for 15 minutes.
2. Toss the sunflower seeds into a powerful blender and blend until it smooth and flour-like.
3. Transfer the sunflower seed flour into a mixing bowl and add the rosemary and xanthan gum. Mix and set aside.
4. Melt the cheese in a microwave. To do this, combine the cream cheese and mozzarella cheese in a microwave-safe dish.
5. Place the microwave-safe dish in the grill and heat the cheese on high for 1 minute.
6. Bring out the dish and stir. Place the dish in the grill and heat for 30 seconds. Bring out the dish and stir until smooth.
7. Pour the melted cheese into a large mixing bowl.
8. Add the sunflower flour mixture to the melted cheese and stir the ingredients are well combined.
9. Add the salt and egg and mix thoroughly to form a smooth dough.
10. Measure out equal pieces of the dough and roll into sticks.
11. Grease a baking sheet with oil and arrange the breadsticks into the baking sheet in a single layer.
12. Use the back of a knife or metal spoon to make lines on the breadsticks.
13. Place the baking sheet on the grill and make for about 12 minutes or until the breadsticks turn golden brown.
14. Remove the baking sheet from the grill and let the breadsticks cool for a few minutes.
15. Serve.

Nutrition: Calories: 23 Total Fat: 1.9 g Saturated Fat: 0.5 g Cholesterol: 7 mg Sodium: 47 mg Total Carbohydrate: 0.6 g Dietary Fiber: 0.2 g Total Sugars: 0.1 g Protein: 1.2 g

Simple Roasted Butternut Squash

Preparation Time: 5 minutes
Cooking Time: 25 minutes
Servings: 8
Ingredients:

· 1(2 pounds) butternut squash
· 2garlic cloves (minced)
· 2tablespoon extra olive virgin oil
· 1tsp paprika
· 1tsp oregano
· 1tsp thyme
· Salt and pepper to taste

Directions:

1. Start your grill on smoke mode and leave the grill open for 5 minutes, until fire Preheat the grill to 400°F.
2. Peel the butternut squash.
3. Cut the butternut squash into two (cut lengthwise).
4. Use a spoon to scoop out the seeds.
5. Cut the butternut squash into 1-inch chunks and wash the chunks with water.
6. In a big bowl, combine the butternut squash chunks and other ingredients.
7. Stir until the chunks are coated with the ingredients.
8. Spread the coated chunks on the sheet pan.
9. Place the sheet pan on the grill and bake for 25 minutes.
10. Remove the baked butternut squash from heat and let it sit to cool.
11. Serve.

Nutrition: Calories: 8 Total Fat: 3.7 g Saturated Fat: 0.5 g Cholesterol: 0 mg Sodium: 331 mg Total Carbohydrate 13.8 g Dietary Fiber 2.6 g Total Sugars: 2.5 g Protein: 1.2 g

Baked Cherry Cheesecake Galette

Preparation Time: 10 minutes
Cooking Time: 20 minutes
Servings: 6-8
Ingredients:

• For the cherry filling:
• 1-pound cherries (thawed, drained)
• ¼ cup of sugar
• 1 tsp. cornstarch
• 1 tsp. coriander
• A pinch of salt
• 1 tbsp. orange zest
• ½ tablespoon lemon zest
• For the cream cheese filling:
• 8 ounces of cream cheese (softened)
• 1 tsp. vanilla
• ¼ cup of sugar
• One egg
• For the galette:
• One refrigerated pie crust
• 1 egg, 1 tbsp. water, cream, or milk
• Granulated sugar
• Vanilla ice cream to serve

Directions:

1. Grab a medium bowl; mix your cherries, orange zest, lemon zest, and coriander, half of the sugar, cornstarch, and a pinch of salt.
2. Grab another bowl, and in it, mix your egg, vanilla, and cream cheese. Whip it up.
3. Get your pie dough onto a sheet tray, and then stretch it out with a rolling pin. Get it to about 1 inch in diameter.
4. Spread out your cream cheese filling in the middle of the pie dough. Be careful to leave a border of an inch around the edge. Then pile your cherry mix on the cream cheese.
5. Now, you're going to fold in the pie dough's edges into little parts over the filling.
6. Next, brush the edges of the pie dough with egg wash, and then sprinkle on some granulated sugar.

On the Grill:

1. Set up your wood pellet smoker grill for indirect cooking.
2. Preheat your wood pellet smoker grill at a temperature of 350 degrees Fahrenheit, keeping it closed for 15 minutes.
3. Set your sheet to try right on the grill grate, and then bake that yummy goodness for 15 to 20 minutes. You want the crust to become nice and golden brown and for the cheesecake filling to be completely set.
4. Dish the galette while warm with some ice cream. And then enjoy.

Nutrition: Calories: 400 Cal Fat: 51 g Carbohydrates: 18 g Protein: 5 g Fiber: 3 g

CHAPTER 15: FISH AND SEAFOOD RECIPES

Baked Salmon Fishcakes

(TOTAL COOK TIME 1 HOUR 20 MINUTES)
INGREDIENTS FOR 3-4 SERVINGS
THE FISH
· Fresh salmon, bones, and skin removed (2-lbs, 0.9-kgs)
THE INGREDIENTS
· Salt and freshly ground black pepper
· ½ small onion, peeled and diced
· 1 celery, trimmed and diced
· 1 red bell pepper, trimmed and diced
· Fresh or dried dill – 1 tablespoon
· Lemon zest – 1 teaspoon
· Sea salt – ¼ teaspoon
· Breadcrumbs – 1½ - 2 tablespoons
· 2 eggs
· Extra-virgin olive oil – 3 tablespoons
THE WOOD PELLET GRILL

· With the lid closed, preheat your wood pellet grill to 275°F (135°C) for 15 minutes

· Maple wood pellets are a good choice for this recipe
METHOD
1. Season the fish with salt and black pepper.
2. Place the salmon directly on the grill grate and cook until the fish registers an internal temperature of 120°F (49°C). Remove the fish from the grill and put aside to cool.
3. Transfer the now cooled salmon to a large bowl, and using a metal for, break the fish up.
4. Add the onion, diced celery, diced bell pepper, dill, lemon zest, sea salt, black pepper, breadcrumbs, and eggs. Mix thoroughly to combine, adding more breadcrumbs if needed for the mixture to hold together.
5. Using clean hands, shape the mixture into 6 even-size patties.

6. Turn the grill heat up to 375°F (190°C) and preheat for 10-12 minutes with the lid closed.
7. Once the oil is hot, add the salmon patties to a cast iron pan, and in batches, cook for 5-6 minutes. Flip the patties over and cook for another 5-6 minutes, until golden.
8. Serve and enjoy.

Grilled Saké Shrimp

Prep. Time: 120 mins
Cook Time: 10 mins
Servings: 4
Ingredients
· Shrimp with Tails 24 (Large)
· Soy Sauce 3 tbsp
· Japanese Sake ½ cup
· Lemon Juice 1 tbsp
· Fresh Ginger 1 inch (peeled and sliced into coins).
· Scallions 1
· Clove Garlic 1
· Sugar 1 tsp
· Sesame Oil 1 tbsp
· Wedges of lemon 1
Instructions
1. Rinse the shrimp and drain them.
2. In a large mixing bowl or plastic container, combine the sake, soy sauce, scallion, garlic, ginger, sugar, lemon juice, and oil to prepare the marinade (resealable).
3. Swirl the shrimp in the bag to coat them. Refrigerate the marinade for 2 hours, stirring the bag occasionally to disperse it.
4. Preheat the to 450°F and keep the lid closed for 15 mins until ready to cook.
5. Drain and pat the shrimp dry before threading three shrimp onto each of the eight skewers. Cook the shrimp skewers and lemon wedges for 3-4 mins each hand on the grill, turning once, or until opaque and cooked through. Have fun with it.

Lobster Tail

Preparation Time: 10 minutes
Cooking Time: 1 hour and 5 minutes
Servings: 2
Ingredients:
• Two lobster tails, each about 8-ounce
• 1/4 teaspoon old bay seasoning
• 1/4 teaspoon garlic salt
• 1/4 teaspoon ground black pepper
• 8 tbsp. butter, unsalted
• 1 tsp. paprika
• 2 tbsp. lemon juice
• 2 tbsp. chopped parsley
Directions:
1.   Open the smoker's hopper, add dry pallets, make sure ash-can is in place, and then open the ash damper, power on the smoker, and close the ash damper.
2.   Set the temperature of the smoker to 450 degrees F, switch smoker to open flame cooking mode, press the open flame 3, remove the grill grates and the batch, replace batch with direct flame insert, then return grates on the grill in the lower position and let preheat for 30 minutes or until the green light on the dial blinks that indicate smoker has reached to set temperature.
3.   Meanwhile, prepare the lobster and for this, use kitchen shears to cut down the middle of the shell and then lift out the meat by using your fingers from it but keep it attached at the base of the tail.
4.   Then butterfly the crab meat by making a slit down the middle and place the lobster tails on a baking sheet.
5.   Put a saucepan over medium-low heat, add butter and when it melts, add garlic salt, black pepper, paprika, parsley, old bay seasoning, and lemon juice, stir well and remove the pan from the heat.
6.   Spoon 1 tablespoon of the butter sauce over each lobster tail, then transfer lobster tails to the smoker grill from the baking sheet and shut with lid.
7.   Smoke the lobster tails for 30 minutes or until its meat is white.
8.   When done, transfer lobster tails to a dish and serve with remaining butter sauce.

Nutrition: Calories: 131.9; Total Fat: 4 g; Saturated Fat: 1 g; Protein: 20.1 g; Carbs: 1.4 g; Fiber: 0.1 g; Sugar: 0 g

Simple Glazed Salmon Fillets

Prep. Time: 5 mins
Cook Time: 25 mins
Servings: 2
Ingredients
·   Salmon Fillets 6-8 Ounces
·   Mayonnaise, ½ Cup
·   Feather and Fin Rub
·   Dijon Mustard 2 tbsp
·   Tarragon or Dill 1 tbsp
·   Lemon Juice 1 tbsp
·   Lemon Wedges
Instructions
1. Season the fillets with Fin and Feather Rub.
2. To make the glaze, combine the mayonnaise and mustard in a shallow mixing cup. In a mixing dish, combine the tarragon or dill and lemon juice.
3. The glaze should be applied to the fleshy side of the fillets.
4. Preheat the grill up to 350°F for 15 mins with the lid closed when ready to cook.
5. Put the salmon fillets on the grill grate skin-side down. Grill the fish for 25-30 mins, or until opaque and flaky when flaked with a fork.
6. Serve immediately with sliced lemons and (minced) dill on a plate or in bowls. Enjoy yourself.

Grilled Lobster Tail

Preparation Time: 10 minutes
Cooking Time: 15 minutes
Servings: 4
Ingredients:
·   2 (8 ounces each) lobster tails
·   1/4 tsp old bay seasoning
·   ½ tsp oregano
·   1 tsp paprika
·   Juice from one lemon

- 1/4 tsp Himalayan salt
- 1/4 tsp freshly ground black pepper
- 1/4 tsp onion powder
- 2 tbsp freshly chopped parsley
- ¼ cup melted butter

Directions:

1. Slice the tail in the middle with a kitchen shear. Pull the shell apart slightly and run your hand through the meat to separate the meat partially
2. Combine the seasonings
3. Drizzle lobster tail with lemon juice and season generously with the seasoning mixture.
4. Preheat your wood pellet smoker to 450°F, using apple wood pellets.
5. Place the lobster tail directly on the grill grate, meat side down. Cook for about 15 minutes.
6. The tails must be pulled off and it must cool down for a few minutes
7. Drizzle melted butter over the tails.
8. Serve and garnish with fresh chopped parsley.

Nutrition: Calories: 146 Cal Fat: 11.7 g Carbohydrates: 2.1 g Protein: 9.3 g Fiber: 0.8 g

Vodka Brined Salmon

Preparation Time: 4 hours 10 minutes
Cooking Time: 2 hours
Servings: 6
Ingredients:
- 2 pounds salmon fillets
- 1/2 cup salt
- 1 cup brown sugar
- 1 tbsp. ground black pepper
- 1 cup vodka

Directions:

1. Pour vodka into a bowl, add salt, sugar, and black pepper and stir until mixed.
2. Place salmon in a large plastic bag, pour in vodka mixture, then seal the bag, turn it upside down to coat salmon with vodka mixture and let marinate in the refrigerator for 4 hours.

3. When ready to cook, open the smoker's hopper, add dry pallets, make sure the ash-can is in place, open the ash damper, power on the smoker, and close the ash damper.
4. Set the smoker's temperature to 180 degrees F, let preheat for 30 minutes or until the green light on the dial blinks that indicate the smoker has reached to set temperature.
5. Remove salmon from the marinade, place it on the smoker grill, and smoke for 30 minutes.
6. Then, increase the smoker's temperature to 225 degrees F and continue smoking the salmon for 1 hour or until the salmon's internal temperature reaches 140 degrees F.
7. When done, transfer salmon to a dish and serve with lemon wedges.

Nutrition: Calories: 456.3; Total Fat: 11.2 g; Saturated Fat: 2 g; Protein: 33.1 g; Carbs: 35.4 g; Fiber: 0 g; Sugar: 35.5 g

Smoked Albacore Tuna

Prep. Time: 10 mins
Cook Time: 240 mins
Servings: 4
Ingredients
- Kosher Salt 1 Cup
- Orange 1
- Brown Sugar 1 Cup
- Albacore Tuna Fillets 8 Oz
- Lemon 1

Instructions

1. In a shallow dish, combine the sugar, salt, and citrus zest. In a container, layer the fish and brine, ensuring that if the fillets are piled, there is enough brine between them so that they don't touch. Refrigerate for at least 6 hours in order to brine.
2. Drain the fillets of any remaining brine. Chill for 30-40 mins on a greased cooling rack after thoroughly drying.
3. Preheat the up to 180°F (covered) for 15 mins when ready to cook. Use Super Smoke if it's available for a better flavor.
4. Remove the fillets from the fridge and place them on the grill for 3 hours.

5. Raise the temperature. Preheat the grill to 225°F and cook for another hour, or until the fish is a light brown color and readily flakes with a fork.

6. Remove the steaks from the grill and serve immediately, or set them aside to cool. It will be good for up to 7 days in the fridge. Have fun with it.

Coriander Rub Smoked Salmon Fillet

(Cooking Time 1 hour 10 minutes)
Ingredients for 10 servings
· Salmon fillet (5-lb., 2.3-kg.)
The Rub
· Ground coriander - 2 tablespoons
· Black peppercorns - 1 teaspoon
· Brown sugar - ½ cup
· Dill weed - 1 teaspoon
· Celery seeds - ½ teaspoon
· Cumin - 1 teaspoon
· Fennel seeds - ½ teaspoon
· Garlic powder - 1 tablespoon
· Onion powder - ½ tablespoon
· Paprika - 1 teaspoon
· Chili powder - ½ teaspoon
· Kosher salt - 1 teaspoon
· Black pepper - ¼ teaspoon
The Heat
· Alder wood pellet
Method

1. Place the ground coriander in a bowl together with black peppercorns, brown sugar, dill weed, celery seeds, cumin, fennel seeds, garlic powder, onion powder, paprika, chili powder, salt, and pepper. Mix until combined.

2. Rub the spice mixture over the salmon fillet and set aside.

3. Next, plug the wood pellet smoker then fill the hopper with the wood pellet. Turn the switch on and set the wood pellet smoker for indirect heat.

4. Adjust the temperature to 200°F (93°C) and let the wood pellet smoker reaches the desired temperature.

5. Place the seasoned salmon fillet in the wood pellet smoker and smoke it for approximately 1 hour.

6. Once the internal temperature of the smoked salmon fillet reaches 145°F (63°C), remove it from the wood pellet smoker. The smoked salmon fillet will flake.

7. Place the smoked salmon fillet on a serving dish and serve.

8. Enjoy!

Baked Whole Fish in Sea Salt

Prep. Time: 10 mins
Cook Time: 30 mins
Servings: 4
Ingredients
· Branzino 3 Pound
· Lemon 1
· Thyme Sprigs 10
· Sea Salt 5 Cup
· Olive Oil
· Egg White 10
· Lemon 1 (Juiced)

Instructions

1. When ready to cook, preheat the on High with the lid covered for approximately 10-15 mins.

2. Gills and fins of the fish should be cut. The cavity should be packed with thyme and lemon slices. After beating the egg whites to soft peaks, fold in the sea salt.

3. Place immediately on the grill and roast for approximately 30 mins, or until an internal temperature of 165°F is reached. When a thermometer is pierced through the salt coating and into the meat of the fish, it reads 135-140°F. Take the salmon from the grill and allow it to cool for 10 mins.

4. Slap the crust open with a wooden spoon to remove any remaining salt from the fish's body.

5. Remove the skin of the fish and cover it in olive oil and lemon juice. Have fun with it.

Teriyaki Salmon

Prep. Time: 60 mins
Cook Time: 10 mins
Servings: 2
Ingredients
- Soy Sauce 1 cup
- Clove Garlic 4
- Brown Sugar 6 tbsp
- Ginger 1 tbsp (Minced)
- Orange Zest 2
- Orange 2 (Juiced)
- Salmon Fillets 6 oz
- Scallions (Chopped)
- Sesame Seeds 1 tbsp
- Sesame Seeds (Toasted)

Instructions

1. Combine everything in a saucepan except the sesame seeds and the fish. Bring to a boil, then lower to a syrupy consistency (about a 50% reduction). Allow cooling before serving.
2. In a dish, mix the sesame seeds and fish and marinate for 1 hour.
3. Take the salmon from the marinade and bring the sauce to a boil in a saucepan.
4. Preheat the grill to high heat with the lid covered for 10-15 mins. Put the salmon fillets on the grill grate, skin side up.
5. Cook the salmon for approximately 3-5 mins on each side, or until done to your liking, brushing it with the "Teriyaki Sauce" as needed.
6. Remove the salmon from the pan after it's cooked to your liking and sprinkle with sliced scallions and toasted sesame seeds. Have fun with it.

Grilled Salmon

Preparation Time: 10 minutes
Cooking Time: 40 minutes
Servings: 8
Ingredients:
- 2 pounds salmon (cut into fillets)
- 1/2 cup low sodium soy sauce
- 2 garlic cloves (grated)
- 4 tbsp olive oil
- 2 tbsp honey

- 1 tsp ground black pepper
- ½ tsp smoked paprika
- ½ tsp Italian seasoning
- 2 tbsp chopped green onion

Directions:
1. Incorporate pepper, paprika, Italian seasoning, garlic, soy sauce and olive oil. Add the salmon fillets and toss to combine. Cover the bowl and refrigerate for 1 hour.
2. Remove the fillets from the marinade and let it sit for about 2 hours, or until it is at room temperature.
3. Start the wood pellet on smoke, leaving the lid opened for 5 minutes, or until fire starts.
4. Keep lid unopened and preheat grill to a temperature 350°F for 15 minutes.
5. Do not open lid for 4 minutes or until cooked
6. Flip the fillets and cook for additional 25 minutes or until the fish is flaky.
7. Remove the fillets from heat and let it sit for a few minutes.
8. Serve warm and garnish with chopped green onion.

Nutrition: Calories: 317 Cal Fat: 18.8 g Carbohydrates: 8.3 g Protein: 30.6 g Fiber: 0.4 g

Grilled Swordfish with Corn Salsa

Prep. Time: 15 mins
Cook Time: 30 mins
Servings: 4
Ingredients
- Ears Corn 4
- Salt
- Olive Oil 2 cups
- Pepper
- Red Onion 1 (Diced)
- Cherry Tomatoes 2 Oz
- Chile, Serrano 1 (Chopped)
- Swordfish Fillet 4 (whole)
- Lime 1 (Juiced)

Instructions

1. Preheat the oven to high heat for 15 mins, then shut the lid until ready to cook.
2. Season corn with pepper and salt and drizzle with olive oil. After 12-15 mins on the grill, the corn should be cooked through and nicely browned. Allow time for the dish to cool before serving.
3. Remove the kernels from the corn when it has cooled and place them in a mixing cup. In a mixing bowl, mix the tomatoes, cilantro, serrano, lime juice and red onion. Toss to combine and season to taste with salt.
4. After coating the fish steaks with olive oil, season them with salt and pepper.
5. Place the fish on the grill grate and cook for 18 mins, or until opaque and flaky when poked with a fork. (If you want your tuna or salmon rare, cook it for a shorter period.)
6. Pile up the corn salsa on top of the cooked swordfish. Have fun with it.

is in place, open the ash damper, power on the smoker, and close the ash damper.
5.   Set the temperature of the smoker to20 degrees F; let preheat for 30 minutes or until the green light on the dial blinks that indicate the smoker has reached to set temperature.
6.   Meanwhile, pat dries the plant, arranges marinated salmon fillets on it, and places them on the smoker grill.
7.   Shut the smoker with a lid, smoke for 1 hour, then baste salmon fillets with half of the chili sauce and continue smoking for 1 hour.
8.   Then, increase the smoker's temperature to 350 degrees F, baste fillets with remaining chili sauce, flip the fillets, and continue smoking the fillets until the salmon's internal temperature reaches 130 degrees F.
9.   Serve straight away.
Nutrition: Calories: 370; Total Fat: 13.1 g; Saturated Fat: 1.8 g; Protein: 38.3 g; Carbs: 20.4 g; Fiber: 0.3 g; Sugar: 12.4 g

Cedar Plank Salmon

Preparation Time: 2 hours 10 minutes
Cooking Time: 2 hours 45 minutes
Servings: 4
Ingredients:
• 2 pounds salmon fillets
• ¼ cup brown sugar
• ¼ cup of soy sauce
• 3 tbsp. apple cider vinegar
• ¼ cup red wine
• ¼ cup sweet Thai chili sauce
• Cedar plank as needed
Directions:
1.   Place sugar in a small bowl, add soy sauce, vinegar, and red wine, and stir well until combined.
2.   Place salmon fillets in a large plastic bag, pour in brown sugar mixture, seal the bag, turn it upside down to coat salmon with the combination and marinate in the refrigerator for 2 hours.
3.   In the meantime, soak the cider plank in the water.
4.   When ready to cook, open the smoker's hopper, add dry pallets, make sure the ash-can

Grilled Shrimp Brochette

Prep. Time: 20 mins
Cook Time: 20 mins
Servings: 6
Ingredients
·   Shrimp 1 lb (Peeled and Deveined)
·   Block Monterey Jack Cheese 8 Oz
·   Whole Jalapeños 6
·   Bacon, 1 lb
·   Some Oil
·   Meat Church the Gospel All-Purpose Rub 2 tbsp
Instructions
1. Peel the shrimp and cut them in half. After removing the seeds, slice the jalapenos into thin slivers. Slice the cheese into slivers about the same size as the peppers. Cut the bacon strips in half.
2. Stuff a jalapeño slice and a piece of cheese inside each shrimp. Secure the filled shrimp in a half-piece of bacon with a toothpick.
3. After assembling all of the shrimp, season lightly the Meat Church with gospel all-purpose rub.

4. Preheat the to 425°F for 15 mins with the lid closed when ready to cook.

5. Lightly grease the grill grate before placing the shrimp straight on it. Cook for approximately 20 mins, turning halfway during the cooking time. The bacon should start to crisp up, and the shrimp should become yellow.

6. Take the steaks from the grill and lay them aside to cool for at least 10 mins. Have fun with it.

Halibut Fish Sticks

(TOTAL COOK TIME 35 MINUTES)
INGREDIENTS FOR 4 SERVINGS
THE FISH
·   Fresh halibut, skinned, rinsed, patted dry (1.5-lbs, 0.7-kgs)
THE INGREDIENTS
·   Extra-virgin olive oil, as needed
·   All-purpose flour – ½ cup
·   Salt – 1½ teaspoons
·   Freshly ground black pepper – 1 teaspoon
·   2 eggs
·   Panko breadcrumbs – 1½ cups
·   Dried parsley – 2 tablespoons
·   Dried dill – 1 teaspoon
·   Seafood sauce, store-bought, of choice, to serve, optional
THE WOOD PELLET GRILL
·   With the lid closed, preheat your wood pellet grill to 500°F (260°C) for 15 minutes
·   Hickory wood pellets are a good choice for this recipe
METHOD
1.   Cut the fish into 1-ins (2.5-cms) strips.
2.   Add a splash of oil to a Dutch oven.
3.   Place the Dutch oven in your pellet grill to preheat for around 10 minutes.
4.   In a bowl, combine the flour with the salt and black pepper.
5.   In a second bowl, beat the eggs.
6.   In a third small bowl, combine the breadcrumbs with the dried parsley and dried dill.

7.   Dip the fish strips first in the flour, then in the beaten egg, and finally in the seasoned breadcrumbs.
8.   Add the fish sticks to the oil, and fry for around 3-4 minutes, or until they register an internal temperature of 130°F (55°C).
9.   Serve and enjoy with your favorite seafood sauce.

Smoked Chilean Sea Bass

Prep. Time: 5 mins
Cook Time: 40 mins
Servings: 4
Ingredients
Marinade
·   Grapeseed ¼ Cup
·   Clove Garlic 1 (Crushed)
·   Lemon 1 (Juiced)
·   Fresh Oregano 1 tbsp
·   Fresh Thyme 1 tbsp
·   Blackened Saskatchewan rub 1 tsp
Main
·   Fresh Chilean Fillets 6 Oz
·   Chicken Rub
·   Pure Irish Kerry gold Butter 8 tbsp
·   Lemon 4 slices (for garnish)

Instructions

1. To make the marinade, combine all of the marinade ingredients in a big (resealable) bag and thoroughly mix them together.

2. Toss in the sea bass with the prepared marinade and chill for at least 30 mins. At the very least, turn it once.

3. Preheat the oven to at least 325°F while keeping the lid covered for 15 mins.

4. Place the butter on a baking dish large enough to hold the fillets flat and melt it completely under the grill.

5. Remove the fish from the marinade and place it on a clean, flat surface. Fill the container with the marinade and butter. The fillets should be thoroughly seasoned with Chicken Rub.

6. After putting the fillets in the pan along with the butter mixture, return them to the grill.

Cook for 30 mins, basting the fillets once or twice with the hot butter mixture.

7. Remove the fish from the after its internal temperature reaches 160°F. As a garnish, fresh lemon and thyme slices may be used. Have fun with it.

Crab Stuffed Tomato

Preparation Time: 10 minutes
Cooking Time: 45 minutes
Serving: 4
Recommended Wood Type: Alder/ Apple/ Cherry
Ingredients
• 1 pound of the fresh lump of crabmeat
• 2 cups of panko bread crumbs
• 1 cup of chopped scallions, with the white and green pats, moved
• Two large eggs, beaten
• ½ a cup of melted butter
• ¼ cup of freshly squeezed lemon juice
• 1 tsp. Of salt
• ½ a teaspoon of freshly ground black pepper
• Eight large tomatoes, hollowed out, making sure to leave enough flesh all around on the bottom to form a nice shell
Directions:
1. Take your drip pan and add water; cover with aluminum foil. Pre-heat your smoker to 200 degrees F
2. Use water fill water pan halfway through and place it over drip pan. Add wood chips to the side tray
3. Take a large-sized bowl and stir in crabmeat, scallions, bread crumbs, eggs, lemon juice, butter, salt, and pepper
4. Stuff the mixture into the tomatoes and transfer to the smoker
5. Smoke for 45 minutes. Enjoy!
Nutrition: Calories: 559 Fats: 5g Carbs: 57g Fiber: 1g

Oyster in Shells

Preparation Time: 25 minutes
Cooking Time: 8 minutes
Servings: 4
Ingredients:
· 12 medium oysters
· 1 tsp oregano
· 1 lemon (juiced)
· 1 tsp freshly ground black pepper
· 6 tbsp unsalted butter (melted)
· 1 tsp salt or more to taste
· 2 garlic cloves (minced)
· 2 ½ tbsp grated parmesan cheese
· 2 tbsp freshly chopped parsley
Directions:
1. Remove dirt
2. Open the shell completely. Discard the top shell.
3. Gently run the knife under the oyster to loosen the oyster foot from the bottom shell.
4. Repeat step 2 and 3 for the remaining oysters.
5. Combine melted butter, lemon, pepper, salt, garlic and oregano in a mixing bowl.
6. Pour ½ to 1 tsp of the butter mixture on each oyster.
7. Start your wood pellet grill on smoke, leaving the lid opened for 5 minutes, or until fire starts.
8. Keep lid unopened to preheat in the set "HIGH" with lid closed for 15 minutes.
9. Gently arrange the oysters onto the grill grate.
10. Grill oyster for 6 to 8 minutes or until the oyster juice is bubbling and the oyster is plump.
11. Remove oysters from heat. Serve and top with grated parmesan and chopped parsley.
Nutrition: Calories: 200 Cal Fat: 19.2 g Carbohydrates: 3.9 g Protein: 4.6 g Fiber: 0.8 g

Citrus Salmon

Prep. Time: 10 mins
Cook Time: 15 mins
Servings: 2

Ingredients
·   Softened Butter 2 Tbsp
·   Lemon Juice 1 tsp
·   Lemon Zest ½ tsp
·   Fresh Sliced dill 2 tsp
·   Black Pepper
·   Salt ½ tsp
·   Lemon 1 (Thinly cut)
·   Salmon Fillets 4 (8 Oz)

Instructions

1. When you're ready to cook, preheat the to 350°F and shut the lid for roughly 15 mins.

2. In a mixing bowl, combine the salt, lemon zest, and pepper, dill, melted butter, and lemon juice.

3. Using the butter dilled with lemon and one lemon slice, generously cover the salmon fillets.

4. Place the salmon fillets on a hot grill, skin-side down, and cook until done. Cook it for 15-20 mins for moderate-rare salmon, or until it's done to your liking, then garnish with dill. Take pleasure in your food.

Lime and Coconut Marinade Smoked Whole Salmon

(Cooking Time 1 hour 30 minutes)

Ingredients for 10 servings
·   Whole salmon (6-lb., 2.7-kg.)

The Marinade
·   Coconut milk - 1 cup
·   Fresh limes - 2
·   Soy sauce - 2 tablespoons
·   Fish sauce - 1 tablespoon
·   Chili powder - ½ teaspoon
·   Kosher salt - ½ teaspoon

The Heat
·   Oak wood pellet

Method

1.   Cut the limes into halves and squeeze the juice over the coconut milk.

2.   Season the liquid mixture with soy sauce, fish sauce, chili powder, and salt. Stir until incorporated.

3.   Put the whole salmon into the liquid mixture and make sure that the seasoning mixture completely covers the salmon.

4.   Marinate the salmon for an hour and store it in the fridge to keep the salmon fresh.

5.   Next, plug the wood pellet smoker then fill the hopper with the wood pellet. Turn the switch on and set the wood pellet smoker for indirect heat.

6.   Adjust the temperature to 225°F (107°C) and let the wood pellet smoker reaches the desired temperature.

7.   When the wood pellet smoker is ready, place the salmon in the wood pellet smoker and smoke it until flakes. It will take for approximately an hour and 30 minutes.

8.   Once it is done, take the smoked salmon out of the wood pellet smoker and place it on a serving dish.

9.   Serve and enjoy!

Grilled Shrimp with Shrimp Butter

Preparation time: 30 minutes
Servings:6
Ingredients:
·   Unsalted butter, 6 tbsp.
·   Finely chopped red onion, ½ cup
·   Red pepper, 1 ½ tsp
·   Malaysian shrimp taste, 1 tsp
·   Fresh lime juice, 1 ½ tsp
·   Salt
·   Black pepper
·   24 large shrimps, shelled and deveined
·   6 large wooden skewers, soaked for half an hour
·   For, garnish, mint leaves and assorted sprouts

Instructions:

·   Add 3 tablespoons of butter to a small skillet and melt it finely. Heat, occasionally stirring, until the onion is translucent, about 3 minutes.

·   Sauté, occasionally whisking, for 2 minutes, until the crushed red pepper and shrimp paste are aromatic. Season with salt and lime juice, as well as the remaining 3 tablespoons of butter. Warm the butter with the shrimp.

· Prepare the wood pellet grill and lubricate it with oil. Sprinkle the shrimp with salt and pepper before threading them onto the skewers (don't overcrowd them).

· Roast for 4 minutes totals over high heat, rotating once, until golden brown and lightly seared through. Transfer to a serving plate and top with the shrimp butter. Serve garnished with mint leaves and sprouts.

Peppercorn Tuna Steak

Preparation Time: 8 hours
Cooking Time: 10 minutes
Serving: 8
Recommended Wood Type: Alder/ Apple/ Cherry
Ingredients
• ¼ cup of salt
• 2 pound of yellow fin tuna
• ¼ cup of Dijon mustard
• Freshly ground black pepper
• 2 tbsp. of peppercorn
Directions:
1. Take a large-sized container and dissolve salt in warm water (enough water to cover fish)
2. Transfer tuna to the brine and cover, refrigerate for 8 hours
3. Take your drip pan and add water; cover with aluminum foil. Pre-heat your smoker to 225 degrees F
4. Use water fill water pan halfway through and place it over drip pan. Add wood chips to the side tray
5. Remove tuna from bring and pat it dry
6. Transfer to grill pan and spread Dijon mustard all over
7. Season with pepper and sprinkle peppercorn on top
8. Transfer tuna to smoker and smoker for 1 hour. Enjoy!
Nutrition: Calories: 707 Fats: 57g Carbs: 10g Fiber: 2g

Spicy Grilled Shrimp

Preparation time:20 minutes
Servings:8
Ingredients:
· Extra virgin olive oil, ¼ cup
· Lime juice, ¼ cup
· 4 garlic cloves, minced
· Honey, 3 tbsp.
· Low-sodium soy sauce, 2 tbsp.
· Chili garlic sauce or Sriracha
· Shrimp, peeled and deveined, 2 pounds
· For garnish, freshly chopped cilantro, ¼ cup
· For serving, lime wedges
Instructions:
· Immerse wooden skewers in water for 30 minutes before using.
· Combine olive oil, garlic, lime juice, soy sauce, honey, and chili sauce in a medium mixing bowl. 1/3 cup marinade should be saved to spray on the shrimp when cooking.
· Prepare the wood pellet grill and lubricate it with oil. Mix the shrimp with the remaining marinade in a large mixing bowl. Put shrimp onto skewers while the grill or grill pan is heating up. Heat the shrimp for 3 minutes per side, basting with the reserved 1/4 cup marinade before and after each turn.
· Serve with lime wedges and cilantro on the side.

Grilled Tilapia

Preparation Time: 10 minutes
Cooking Time: 20 minutes
Servings: 6
Ingredients:
· 2 tsp dried parsley
· ½ tsp garlic powder
· 1 tsp cayenne pepper
· ½ tsp ground black pepper
· ½ tsp thyme
· ½ tsp dried basil
· ½ tsp oregano
· 3 tbsp olive oil
· ½ tsp lemon pepper
· 1 tsp kosher salt

- 1 lemon (juiced)
- 6 tilapia fillets
- 1 ½ tsp creole seafood seasoning

Directions:
1. In a mixing bowl, combine spices
2. Brush the fillets with oil and lemon juice.
3. Liberally, season all sides of the tilapia fillets with the seasoning mix.
4. Preheat your grill to 325°F
5. Place a non-stick BBQ grilling try on the grill and arrange the tilapia fillets onto it.
6. Grill for 15 to 20 minutes
7. Remove fillets and cool down

Nutrition: Calories: 176 Cal Fat: 9.6 g Carbohydrates: 1.5 g Protein: 22.3 g Fiber: 0.5 g

Barbecue Halibut Steak

Preparation time:25 minutes
Servings:3
Ingredients:
- Butter, 2 tbsp.
- Brown sugar, 2 tbsp.
- 2 garlic cloves, minced
- Lemon juice, 1 tbsp.
- Soy sauce, 2 tsp
- Freshly ground black pepper, ½ tsp
- 1 halibut steak

Instructions:
- Heat the grill to medium-high.
- In a small saucepan, combine the butter, brown sugar, garlic, lemon juice, soy sauce, and pepper. Heat, frequently mixing, over medium heat until sugar is fully dissolved.
- Prepare the wood pellet grill and lubricate it with oil. Grease the grill grate generously. Put the fish on the grill after coating it with brown sugar sauce. Heat for 5 minutes per side, brushing with sauce until fish can easily split with a fork. Remove and dump any remaining basting sauce.

Grilled Crab Legs With Lime Butter

(TOTAL COOK TIME 10 MINUTES)
INGREDIENTS FOR 2 SERVINGS
THE SEAFOOD
- King crab legs, split lengthwise (2-lbs, 0.9-kgs)

THE BUTTER
- Salted butter– 6 tablespoons
- Freshly squeezed juice and zest of 2 limes
- Chicken rub – 1 tablespoon
- Cumin – 1 teaspoon

THE WOOD PELLET GRILL
- Prepare your smoker grill for smoking at 225°F (107°C)
- Add your choice of wood pellets

METHOD
1. In a microwave-safe bowl, combine the salted butter with the lime zest and juice, chicken rub, and cumin. Microwave for 25-30 seconds until melted.
2. Makes sure that all of the crab legs are free from any shell fragments and lay them split side facing upwards on the grill. Cook for 7 minutes, flipping over once.
3. Transfer to a platter and serve with the melted lime butter.

Grilled Sea Scallops with Corn Salad

Preparation time: 20 minutes
Servings:6
Ingredients:
- 6 ears of corn, shucked
- 1-pint grape tomatoes, halved
- 3 scallions, white and light green parts only, thinly sliced
- 1/3 cup basil leaves, thinly sliced
- Salt and freshly ground black pepper
- 1 small shallot, minced
- Balsamic vinegar, 2 tbsp.
- Hot water, 2 tbsp.
- Dijon mustard, 1 tsp
- Sunflower oil, ¼ cup plus 3 tbsp.
- 1.5 pounds sea scallops (about 30)

Instructions:

· Stir the corn until golden in a large pot of boiling salted water, about 5 minutes. Strain and set aside to cool. Remove the kernels from the corn and place them in a big bowl. Sprinkle with salt and add the tomatoes, scallions, and basil.

· Sautee the shallot with vinegar, hot water, and mustard in a blender. Slowly drizzle in 6 tablespoons of safflower oil while the mixer is running. Toss the corn salad with the vinaigrette, sprinkling it with salt and pepper.

· Prepare the wood pellet grill and lubricate it with oil. Stir the scallops with the remaining 1 tablespoon of oil in a large mixing bowl; add salt and pepper. A large grill pan should be heated. Half of the scallops should be transferred to the pan and cooked, rotating once until golden.

Stuffed Tilapia and Shrimp

Preparation Time: 20 minutes
Cooking Time: 45 minutes
Serving: 6
Recommended Wood Type: Alder/ Apple/ Cherry
Ingredients
• 5 ounce of fresh, farmed tilapia fillets
• 2 tbsp. of extra virgin olive oil
• 1 and a ½ tsp. of smoked paprika
• 1 and a ½ tsp. of old Bay Seasoning
For Shrimp Stuffing
• 1 pound of cooked and deveined shrimp (tail off)
• 1 tbsp. of salted butter
• 1 cup of red onion, diced
• 1 cup of Italian bread crumbs
• ½ a cup of Italian bread crumbs
• ½ a cup of mayonnaise
• One beaten large eggs
• 2 tsp. of freshly chopped parsley
• 1 and a ½ tsp. of salt and pepper
Directions:
1. Take a food processor and add shrimp, chop them up
2. Take a skillet and place it over medium-high heat, add butter and allow it to melt

3. Sauté the onions for 3 minutes
4. Add chopped shrimp with cooled Sautéed onion alongside remaining ingredients listed under stuffing ingredients and transfer to a bowl
5. Cover it and allow the mix to refrigerate for 60 minutes
6. Rub both sides of the fillet with olive oil
7. Spoon 1/3 cup of the stuffing to the fillet
8. Flatten out the stuffing onto the bottom half of the fillet and fold the Tilapia in half
9. Secure with two toothpicks
10. Dust each fillet with smoked paprika and Old Bay seasoning
11. Take your drip pan and add water; cover with aluminum foil. Pre-heat your smoker to 400 degrees F
12. Use water fill water pan halfway through and place it over drip pan. Add wood chips to the side tray
13. Add your preferred wood chips and transfer the fillets to a non-stick grill tray
14. Transfer to your smoker and smoker for 30-45 minutes until the internal temperature reaches 145 degrees Fahrenheit
15. Let the fish to rest for 5 minutes and enjoy!
Nutrition: Calories: 620 Fats: 50g Carbs: 6g Fiber: 1g

Grilled Salmon Kyoto

Preparation time: 1 hour and 20 minutes
Servings:4
Ingredients:
· Soy sauce, 1/3 cup
· Concentrated orange juice, ¼ cup
· Vegetable oil, 2 tbsp.
· Tomato sauce, 2 tbsp.
· Lemon juice, 1 tsp
· Prepared mustard, ½ tsp
· Green onion, minced, 1 tbsp.
· 1 garlic clove, minced
· Minced fresh ginger root, ½ tsp
· 4 salmon steaks
· Olive oil, 1 tbsp.
Instructions:

· Mix orange juice concentrate, soy sauce, oil, lemon juice, tomato sauce, mustard, green onion, ginger, and garlic, in a shallow glass baking dish. Toss the fish in the marinade to coat it. Refrigerate for 30 minutes to 1 hour, wrapped.

· Heat an outside barbecue to high temperatures.

· Take the salmon out of the marinade. Fill a small saucepan halfway with marinade. Bring to a simmer, then reduce to a cook for 1 minute.

· Prepare the wood pellet grill and lubricate it with oil. Lubricate the grill grate generously. Olive oil should be sprayed or drizzled on the fish. Heat for 5 to 10 minutes on the grill or until the salmon flakes easily with a fork. Midway through the cooking time, rotate the salmon and coat it with the boiling marinade.

Wood Rockfish

Preparation Time: 10 Minutes
Cooking Time: 20 Minutes
Servings: 6
Ingredients:
· Six rockfish fillets
· One lemon, sliced
· 3/4 tbsp salt
· 2 tbsp fresh dill, chopped
· 1/2 tbsp garlic powder
· 1/2 tbsp onion powder
· 6 tbsp butter

Directions:
1. Preheat your Wood Pellet Grill Smoker to 400ºF.
2. Season the fish with salt, dill, garlic, and onion powder on both sides, then place it in a baking dish.
3. Place a pat of butter and a lemon slice on each fillet. Place the baking dish in the Wood Pellet Grill Smoker and close the lid.
4. Cook for 20 minutes or until the fish is no longer translucent and is flaky.
5. Remove from Wood Pellet Grill Smoker and let rest before serving.

Nutrition: Calories 270 Total fat 17g Saturated fat 9g Total carbs 2g Net carbs 2g Protein 28g Sodium 381mg

Halibut Soft Tacos

Preparation time:30 minutes
Servings:4
Ingredients:
· 1 mango, diced
· Diced avocado, ½ cup
· Red onion, ¼ cup
· 2 tomatoes, chopped
· 2 jalapeno peppers
· Minced parsley, 2 tbsp.
· Olive oil, 2 tsp
· Lemon juice, 1 tsp
· Honey, 1 tsp
· Salt, ½ tsp
· 1-pound halibut steak
· Black pepper, ¼ tsp
· Garlic salt, ¼ tsp
· 4 Bibb lettuce leaves
· 4 flour tortillas
· Taco sauce, 4 tsp

Instructions:
· Heat an outside grill to high heat and brush the grate gently with oil.

· In a small mixing dish, combine mango, avocado, onion, tomatoes, jalapeño pepper, parsley, 2 teaspoons olive oil, lemon juice, and honey.

· Sprinkle halibut steaks with salt, black pepper, and garlic salt after spraying with 1 teaspoon olive oil.

· Prepare the wood pellet grill and lubricate it with oil. Put the halibut on the grill and shut the lid; grill for 3 to 5 minutes per side, or until the fish flakes easily with a fork.

· Top each tortilla with a Bibb lettuce leaf. Halibut should be split into 4 chunks and tucked within lettuce leaves. To serve, garnish with the mango mixture and sprinkle with taco sauce.

Buttery Smoked Lobster Tails Garlic

(Cooking Time 45 minutes)
Ingredients for 10 servings
· Lobster tail (4-lbs., 1.8-kg.)
The Spices
· Salted butter - ¼ cup
· Garlic powder - 1 teaspoon
· Pepper - ¼ teaspoon
The Heat
· Mesquite wood pellet
Method
1. Using scissors cut the lobster tails lengthwise along the top and gently pull the shells into halves apart from each other. Set aside.
2. Melt the salted butter over low heat then season it with garlic and pepper. Stir well.
3. Pour the melted butter over the tail meat and set aside.
4. Next, plug the wood pellet smoker then fill the hopper with the wood pellet. Turn the switch on and set the wood pellet smoker for indirect heat.
5. Adjust the temperature to 225°F (107°C) and let the wood pellet smoker reaches the desired temperature.
6. Arrange the lobster tails in the wood pellet smoker and smoke them for 45 minutes.
7. Baste the remaining butter mixture over the lobster tails once every 15 minutes.
8. Once the internal temperature of the smoked lobster tails reaches 140°F (60°C), remove them from the wood pellet smoker.
9. Transfer the smoked lobster tails to a serving dish and serve.
10. Enjoy!

Grilled Oysters with Spiced Tequila Butter

Preparation time:
25 minutes
Servings:
6
Ingredients:
· Fennel seeds, ½ tsp
· Crushed red pepper, ¼ tsp
· Unsalted butter, 7 tbsp.
· Sage leaves
· Dried oregano, 1 tsp
· Lemon juice, 2 tbsp.
· Tequila, 2 tbsp.
· Salt
· Rock salt, for serving
· 34-36 medium oysters
Instructions:
· Heat the fennel seeds and crushed red pepper in a pan over medium heat for 1 minute or until aromatic. Allow cooling completely before moving to a mortar. Blend the spices to a fine powder using a pestle and transfer to a container.
· Prepare the wood pellet grill and lubricate it with oil. Heat 3 1/2 tablespoons butter in the same skillet over moderate heat for 2 minutes or until it begins to golden. Heat, rotating once, until the sage is crunchy, about 2 minutes. Move the sage to a plate using a slotted spoon. In the same dish as the spices, add the browned butter. Continue with the remaining butter and 36 sage leaves, saving the leaves for garnish.
· Fill the mortar with the first batch of fried sage leaves and smash them with the pestle. Sprinkle with salt after adding the crushed sage, oregano, lemon juice, and tequila to the butter. Hold it warm.
· Preheat the grill. Using rock salt, cover a dish. Cook the oysters over high heat, flat side up, for 1 to 2 minutes, or until they split. Remove the flat top shell from the oysters and set them on the rock salt, careful not to spill their juice. Serve the oysters with a dollop of warm tequila butter and a crisp sage leaf on top.

Fancy Garlic and Citrus Scallops

Preparation Time: 10 minutes
Cooking Time: 30-40 minutes
Serving: 8
Recommended Wood Type: Alder/Apple/Cherry

Ingredients
• 2-3 pounds of fresh scallops
• 1 tbsp. Of freshly squeezed lemon juice
• 1 tbsp. of freshly squeezed orange juice
• 1 tbsp. of ground black pepper
• 2 tsp. of salt
• One garlic, minced
• Zest of 1 orange

Directions:
1. Take your drip pan and add water. Cover with aluminum foil. Pre-heat your smoker to 200 degrees F
2. Use water fill water pan halfway through and place it over drip pan. Add wood chips to the side tray
3. Take a large bowl and stir in scallops with orange juice and lemon
4. Season with salt, pepper, and garlic
5. Transfer the scallops to your smoker and smoke for 30-40 minutes
6. Sprinkle zest over your scallops, and serve warm!

Nutrition: Calories: 346 Fats: 28g Carbs: 22g Fiber: 2g

Grilled Halibut

Preparation time:
20 minutes
Servings:
4
Ingredients:
· 4 halibut steaks
· Olive oil, 2 tbsp.
· Kosher salt
· Black pepper
· 1 mango, diced
· 1 red pepper, chopped
· ½ red onion, diced
· 1 jalapeno
· Chopped cilantro, 1 tbsp.
· Juice of 1 lime

Instructions:
· Prepare the grill to medium-high and spray both sides of the halibut with oil before sprinkling with salt and pepper.

· Prepare the wood pellet grill and lubricate it with oil. Heat 5 minutes per side on the grill until halibut is done completely.
· To prepare salsa, follow these steps: Combine all ingredients and add salt and pepper in a medium mixing bowl. Dish the salsa alongside the halibut.

Crab Stuffed Lingcod

Preparation Time: 20 Minutes
Cooking Time: 30 Minutes
Servings: 6
Ingredients:
Lemon cream sauce
· Four garlic cloves
· One shallot
· One leek
· 2 tbsp olive oil
· 1 tbsp salt
· 1/4 tbsp black pepper
· 3 tbsp butter
· 1/4 cup white wine
· 1 cup whipping cream
· 2 tbsp lemon juice
· 1 tbsp lemon zest
Crab mix
· 1 lb. crab meat
· 1/3 cup mayo
· 1/3 cup sour cream
· 1/3 cup lemon cream sauce
· 1/4 green onion, chopped
· 1/4 tbsp black pepper
· 1/2 tbsp old bay seasoning
Fish
· 2 lb. lingcod
· 1 tbsp olive oil
· 1 tbsp salt
· 1 tbsp paprika
· 1 tbsp green onion, chopped
· 1 tbsp Italian parsley

Directions:
Lemon cream sauce
1. Chop garlic, shallot, and leeks, then add to a saucepan with oil, salt, pepper, and butter.
2. Sauté over medium heat until the shallot is translucent.

3.   Deglaze with white wine, then add whipping cream. Bring the sauce to boil, reduce heat, and simmer for 3 minutes.

4.   Remove from heat and add lemon juice and lemon zest. Transfer the sauce to a blender and blend until smooth.

5.   Set aside 1/3 cup for the crab mix

Crab mix

1.   Add all the fixings to a mixing bowl and mix thoroughly until well combined.

2.   Set aside

Fish

1.   Fire up your Wood Pellet Grill Smoker to high heat, then slice the fish into 6-ounce portions.

2.   Lay the fish on its side on a cutting board and slice it 3/4 way through the middle leaving a 1/2 inch on each end to have a nice pouch.

3.   Rub the oil into the fish, then place them on a baking sheet. Sprinkle with salt.

4.   Stuff crab mix into each fish, then sprinkle paprika and place it on the grill.

5.   Cook for 15 minutes or more if the fillets are more than 2 inches thick.

6.   Remove the fish and transfer to serving platters. Pour the remaining lemon cream sauce on each fish and garnish with onions and parsley.

Nutrition: Calories 476Total fat 33g Saturated fat 14g Total carbs 6g Net carbs 5g Protein 38g Sugars 3g Fiber 1g Sodium 1032mg

Grilled Prawns with a Spicy Peanut-Lime Vinaigrette

Preparation time:
1 hour and 24 minutes
Servings:
8
Ingredients:
·   Minced lemongrass, ¼ cup
·   Ginger root, ¼ cup minced
·   Minced garlic, 2 tbsp.
·   Chopped cilantro, ¼ tbsp.
·   1 Thai Chile pepper, minced
·   Canola oil, ¾ cup
·   2 pounds shrimp, tail left on
·   Lime juice, ¼ cup
·   Rice wine vinegar, ¼ cup
·   Mirin, ½ cup
·   Dark soy sauce, 2 tbsp.
·   Coldwater, 2 tbsp.
·   Lime zest, 3 tbsp.
·   Fish sauce, 2 tsp.
·   2 fresh Thai pepper, deseeded
·   Unsalted peanut butter, ½ cup
·   Peanut oil, ¼ cup
·   Chopped mint, 2 tbsp.
·   Roasted peanuts, unsalted, ¼ cup
·   Kosher salt

Instructions:
·   In a large mixing bowl, combine lemongrass, 1/4 cup ginger, cilantro, garlic, 3/4 cup peanut oil, and 1 minced chile. Mix in the shrimp and set aside to marinate for 20 to 30 minutes at room temperature.

·   Prepare the grill to medium-high. Prepare the wood pellet grill and lubricate it with oil.

·   Then, in a blender or food processor, combine soy sauce, lime juice, mirin, rice vinegar, and water. Blend until homogeneous, including the lime zest, 1 tablespoon ginger, 2 Chile peppers, fish sauce, peanut butter, and garlic. Gradually drizzle in the peanut oil while mixing; continue to process until light and fluffy. In a mixing dish, combine the mint, cilantro, and chopped peanuts; sprinkle with salt to taste.

·   Squeeze off any extra marinade from the shrimp. Heat for 2 minutes per side on a hot grill until red and hard. Serve right away with the sauce.

Spicy Cajun Shrimp

Preparation Time: 10-15 minutes
Cooking Time: 10 minutes
Serving: 4
Recommended Wood Type: Seaweed
Ingredients
• 4 tbsp. extra virgin olive oil
• One lemon, juiced
• Two garlic cloves, finely minced

• 1 tbsp. Cajun shake
• 1 tsp. salt
• 2 pounds shrimp raw, peeled, and deveined

Directions:

1. Take a zip bag and add listed ingredients, shake well and toss well
2. Cover shrimp and let it sit in the marinade for 3 hours
3. Pre-heat your Master built smoker on HIGH settings for 5 minutes; once done, thread shrimps into skewers and transfer to the smoking rack
4. Let both sides cook for 4 minutes each, making sure that they are smoked thoroughly
5. Serve and enjoy!

Nutrition: Calories: 250 Fat: 6g Carbohydrates: 33g Protein: 29g

Maui Wowie Shrimp

Preparation time:

25 minutes

Servings:

6

Ingredients:

· Uncooked medium shrimp, 2 pounds
· 1 pinch garlic salt
· Black pepper
· Cayenne pepper, ¼ tsp
· Mayonnaise, 1 cup
· Wedges of lemon

Instructions:

· Heat the outdoor grill to medium heat and brush the grate gently with oil.
· Using skewers, insert shrimp onto the skewers. Dress garlic salt and black pepper on both sides of the shrimp; consult Cook's Note when using cayenne.
· Mayonnaise should be liberally applied to both sides of the shrimp.
· Prepare the wood pellet grill and lubricate it with oil. Grill for 5 to 10 minutes on each side on a hot grill until the shrimp are hot pink on the exterior and translucent on the core, and the mayonnaise turns nicely browned. Present with lemon slices on the side.

Ginger and Mint Smoked Scallops

(**Cooking Time** 45 minutes)

Ingredients for 10 **servings**

· Scallops (4-lbs., 1.8-kg.)

The Spices

· Ginger powder - ½ teaspoon
· Diced mint leaves - 1 teaspoon
· Brown sugar - 3 tablespoons
· Lemon juice - 2 tablespoons
· Olive oil - 3 tablespoons
· Kosher salt - ½ teaspoon
· Tamari - 3 tablespoons
· Black pepper - ½ teaspoon

The Heat

· Alder wood pellet

Method

1. Mix ginger with chopped mint leaves, brown sugar, salt, and black pepper.
2. Drizzle olive oil, lemon juice, and tamari over the spices. Stir until becoming a paste.
3. Carefully season the scallops with the seasoning mixture and spread them in a disposable aluminum pan.
4. Next, plug the wood pellet smoker then fill the hopper with the wood pellet. Turn the switch on and set the wood pellet smoker for indirect heat.
5. Adjust the temperature to 225°F (107°C) and let the wood pellet smoker reaches the desired temperature.
6. Insert the aluminum pan into the wood pellet smoker and smoke the scallops for 45 minutes.
7. Once the internal temperature of the smoked scallops reaches 145°F (63°C), remove them from the wood pellet smoker.
8. Transfer the smoked o
9. Once it is done, take the smoked oysters out of the wood pellet smoker and transfer them to a serving dish.
10. Serve and enjoy!

Grilled Lobsters with Miso-Chile Butter

Preparation time:

40 minutes
Servings:
4
Ingredients:
· White miso, 2 tbsp.
· Sriracha, 1 tbsp.
· 1 stick butter, unsalted
· 2 bunches of scallions:
· Canola oil, 1 tbsp.
· Lemon juice, 2 tbsp.
· Black pepper
· Salt
· 8 long metal skewers
· Four 1.5 pounds' lobsters, claws detached

Instructions:
· Heat the butter in a small pot. Combine the miso, Sriracha, and lemon juice in a mixing bowl. Save 1/4 cup Miso-Chile butter is set aside for presentation.

· Preheat the grill. Prepare the wood pellet grill and lubricate it with oil. Mix the scallions with the oil in a large mixing bowl and add salt and pepper. Heat 5 minutes over moderate heat, rotating once, until slightly caramelized and soft. Stir 1 tablespoon of the Miso-Chile butter with the scallions.

· To maintain the lobster bodies upright, pierce them from the tail towards the head. Apply 2 tablespoons Miso-Chile butter, spread over lobster meat. Turn and baste the lobster bodies and claws with the remaining Miso-Chile butter over moderate heat until the shells are brilliant red, 7 to 8 minutes for the tails and 12 to 15 minutes for the claws. Pull the fillets from the skewer.

· Arrange the scallions on top of the lobsters on a tray or plates. End up serving with lemon wedges and the 1/4 cup Miso-Chile butter that was set aside.

Grilled Shrimp Kabobs

Preparation Time: 5 Minutes
Cooking Time: 10 Minutes
Servings: 4
Ingredients:
· 1 lb. colossal shrimp, peeled and deveined

· 2 tbsp. oil
· 1/2 tbsp. garlic salt
· 1/2 tbsp. salt
· 1/8 tbsp. pepper
· Six skewers

Directions:
1. Preheat your Wood Pellet Grill Smoker to 3750F.
2. Pat the shrimp dry with a paper towel.
3. In a mixing bowl, mix oil, garlic salt, salt, and pepper
4. Toss the shrimp in the mixture until well coated.
5. Skewer the shrimps and cook in the Wood Pellet Grill Smoker with the lid closed for 4 minutes.
6. Open the lid, flip the skewers, cook for another 4 minutes, or wait until the shrimp is pink and the flesh is opaque.
7. Serve.

Nutrition: Calories 325 Protein 20g Sodium 120mg

Grilled Oysters with Spicy Tarragon Butter

Preparation time: 40 minutes
Servings: 6
Ingredients:
· Salt, ½ tsp
· Black pepper, ¼ tsp
· 36 medium to large oysters
· Hot sauce, 2 tbsp.
· Tarragon, chopped, 3 tbsp.
· Unsalted butter, 2 sticks

Instructions:
· Preheat the grill. Blend the butter, tarragon, hot sauce, salt, and pepper in a processor until creamy.

· Wrap the tarragon butter into a 2-inch-thick log using a sheet of plastic wrap. Chill the butter for about 15 minutes, or until it is somewhat hard. Divide the butter into 36 parts with a knife. Prepare the wood pellet grill and lubricate it with oil.

· Put the oysters flat-side up on the heated grill. Wrap the grill and heat for 5 minutes or until the oysters split. Then, move the oysters to a tray with tongs, attempting to preserve the fluid within.

·   Pull the top shells as soon as possible, and dislodge the oysters from the bottom shells. Place the oysters on the grill with a pat of tarragon butter on top of each one. Heat, wrapped until the butter has melted.

Full-On Trout

Preparation Time: 10-15 minutes + 6 hours
Cooking Time: 3 hours
Servings: 4
Recommended Wood Type: Alder Wood
Ingredients
• Four trout fillets
• 1 cup white cooking wine
• ¼ cup of soy sauce
• ¼ cup lemon juice
Directions:
1.   Take your drip pan and add water; cover with aluminum foil. Pre-heat your smoker to 150 degrees F
2.   Take a small bowl and add listed ingredients (except trout) and mix well
3.   Transfer trout fillets on a plate and pour marinade all over. Mix well to ensure that the fillets are covered in marinade
4.   Let it sit for 6 hours
5.   Transfer marinated trout fillets to your smoking tray and let it rest for 30 minutes
6.   Use water fill water pan halfway through and place it over drip pan. Add wood chips to the side tray.
7.   Place fish inside your smoker and smoke for 3 hours, take the trout out and serve. Enjoy!
Nutrition: Calories: 382   Fat: 16g Carbohydrates: 24g Protein: 63g

Wood Pellet Grill Smoker Spot Prawn Skewers

Preparation Time: 10 Minutes
Cooking Time: 10 Minutes
Servings: 6
Ingredients:
·   2 lb. spot prawns
·   2 tbsp oil
·   Salt and pepper to taste
Directions:
1.   Preheat your Wood Pellet Grill Smoker to 4000F.
2.   Skewer your prawns with soaked skewers, then generously sprinkle with oil, salt, and pepper.
3.   Place the skewers on the grill, then cook with the lid closed for 5 minutes on each side.

4.   Remove the skewers and serve when hot.
Nutrition: Calories 221 Total fat 7g Saturated fat 1g Total carbs 2g Net carbs 2g Protein 34g Sodium 1481mg

Cilantro Lime Grilled Salmon

Preparation time:25 minutes
Servings:4
Ingredients:
·   Butter, 4 tbsp.
·   Lime juice, ½ cup
·   Honey, ¼ cup
·   2 cloves of garlic, minced
·   Chopped cilantro, 2 tbsp.
·   Salt
·   Black pepper
·   4 salmon fillets (6-oz.)
Instructions:
·   Dress the salmon with salt and pepper before cooking. Preheat the grill and set the salmon flesh side down on it. Prepare the wood pellet grill and lubricate it with oil. Heat for 8 minutes on one side, then rotate and heat for another 6 minutes until salmon is done through. Allow 5 minutes for resting.
·   Now, prepare the sauce: Put butter, lime juice, honey, and garlic in a medium saucepan over medium heat. Whisk until all of the ingredients are mixed, and the butter has liquefied. Remove the pan from the heat and stir in the cilantro.

· Serve the fish with the sauce.

Wood Pellet Grill Smoker Lobster Tail

Preparation Time: 10 Minutes
Cooking Time: 15 Minutes
Servings: 2
Ingredients:
· 10 oz lobster tail
· 1/4 tbsp old bay seasoning
· 1/4 tbsp Himalayan salt
· 2 tbsp butter, melted
· 1 tbsp fresh parsley, chopped
Directions:
1. Preheat your Wood Pellet Grill Smoker to 4500F.
2. Slice the tail down the middle, then season it with bay seasoning and salt.
3. Place the tails directly on the grill with the meat side down. Grill for 15 minutes or until the internal temperature reaches 1400F.
4. Remove from the Wood Pellet Grill Smoker and drizzle with butter.
5. Serve when hot garnished with parsley.
Nutrition: Calories 305 Total fat 14g Saturated fat 8g Total carbs 5g Net carbs 5g Protein 38g Sodium 684mg

Taco Lime Shrimp

Preparation time:35 minutes
Servings:4
Ingredients:
· Vegetable oil, 2 tbsp.
· Garlic powder, 1 tsp.
· Taco seasoning mix, 2 tbsp.
· 1 lb. medium shrimp
· Red enchilada sauce, ¼ cup
· Freshly ground black pepper
· Lemon wedges
· Lemon juice
· Chopped cilantro
Instructions:

· Combine lime juice, enchilada sauce, taco seasoning, vegetable oil, and garlic powder in a large mixing bowl and sprinkle with pepper. Mix in the shrimp until well seasoned.
· Allow 20 minutes to marinate.
· Prepare the wood pellet grill and lubricate it with oil. Preheat the grill to medium-high heat. 3 minutes per side, skewer shrimp and cook until rosy and crispy.
· Before plating, dress with cilantro and sprinkle extra lime.

Halibut with Garlic Pesto

Preparation Time: 20 minutes
Cooking Time: 10 minutes
Servings: 4
Ingredients:
· 4 halibut fillets
· 1 cup olive oil
· Salt and pepper to taste
· 1/4 cup garlic, chopped
· 1/4 cup pine nuts
Direction:
1. Set the Wood Pellet Grill Smoker grill to smoke.
2. Establish fire for 5 minutes.
3. Set temperature to high.
4. Place a cast iron on a grill.
5. Season fish with salt and pepper.
6. Add fish to the pan.
7. Drizzle with a little oil.
8. Sear for 4 minutes per side.
9. Prepare the garlic pesto by pulsing the remaining ingredients in the food processor until smooth.
10. Serve fish with garlic pesto.
Serving Suggestion: Sprinkle with fresh herbs before serving.
Preparation / Cooking Tips: You can also use other white fish fillets for this recipe.
Nutrition: Calories: 298 Protein: 32g Carbohydrates: 20g Fat: 16 Fiber 0g

Blackened Salmon

Preparation Time: 10 Minutes
Cooking Time: 20 Minutes
Servings: 4
Ingredients:
· 2 lb. salmon, fillet, scaled and deboned
· Two tablespoons olive oil
· Four tablespoons sweet dry rub
· One tablespoon cayenne pepper
· Two cloves garlic, minced
Directions:
1. Turn on your wood pellet grill.
2. Set it to 350 degrees F.
3. Brush the salmon with the olive oil.
4. Sprinkle it with the dry rub, cayenne pepper, and garlic.
5. Grill for 5 minutes per side.
Nutrition: Calories 119 Total fat 10g Saturated fat 2g Sodium 720mg

Salmon with Pineapple Salsa

Preparation time:25 minutes
Servings:4
Ingredients:
· Chopped pineapple, 1 ½ cup
· ¼ chopped red onion
· 4 skin-on salmon fillets (6-oz.)
· Chopped fresh cilantro, 1 tbsp.
· Honey, 1 tsp.
· Extra virgin olive oil, 2 tbsp.
· Kosher salt
· Juice of 3 limes
· Ground black pepper
Instructions:
· To prepare the sauce, stir together the olive oil, lemon juice, and honey in a large mixing bowl.
· Preheat the grill to medium-high heat. Prepare the wood pellet grill and lubricate it with oil. Heat until salmon is roasted through, 5 to 6 minutes per side, after basting with honey-lime sauce.
· Now, prepare pineapple salsa by tossing pineapple, onion, remaining lime juice, and cilantro in a medium mixing bowl and sprinkling with salt and pepper.

· Serve the salmon with salsa while it's still warm.

Salmon Cakes

Preparation Time: 5 Minutes
Cooking Time: 25 Minutes
Servings: 4
Ingredients:
· 1 cup cooked salmon, flaked
· 1/2 red bell pepper, chopped
· Two eggs, beaten
· 1/4 cup mayonnaise
· 1/2 tablespoon dry sweet rub
· 1 1/2 cups breadcrumbs
· One tablespoon mustard
· Olive oil
Directions:
1. Combine all the fixings except the olive oil in a bowl.
2. Form patties from this mixture.
3. Let sit for 15 minutes.
4. Turn on your wood pellet grill.
5. Set it to 350 degrees F.
6. Add a baking pan to the grill.
7. Drizzle a little olive oil on top of the pan.
8. Add the salmon cakes to the pan.
9. Grill each side for 3 to 4 minutes.
Nutrition: Calories 119 Total fat 10g Saturated fat 2g Sodium 720mg

Sweet Chili Grilled Salmon with lime

Preparation time:3 hours and 20 minutes
Servings:4
Ingredients:
· Soy sauce, ¼ cup
· 4 salmon fillets with skin
· Lime juice
· Green onions
· Lemon wedges
· Sweet chili sauce, 1 cup
Instructions:

·   To prepare the marinade, stir together the lime juice, sweet chili sauce, and soy sauce in a large basin. Half of the marinade should be saved for brushing the fish after it has been barbecued.

·   Drizzle the marinade over the salmon in a baking dish. Allow at least 3 hours and up to overnight to marinate in the refrigerator.

·   Prepare the wood pellet grill and lubricate it with oil. Preheat the grill to high when you're ready to cook. Grates should be oiled before introducing the salmon. Brush with marinade and cook for 5 minutes per side, or until roasted through.

·   Finish with a brushing of the reserved marinade and a sprinkling of green onions. Lime wedges are recommended with serving.

Grilled Herbed Tuna

Preparation Time: 4 hours and 15 minutes
Cooking Time: 10 minutes
Servings: 6
Ingredients:
·   6 tuna steaks
·   1 tablespoon lemon zest
·   1 tablespoon fresh thyme, chopped
·   1 tablespoon fresh parsley, chopped
·   Garlic salt to taste
Direction:
1.   Sprinkle the tuna steaks with lemon zest, herbs and garlic salt.
2.   Cover with foil.
3.   Refrigerate for 4 hours.
4.   Grill for 3 minutes per side.
Serving Suggestion: Top with lemon slices before serving.
Preparation / Cooking Tips: Take the fish out of the refrigerator 30 minutes before cooking.
Nutrition: Calories: 234 Protein: 25g Carbohydrates: 17g Fat: 11g Fiber 0g

Smoked Catfish Recipe

Preparation Time: 10 minutes

Cooking Time: 5 Minutes
Servings: 3 Servings
Ingredients:
Ingredients
·   for The Rub
·   2 tablespoons paprika
·   1/4 teaspoon salt
·   1 tablespoon garlic powder
·   1 tablespoon onion powder
·   1/2 tablespoon dried thyme
·   1/2 tablespoon cayenne
Other ingredients
·   2 pounds fresh catfish fillets
·   4 tablespoons butter, soften
Directions:
1.   Take a mixing bowl, and combine all the rub ingredients in it, including the paprika, salt, garlic powder, onion powder, and thyme and cayenne paper.
2.   Rub the fillet with the butter, and then sprinkle a generous amount of rub on top
3.   Coat fish well with the rub.
4.   Preheat the smoker grill at 200 degrees Fahrenheit for 15 minutes.
5.   Cook fish on the grill for 10 minutes, 5minutes per side.
6.   Once done, serve and enjoy.
Nutrition: Calories 146 - Total Fat 4.2g - Saturated Fat 2.5g - Cholesterol 61mg Sodium 28mg

Shrimp with Feta-Dill Sauce and Lemon Skewers

Preparation time:30 minutes
Servings:6
Ingredients:
·   Crumbled feta cheese, ½ cup
·   Salt and black pepper
·   Finely chopped dill, 2 ½ tbsp.
·   Olive oil, ¼ cup
·   4 large garlic cloves, minced
·   2-pounds large shrimp
·   1 scallion, thinly sliced
·   2 lemons
·   Plain low-fat yogurt, ½ cup
Instructions:

·   Preheat the grill. Combine the yogurt, scallion, 1/4 teaspoon garlic, and 1/2 tablespoon dill in a medium mixing basin. Mix in the feta, softly pressing it in. Sprinkle salt & pepper to taste.

·   Mix the remaining minced garlic and 2 tablespoons dill with the olive oil in a large mixing basin. Sprinkle with salt and stir to coat the shrimp and lemons. On each of the 12 skewers, insert 4 shrimp and 2 lemon wedges.

·   Prepare the wood pellet grill and lubricate it with oil. Dress with salt and pepper and cook, frequently rotating, over medium-hot heat until the shrimp are roasted and heated for about 5 minutes. Move the skewers to a plate and top with the feta sauce right away.

Cajun Smoked Shrimp

Preparation Time: 10 minutes
Cooking Time: 10 Minutes
Servings: 2 Servings
Ingredients:
·   2 tablespoons of virgin olive oil
·   1/2 lemon, juiced
·   3 cloves garlic, finely minced
·   2 tablespoons of Cajun spice
·   Salt, to taste
·   1.5 pounds of shrimp, raw, peeled, deveined

Directions:
1.   Take a zip lock bag and combine olive oil, lemon juice, garlic cloves, Cajun spice, salt, and shrimp.
2.   Toss the ingredients well for fine coating.
3.   Preheat the smoker grill for 10 minutes until the smoke starts to establish.
4.   Put the fish on the grill grate and close lid.
5.   Turn the temperature to high and allow the fish to cook the shrimp for 10 minutes, 5 minutes per side.
6.   Once done, serve.

Nutrition: Calories 446 Total Fat 4.8g Saturated Fat 6.5g Cholesterol 53mg Sodium 48mg

Grilled Scallops with Avocado Salsa

Preparation time: 30 minutes
Servings: 4
Ingredients:
·   1 Hass avocado
·   Black pepper
·   Salt
·   Olive oil
·   2-pounds large sea scallops
·   Grated lemon zest,
·   Lemon juice, 2 tbsp.

Instructions:
·   Preheat the grill. Mix the lime juice and zest with 1 tablespoon olive oil in a mixing bowl. Toss in the avocado with a rubber spatula. Sprinkle the salsa with black pepper and salt.

·   Prepare the wood pellet grill and lubricate it with oil. Garnish the scallops with salt and black pepper after showering them with olive oil. Heat 3 to 4 minutes per side over moderately high heat, rotating once until well browned and almost roasted through. Move the scallops to plates and serve with the salsa on the side.

Grilled Blackened Salmon

Preparation Time: 15 minutes
Cooking Time: 30 minutes
Servings: 4
Ingredients:
·   4 salmon fillet
·   Blackened dry rub
·   Italian seasoning powder
Direction:
1.   Season salmon fillets with dry rub and seasoning powder.
2.   Grill in the Wood Pellet Grill Smoker grill at 325 degrees F for 10 to 15 minutes per side.
Serving Suggestion: Garnish with lemon wedges.
Preparation / Cooking Tips: You can also drizzle salmon with lemon juice
Nutrition: Calories: 258 Protein: 23g Carbohydrates: 20g Fat: 12g Fiber 0g

Juicy Lime Smoked Tuna Belly

Preparation Time: 10 minutes
Cooking Time: 2 Hours 10 Minutes
Servings: 10 servings
Ingredients:
· Tuna belly (3-lb., 1.4-kg.)
The Marinade
· Fresh limes – 2
· White sugar – 2 tablespoons
· Brown sugar – 3 tablespoons
· Pepper – ½ teaspoon
· Soy sauce – 1 tablespoon
· Sriracha sauce – 2 tablespoons
Directions:
1. Cut the limes into halves then squeeze the juice over the tuna belly. Marinate the tuna belly with the juice for 10 minutes. Meanwhile, combine white sugar with brown sugar, pepper, soy sauce, and Sriracha sauce then mix well. Wash and rinse the tuna belly then pat it dry. Then, plug the wood pellet smoker then fill the hopper with the wood pellet. Turn the switch on.
2. Set the wood pellet smoker for indirect heat then adjust the temperature to 225°F (107°C).
3. Wait until the wood pellet smoker reaches the desired temperature then place the seasoned tuna belly in it. Smoke the tuna belly for 2 hours or until it flakes and once it is done, remove it from the wood pellet smoker.
4. Serve and enjoy.
Nutrition: Calories: 392 Fats: 27g Carbs: 2g Fiber: 0g

Mediterranean Salmon Skewers

Preparation time:20 minutes
Servings:4
Ingredients:
· Extra virgin olive oil
· Kosher salt
· 3 lemons, sliced
· Black pepper
· 1-pound salmon fillets
· Torn fresh dill
Instructions:

· Prepare the wood pellet grill and lubricate it with oil. Preheat the grill to high heat. Using skewers, hook the salmon and lemon slices, then drizzle with olive oil and dress with salt and pepper all over.
· Heat it 6 to 12 minutes on the grill, rotating once until salmon is done through.
· Serve with a dill garnish.

Smoked Crab Paprika Garlic with Lemon Butter Flavor

Preparation Time: 5 minutes
Cooking Time: 30 Minutes
Servings: 10 servings
Ingredients:
· Fresh Crabs (7-lb., 3.2-kg.)
The Sauce
· Salt – 1 tablespoon
· Cayenne pepper – 1 ½ teaspoon
· Salted butter – 2 cups
· Lemon juice – ½ cup
· Worcestershire sauce – 1 tablespoon
· Garlic powder – 2 teaspoons
· Smoked paprika – 2 teaspoons
Directions:
1. Preheat a saucepan over low heat then melt the butter. Let it cool.
2. Season the melted butter with salt, cayenne pepper, Worcestershire sauce, garlic powder, and smoked paprika, then pour lemon juice into the melted butter. Stir until incorporated and set aside.
3. Then, plug the wood pellet smoker then fill the hopper with the wood pellet. Turn the switch on.
4. Set the wood pellet smoker for indirect heat then adjust the temperature to 350°F (177°C).
5. Arrange the crabs in a disposable aluminum pan then drizzle the sauce over the crabs.
6. Smoke the crabs for 30 minutes then remove from the wood pellet smoker.
7. Transfer the smoked crabs to a serving dish then serve.
8. Enjoy!

Nutrition: Calories: 455 Fats: 53g Carbs: 3g Fiber: 0g

Shrimp with Miso Butter

Preparation time:30 minutes
Servings:4
Ingredients:
- 1-pound large shrimp
- Thinly sliced scallions
- Canola oil, 2 tbsp.
- Fresh lemon juice, 1 tbsp.
- 1 large garlic clove, minced
- Grated lemon zest, ½ tsp
- Korean chili powder, 1 tsp
- White miso, 2 tbsp.
- Salt, 1 tsp
- 1 stick unsalted butter
- Pickled mustard seeds in brine, 1 ½ tsp

Instructions:
- Blend the butter with lemon zest, miso and lemon juice in a food processor until creamy. Blend in the 1 tbsp of scallion until it is all combined. Set aside the miso butter in a large mixing dish.
- Combine the shrimp with the oil, garlic, chili powder, and salt in a separate large mixing dish and set aside for 10 minutes.
- Prepare the wood pellet grill and lubricate it with oil. Preheat the grill or a grill pan. Cook the shrimp over high heat, rotating once, for about 4 minutes, or until just roasted through. Toss the shrimp in the miso butter right away until fully covered. Serve the shrimp topped with scallions, pickled mustard seeds, and brine.

Salmon with Avocado Salsa

Preparation Time: 30 minutes
Cooking Time: 20 minutes
Servings: 6
Ingredients:
- 3 lb. salmon fillet
- Garlic salt and pepper to taste
- 4 cups avocado, sliced into cubes
- 1 onion, chopped
- 1 jalapeño pepper, minced
- 1 tablespoon lime juice
- 1 tablespoon olive oil
- ¼ cup cilantro, chopped
- Salt to taste

Direction:
1. Sprinkle both sides of salmon with garlic salt and pepper.
2. Set the Wood Pellet Grill Smoker grill to smoke.
3. Grill the salmon for 7 to 8 minutes per side.
4. While waiting, prepare the salsa by combining the remaining ingredients in a bowl.
5. Serve salmon with the avocado salsa.

Serving Suggestion: Garnish with lemon wedges.

Preparation / Cooking Tips: You can also use tomato salsa for this recipe if you don't have avocados.

Nutrition: Calories: 278 Protein: 20g Carbohydrates: 17g Fat: 11g Fiber 0g

Cinnamon Ginger Juicy Smoked Crab

Preparation Time: 10 minutes
Cooking Time: 30 Minutes
Servings: 10 servings
Ingredients:
- Fresh Crabs (7-lb., 3.2-kg.)

The Spices
- Salt – 1 tablespoon
- Ground celery seeds – 3 tablespoons
- Ground mustard – 2 teaspoons
- Cayenne pepper – ½ teaspoon
- Black pepper – ½ teaspoon
- Smoked paprika – 1 ½ teaspoon
- Ground clove – A pinch
- Ground allspice – ¾ teaspoon
- Ground ginger – 1 teaspoon
- Ground cardamom – ½ teaspoon
- Ground cinnamon – ½ teaspoon
- Bay leaves - 2

Directions:

1. Combine the entire spices—salt, ground celery seeds, mustard, cayenne pepper, black pepper, smoked paprika, clove, allspice, ginger, cardamom, and cinnamon in a bowl then mix well. Sprinkle the spice mixture over the crabs then wrap the crabs with aluminum foil. Then, plug the wood pellet smoker then fill the hopper with the wood pellet. Turn the switch on. Set the wood pellet smoker for indirect heat then adjust the temperature to 350°F (177°C). Place the wrapped crabs in the wood pellet smoker and smoke for 30 minutes. Once it is done, remove the wrapped smoked carbs from the wood pellet smoker and let it rest for approximately 10 minutes.

2. Unwrap the smoked crabs and transfer it to a serving dish.

3. Serve and enjoy!

Nutrition: Calories: 355 - Fats: 22g - Carbs: 8g - Fiber: 0g

Baked Steelhead

Preparation Time: 15 minutes
Cooking Time: 20 minutes
Servings: 4 - 6
Ingredients:

- 1 Lemon
- 2 Garlic cloves, minced
- ½ Shallot, minced
- 3 tbsp. Butter, unsalted
- Saskatchewan seasoning, blackened
- Italian Dressing
- 1 Steelhead, (a fillet)

Directions:

1. Preheat the grill to 350F with closed lid.

2. In an iron pan place the butter. Place the pan in the grill while preheating so that the butter melts. Coat the fillet with Italian dressing. Rub with Saskatchewan rub. Make sure the layer is thin.

3. Mince the garlic and shallot. Remove the pan from the grill and add the garlic and shallots.

4. Spread the mixture on the fillet. Slice the lemon into slices. Place the slice on the butter mix.

5. Place the fish on the grate. Cook 20 - 30 minutes.

6. Remove from the grill and serve. Enjoy!

Nutrition: Calories: 230 Protein: 28g Carbs 2g: Fat: 14g

Simple Mahi-Mahi

Preparation Time: 10 minutes
Cooking Time: 10 minutes
Servings: 4
Ingredients:

- 4 (6-ounce) mahi-mahi fillets
- 2 tablespoons olive oil
- Salt and ground black pepper, as required

Directions:

1. Preheat the Z Grills Wood Pellet Grill Smoker Grill & Smoker on grill setting to 350 degrees F.

2. Coat fish fillets with olive oil and season with salt and black pepper evenly.

3. Place the fish fillets onto the grill and cook for about 5 minutes per side.

4. Remove the fish fillets from grill and serve hot.

Nutrition: Calories 195 Total Fat 7 g Saturated Fat 1 g Cholesterol 60 mg Sodium 182 mg Total Carbs 0 g Fiber 0 g Sugar 0 g Protein 31.6g

Smoked Shrimp

Preparation Time: 4 hours and 15 minutes
Cooking Time: 10 minutes
Servings: 4
Ingredients:

- 4 tablespoons olive oil
- 1 tablespoon Cajun seasoning
- 2 cloves garlic, minced
- 1 tablespoon lemon juice
- Salt to taste
- 2 lb. shrimp, peeled and deveined

Direction:
1. Combine all the ingredients in a sealable plastic bag.
2. Toss to coat evenly.
3. Marinate in the refrigerator for 4 hours.
4. Set the Wood Pellet Grill Smoker grill to high.
5. Preheat it for 15 minutes while the lid is closed.
6. Thread shrimp onto skewers.
7. Grill for 4 minutes per side.

Serving Suggestion: Garnish with lemon wedges.

Preparation / Cooking Tips: Soak skewers first in water if you are using wooden skewers.

Nutrition: Calories: 298Protein: 42g Carbohydrates: 10g Fat: 10g Fiber 0g

Sesame Seeds Flounder

Preparation Time: 15 minutes
Cooking Time: 2½ hours
Servings: 4
Ingredients:
· ½ cup sesame seeds, toasted
· ½ teaspoon kosher salt flakes
· 1 tablespoon canola oil
· 1 teaspoon sesame oil
· 4 (6-ounce) flounder fillets

Directions:
1. Preheat the Z Grills Wood Pellet Grill Smoker Grill & Smoker on grill setting to 225 degrees F.
2. With a mortar and pestle, crush sesame seeds with kosher salt slightly.
3. In a small bowl, mix together both oils.
4. Coat fish fillets with oil mixture generously and then, rub with sesame seeds mixture.
5. Place fish fillets onto the lower rack of grill and cook for about 2-2½ hours.
6. Remove the fish fillets from grill and serve hot.

Nutrition: Calories 343 Total Fat 16.2 g Saturated Fat 2.3 g Cholesterol 116 mg Sodium 476 mg Total Carbs 4.2 g Fiber 2.1 g Sugar 0.1 g Protein 44.3 g

Chili Lime Cod In Parchment Paper

(TOTAL COOK TIME 35 MINUTES)
INGREDIENTS FOR 2 SERVINGS
THE FISH
· 1 cod fillet (8-ozs, 226-gms)
THE INGREDIENTS
· ½ jalapeno, sliced into rounds
· 3-4 garlic cloves, peeled and thinly sliced
· A thumb of fresh ginger, peeled and thinly sliced 1-ins (2.5-cms)
· A small handful of fresh cilantro, chopped
· Olive oil, as needed
· Freshly squeezed juice of 1 lime
· Carne Asada seasoning, as needed
· Brown sugar – 1 teaspoon
· 1 lime, sliced
THE SLAW
· 1 small cucumber
· 1 large carrot, peeled and shredded
· Cilantro leaves – 1 cup
· Peanuts, crushed – 3 tablespoons
· Spicy peanut sauce, store-bought, as needed
THE WOOD PELLET GRILL
· Preheat your wood pellet grill to 400°F (204°C)
· Choose your favorite wood pellets for this recipe
METHOD
1. First, fold a piece of parchment paper measuring 24x24-ins (61x61-cms) in half. Cut the paper into a large heart shape, discard the unwanted paper.
2. In a bowl, combine the jalapeno with garlic, ginger, and cilantro. Drizzle over a drop of olive oil and a squeeze of fresh lime juice. Toss to coat evenly.
3. Add the mixture to the middle of one half of the heart.
4. Top the heart with the fish.
5. Rub a fine layer of oil over the fish and season lightly with Carne Asada seasoning.
6. Scatter with brown sugar and a few lime slices.
7. Fold the opposite side of the heart over the fish. Beginning at the fold, on the rounder side of the heart shape. Make a small, firm fold towards the fish. Continue to work your way

around the half heart, folding and creating firm creases. Once you reach the pointy end of the heart, fold the paper overhang under the parcel. All of the folds and creases need to be firm and sealed.

8.   Lay the parcel on the grill while you prepare the slaw.

9.   Slice the cucumber into 2-ins (5-cms) sections and half lengthwise. Scoop out the seeds.

10. In a bowl, combine the cucumber with carrots, cilantro, and peanuts. Add a drizzle of peanut sauce to taste and to coat.

11. When the cod has been cooking for 12-15 minutes, test the fish for firmness. The cooking time will be around 15-18 minutes. The cod is cooked when it registers an internal temperature of 145°F (63°C).

12. Serve the chili lime cod in the paper parcel with a side of slaw.

Buttered Shrimp

Preparation Time: 15 minutes
Cooking Time: 30 minutes
Servings: 6
Ingredients:
·   8 ounces salted butter, melted
·   ¼ cup Worcestershire sauce
·   ¼ cup fresh parsley, chopped
·   1 lemon, quartered
·   2 pounds jumbo shrimp, peeled and deveined
·   3 tablespoons BBQ rub
Directions:
1.   In a metal baking pan, add all ingredients except for shrimp and BBQ rub and mix well.
2.   Season the shrimp with BBQ rub evenly.
3.   Add shrimp in the pan with butter mixture and coat well.
4.   Set aside for about 20-30 minutes.
5.   Preheat the Z Grills Wood Pellet Grill Smoker Grill & Smoker on grill setting to 250 degrees F.
6.   Place the pan onto the grill and cook for about 25-30 minutes.
7.   Remove the pan from grill and serve hot.

Nutrition: Calories 462 Total Fat 33.3 g Saturated Fat 20.2 g Cholesterol 400 mg Sodium 485 mg Total Carbs 4.7 g Fiber 0.2 g Sugar 2.1 g Protein 34.9 g

Smoked Striped Sea Bass

(TOTAL COOK TIME 40 MINUTES)
INGREDIENTS FOR 4 SERVINGS
THE FISH
·   4 fresh striped sea bass fillets (6-ozs, 170-gms) each
THE RUB
·   Paprika – ¼ cup
·   Salt – 1 tablespoon
·   Black pepper – 1 tablespoon
·   Brown sugar – 1 tablespoon
·   Chili powder – 1 teaspoon
·   Garlic powder – 1 teaspoon
·   Red cayenne pepper -1 teaspoon
·   Dry mustard – ⅛ teaspoon
THE INGREDIENTS
·   Grapeseed oil – 2 tablespoons
·   Freshly squeezed juice of 1 lemon
·   8 garlic cloves, peeled and crushed
·   Fresh oregano – 1 tablespoon
·   Fresh thyme – 1 tablespoon
·   Blackened Saskatchewan rub, see recipe above– 1 teaspoon
·   Butter – 8 tablespoons
·   Fish and poultry rub, as needed
·   Fresh thyme, to serve
·   Lemon slices, to serve
THE WOOD PELLET GRILL
·   Preheat your wood pellet grill with the lid closed, for smoking to 325°F (163°C) for 15 minutes
·   Choose your favorite wood pellets for this recipe
METHOD
1.   For the Blackened Saskatchewan rub, combine all the ingredients and use as directed. This recipe will yield approximately ½ cup. Store any used rub in a resealable spice jar.
2.   For the marinade: In a ziplock bag, combine the grapeseed oil with fresh lemon

juice, garlic, oregano, thyme, and blackened Saskatchewan rub.

3.   Add the fish to the bag, and transfer to the fridge for 30 minutes, turning the fish over a couple of times.

4.   Add the butter to a skillet that is large enough to accommodate all the fillets and place on the grill for 2-3 minutes to melt.

5.   Take the fish out of the marinade, and transfer to a platter or clean work surface. Pour the marinade into the pan with the melted butter.

6.   Season the fish generously with fish and poultry rub.

7.   Place the fish in the pan and return to the grill.

8.   Cook the fillets for approximately 30 minutes, basting once or twice during cooking with the hot butter.

9.   Take the fish out of the grill when it registers an internal temperature of 160°F (71°C).

10. Garnish with thyme and slices of lemon, and enjoy.

Buttered Clams

Preparation Time: 15 minutes
Cooking Time: 8 minutes
Servings: 6
Ingredients:

· 24 littleneck clams
· ½ cup cold butter, chopped
· 2 tablespoons fresh parsley, minced
· 3 garlic cloves, minced
· 1 teaspoon fresh lemon juice

Directions:

1.   Preheat the Z Grills Wood Pellet Grill Smoker Grill & Smoker on grill setting to 450 degrees F.

2.   Scrub the clams under cold running water.

3.   In a large casserole dish, mix together remaining ingredients.

4.   Place the casserole dish onto the grill.

5.   Now, arrange the clams directly onto the grill and cook for about 5-8 minutes or until they are opened. (Discard any that fail to open).

6.   With tongs, carefully transfer the opened clams into the casserole dish and remove from the grill.

7.   Serve immediately.

Nutrition: Calories 306 Total Fat 17.6 g Saturated Fat 9.9 g Cholesterol 118 mg Sodium 237 mg Total Carbs 6.4 g Fiber 0.1 g Sugar 0.1 g Protein 29.3 g

Halibut Fish Sticks

(TOTAL COOK TIME 35 MINUTES)
INGREDIENTS FOR 4 SERVINGS
THE FISH

· Fresh halibut, skinned, rinsed, patted dry (1.5-lbs, 0.7-kgs)

THE INGREDIENTS

· Extra-virgin olive oil, as needed
· All-purpose flour – ½ cup
· Salt – 1½ teaspoons
· Freshly ground black pepper – 1 teaspoon
· 2 eggs
· Panko breadcrumbs – 1½ cups
· Dried parsley – 2 tablespoons
· Dried dill – 1 teaspoon
· Seafood sauce, store-bought, of choice, to serve, optional

THE WOOD PELLET GRILL

· With the lid closed, preheat your wood pellet grill to 500°F (260°C) for 15 minutes
· Hickory wood pellets are a good choice for this recipe

METHOD

1.   Cut the fish into 1-ins (2.5-cms) strips.

2.   Add a splash of oil to a Dutch oven.

3.   Place the Dutch oven in your pellet grill to preheat for around 10 minutes.

4.   In a bowl, combine the flour with the salt and black pepper.

5.   In a second bowl, beat the eggs.

6.   In a third small bowl, combine the breadcrumbs with the dried parsley and dried dill.

7.   Dip the fish strips first in the flour, then in the beaten egg, and finally in the seasoned breadcrumbs.
8.   Add the fish sticks to the oil, and fry for around 3-4 minutes, or until they register an internal temperature of 130°F (55°C).
9.   Serve and enjoy with your favorite seafood sauce.

Grilled Scallops with Lemony Salsa Verde

Preparation Time: 15 minutes
Cooking Time: 15 minutes
Servings: 2
Ingredients:
·   2 tbsp of vegetable oil and more for the grill
·   12 large sea scallops, side muscle removed
·   Kosher salt and grounded black pepper
·   Lemony Salsa Verde
Intolerances:
·   Gluten-Free - Egg-Free - Lactose-Free
Directions:
1.   Set up the grill for medium-high heat, then oil the grate. Toss the scallops with 2 tbsp of oil on a rimmed baking sheet and season with salt and pepper.
2.   Utilizing a fish spatula or your hands, place the scallops on the grill.
3.   Grill them, occasionally turning, until gently singed and cooked through, around 2 minutes for each side.
4.   Serve the scallops with Lemony Salsa Verde.
Nutrition: Calories: 30 Fat: 1g Cholesterol: 17mg Carbs: 1g Protein: 6g

Garlic Shrimp Pesto Bruschetta

(TOTAL COOK TIME 20 MINUTES)
INGREDIENTS FOR 12 SERVINGS
THE SEAFOOD
·   12 jumbo shrimp, peeled and deveined
THE INGREDIENTS
·   12 slices of baguette

·   Olive oil – 2 tablespoons
·   4 garlic cloves, peeled and minced
·   Chili pepper flakes – ½ teaspoon
·   Garlic powder – ½ teaspoon
·   Smoked paprika – ½ teaspoon
·   Salt, to season
·   Black pepper, to season
·   Pesto, store-bought, as needed
·   Fresh parsley leaves – ¼ teaspoons
THE WOOD PELLET GRILL
·   Prepare your wood pellet grill for smoking with the lid open and preheat to 350°F (177°C)
·   Use your favorite wood pellets
METHOD
1.   Arrange the slices of baguette in a single layer on a foil-lined baking sheet.
2.   In a small bowl, combine the olive oil with the minced garlic and brush the mixture over both sides of the bread. Transfer the baking sheet to the grill and bake for approximately 10-15 minutes.
3.   In a frying pan, heat a splash of oil. Add the shrimp, chili flakes, garlic powder, smoked paprika, salt, and pepper. Grill on moderate to high heat for around 5 minutes, or until the shrimp are pink. You will need to frequently stir during this process.
4.   When the shrimp are pink, remove the pan from the heat.
5.   Set the toasted baguettes aside to cool for a few minutes.
6.   Spread the pesto onto each slice of toasted bread, top with shrimp, garnish with parsley and enjoy.

Grilled Sea Scallops with Corn Salad

Preparation Time: 25 minutes
Cooking Time: 30 minutes
Servings: 6
Ingredients:
·   6 shucked ears of corn
·   1-pint grape tomatoes, halved
·   3 sliced scallions, white and light green parts only
·   1/3 cup basil leaves, finely shredded

- Salt and grounded pepper
- 1 small shallot, minced
- 2 tbsp balsamic vinegar
- 2 tbsp hot water
- 1 tsp Dijon mustard 1/4 cup
- 3 tbsp sunflower oil
- 1 1/2 pounds sea scallops

Intolerances:
- Gluten-Free
- Egg-Free
- Lactose-Free

Directions:
1. In a pot of boiling salted water, cook the corn for about 5 minutes. Drain and cool.
2. Place the corn into a big bowl and cut off the kernels. Add the tomatoes, the scallions and basil then season with salt and grounded pepper.
3. In a blender, mix the minced shallot with the vinegar, heated water, and mustard. With the blender on, gradually add 6 tbsp of the sunflower oil.
4. Season the vinaigrette with salt and pepper; at that point, add it to the corn salad.
5. In a huge bowl, toss the remaining 1 tbsp of oil with the scallops, then season with salt and grounded pepper.
6. Heat a grill pan. Put on half of the scallops and grill over high heat, turning once, until singed, around 4 minutes.
7. Repeat with the other half of the scallops. Place the corn salad on plates, then top with the scallops and serve.

Nutrition: Calories: 230 Fat: 5g Cholesterol: 60mg Carbs: 13g Protein: 33g

Citrus Soy Squid

Preparation Time: 15 minutes
Cooking Time: 45 minutes
Servings: 4
Ingredients:
- 1 cup mirin
- 1 cup of soy sauce
- 1/3 cup yuzu juice or fresh lemon juice
- 2 cups of water

- 2 pounds squid tentacles left whole; bodies cut crosswise 1 inch thick

Intolerances:
- Gluten-Free
- Egg-Free
- Lactose-Free

Directions:
1. In a bowl, mix the mirin, soy sauce, the yuzu juice, and water.
2. Put a bit of the marinade in a container and refrigerate it for later use.
3. Add the squid to the bowl with the rest of the marinade and let it sit for about 30 minutes or refrigerate for 4 hours.
4. Set up the grill. Drain the squid.
5. Grill over medium-high heat, turning once until white all through for 3 minutes.
6. Serve hot.

Nutrition: Calories: 110 Fat: 6g Carbs: 6g Protein: 8g

Grilled Crawfish With Spicy Tarragon Butter Sauce

(TOTAL COOK TIME 35 MINUTES)
INGREDIENTS FOR 2 SERVINGS
THE SEAFOOD
- Live crawfish, picked over and cleaned (5.5-lbs, 2.5-kgs)
- Salt – 1 teaspoon

THE SAUCE
- Salted butter, softened – 2 cups
- Tarragon – 1 tablespoon
- Cayenne pepper – ½ teaspoon
- Hot sauce, of choice – ¼ cup
- Freshly squeezed juice of ½ lemon
- Chicken seasoning – 1-2 tablespoons

THE WOOD PELLET GRILL
- Preheat your wood pellet grill to 400°F (204°C)
- Use your favorite wood pellets

METHOD
1. Over high heat, bring a water-filled stockpot to a rolling boil. Liberally salt the water, and add the crawfish. Boil the crawfish for around 10 minutes, or until their shells became a vivid red color. Remove the crawfish

from the pot, strain, and place in an ice-filled bowl. This process will halt the cooking process.

2. White the crawfish are in the ice, prepare the sauce. Using a food blender or processor, combine the softened butter with the tarragon, cayenne, hot sauce, freshly squeezed lemon juice, and chicken seasoning (to taste). Mix thoroughly and put to one side, until needed.

3. Transfer the crawfish to a grill basket and grill for 10-20 minutes, until the meat is opaque and the shells are vivid red. Remove the crawfish from the grill.

4. In a pan, melt the tarragon butter, transfer it to a bowl and serve alongside the grilled crawfish.

5. Enjoy.

Smoked Scallops with Citrus and Garlic Butter Sauce

Preparation Time: 10 minutes
Cooking Time: 1 hour and 40 minutes
Servings: 4
Ingredients:
• 2 pounds large scallops
• ½ teaspoon minced garlic
• 2 tsp. salt
• 1/2 small orange zest
• 1 tsp. Ground black pepper
• 1/4 teaspoon Worcestershire sauce
• 8 tbsp. butter, salted, melted
• 1/2 small orange juice
• 1 1/2 teaspoon chopped parsley
Directions:
1. Open the smoker's hopper, add dry pallets, make sure ash-can is in place, and then open the ash damper, power on the smoker, and close the ash damper.

2. Set the smoker's temperature to 225 degrees F, let preheat for 30 minutes or until the green light on the dial blinks that indicate the smoker has reached to set temperature.

3. Meanwhile, rinse scallops, pat dry, and then season with salt and black pepper.

4. Take a baking sheet, place a wire rack on it, arrange seasoned scallops on it, place the baking sheet on the smoker grill, shut the smoker with a lid, and smoke scallops for 20 minutes.

5. Then remove the baking sheet containing scallops from the smoker and set aside until required.

6. Set the temperature of the smoker to 400 degrees F, switch smoker to open flame cooking mode, press the open flame 3, remove the grill grates and the batch, replace batch with direct flame insert, then return grates on the grill in the lower position and let preheat for 30 minutes or until the green light on the dial blinks that indicate smoker has reached to set temperature.

7. Return the baking sheet with scallops on the grill grate, shut with lid, and continue smoking the scallops for 15 minutes or until opaque and tender.

8. Meanwhile, place a saucepan over medium-low heat, add butter and when it melts, add garlic, parsley, and orange zest along with Worcestershire sauce and orange juice, stir until mixed.

9. Boil the sauce for 5 minutes, then remove the saucepan from the heat and keep it warm.

10. When done, transfer scallops to a dish and serve with prepared butter sauce.

Nutrition: Calories: 184; Total Fat: 9 g; Saturated Fat: 5 g; Protein: 21 g; Carbs: 1 g; Fiber: 0 g; Sugar: 0 g

Zesty Shrimp Cocktail

Preparation Time: 10 minutes
Cooking Time: 1 hour and 15 minutes
Servings: 6
Ingredients:
• 12 ounces smoked shrimp, peeled, deveined
• 1-pound tomatoes
• Two jalapeno pepper, diced
• One small red onion, peeled, sliced 1/4 inch thick
• Three garlic cloves, peeled, halved
• 1 tbsp. olive oil
• 2 tbsp. apple wine vinegar

• 1 ½ teaspoon salt
• 2 tbsp. brown sugar
• 1/4 cup Tabasco sauce
• 1/2 lemon, juiced
• 3 tbsp. cilantro, chopped
• One small avocado, peeled, pitted, flesh cut into 1/2-inch cubes
• 1 ¼ tsp. salt

Directions:

1. Open the smoker's hopper, add dry pallets, make sure ash-can is in place, and then open the ash damper, power on the smoker, and close the ash damper.

2. Set the temperature of the smoker to 350 degrees F, switch smoker to open flame cooking mode, press the open flame 3, remove the grill grates and the batch, replace batch with direct flame insert, then return grates on the grill in the lower position and let preheat for 30 minutes or until the green light on the dial blinks that indicate smoker has reached to set temperature.

3. Then place tomatoes on a rimmed baking sheet, put it on the smoker grill, shut with lid, and smoke for 30 to 45 minutes or until tender and blackened.

4. Meanwhile, take another rimmed baking sheet, add onion and garlic drizzle with oil, and toss until mixed.

5. Place the baking sheet containing onion and garlic on the smoker grill and roast for 15 minutes or until nicely browned, set aside until required.

6. When tomatoes are done, let them rest for 5 minutes, remove their blackened skin, place tomatoes in a food processor, pulse for several times or chopped into small pieces, and then tip tomatoes in a bowl and set aside.

7. Add onion and garlic into the food processor and continue blending until coarsely chopped.

8. Tip onion and garlic mixture in a large bowl, add tomatoes and salt, sugar, vinegar, lemon juice, and hot sauce, and stir until well mixed.

9. Add shrimps and remaining ingredients, stir until combined, and serve.

Nutrition:

Calories: 234; Total Fat: 12 g; Saturated Fat: 2 g; Protein: 24 g; Carbs: 7 g; Fiber: 4 g; Sugar: 1 g

Swordfish with Sicilian Olive Oil Sauce

Prep. Time: 15 mins
Cook Time: 10 mins
Servings: 4

Ingredients

· Olive Oil ½ Cup and for Oiling the Fish extra 2 tbsp
· Clove Garlic 2 (Minced)
· Lemon 1 (Juiced)
· Fresh Parsley 3 tbsp (Finely Chopped)
· Brined Capers 1 tbsp
· Fresh Oregano 1 tbsp (Finely Chopped)
· Swordfish, Halibut, Tuna 6 To 8 Ounces
· Salt and Pepper

Instructions

1. Melt ½ cup olive oil in a saucepan over medium heat.

2. Combine 2 tablespoons of hot water and lemon juice in a mixing bowl. Add the garlic, oregano, parsley, capers, and season to taste with salt and pepper. It's critical to keep things warm.

3. When ready to cook, preheat the to 400°F with the lid closed for 15 mins.

4. After coating the fish steaks with 2 tbsp olive oil, season them with salt and pepper.

5. Place the fish on the grill and cook for 18 mins, or until opaque and flaky when pressed with a fork. (Cook it for a shorter period of time.)

6. On a tray or on separate plates, drizzle the "warm" olive oil sauce over the fish steaks. The leftover sauce should be served on the side. Take pleasure in it.

Nutrition: Energy (calories): 413 kcal Protein: 51.28 g Fat: 13.55 g Carbohydrates: 19.99 g

Smoked Lamb Leg

Preparation Time: 10 minutes
Cooking Time: 4 hours
Servings: 4-6
Ingredients:
The Meat
• 1 Lamb leg.
The Mixture
• Honey – ¼ cup.
• Sierra Dijon Mustard – 2 tbsp.
• Chopped rosemary – 2 tbsp.
• Lemon zest – 1 tsp.
• Garlic (minced) – 3 cloves.
• Ground black pepper – 1 tsp.
The Fire
• Wood pellet smoker.
Directions:
1.   It is better to have frozen piece of lamb leg. So, you can shave off as much fat as you like.

2.   Mix garlic, lemon zest, chopped rosemary, mustard, pepper, and honey in a bowl. Put a saran wrap and place the leg of lamb on top of it. Pour the mixture on top of it.
3.   Alternatively, you can use zip lock bag for this process Wrap the lamb leg up and put it in the refrigerator.
4.   Let it sit in the fridge overnight. Take the wrap off the meat or take it out of zip lock bag if you have used it.
5.   Take 3-4 garlic cloves and insert it in the meat. Sprinkle over the meat some seasonings, which include salt, pepper, and cayenne. Slow smoking is the method of cooking used for the lamb meat in this recipe.
6.   Set the temperature at 200 and watch your meat thermometer probe. When it reaches 130 degrees take it out and let it rest for 20 minutes.
7.   Make ¼ inch standards cut for serving meat and pour the juices on top of it to serve.

Ground Lamb Kebabs

Preparation Time: 10 minutes
Cooking Time: 1 hour
Servings: 2-4
Ingredients:
The Meat
• Ground Lamb – 1-1/2 lb.
The Mixture
• Minced onions – 1/3 cup.
• Minced garlic – ½ cloves.
• Cilantro – 3 tbsp.
• Minced fresh mint – 1 tbsp.
• Ground cumin 1 tsp.
• Paprika – 1 tsp.
• Salt – 1 tsp.
• Ground coriander – ½ tsp.
• Cinnamon – ¼ tsp.
• Pita bread - to serve.
The Fire
• Wood pellet smoker, cherry wood pellets.
Directions:
1.   Take a large mixing bowl. Put in all of the ingredients except for the pita bread. Now start making meatballs out of the mixture. The meatballs should be about 2 inches in diameter.
2.   Take a bamboo skewer for each of the meatballs. Now, wet your hands to easily mold the skewered meal. Mold them each into a cigar shape.
3.   Place it in the refrigerator for at least 30 minutes at least or preferably overnight. Set your wood pellet smoker on the smoke option and with the lid open the fire establishes. It takes about 4-5 minutes.
4.   Then after that set the temperature to 350F and preheat it for about 10-15 minutes. During preheating keep the lid closed. Place the kebabs on the grill.
5.   After 30 minutes turn them over.

6.   Also, if the internal temperature reads 160F then it is time to turn them over. Warm the bread before serving it with kebobs.

Nutrition: Energy (calories): 173 kcal Protein: 17.62 g Fat: 10.76 g Carbohydrates: 1.72 g

Basil Shrimp Appetizer

Preparation Time: 5-10 minutes
Cooking Time: 8 minutes
Servings: 4-6
Ingredients:
- 2 tsp. olive oil
- Black pepper (ground) and salt to taste
- 1-lb. shrimp, peeled and deveined
- 1 tbsp. basil, chopped

Preparation:
1.   Take a Ninja Foodi Grill, arrange it over a cooking platform and open the top lid.
2.   In the unit, place the basket. Add all the ingredients and combine them.
3.   Select the "Air Fryer" mode and adjust the 370°F temperature level. Then, set the timer to 8 minutes and press "STOP/START," which will start the cooking process.
4.   When the timer goes off, open the lid. Serve it warm.

Nutritional Information Per Serving:
Calories: 117, Fat: 5g| Saturated Fat: 1g| Trans Fat: 0g| Carbohydrates: 2g| Fiber: 0g| Sodium: 924mg| Protein: 15g.Bacon BBQ Bites

Method of preparation: Grilling
Preparation time: 10 minutes
Cooking time: 30 minutes
Servings: 4
Ingredients:
1 tbsp. fennel, ground
½ cup of brown sugar
1 lb. slab bacon, cut into cubes (1 inch)
1 tsp. black pepper
salt

Dircctions:
Take an aluminum foil and then fold in half. Once you do that, and then turn the edges so that a rim is made. With a fork, make small holes on the bottom. In this way, the excess fat will escape and will make the bites crispy.
Preheat the grill to 350°F with a closed lid.
In a bowl, combine the black pepper, salt, fennel, and sugar. Stir.

Place the pork in the seasoning mixture. Toss to coat. Transfer on the foil.
Place the foil on the grill. Bake for 25 minutes, or until crispy and bubbly.
Serve and enjoy!
Nutrition:
Calories: 300 Protein: 27 g Carbs: 4 g Fat: 36 g

Atomic Buffalo Turds

Method of preparation: Grilling
Preparation time: 30 to 45 minutes
Cooking time: 1.5 hours to 2 hours
Servings: 6
Ingredients:
10 medium Jalapeno Pepper
8 ounces regular cream cheese at room temperature
¾ cup Monterey Jack and Cheddar Cheese Blend Shred (optional)
1 tsp. smoked paprika
1 tsp. garlic powder
½ tsp. cayenne pepper
Red pepper flakes (optional)
20 smoky sausages
10 sliced bacon, cut in half
Directions:
Wear food service gloves when using. Jalapeno peppers are washed vertically and sliced. Carefully remove seeds and veins using a spoon or paring knife and discard. Place Jalapeno on a grilled vegetable tray and set aside.
In a small bowl, mix cream cheese, shredded cheese, paprika, garlic powder, cayenne pepper is used, and red pepper flakes if used until thoroughly mixed.

Mix cream cheese with half of the jalapeno pepper.

Place the Little Smokiness sausage on half of the filled jalapeno pepper.

Wrap half of the thin bacon around half of each jalapeno peppers.

Fix the bacon to the sausage with a toothpick so that the pepper does not pierce. Place the ABT on the grill tray or pan.

Set the wood pellet smoker and grill for indirect cooking and preheat to 250°F using wood pellets

Suck jalapeno peppers at 250°F for about 1.5 to 2 hours until the bacon is cooked and crisp.

Remove the ABT from the grill and let it rest for 5 minutes before hors d'oeuvres.

Nutrition:

Calories: 131 Carbs: 1 g Fat: 1 2g Protein: 5 g

7.In the meantime, season the pizza bases. First, put the tomato pulp, helping to distribute it evenly with a spoon.

8.Put the mozzarella on top, then the olives and finally the capers.

9.Season with a drizzle of oil and with the help of the pizza shovel, place the pizza on the stone.

10.Close the lid and cook for 15 minutes.

11.As soon as the pizza is cooked, proceed to cooking the others.

12.Cut the pizzas into four slices each and serve.

Nutrition:

calories for 100 grams: 346

fat for 100 grams: 13

carbohydrates for 100 grams: 49

proteins for 100 grams: 11

Pizza with olives and capers

Preparation time: 15 minutes
Smoking time: 15 minutes for pizza
Temperature: 450°F
Portion: 4
Recommended pellets: Maple or Cherry Blend pellets
INGREDIENTS:
•850 grams of pizza dough
•400 grams of tomato pulp
•130 grams of black olives
•200 grams of buffalo mozzarella
•30 grams of capers
•Salt and pepper to taste
•Olive oil to taste
DIRECTIONS
1.Start by preparing the dressing.
2.Cut the mozzarella into thin slices and set aside.
3.Rinse and dry the capers.
4.Now take 4 loaves of pizza dough and stretch them until you get a thin disc.
5.Preheat the grill for indirect cooking at 500 ° F for 10 minutes.
6.Place the pizza stone in the center of the grill and let it heat for 10 minutes.

Caprese Tomato Salad

Preparation Time: 5 Minutes
Cooking Time: 60 Minutes
Servings: 4
Ingredients:
·   3 - cups halved multicolored cherry tomatoes
·   1/8 - teaspoon kosher salt
·   ½ - cup fresh basil leaves
·   1 - tablespoon extra-virgin olive oil
·   1 - tablespoon balsamic vinegar
·   ½ - teaspoon black pepper
·   ¼ - teaspoon kosher salt
·   1 - ounce diced fresh mozzarella cheese (about 1/3 cup)
Directions:
1. Join tomatoes and 1/8 tsp. legitimate salt in an enormous bowl. Let represent 5mins. Include basil leaves, olive oil, balsamic vinegar, pepper, 1/4 tsp. fit salt, and mozzarella; toss.
Nutrition: Calories 80 Fat 5.8g Protein 2g Carb 5g Sugars 4g

Smoked Vegetables

Method of preparation: Smoking
Preparation time: 5 minutes
Cooking time: 20 minutes
Servings: 4
Ingredients:
1 head of broccoli
4 carrots
16 oz. snow peas
1 tbsp. olive oil
1 cup mushrooms, chopped
1-1/2 tbsp. pepper
1 tbsp. garlic powder
Directions:
Cut broccoli and carrots into bite-size pieces. Add snow peas and combine.
Toss the veggies with oil and seasoning.
Now cover a pan, sheet, with parchment paper. Place veggies on top.
Meanwhile, set your wood pellet smoker to 180°F.
Place the pan into the smoker. Smoke for about 5 minutes.
Adjust smoker temperature to 400°F and continue cooking for another 10-15 minutes until slightly brown broccoli tips.
Remove, serve, and enjoy.
Nutrition:
Calories: 111 Total Fat: 4 g Saturated Fat: 1 g Total Carbs: 15 g Net Carbs: 9 g Protein: 5 g Sugar: 7 g Fiber: 6 g Sodium: 0 mg Potassium: 109 mg

Potato focaccia with rosemary

Preparation time: 30 minutes+ 2 hours for leavening
Smoking time: 20 minutes
Temperature: 220-464°F
Portion: 8
Recommended pellets: Apple Wood
ingredients
•300 grams of flour
•200 grams of potatoes
•140 ml of warm water
•1 teaspoon of brown sugar
•7 grams of brewer's yeast
•Olive oil to taste
•Salt and pepper to taste
•1 tablespoon of rosemary needles
DIRECTIONS
1.Start with the potatoes; wash them thoroughly under running water without peeling them.
2.Cook them for 25 minutes in plenty of boiling salted water.
3.Just cooked, drain, pass them under cold water and peel them.
4.Mash them with a potato masher and collect them in a bowl.
5.Add the flour, baking powder, 2 teaspoons of salt, sugar and water.
6.Knead vigorously for at least 15 minutes until the mixture is soft.
7.Compact it with your hands and give it the usual shape of a ball. Cover with cling film and let it rise for 2 hours.
8.Preheat the grill at 464 ° F for 15 minutes.
9.Put on the pizza stone and let it heat up for 15 minutes.
10.Brush a round baking pan with olive oil and put the dough inside.
11.Roll it out with your hands and brush the surface with olive oil.
12.Sprinkle with a little salt and rosemary needles and put the baking pan on the pizza stone.
13.Close the lid and cook for 20 minutes.
14.Check the cooking and if the focaccia is golden brown, remove it from the barbecue otherwise continue cooking for another 5 minutes.
15.Just cooked, remove it from the barbecue and let it rest for 5 minutes.
16.After 5 minutes, cut it into 8 slices and serve.
Nutrition:
calories for 100 grams: 343
fat for 100 grams: 6
carbohydrates for 100 grams: 40
proteins for 100 grams: 5

Spinach Salad with Avocado and Orange

Preparation Time: 5 Minutes
Cooking Time: 20 Minutes
Servings: 4
Ingredients:
· 1 ½ - tablespoons fresh lime juice
· 4 - teaspoons extra-virgin olive oil
· 1 - tablespoon chopped fresh cilantro
· 1/8 - teaspoon kosher salt
· ½ - cup diced peeled ripe avocado
· ½ - cup fresh orange segments
· 1 - (5-ounce) package baby spinach
· 1/8 - teaspoon freshly ground black pepper

Directions:
1. Combine first 4 substances in a bowl, stirring with a whisk.
2. Combine avocado, orange segments, and spinach in a bowl. Add oil combination; toss. Sprinkle salad with black pepper.

Nutrition: Calories 103 Fat 7.3g Sodium 118mg

Bacon Cheddar Slider

Method of preparation: Smoking
Preparation time: 30 minutes
Cooking time: 15 minutes
Servings: 6-10 (1-2 sliders each as an appetizer)
Recommended pellet: Optional
Ingredients:
1-pound ground beef (80% lean)
1/2 tsp. of garlic salt
1/2 tsp. salt
1/2 tsp. of garlic
1/2 tsp. onion
1/2 tsp. black pepper
6 bacon slices, cut in half
½ Cup mayonnaise
2 tsp. of creamy wasabi (optional)
6 (1 oz.) sliced sharp cheddar cheese, cut in half (optional)
Sliced red onion
½ Cup sliced kosher dill pickles
12 mini pieces of bread sliced horizontally
Ketchup

Directions:
Place ground beef, garlic salt, seasoned salt, garlic powder, onion powder, and black hu
Divide the meat mixture into 12 equal parts, shape it into small thin round patties (about 2 ounces each) and save.
Cook the bacon on medium heat over medium heat for 5-8 minutes until crunchy. Set aside.
To make the sauce, mix the mayonnaise and horseradish in a small bowl if using.
Set up a wood pellet smoker grill for direct cooking to use griddle accessories. Contact the manufacturer to see, if there is a griddle accessory that works with the wood pellet smoker grill.
Spray a cooking spray on the griddle-cooking surface for best non-stick results.
Preheat wood pellet smoker grill to 350°F using selected pellets. The griddle surface should be approximately 400°F.
Grill the putty for 3-4 minutes each until the internal temperature reaches 160°F.
If necessary, place a sharp cheddar cheese slice on each patty while the patty is on the griddle, or after the patty is removed from the griddle. Place a small amount of mayonnaise mixture, a slice of red onion, and a hamburger pate in the lower half of each roll. Pickled slices, bacon, and ketchup.

Nutrition:
Calories: 77 Total Fat: 1 g Saturated Fat: 1 g Total Carbs: 17 g Net Carbs: 15 g Protein: 3 g Sugar: 6 g Fiber: 2 g Sodium: 14 mg Potassium: 243 mg

Rustic pie with zucchini and ricotta

Preparation Time: 25 Minutes
Smoking Time: 25 minutes
Temperature: 500ºF
Portion: 4
Recommended pellets: Applewood Pellets
Ingredients
•1 roll of puff pastry
•300 grams of zucchini
•4 zucchini flowers

•100 grams of Taleggio
•300 grams of cottage cheese
•2 eggs
•50 grams of grated Parmesan cheese
•Olive oil to taste
•Salt and pepper to taste

Directions

1. Wash the zucchinis, and then cut them into thin slices.
2. Put a tablespoon of oil in a pan and as soon as it is hot, sauté the courgettes for 5 minutes. Season with salt and pepper and turn off.
3. Wash and dry the zucchinis flowers and then cut them into thin slices.
4. Put the ricotta in a bowl. Add the parmesan, eggs, salt, pepper, and mix. Put the zucchinis flowers and mix again.
5. Brush a round baking pan with olive oil and line it with the puff pastry.
6. Prick the bottom of the puff pastry with a fork and put the zucchinis on the bottom. Pour over the ricotta mixture and then put the Taleggio cheese cut into cubes on top.
7. Preheat the grill at 500 ° F for 15 minutes.
8. Place the pizza stone and let it heat for 10 minutes.
9. Now put the baking pan on the stone and cook, with the lid closed, for 25 minutes.
10. As soon as it is ready, remove the pie from the barbecue and let it rest for 10 minutes, then cut it into slices and serve.

Nutrition:

calories for 100 grams: 354
fat for 100 grams: 25
carbohydrates for 100 grams: 21
proteins for 100 grams: 11

Brisket Baked Beans

Method of preparation: Grilling

Preparation time: 20 minutes

Cooking time: 2 hours

Servings: 10

Ingredients:

2 tbsp. extra virgin olive oil
1 large diced onion

1 diced green pepper
1 red pepper diced
2 to 6 jalapeno peppers diced
3 pieces Texas-style brisket flat chopped
1 baked bean, like Bush's country-style baked beans
1 pork and beans
1 red kidney beans, rinse, drain
1 cup barbecue sauce like Sweet Baby Ray's barbecue sauce
½ cup stuffed brown sugar
3 garlic, chopped
2 tsp. of mustard
½ tsp. kosher salt
½ tsp. black pepper

Directions:

Heat the skillet with olive oil over medium heat and add the diced onion, peppers, and jalapeno. Sauté the food for about 8-10 minutes until the onion is translucent.

In a 4-quart casserole dish, mix chopped brisket, baked beans, pork beans, kidney beans, cooked onions, peppers, barbecue sauce, brown sugar, garlic, mustard, salt, and black pepper.

Using the selected pellets, configure a wood pellet-smoking grill for indirect cooking and preheat to 325°F. Cook the beans baked in the brisket for 1.5 to 2 hours until they become bare beans. Rest for 15 minutes before eating.

Nutrition:

Calories: 199 Carbs: 35 g Fat: 2 g Protein: 9 g

Tequila Slaw with Lime and Cilantro

Preparation Time: 5 Minutes

Cooking Time: 5 Minutes

Servings: 6

Ingredients:

- ¼ - cup canola mayonnaise (such as Hellmann's)
- 3 - tablespoons fresh lime juice
- 1 - tablespoon silver tequila
- 2 - teaspoons sugar
- ¼ - teaspoon kosher salt
- 1/3 - cup thinly sliced green onions

· ¼- cup chopped fresh cilantro
· 1 - (14-ounce) package coleslaw

Directions:

1. Add the first 5 ingredients in a big bowl. Add remaining ingredients; toss.

Nutrition: Calories 64 Fat 3g Protein 0.8g Carb 6.4g

Spinach Salad with Avocado and Orange

Preparation Time: 5 Minutes

Cooking Time: 20 Minutes

Servings: 4

Ingredients:

- 1 ½ - tablespoons fresh lime juice
- 4 - teaspoons extra-virgin olive oil
- 1 - tablespoon chopped fresh cilantro
- 1/8 - teaspoon kosher salt
- ½ - cup diced peeled ripe avocado
- ½ - cup fresh orange segments
- 1 - (5-ounce) package baby spinach
- 1/8 - teaspoon freshly ground black pepper

Directions:

1. Combine first 4 substances in a bowl, stirring with a whisk.
2. Combine avocado, orange segments, and spinach in a bowl. Add oil combination; toss. Sprinkle salad with black pepper.

Nutrition: Calories 103 Fat 7.3g Sodium 118mg

Potato pie with cheese and herbs

Preparation Time: 20 Minutes
Smoking Time: 20 Minutes
Temperature: 446ºF
Portion: 4
Recommended pellets: Hickory, mesquite, apple

Ingredients
•600 grams of potatoes
•200 grams of emmenthal
•200 ml of milk
•40 grams of shelled walnuts
•1 small piece of thyme
•1 sprig of rosemary
•6 sage leaves
•1 sprig of chopped parsley
•1 egg
•Butter to taste
•Breadcrumbs to taste
•Salt and pepper to taste
•Olive oil to taste

Directions

1.Bring a saucepan with plenty of salted water to a boil.
2.In the meantime, peel the potatoes, wash them and then cut them into thin slices.
3.Put the potato slices to cook for 5 minutes, then drain and let them cool.
4.Wash and dry thyme, sage and rosemary. Remove the sprigs of thyme and rosemary and then put everything in the glass of the blender.
5.Add the walnuts, milk, egg, salt and pepper and blend until the mixture is liquid and homogeneous.
6.Brush a baking dish with olive oil and put a layer of potatoes at the bottom.
7.Put a little herb sauce on top and then a few slices of Emmenthal and repeat the same operation until all the ingredients are used up.
8.Sprinkle the surface with breadcrumbs and a few tufts of butter and then cover the pan with aluminum foil.
9.Preheat the grill at 446 ° F for 15 minutes.
10.Place the grill and place the pan with the potatoes in the center.
11.Cook for 10 minutes, and then remove the aluminum foil.
12.Continue cooking for another 10 minutes and then remove from the grill.
13.Let it rest for 10 minutes, then divide the portions and serve.

Nutrition:
calories for 100 grams: 165
fat for 100 grams: 10
carbohydrates for 100 grams: 10
proteins for 100 grams: 9

Grilled Watermelon juice

Preparation Time: 10 Minutes
Cooking Time: 15 Minutes
Servings: 4
Ingredients:
- 2 Limes
- 2 tbsp. oil
- ½ Watermelon, sliced into wedges
- ¼ Tsp. Pepper flakes
- 2 tbsp. Salt

Directions:
1. Preheat the grill to high with closed lid.
2. Brush the watermelon with oil. Grill for 15 minutes. Flip once.
3. In a blender mix the salt and pepper flakes until combined.
4. Transfer the watermelon on a plate.
5. Serve and enjoy!
Nutrition: Calories: 40 Protein: 1g Carbs: 10g Fat: 0

Grilled French Dip

Preparation Time: 15 Minutes
Cooking Time: 35 Minutes
Servings: 8 to 12
Ingredients:
- 3 lbs. onions, thinly sliced (yellow)
- 2 tbsp. oil
- 2 tbsp. of Butter
- Salt to taste
- Black pepper to taste
- 1 tsp. Thyme, chopped
- 2 tsp. of Lemon juice
- 1 cup Mayo
- 1 cup of Sour cream

Directions:
1. Preheat the grill to high with closed lid.
2. In a pan combine the oil and butter. Place on the grill to melt. Add 2 tsp. salt and add the onions.
3. Stir well and close the lid of the grill. Cook 30 minutes stirring often.
4. Add the thyme. Cook for an additional 3 minutes. Set aside and add black pepper.
5. Once cooled add lemon juice, mayo, and sour cream. Stir to combine.

6. Serve with veggies or chips. Enjoy!
Nutrition: Calories: 60 Protein: 4g Carbs: 5g Fat: 6g

Quiche with salmon and shallots

Preparation Time: 15 Minutes
Smoking Time: 25 Minutes
Temperature: 482°F
Portion: 4
Recommended pellets: hickory, cherry, apple, pecan and mesquite
Ingredients
- 1 roll of short crust pastry
- 2 shallots
- 3 eggs
- 200 ml of cooking cream
- 100 grams of smoked salmon
- Olive oil to taste
- Salt and pepper to taste

Directions
1. Start by peeling and washing the shallots, and then cut them into thin slices.
2. Heat a tablespoon of oil in a pan and then sauté the shallots for two minutes. Season with salt and pepper and turn off.
3. Put the eggs in a bowl and beat them with a fork.
4. Add the cooking cream, salt and pepper and mix well.
5. Now put the shallots in the bowl and mix everything together.
6. Take a round baking pan and put the short crust pastry inside.
7. Put the shallots mixture inside and then the salmon cut into thin slices.
8. Preheat the grill at 482 ° F for 15 minutes.
9. Put on the pizza stone and let it heat for 10 minutes.
10. Put the baking pan on top of the stone and cook, with the lid closed, for 25 minutes.
11. Just cooked, remove the quiche from the grill and let it rest for 10 minutes.
12. After 10 minutes, cut it into slices, put it on plates and serve.
Nutrition:
calories for 100 grams: 283

fat for 100 grams: 17
carbohydrates for 100 grams: 21
proteins for 100 grams: 9

Atomic Buffalo Turds

Preparation Time: 30 to 45 Minutes
Cooking Time: 1.5 Hours to 2 Hours
Servings: 6
Ingredients:
· 10 Medium Jalapeno Pepper
· 8 ounces regular cream cheese at room temperature
· ¾Cup Monterey Jack and Cheddar Cheese Blend Shred (optional)
· One teaspoon smoked paprika
· One teaspoon garlic powder
· ½ teaspoon cayenne pepper
· Teaspoon red pepper flakes (optional)
· 20 smoky sausages
· Ten sliced bacon, cut in half
Directions:
1. Wear food service gloves when using. Jalapeno peppers are washed vertically and sliced. Carefully remove seeds and veins using a spoon or paring knife and discard. Place Jalapeno on a grilled vegetable tray and set aside.
2. A small bowl, mix cream cheese, shredded cheese, paprika, garlic powder, cayenne pepper is used, and red pepper flakes if used until thoroughly mixed.
3. Mix cream cheese with half of the jalapeno pepper.
4. Place the Little Smokiness sausage on half of the filled jalapeno pepper.
5. Wrap half of the thin bacon around half of each jalapeno peppers.
6. Fix the bacon to the sausage with a toothpick so that the pepper does not pierce. Place the ABT on the grill tray or pan.
7. Set the wood pellet smoker and grill for indirect cooking and preheat to 250 degrees Fahrenheit using hickory pellets or blends.
8. Suck jalapeno peppers at 250 ° F for about 1.5 to 2 hours until the bacon is cooked and crisp.

9. Remove the ABT from the grill and let it rest for 5 minutes before hors d'oeuvres.
Nutrition: Calories: 131 Carbs: 1g Fat: 12g Protein: 5g

Pizza with gorgonzola, pears and walnuts

Preparation Time: 15 Minutes
Smoking Time: 12 Minutes For Pizza
Temperature: 482ºF
Portion: 4
Recommended pellets: cherrywood/pearwood, maple
Ingredients
•800 grams of pizza dough
•4 mozzarella
•2 pears
•200 grams of gorgonzola
•4 chopped walnut kernels
•Salt and pepper to taste
•Olive oil to taste
Directions
1.Divide the pizza dough into 4 loaves.
2.Put them on a lightly floured work surface and roll them out with your hands until you have 4 circles of dough.
3.Lightly brush the surface of the pizza with oil.
4.Cut the mozzarella into slices and place them on top of each pizza.
5.Wash and dry the pears, remove the seeds and then cut them into slices. Divide the slices of pears in each pizza.
6.Now cut the gorgonzola into cubes and place it on top of the pizzas.
7.Season with salt, pepper and olive oil, and sprinkle with chopped walnuts.
8.Preheat the grill for 15 minutes at 482 ° F.
9.Put the pizza stone to heat for 10 minutes.
10.After 10 minutes, put the first pizza to cook for 12 minutes, with the lid closed.
11.Repeat the same operation for the other pizzas.
12.As soon as they are ready, cut the pizzas into four parts and serve.
Nutrition:

calories for 100 grams: 247
fat for 100 grams: 10
carbohydrates for 100 grams: 28
proteins for 100 grams: 11

Thyme - Rosemary Mash Potatoes

Preparation Time: 20 minutes
Cooking Time: 1 hour
Servings: 6
Ingredients:
· 4 ½ lbs. Potatoes, russet
· Salt
· 1 pint of Heavy cream
· 3 Thyme sprigs + 2 tablespoons for garnish
· 2 Rosemary sprigs
o - 7 Sage leaves
o - 7 Black peppercorns
· Black pepper to taste
· Two stick Butter softened
· 2 Garlic cloves, chopped
Directions:
1. Preheat the grill to 350F with a closed lid.
2. Peel the russet potatoes.
3. Cut into small pieces and place them in a baking dish. Fill it with water (1 ½ cups). Place on the grill and cook with a closed lid for about 1 hour.
4. In the meantime, in a saucepan, combine the garlic, peppercorns, herbs, and cream. Place on the grate and cook covered for about 15 minutes. Once done, strain to remove the garlic and herbs. Keep warm.
5. Take out the water of the potatoes and place them in a stockpot. Rice them with a fork and pour 2/3 of the mixture. Add one stick of softened butter and salt.
6. Serve right away.
Nutrition: Calories: 180 Protein: 4g Carbs: 28g Fat: 10g

The Best Potato Roast

Preparation Time: 15 minutes
Cooking Time: 35 minutes

Servings: 6
Ingredients:
· 4 Potatoes, large (scrubbed)
· 1 ½ cups gravy (beef or chicken)
· Rib seasoning to taste
· 1 ½ cups Cheddar cheese
· Black pepper and salt to taste
· Two tablespoons sliced Scallions
Directions:
1. Preheat the grill to high with a closed lid.
2. Slice each potato into wedges or fries. Transfer into a bowl and drizzle with oil—season with Rib seasoning.
3. Spread the wedges/fries on a baking sheet (rimmed)—roast for about 20 minutes. Turn the wedges/fries and cook for 15 minutes more.
4. In the meantime, in a saucepan, warm the chicken/beef gravy. Cut the cheese into small cubes.
5. It was once done cooking, place the potatoes on a plate or into a bowl. Distribute the cut cheese and pour hot gravy on top.
6. Serve garnished with scallion—season with pepper. Enjoy!
Nutrition: Calories: 220 Protein: 3g Carbs: 38g Fat: 15g

Baked cod au gratin

Preparation Time: 25 Minutes
Smoking Time: 15 Minutes
Temperature: 410°F
Portion: 4
Recommended pellets: pecan
Ingredients
•400 grams of cod fillet
•3 fennel
•200 grams of béchamel
•60 grams of grated Parmesan cheese
•Salt and pepper to taste
•Olive oil to taste
Directions
1.Remove the beard and the hardest leaves from the fennel and then cut them into 4.
2.Cook them for 7 minutes in boiling salted water, then drain and set aside.

3.Wash and dry the cod fillets, remove skin and bones if present and then cut them into cubes of 3 cm each.

4.As soon as the fennels have cooled, cut them into slices.

5.Brush a baking dish with olive oil and then put the fennel on the bottom.

6.Put the cod on top and then sprinkle with salt and pepper.

7.Sprinkle with the béchamel and then spread over the parmesan.

8.Preheat the grill to 410 ° F for 15 minutes.

9.Place the grill and then put the pan with the fish on top.

10.Close the lid and cook for 15 minutes.

11.Just cooked, remove the fish from the barbecue and let it rest for 5 minutes.

12.Divide the fennel and fish in serving plates and serve.

Nutrition:

calories for 100 grams: 120

fat for 100 grams: 4

carbohydrates for 100 grams: 6

proteins for 100 grams: 17

Watermelon-Cucumber Salad

Preparation Time: 12 Minutes

Cooking Time: 0 Minutes

Servings: 4

Ingredients:

- 1 - tablespoon olive oil
- 2 - teaspoons fresh lemon juice
- ¼ - teaspoon salt
- 2 - cups cubed seedless watermelon
- 1 - cup thinly sliced English cucumber
- ¼ - cup thinly vertically sliced red onion
- 1 - tablespoon thinly sliced fresh basil

Directions:

1. Consolidate oil, squeeze, and salt in a huge bowl, mixing great. Include watermelon, cucumber, and onion; toss well to coat. Sprinkle plate of mixed greens equally with basil.

Nutrition: Calories 60 Fat 3.5g Protein 0.8g Carb 7.6g

Salty plum cake with spinach, cherry tomatoes and feta

Preparation Time: 40 Minutes

Smoking Time: 35 Minutes

Temperature: 482ºF

Portion: 6

Recommended pellets: Hudson Oak & Apple Pellets

Ingredients

•4 eggs

•30 grams of brown sugar

•120 ml of seed oil

•180 ml of milk

•460 grams of flour

•150 grams of cooked spinach

•16 grams of yeast

•100 grams of feta

•80 grams of cherry tomatoes

•2 shallots

•Olive oil to taste

•Salt and pepper to taste

Directions

1.Peel and wash the shallots and then cut them into slices.

2.Finely chop the spinach.

3.In a large bowl, break 4 eggs, start beating them with a whisk.

4.Add the salt, sugar, seed oil, milk and half of the flour and mix everything well.

5.Proceed by combining the boiled spinach and baking powder and continue stirring.

6.Add the remaining flour and mix until the mixture is smooth and free of lumps.

7.Wash and dry the cherry tomatoes and then cut them into small pieces.

8.Finally add the crumbled feta, cherry tomatoes, black olives and shallots. Mix again and add everything to the dough.

9.Season with salt and pepper and then pour the mixture into a previously oiled and floured plum cake mold.

10.Preheat the grill at 482 ° F for 15 minutes.

11.Preheat the pizza stone for 10 minutes.

12.Put the mold on the stone and cook for 30 minutes.

13.After 30 minutes, check the cooking with a toothpick and if it is cooked then remove it from the barbecue, otherwise continue cooking for another 5 minutes.

14.Just cooked, remove the plum cake from the grill and let it rest for 15 minutes.

15.Remove the plum cake from the mold, cut it into slices and serve.

Nutrition:

calories for 100 grams: 300

fat for 100 grams: 13

carbohydrates for 100 grams: 18

proteins for 100 grams: 7

Crunchy Zucchini Chips

Preparation Time: 15 Minutes

Cooking Time: 25 Minutes

Servings: 4

Ingredients:

- 1/3 - cup whole-wheat panko
- 3 - tablespoons uncooked amaranth
- ½ - teaspoon garlic powder
- ¼ - teaspoon kosher salt
- ¼ - teaspoon freshly ground black pepper
- 1 - ounce Parmesan cheese, finely grated
- 12 - ounces zucchini, cut into
- ¼ - inch-thick slices
- 1 - tablespoon olive oil Cooking spray

Directions:

1. Preheat stove to 425°. Join the initial 6 ingre-dients in a shallow dish. Join zucchini and oil in an enormous bowl; toss well to coat. Dig zucchini in panko blend, squeezing tenderly to follow. Spot covered cuts on an ovenproof wire rack covered with cooking shower; place the rack on a preparing sheet or jam move dish.

2. Heat at 425° for 26 minutes or until cooked and fresh. Serve chips right away.

Nutrition: Calories 132 Fat 6.5g Protein 6g Carb 14g Sugars 2g

Smoked Popcorn with Parmesan Herb

Preparation Time: 10 Minutes

Cooking Time: 10 Minutes

Servings: 2 to 4

Ingredients:

- ¼ cup of Popcorn Kernels
- 1 tsp. of salt
- 1 tsp. of Garlic powder
- ½ cup grated Parmesan
- 2 tsp. of Italian seasoning
- 2 tbsp. oil
- 4 tbsp. of Butter

Directions:

1. Preheat the grill to 250F with closed lid.

2. In a saucepan add the butter and oil. Melt and add the salt, garlic powder, and Italian seasoning.

3. Add the kernels in a paper bag. Fold it two times to close.

4. Place in the microwave. Turn on high heat and set 2 minutes.

5. Open and transfer into a bowl.

6. Pour the butter. Toss. Transfer on a baking tray and grill for about 10 minutes.

7. Serve and enjoy!

Nutrition: Calories: 60 Protein: 1g Carbs: 5g Fat: 3g

Pizza with raw ham, buffalo mozzarella and pistachios

Preparation Time: 15 Minutes

Smoking Time: 15 Minutes For Pizza

Temperature: 500ºF

Serving: 4

Recommended pellets: hickory

Ingredients

- 800 grams of pizza dough
- 250 grams of tomato pulp
- 2 mozzarella
- 4 buffalo mozzarella
- 100 grams of raw ham
- 40 grams of chopped pistachios
- Salt and pepper to taste
- Olive oil to taste

Directions

1.Divide the pizza dough into 4 loaves of 200 grams each.

2.Put them on a lightly floured work surface and spread them with your hands until you get 4 thin circles.

3.Place the tomato pulp and the sliced mozzarella on each pizza.

4.Preheat the grill at 500 ° F for 15 minutes with the lid closed.

5.Put the pizza stone to heat for 10 minutes.

6.After 10 minutes, place the pizza on the stone, using a pizza shovel.

7.Cook for 15 minutes and then remove from the barbecue.

8.Repeat the same operation also with the other 3 pizzas.

9.Let the pizza rest for 5 minutes and in the meantime put the buffalo mozzarella cut into pieces, the raw ham and finally the pistachio on top of the pizza.

10.Season with oil, salt and pepper, cut into slices and serve.

Nutrition:

calories for 100 grams: 301

fat for 100 grams: 6

carbohydrates for 100 grams: 36

proteins for 100 grams: 8

Buffalo Mini Sausages

Preparation Time:30 Min

Cooking time:1h – 1 ½ hrs.

Servings:10

Ingredients:

·   8 ounces regular cream cheese (room temp)

·   ¾ cup cheddar cheese blend and shredded Monterey Jack (not necessary)

·   1 teaspoon smoked paprika

·   1 teaspoon garlic powder

·   ½ teaspoon red pepper flakes (not necessary)

·   ¾ cup sour cream

·   Little Smokies sausages (20)

·   10 bacon strips, thinly sliced and halved

·   10 jalapeno peppers (medium)

Directions:

1.   Wash the jalapenos, then slice them up along the length. Get a spoon, or a paring knife if you prefer, and use that to take out the seeds and the veins.

2.   Place the scooped-out jalapenos on a veggie grilling tray and put it all aside.

3.   Get a small bowl and mix the shredded cheese, cream cheese, paprika, cayenne pepper, garlic powder, and red pepper flakes. Mix them thoroughly.

4.   Get your jalapenos which you've hollowed out, and then stuff them with the cream cheese mix.

5.   Get your little Smokies sausage, and then put it right onto each of the cheese stuffed jalapenos.

6.   Grab some of the thinly sliced and halved bacon strips and wrap them around each of the stuffed jalapenos and their sausage.

7.   Grab some toothpicks. Use them to keep the bacon nicely secured to the sausage.

8.   Set up your wood pellet smoker grill so it's ready for indirect cooking. Get it preheated to 250°F. Use hickory or blends for your wooden pellets.

9.   Put your jalapeno peppers in and smoke them at 250°F for anywhere from 90 minutes to 120 minutes. You want to keep it going until the bacon is nice and crispy.

10. Take out the atomic buffalo turds, and then let them rest for about 5 minutes.

11. Serve!

Nutrition: Calories: 198 Fat: 17g Cholesterol: 48mg Carbs: 3g Protein: 8g Intolerances: Egg-Free

Buffalo Mini Sausages

Preparation Time:30 Min

Cooking time:1h – 1 ½ hrs.

Servings:10

Ingredients:

·   8 ounces regular cream cheese (room temp)

·   ¾ cup cheddar cheese blend and shredded Monterey Jack (not necessary)

·   1 teaspoon smoked paprika

·   1 teaspoon garlic powder

·   ½ teaspoon red pepper flakes (not necessary)

·   ¾ cup sour cream

- Little Smokies sausages (20)
- 10 bacon strips, thinly sliced and halved
- 10 jalapeno peppers (medium)

Directions:

1. Wash the jalapenos, then slice them up along the length. Get a spoon, or a paring knife if you prefer, and use that to take out the seeds and the veins.

2. Place the scooped-out jalapenos on a veggie grilling tray and put it all aside.

3. Get a small bowl and mix the shredded cheese, cream cheese, paprika, cayenne pepper, garlic powder, and red pepper flakes. Mix them thoroughly.

4. Get your jalapenos which you've hollowed out, and then stuff them with the cream cheese mix.

5. Get your little Smokies sausage, and then put it right onto each of the cheese stuffed jalapenos.

6. Grab some of the thinly sliced and halved bacon strips and wrap them around each of the stuffed jalapenos and their sausage.

7. Grab some toothpicks. Use them to keep the bacon nicely secured to the sausage.

8. Set up your wood pellet smoker grill so it's ready for indirect cooking. Get it preheated to 250°F. Use hickory or blends for your wooden pellets.

9. Put your jalapeno peppers in and smoke them at 250°F for anywhere from 90 minutes to 120 minutes. You want to keep it going until the bacon is nice and crispy.

10. Take out the atomic buffalo turds, and then let them rest for about 5 minutes.

11. Serve!

Nutrition: Calories: 198 Fat: 17g Cholesterol: 48mg Carbs: 3g Protein: 8g Intolerances: Egg-Free

Hearty Peaches

Preparation Time: 10-15 minutes
Cooking Time: 30 minutes
Servings: 4
Ingredients
- fresh peaches

Directions:

1. Take your drip pan and add water, cover with aluminum foil. Pre-heat your smoker to 200 degrees F

2. Use water fill water pan halfway through and place it over drip pan. Add wood chips to the side tray

3. Transfer peaches directly onto your smoker and smoke for 30 minutes, the first 20 minutes should be skin side down while the final 10 should be skin side up

4. Remove from smoker and serve, enjoy!

Nutrition; Calories: 117 Fat: 0.8g Carbohydrates: 28g Protein: 3g

Stuffed Up Chorizo Pepper

Preparation Time: 10-15 minutes
Cooking Time: 2 hours
Servings: 4
Ingredients
- 3 cups cheese, shredded
- 2 pounds chorizo, ground
- 4 poblano pepper, halved and seeded
- 8 bacon slices, uncooked

Directions:

1. Take your drip pan and add water, cover with aluminum foil. Pre-heat your smoker to 225 degrees F

2. Use water fill water pan halfway through and place it over drip pan. Add wood chips to the side tray

3. Divide the mix into 8 portions and press one portion into each pepper half

4. Sprinkle rest of the cheddar on top

5. Wrap each pepper half with 1 bacon slice, making sure to tuck in the edges to secure it

6. Transfer peppers to your smoker and smoke for 2 hours until the internal temperature of the sausage reach 165-degree Fahrenheit

7. Enjoy!

Nutrition: Calories: 834 Fats: 51g Carbs: 55g Fiber: 2g

Grill Buttered Potatoes

Prep time: 10 minutes | **Cook time**: 60 minutes | Serves 8

1, 32 oz., package frozen hash browns
½ cup cheddar cheese, grated
1 can cream chicken soup
1 cup sour cream
1 cup Mayonnaise
3 cups corn flakes, whole or crushed
¼ cup melted butter

1. Preheat your grill to 350°F.
2. Spray a 13 x 9 baking pan, aluminum, using a cooking spray, non-stick.
3. Mix hash browns, cheddar cheese, chicken soup cream, sour cream, and mayonnaise in a bowl, large.
4. Spoon the mixture into a baking pan gently.
5. Mix corn flakes and melted butter then sprinkle over the casserole.
6. Grill for about 1-½ hours until potatoes become tender. If the top browns too much, cover using a foil until potatoes are done.
7. Remove from the grill and serve hot.

Per Serving
Calories: 403 | Fat: 37g | Carbs: 14g | Protein: 4g | Sugar: 2g | Sodium: 620mg

Queso Chorizo Meal

Serving: 4
Preparation Time: 10-15 minutes
Cooking Time: 60 minutes
Servings: 4

Ingredients
· 16 ounces cubed Velveeta cheese
· 4 ounces cream cheese, cubed
· 10 ounces Rotel
· 1 pound cooked Chorizo, chopped

How To
1. Take your drip pan and add water, cover with aluminum foil. Pre-heat your smoker to 200 degrees F
2. Use water fill water pan halfway through and place it over drip pan. Add wood chips to the side tray
3. Add all of the ingredients in an aluminum foil pan and smoke for 1 hour, stirring after every 15 minutes
4. Serve with tortilla chips
5. Enjoy!

Nutrition: Calories: 372 Fat: 30g Carbohydrates: 6g Protein: 6g

Smoky Caramelized Onions on the Grill

Prep time: 5 minutes | **Cook time**: 60 minutes | **Serves** 4

5 large, sliced onions
½ cup fat your choice
Pinch Sea salt

1. Place all the ingredients into a pan. For a deep rich brown caramelized onion, cook them off for about 1hour on a stovetop.
2. Keep the grill temperatures not higher than 250 - 275°F.
3. Now transfer the pan into the grill.
4. Cook for about 1-1½ hours until brown in color. Check and stir with a spoon, wooden, after every 15 minutes. Make sure not to run out of grill.
5. Now remove from the grill and season with more salt if necessary.
6. Serve immediately or place in a refrigerator for up to 1 week.

Per Serving
Calories: 286 | Fat: 26g | Carbs: 13g | Protein: 2g | Sugar: 6g | Sodium: 6mg

Grilled Mushroom Skewers

Prep time: 5 minutes | **Cook time**: 60 minutes | **Serves** 6

16 - oz. 1 pound Baby Portobello Mushrooms
For the marinade:
¼ cup olive oil
¼ cup lemon juice
Small handful parsley
1 teaspoon sugar
1 teaspoon salt

¼ teaspoon pepper
¼ teaspoon cayenne pepper
1 to 2 garlic cloves
1 tablespoon balsamic vinegar
What you will need:
10-inch bamboo/wood skewers
1.   Add the beans to the plate of a lipped container, in an even layer. Shower the softened spread uniformly out ludicrous and utilizing a couple of tongs tenderly hurl the beans with the margarine until all around covered.
2.   Season the beans uniformly, and generously, with salt and pepper.
3.   Preheat the smoker to 275°. Include the beans, and smoke 3-4 hours, hurling them like clockwork or until delicate wilted, and marginally seared in spots.
4.   Spot 10 medium sticks into a heating dish and spread with water. It's critical to douse the sticks for in any event 15 minutes (more is better) or they will consume too rapidly on the flame broil.
5.   Spot most of the marinade mixture in a nourishment processor and heartbeat a few times until the marinade is almost smooth.
6.   Flush your mushrooms and pat dry. Cut each mushroom down the middle, so each piece has half of the mushroom stem.
7.   Spot the mushroom parts into a big gallon-size Ziploc sack, or a medium bowl and pour in the marinade. Shake the pack until most of the mushrooms are equally covered in marinade. Refrigerate and marinate for 30mins to 45mins.
8.   Preheat your barbecue to about 300°F
9.   Stick the mushrooms cozily onto the bamboo/wooden sticks that have been dousing (no compelling reason to dry the sticks). Piercing the mushrooms was a bit irritating from the outset until I got the hang of things.
10. I've discovered that it's least demanding to stick them by bending them onto the stick. If you simply drive the stick through, it might make the mushroom break.
11. Spot the pierced mushrooms on the hot barbecue for around 3mins for every side, causing sure the mushrooms don't consume the flame broil. The mushrooms are done when they are delicate; as mushrooms ought to be.
12. Remove from the barbecue. Spread with foil to keep them warm until prepared to serve
Per Serving
Calories: 230 | Fat: 20g | Carbs: 10g | Protein: 5g | Sugar: 2g | Sodium: 393mg

A Meaty Bologna

Preparation Time: 20 minutes
Cooking Time:60 minutes
Serving: 6-8
Ingredients
· Salt and pepper to taste
· ¼ cup yellow mustard
· pounds all-beef bologna chub
· 1 teaspoon garlic powder
· 1 teaspoon ground nutmeg
· 1 teaspoon ground coriander
· 2 tablespoons packed brown sugar
· 2 tablespoons chili powder
Directions:
1.   Take your drip pan and add water, cover with aluminum foil. Pre-heat your smoker to 250 degrees F
2.   Use water fill water pan halfway through and place it over drip pan. Add wood chips to the side tray
3.   Take a small-sized bowl and add chili powder, coriander, nutmeg, brown sugar, garlic
4.   Mix well and keep it on the side
5.   Cut bologna into ½ inch slices, making sure that there are few small cuts all around the edges
6.   Coat them generously with mustard mix
7.   Season generously with salt and pepper, spice mix
8.   Transfer to Smoker and smoke for 1 hour
9.   Serve and enjoy once done!
Nutrition: Calories: 819 Fats: 46g Carbs: 1g Fiber: 2g

Roasted Cashews

Prep time: 15 minutes | **Cook time**: 12 minutes | **Serves** 6

¼ cup Rosemary, chopped

2 ½ tablespoon Butter, melted

2 cups Cashews, raw

½ teaspoon Cayenne pepper

1 teaspoon salt

1.   Preheat the grill to 350°F with a closed lid.
2.   In a baking dish layer, the nuts. Combine the cayenne, salt rosemary, and butter. Add on top.
3.   Grill for 12 minutes.
4.   Serve and enjoy!

Per Serving

Calories: 150 | Fat: 15g | Carbs: 7g | Protein: 5g | Sugar: 1g | Sodium: 415mg

Grilled Green Onions and Orzo and Sweet Peas

Prep time: 5 minutes | **Cook time**: 15 minutes | **Serves** 4

¾ cup whole-wheat orzo

1 cup frozen peas

1 bunch green onions, trimmed

1 teaspoon olive oil

½ teaspoon grated lemon rind

1 tablespoon lemon juice

1 teaspoon olive oil

¼ teaspoon salt

1-ounce shaved Montego cheese

1.   Plan orzo as indicated by way of headings, discarding salt, and fat. Include peas throughout the most recent 2mins of cooking, channel.
2.   Warm a fish fry skillet over high warmness. Toss inexperienced onions with 1 teaspoon olive oil.
3.   Cook 2 minutes on each facet. Cleave onions, upload to orzo. Include lemon skin, lemon juice, 1 teaspoon olive oil, and salt: toss. Sprinkle with shaved Manchego cheddar.

Per Serving

Calories: 197 | Fat: 6g | Carbs: 12g | Protein: 4g | Sugar: 2g | Sodium: 204mg

Smoked Guacamole

Prep time: 25 minutes | **Cook time**: 30 minutes | **Serves** 6 to 8

¼ cup chopped Cilantro

7 Avocados, peeled and seeded

¼ cup chopped Onion, red

¼ cup chopped tomato

3 ears corn

1 teaspoon Chile Powder

1 teaspoon Cumin

2 tablespoon Lime juice

1 tablespoon minced Garlic

1 Chile, poblano

Black pepper and salt to taste

1.   Preheat the grill to 180°F with a closed lid.
2.   Smoke the avocado for 10 min.
3.   Set the avocados aside and increase the temperature of the girl to high.
4.   Once heated grill the corn and chili. Roast for 20 minutes.
5.   Cut the corn. Set aside. Place the chili in a bowl.
6.   In a bowl mash the avocados, leave few chunks. Add the remaining ingredients and mix.
7.   Serve right away because it is best eaten fresh. Enjoy!

Per Serving

Calories: 51 | Fat: 4g | Carbs: 3g | Protein: 1g | Sugar: 2g | Sodium: 16mg

Twice Grilled Potatoes

Prep time: 10 minutes | **Cook time**: 4 hours | **Serves** 6

6 russet potatoes

2 teaspoon olive oil

Salt, to taste

8 cooked bacon slices, crumbled

½ cup heavy whipping cream

4 oz. cream cheese, softened

4 teaspoon butter, softened

4 jalapeño peppers, seeded and chopped

1 teaspoon seasoned salt

2 cup Monterrey Jack cheese, grated and divided

1. Set the temperature of Grill to 225 degrees F and preheat with closed lid for 15 minutes.

2. With paper towels, pat dry the washed potatoes completely.

3. Coat the potatoes with olive oil sprinkle with some salt.

4. Arrange potatoes onto the grill and cook for about 3-3½ hours.

5. Remove the potatoes from grill and cut them in half lengthwise.

6. With a large spoon carefully, scoop out the potato flesh from skins, leaving a little potato layer.

7. In a large bowl, add potato flesh and mash it slightly.

8. Add bacon, cream, cream cheese, butter, jalapeno, seasoned salt and 1 C. of Monterrey Jack cheese and gently, stir to combine.

9. Stuff the potato skins with bacon mixture and top with remaining Monterrey Jack cheese.

10. Arrange the stuffed potatoes onto a baking sheet.

11. Place the baking sheet in grill and cook for about 30 minutes.

12. Serve hot.

Per Serving

Calories: 539 | Fat: 37g | Carbs: 36g | Protein: 18g | Sugar: 3g | Sodium: 1355mg

· ¼ cup barbecue sauce, like Sweet Baby Ray's ½ pound thinly sliced bacon, cut in half PREPPING

Instructions:

· In a large bowl, combine the ground beef, ground pork sausage, egg, bread crumbs, onion, Parmesan cheese, parsley, milk, garlic, salt, oregano, and pepper. Do not overwork the meat.

· Form 1½-ounce meatballs, approximately 1½ inches in diameter, and place on a Teflon-coated fiberglass mat.

· Wrap each meatball with half a slice of thin bacon. Spear the Moink balls onto 6 skewers (3 balls per skewer).

· Configure your wood pellet smoker-grill for indirect cooking.

· Preheat your wood pellet smoker-grill to 225°F using hickory pellets.

· Smoke the Moink ball skewers for 30 minutes.

· Increase your pit temperature to 350°F until the meatballs' internal temperature reaches 175°F and the bacon is crispy (approximately 40 to 45 minutes).

· Brush the Moink balls with your favorite barbecue sauce during the last 5 minutes.

· Serve the Moink ball skewers while they're still hot.

Hickory-Smoked Moink Ball Skewers

Ingredients:

· ½ pound ground beef (80% lean)
· ½ pound ground pork sausage
· 1 large egg
· ½ cup Italian bread crumbs
· ½ cup minced red onions
· ½ cup grated Parmesan cheese
· ¼ cup finely chopped parsley
· ¼ cup whole milk
· 2 garlic cloves, minced, or 1 teaspoon crushed garlic 1 teaspoon oregano
· ½ teaspoon kosher salt
· ½ teaspoon black pepper

Jalapeno Poppers

Preparation Time: 15 Minutes
Cooking Time: 60 Minutes
Servings: 4 to 6
Ingredients:

· 6 Bacon slices halved
· 12 Jalapenos, medium
· 1 cup grated Cheese
· 8 oz. softened Cream cheese
· 2 tbsp. Poultry seasoning

Directions:

1. Preheat the grill to 180F with closed lid.

2. Cut the jalapenos lengthwise. Clean them from the ribs and seeds.

3. Mix the poultry seasoning, grated cheese, and cream cheese.

4. Fill each jalapeno with the mixture and wrap with 1 half bacon. Place a toothpick to secure it. Place them on a baking sheet and smoke and grill 20 minutes.
5. Increase the temperature of the grill to 375F. Cook for 30 minutes more.
6. Serve and enjoy!
Nutrition: Calories: 60 Protein: 4g Carbs: 2g Fat: 8g

Deviled Eggs

Preparation Time: 15 Minutes
Cooking Time: 30 Minutes
Servings: 4 to 6
Ingredients:
- 3 tsp. diced chives
- 3 tbsp. Mayo
- 7 Eggs, hard - boiled, peeled
- 1 tsp. Cider vinegar
- 1 tsp. Mustard, brown
- 1/8 tsp. Hot sauce
- 2 tbsp. crumbled Bacon
- Black pepper and salt to taste
- For dusting: Paprika

Directions:
1. Preheat the grill to 180F with closed lid.
2. Place the cooked eggs on the grate. Smoke 30 minutes. Set aside and let them cool.
3. Slice the eggs in half lengthwise. Scoop the yolks and transfer into a zip lock bag. Now add the black pepper, salt, hot sauce, vinegar, mustard, chives, and mayo. Close the bag and knead the ingredients until smooth.
4. Cut one corner and squeeze the mixture into the egg whites.
5. Top with bacon and dust with paprika.
6. Serve and enjoy! Or chill in the fridge until serving.
Nutrition: Calories: 140 Protein: 6g Carbs: 2g Fat: 6g

Roasted Tomatoes

Preparation Time: 10 Minutes

Cooking Time: 3 Hours
Servings: 2-4
Ingredients:
- 3 ripe Tomatoes, large
- 1 tbsp. black pepper
- 2 tbsp. Salt
- 2 tsp. Basil
- 2 tsp. of Sugar
- Oil

Directions:
1. Place a parchment paper on a baking sheet. Preheat the grill to 225F with closed lid.
2. Remove the stems from the tomatoes. Cut them into slices (1/2 inch).
3. In a bowl combine the basil, sugar, pepper, and salt. Mix well.
4. Pour oil on a plate. Dip the tomatoes (just one side) in the oil. Transfer on the Prepared baking sheet.
5. Dust each slice with the mixture.
6. Grill the tomatoes for 3 hours.
7. Serve and enjoy! (You can serve it with mozzarella pieces).
Nutrition: Calories: 40 Protein: 1g Carbs: 2g Fat: 3g

Smoked Veggie Medley

Preparation Time: 30 mins.
Cooking Time: 1 hr.
Servings: 4
Ingredients:
- 1 Spanish red onion, peeled and cut into quarters
- 1 red pepper, seeded and sliced
- 2 zucchinis, sliced
- 1 yellow summer squash, sliced
- Olive oil – 2 tablespoons
- Balsamic vinegar – 2 tablespoons
- 6 garlic cloves, peeled, minced
- Sea salt – 1 teaspoon
- Black pepper – ½ teaspoon

Directions:
1.Preheat the pellet grill to 350°F.
2.In a large bowl, combine the red onion, red pepper, zucchinis, summer squash, olive oil,

balsamic vinegar, garlic, sea salt, and black pepper. Toss to combine.

3.Transfer the veggies to the smoker and with the lid closed cook for between 30-45 minutes, until cooked through and caramelized.

4.Serve and enjoy.

Nutrition: Calories: 63 Protein: 3g Carbs: 9g Fat: 3g

Butternut Squash

Preparation Time: 30 mins.

Cooking Time: 2 hrs.

Servings: 4-6

Ingredients:

- Brown sugar
- Maple syrup
- 6 T. butter

Butternut squash

Directions:

1.Add wood pellets to your smoker and follow your cooker's startup procedure. Preheat your smoke, with your lid closed, until it reaches 300.

2.Slice the squash in half, lengthwise. Clean out all the seeds and membrane.

3.Place this cut-side down on the grill and smoke for 30 minutes. Flip the squash over and cook for another 30 minutes.

4.Place each half of the squash onto aluminum foil. Sprinkle each half with brown sugar and maple syrup, and put 3 T. of butter onto each. Wrap foil around to create a tight seal.

5.Increase temperature to 400 and place onto the grill for another 35 minutes.

6.Carefully unwrap each half making sure to reserve juices in the bottom. Place onto serving platter and drizzle juices over each half. Use a spoon to scoop out and enjoy.

Nutrition: Calories: 82 Protein: 1.8g Carbs: 21.5g Fat: 0.18g

Corn Salsa

Preparation Time: 10 Minutes

Cooking Time: 15 Minutes

Servings: 4

Ingredients:

- 4 Ears Corn, large with the husk on
- 4 Tomatoes (Roma) diced and seeded
- 1 tsp. of Onion powder
- 1 tsp. of Garlic powder
- 1 Onion, diced
- ½ cup chopped Cilantro
- Black pepper and salt to taste
- 1 lime, the juice
- 1 grille jalapeno, diced

Directions:

1. Preheat the grill to 450F.

2. Place the ears corn on the grate and cook until charred. Remove husk. Cut into kernels.

3. Combine all ingredients, plus the corn and mix well. Refrigerate before serving.

4. Enjoy!

Nutrition: Calories: 120 Protein: 2f Carbs: 4g Fat: 1g

CHAPTER 17: TRADITIONAL RECIPES

Chicken Casserole

Preparation Time: 15 minutes
Cooking Time: 55 minutes
Servings: 8
Ingredients:
- 2 (15-ounce) cans cream of chicken soup
- 2 cups milk
- 2 tablespoons unsalted butter
- ¼ cup all-purpose flour
- 1 pound skinless, boneless chicken thighs, chopped
- ½ cup hatch chiles, chopped
- 2 medium onions, chopped
- 1 tablespoon fresh thyme, chopped
- Salt and ground black pepper, as required
- 1 cup cooked bacon, chopped
- 1 cup tater tots

Directions:

1. Preheat the Wood Pellet Grill Smoker grill & Smoker on grill setting to 400 degrees F.
2. In a large bowl, mix together chicken soup and milk.
3. In a skillet, melt butter over medium heat.
4. Slowly, add flour and cook for about 1-2 minutes or until smooth, stirring continuously.
5. Slowly, add soup mixture, beating continuously until smooth.
6. Cook until mixture starts to thicken, stirring continuously.
7. Stir in remaining ingredients except bacon and simmer for about 10-15 minutes.
8. Stir in bacon and transfer mixture into a 2½-quart casserole dish.
9. Place tater tots on top of casserole evenly.
10. Arrange the pan onto the grill and cook for about 30-35 minutes.
11. Serve hot.

Nutrition: Calories 440 Total Fat 25.8 g Saturated Fat 9.3 g Cholesterol 86 mg Sodium 1565 mg
Total Carbs 22.2 g Fiber 1.5 g Sugar 4.6 g Protein 28.9 g

Sweet & Spicy Chicken Thighs

Preparation Time: 15 minutes
Cooking Time: 15 minutes
Servings: 4
Ingredients:
- 2 garlic cloves, minced
- ¼ cup honey
- 2 tbsp. soy sauce
- ¼ tsp. red pepper flakes, crushed
- 4 (5-ounce) skinless, boneless chicken thighs
- 2 tbsp. olive oil
- 2 tsp. sweet rub
- ¼ tsp. red chili powder
- Ground black pepper, as required

Directions

1. Preheat the grill & Smoker on grill setting to 400°F.
2. In a small bowl, add garlic, honey, soy sauce, and red pepper flakes and with a wire whisk, beat until well combined.
3. Coat chicken thighs with oil and season with sweet rub, chili powder, and black pepper generously.
4. Arrange the chicken drumsticks onto the grill and cook for about 15 minutes per
5. In the last 4-5 minutes of cooking, coat drumsticks with garlic mixture.
6. Serve immediately.

Nutrition:
- Calories: 309
- Fat: 12.1 g
- Saturated Fat: 2.9 g
- Cholesterol: 82 mg
- Sodium: 504 mg
- Carbs: 18.7 g
- Fiber: 0.2 g
- Sugar 17.6 g

· Protein: 32.3 g

Crispy Duck

Preparation Time: 15 minutes
Cooking Time: 4 hours 5 minutes
Servings: 6
Ingredients:
• ¾ cup honey
• ¾ cup soy sauce
• ¾ cup red wine
• 1 teaspoon paprika
• 1½ tablespoons garlic salt
• Ground black pepper, as required
• 1 (5-pound) whole duck, giblets removed and trimmed
Directions:
1. Preheat the Wood Pellet Grill Smoker grill & Smoker on grill setting to 225-250 degrees F.
2. In a bowl, add all ingredients except for duck and mix until well combined.
3. With a fork, poke holes in the skin of the duck.
4. Coat the duck with honey mixture generously.
5. Arrange duck in Wood Pellet Grill Smoker gill, breast side down and cook for about 4 hours, coating with honey mixture one after 2 hours.
6. Remove the duck from grill and place onto a cutting board for about 15 minutes before carving.
7. With a sharp knife, cut the duck into desired-sized pieces and serve.
Nutrition: Calories 878 Total Fat 52.1 g Saturated Fat 13.9 g Cholesterol 3341 mg Sodium 2300 mg Total Carbs 45.4 g Fiber 0.7 g Sugar 39.6 g Protein 51 g

Premium Salmon Nuggets

Preparation Time: 20 minutes +marinate time

Cooking Time: 1-2 hours
Servings: 8
Ingredients:
· 3 cups of packed brown sugar
· 1 cup of salt
· 1 tablespoon of onion, minced
· 2 teaspoons of chipotle seasoning
· 2 teaspoons of fresh ground black pepper
· 1 garlic clove, minced
· 1-2 pound of salmon fillets, cut up into bite-sized portions
Directions:
1. Take a large-sized bowl and stir in brown sugar, salt, chipotle seasoning, onion, garlic and pepper
2. Transfer salmon to a large shallow marinating dish
3. Pour dry marinade over fish and cover, refrigerate overnight
4. Take your drip pan and add water, cover with aluminum foil. Pre-heat your smoker to 180 degrees F
5. Use water fill water pan halfway through and place it over drip pan. Add wood chips to the side tray
6. Rinse the salmon chunks thoroughly and remove salt
7. Transfer them to grill rack and smoke for 1-2 hours
8. Remove the heat and enjoy it!
Nutrition: Calories: 120 Fats: 18g Carbs: 3g Fiber: 2g

Glazed Chicken Wings

Preparation Time: 15 minutes
Cooking Time: 2 hours
Servings: 6
Ingredients:
· 2 pounds' chicken wings
· 2 garlic cloves, crushed
· 3 tbsp. hoisin sauce
· 2 tbsp. soy sauce
· 1 tsp. dark sesame oil
· 1 tbsp. honey
· ½ tsp. ginger powder
· 1 tbsp. sesame seeds, toasted lightly

Directions:
1. Preheat the grill & Smoker on grill setting to 225°F.
2. Arrange the wings onto the lower rack of the grill and cook for about 1½ hours.
3. Meanwhile, in a large bowl, mix together remaining all ingredients.
4. Remove wings from grill and place in the bowl of garlic mixture.
5. Coat wings with garlic mixture generously.
6. Now, set the grill to 375°F.
7. Arrange the coated wings onto a foil-lined baking sheet and sprinkle with sesame seeds.
8. Place the pan onto the lower rack of the grill and cook for about 25-30 minutes.
9. Serve immediately.
Nutrition:
Calories: 336
Fat: 13 g
Saturated Fat: 3.3 g
Cholesterol: 135 mg
Sodium: 560 mg
Carbs: 7.6 g
Fiber: 0.5 g
Sugar: 5.2 g
Protein: 44.7 g

Halibut Delight

Preparation Time: 4-6 hours
Cooking Time: 15 minutes
Servings: 4-6
Ingredients:
· ½ a cup of salt
· ½ a cup of brown sugar
· 1 teaspoon of smoked paprika
· 1 teaspoon of ground cumin
· 2 pound of halibut
· 1/3 cup of mayonnaise
Directions:
1. Take a small bowl and add salt, brown sugar, cumin, and paprika
2. Coat the halibut well and cover, refrigerate for 4-6 hours
3. Take your drip pan and add water, cover with aluminum foil. Pre-heat your smoker to 200 degrees F

4. Use water fill water pan halfway through and place it over drip pan. Add wood chips to the side tray
5. Remove the fish from refrigerator and rinse it well, pat it dry
6. Rub the mayonnaise on the fish
7. Transfer the halibut to smoker and smoke for 2 hours until the internal temperature reaches 120 degrees Fahrenheit
Nutrition: Calories: 375 Fats: 21g Carbs: 10g Fiber: 2g

Grilled Tuna

Preparation Time: 20 minutes
Cooking Time: 4 hours
Servings: 6
Ingredients:
· Albacore tuna fillets – 6, each about 8 ounces
· Salt – 1 cup
· Brown sugar – 1 cup
· Orange, zested – 1
· Lemon, zested – 1
Directions:
1. Before preheating the grill, brine the tuna, and for this, prepare brine stirring together all of its ingredients until mixed.
2. Take a large container, layer tuna fillets in it, covering each fillet with it, and then let them sit in the refrigerator for 6 hours.
3. Then remove tuna fillets from the brine, rinse well, pat dry and cool in the refrigerator for 30 minutes.
4. When the grill has preheated, place tuna fillets on the grilling rack and let smoke for 3 hours, turning halfway.
5. Check the fire after one hour of smoking and add more wood pallets if required.
6. Then switch temperature of the grill to 225 degrees F and continue grilling for another 1 hour until tuna has turned nicely golden and fork-tender.
7. Serve immediately.
Nutrition: Calories: 311; Fiber: 3 g; Saturated Fat: 1.2 g; Protein: 45 g; Carbs: 11 g; Total Fat: 8.8 g; Sugar: 1.3 g

Roasted Christmas Goose

Prep time: 30 min
Cook time: 2 hr.
Serving: 8
Pellets any blend
Difficulty: medium
Ingredients
- 5 1/2 Pound Goose
- 2 Lemons
- 2 Teaspoon Salt
- 3 Tablespoon Honey
- Two lemons
- 2 Sprigs of Sage
- Two sprigs thyme
- One apple, medium green

Instructions
- When ready to cook, preheat the grill on high for 15 minutes with the lid covered.
- In a criss-cross pattern, lightly score the breast and leg skin. This will aid in the faster rendering of fat during cooking.
- Lemon and limes should be grated. 2 tablespoons fine sea salt, plus citrus zest Lemons and limes should be cut into wedges.
- Season the goose cavity liberally with salt, then massage the citrus mixture into the skin and into the cavity.
- Sage, thyme, lemons, limes, and apple wedges should be stuffed inside the goose. Cook the goose for 40 minutes directly on the grill grate. Reduce the temperature to 325°F and brush the geese with honey.
- Cook for 1 1/2 to 2 hours, or until a thermometer inserted into the thickest portion of the breast registers 160°F.
- Remove off the grill, tent with foil, and set aside for 30 minutes to rest. In the thickest portion of the breast, the final internal temperature should be 165°F. Enjoy!

Nutritional facts
- Fats74.8 g
- Calories874.9
- Carbs11.6 g
- Protein36.6 g

Buttered Turkey

Preparation Time: 15 minutes
Cooking Time: 4 hours
Servings: 16
Ingredients:
- ½ pound butter, softened
- 2 tbsp. fresh thyme, chopped
- 2 fresh rosemary, chopped
- 6 garlic cloves, crushed
- 1 (20-pound) whole turkey, neck and giblets removed
- Salt and ground black pepper, as required

Directions:
1. Preheat the grill & Smoker on smoke setting to 300°F, using charcoal.
2. In a bowl, place butter, fresh herbs, garlic, salt and black pepper and mix well.
3. With your fingers, separate the turkey skin from breast to create a pocket.
4. Stuff the breast pocket with ¼-inch thick layer of butter mixture.
5. Season the turkey with salt and black pepper evenly.
6. Arrange the turkey onto the grill and cook for 3-4 hours.
7. Remove turkey from pallet grill and place onto a cutting board for about 15-20 minutes before carving.
8. With a sharp knife, cut the turkey into desired-sized pieces and serve.

Nutrition:
Calories: 965
Fat: 52 g
Saturated Fat: 19.9 g
Cholesterol: 385 mg
Sodium: 1916 mg
Carbs: 0.6 g
Fiber: 0.2 g
Sugar: 0 g
Protein: 106.5 g

Lamb Kebabs

Preparation Time: 15 minutes
Cooking Time: 10 minutes
Servings: 4
Ingredients:

Wood Pellet Grill Smokers: Mesquite
· 1/2 tablespoon salt
· 2 tablespoons fresh mint
· 3 lbs. leg of lamb
· 1/2 cup lemon juice
· 1 tablespoon lemon zest
· 15 apricots, pitted
· 1/2 tablespoon cilantro
· 2 teaspoons black pepper
· 1/2 cup olive oil
· 1 teaspoon cumin
· 2 red onion

Directions:

1. Combine the olive oil, pepper, lemon juice, mint, salt, lemon zest, cumin, and cilantro. Add lamb leg, then place in the refrigerator overnight.

2. Remove the lamb from the marinade, cube them, and then thread onto the skewer with the apricots and onions.

3. When ready to cook, turn your smoker to 400F and preheat.

4. Lay the skewers on the grill and cook for ten minutes.

5. Remove from the grill and serve.

Nutrition: Calories: 50 Carbs: 4g Fiber: 2g Fat: 2.5g Protein: 2g

Jerked Up Tilapia

Preparation Time: 20 minutes
Cooking Time: 45 minutes
Serving: 8
Ingredients:
· 5 cloves of garlic
· 1 small sized onion
· 3 Jalapeno Chiles
· 3 tsp. of ground ginger
· 3 tbsp. of light brown Sugar:
· 3 tsp. of dried thyme
· 2 tsp. of salt
· 2 tsp. of ground cinnamon
· 1 tsp. of black pepper
· 1 tsp. of ground allspice
· ¼ tsp. of cayenne pepper
· 4 -6 ounce of tilapia fillets
· ¼ cup of olive oil

· 1 cup of sliced up carrots
· 1 bunch of whole green onions
· 2 tbsp. of whole allspice

Directions:

1. Take a blending bowl and combine the first 11 of the listed ingredients and puree them nicely using your blender or food processor

2. Add the fish pieces in a large-sized zip bag and toss in the pureed mixture alongside olive oil

3. Seal it up and press to make sure that the fish is coated well

4. Let it marinate in your fridge for at least 30 minutes to 1 hour

5. Take your drip pan and add water, cover with aluminum foil. Pre-heat your smoker to 225°F

6. Use water fill water pan halfway through and place it over drip pan. Add wood chips to the side tray

7. Take a medium-sized bowl and toss in some pecan wood chips and soak them underwater alongside whole allspice

8. Prepare an excellent 9x 13-inch foil pan by poking a dozen holes and spraying it with non-stick cooking spray

9. Spread out the carrots, green onions across the bottom of the pan

10. Arrange the fishes on top of them

11. Place the container in your smoker

12. Smoke for about 45 minutes making sure to add more chips after every 15 minutes until the internal temperature of the fish rises to 145°Fahrenheit

13. Serve hot

Nutrition:
· Calories: 347
· Fats: 19g
· Carbs: 18g
· Fiber: 1g

Creative Sablefish

Preparation Time: 15 minutes
Cooking Time: 3 hours
Servings: 8
Ingredients:

- 2-3 pounds of sablefish fillets
- 1 cup of kosher salts
- ¼ cup of Sugar:
- 2 tbsp. of garlic powder
- Honey for glazing
- Sweet paprika for dusting

Directions:

1. Take a bowl and mix salt, garlic powder, and Sugar:
2. Pour on a healthy layer of your mix into a lidded plastic tub, large enough to hold the fish
3. Cut up the fillet into pieces
4. Gently massage the salt mix into your fish meat and place them with the skin side down on to the salt mix in the plastic tub
5. Cover up the container and keep it in your fridge for as many hours as the fish weighs
6. Remove the sablefish from the tub and place it under cold water for a while
7. Pat, it dries using a kitchen towel and puts it back to the fridge, keep it uncovered overnight
8. Take your drip pan and add water, cover with aluminum foil. Pre-heat your smoker to 225°F
9. Use water fill water pan halfway through and place it over drip pan. Add wood chips to the side tray
10. Smoke for 2-3 hours
11. After the first hour of smoking, make sure to baste the fish with honey and keep repeating this after every hour
12. One done, move the fish to a cooling rack and baste it with honey one last time
13. Let it cool for about an hour
14. Use tweezers to pull out the bone pins
15. Dust the top with some paprika and wait for 30 minutes to let the paprika sink in
16. Put the fish in your fridge
17. Serve hot or chilled!

Nutrition:

- Calories: 171
- Fats: 10g
- Carbs: 13g
- Fiber: 1g

Grilled Swordfish

Preparation Time: 10 minutes
Cooking Time: 18 minutes
Servings: 4
Ingredients:

- Swordfish fillets – 4
- Salt – 1 tbsp.
- Ground black pepper – ¾ tbsp.
- Olive oil – 2 tbsp.
- Ears of corn – 4
- Cherry tomatoes – 1 pint
- Cilantro, chopped – 1/3 cup
- Medium red onion, peeled, diced – 1
- Serrano pepper, minced – 1
- Lime, juiced – 1
- Salt – ½ tsp.
- Ground black pepper – ¼ tsp.

Directions:

1. In the meantime, prepare fillets and for this, brush them with oil and then season with salt and black pepper.
2. Prepare the corn, and for this, brush with olive oil and season with ¼ tsp. each of salt and black pepper.
3. When the grill has preheated, place fillets on the grilling rack along with corns and grill corn for 15 minutes until light brown and fillets for 18 minutes until fork tender.
4. When corn has grilled, cut kernels from it, place them into a medium bowl, add remaining ingredients for the salsa and stir until mixed.
5. When fillets have grilled, divide them evenly among plates, top with corn salsa and then serve.

Nutrition:

- Calories: 311;
- Fat: 8.8 g;
- Saturated Fat: 1.2 g;
- Fiber: 3 g;
- Protein: 45 g;
- Sugar: 1.3 g
- Carbs: 11 g;

Butter Braised Green Beans

Servings: 6

Cooking Time: 20 Minutes
Ingredients:
·   24 ounces Green Beans, trimmed
·   8 tablespoons butter, melted
·   Salt and pepper to taste
Directions:
1.   Fire the Grill to 500F. Use desired wood pellets when cooking. Close the lid and preheat for 15 minutes.
2.   Place all ingredients in a bowl and toss to coat the beans with the seasoning.
3.   Place the seasoned beans in a sheet tray.
4.   Cook in the grill for 20 minutes.
Nutrition Info: Calories per serving: 164; Protein: 1.6g; Carbs: 5.6 g; Fat: 15.8g Sugar: 1.3g

Roasted Parmesan Cheese Broccoli

Servings: 3 To 4
Cooking Time: 45 Minutes
Ingredients:
·   3cups broccoli, stems trimmed
·   1tbsp lemon juice
·   1tbsp olive oil
·   2garlic cloves, minced
·   1/2 tsp kosher salt
·   1/2 tsp ground black pepper
·   1tsp lemon zest
·   1/8 cup parmesan cheese, grated
Directions:
1.   Preheat pellet grill to 375°F.
2.   Place broccoli in a resealable bag. Add lemon juice, olive oil, garlic cloves, salt, and pepper. Seal the bag and toss to combine. Let the mixture marinate for 30 minutes.
3.   Pour broccoli into a grill basket. Place basket on grill grates to roast. Grill broccoli for 14-18 minutes, flipping broccoli halfway through. Grill until tender yet a little crispy on the outside.
4.   Remove broccoli from grill and place on a serving dish—zest with lemon and top with grated parmesan cheese. Serve immediately and enjoy!

Nutrition Info: Calories: 82.6 Fat: 4.6 g Cholesterol: 1.8 mg Carbohydrate: 8.1 g Fiber: 4.6 g Sugar: 0 Protein: 5.5

Chicken Tortilla Soup

Servings: 4
Cooking Time: 35 Minutes
Ingredients:
·   1/2 cup Black Beans, canned
·   1Jalapeno Pepper, halved and seeds removed
·   1-1/2 cup Chicken Stock
·   2Carrots, sliced into ¼-inch pieces
·   1/2 of 1 Onion, peeled and halved
·   1/2 cup Corn
·   3 Garlic cloves
·   14-1/2 oz. Fire Roasted Tomatoes
·   1/4 cup Cilantro Leaves
·   10 oz. Chicken Breast, diced into ½ inch
·   For the seasoning mix:
·   1/4 tsp. Chipotle
·   1tsp. Cuminutes
·   1/2 tsp. Sea Salt
·   1/2 tsp. Smoked Paprika
Directions:
1.   Place pepper, carrots, onion, garlic cloves, and cilantro in the blender pitcher.
2.   Pulse the mixture for 3 minutes and then pour the chicken stock to it.
3.   Pulse again for another 3 minutes.
4.   Next, stir in the remaining ingredients and press the 'hearty soup' button.
5.   Finally, transfer to the serving bowl.
Nutrition Info: Calories: 260 Fat: 4 g Total Carbs: 40 g Fiber: 5.9 g Sugar: 8 g Protein: 14 g Cholesterol: 20 mg

Nectarine and Nutella Sundae

Preparation Time: 10 Minutes
Cooking Time: 25 Minutes
Servings: 4
Ingredients:
· 2nectarines halved and pitted
· 2tsp honey
· 4tbsp Nutella
· 4scoops vanilla ice cream
· 1/4 cup pecans, chopped
· Whipped cream, to top
· 4cherries, to top

Directions:
1. Preheat pellet grill to 400°F.
2. Slice nectarines in half and remove the pits.
3. Brush the inside (cut side) of each nectarine half with honey.

4. Place nectarines directly on the grill grate, cut side down—Cook for 5-6 minutes, or until grill marks develop.
5. Flip nectarines and cook on the other side for about 2 minutes.
6. Remove nectarines from the grill and allow it to cool.
7. Fill the pit cavity on each nectarine half with 1 tbsp Nutella.
8. Place one scoop of ice cream on top of Nutella. Top with whipped cream, cherries, and sprinkle chopped pecans. Serve and enjoy!
Nutrition: Calories: 90 Fat: 3 g Carbohydrate: 15g Sugar: 13 g Protein: 2 g

Grilled Pound Cake with Fruit Dressing

Prep Time: 20 minutes | **Cooking Time**: 50 minutes | **Temperature**: 400F| **Servings**: 12
Ingredients:
• 1 buttermilk pound cake, sliced into 3/4-inch slices
• 1/8 cup butter, melted
• 1 ½ cup whipped cream
• 1/2 cup blueberries
• 1/2 cup raspberries
• 1/2 cup strawberries, sliced

Directions:
1. Preheat the grill to 400F.
2. Brush both sides of each pound cake slice with melted butter.
3. Place directly on the grill grate and cook for 5 minutes per side. Turn 90F halfway through cooking each side of the cake for checkered grill marks.
4. Remove and cool.
5. Top slices with whipped cream, blueberries, raspberries, and sliced strawberries. Serve.
NUTRITION:
Calories: 222.1|Fat: 8.7g| Carb: 33.1g| Protein: 3.4g

Pumpkin Pie

Prep. Time: 5 Mins
Cook Time: 65 Mins
Servings: 6
Ingredients
· Ground cinnamon 1 tsp
· 2 Egg (large)
· Ground cloves 1/4 tsp
· Evaporated milk 1
· Ground ginger 1/2 tsp

- Can of pumpkin pie 1
- Deep 9" pie shell 1
- Sugar 3/4 cup
- Salt 1/2 tsp

Instructions

1. Pre-heat the grill over high heat with the lid open until the fire in the burn pot is ready (3-7 mins). Preheat the oven to 400 degrees Fahrenheit.

2. In a bowl, combine the cinnamon, ginger, cloves, salt, and sugar. In a large mixing basin, whisk together the eggs, pumpkin, and sugar-spice mixture.

3. Mix in the evaporated milk slowly. Pour into a pie crust after everything is combined.

Nectarine and Nutella Sundae

Prep Time: 10 minutes| **Cooking Time**: 25 minutes | **Temperature:** 400F| **Servings**: 4

Ingredients:

o 2 nectarines, halved and pitted
o 2 tsp honey
o 4 tbsp Nutella
o 4 scoops vanilla ice cream
o 1/4 cup pecans, chopped
o Whipped cream, to top
o 4 cherries, to top

Directions:

1. Preheat the grill to 400F.
2. Slice nectarines in half and remove the pits.
3. Brush the cut side of each nectarine half with honey.
4. Place nectarines directly on the grill grate, cut side down. Cook for 5 to 6 minutes or until grill marks develop.
5. Flip nectarines and cook on the other side for 2 minutes.
6. Remove nectarines and cool.
7. Fill the pit cavity on each nectarine half with 1 tbsp. Nutella.
8. Place 1 scoop of ice cream on top of Nutella. Top with whipped cream, cherries, and sprinkle chopped pecans. Serve.

NUTRITION:

Calories: 90|Fat: 3g| Carb: 15g | Protein:2g

Pellet Grill Chocolate Chip Cookies

Preparation Time: 20 Minutes
Cooking Time: 45 Minutes
Servings: 12

Ingredients:

- 1cup salted butter softened
- 1cup of sugar
- 1cup light brown sugar
- 2tsp vanilla extract
- 2large eggs
- 3cups all-purpose flour
- 1tsp baking soda
- 1/2 tsp baking powder
- 1tsp natural sea salt
- 2cups semi-sweet chocolate chips or chunks

Directions:

1. Preheat pellet grill to 375°F.
2. Line a large baking sheet with parchment paper and set aside.
3. In a medium bowl, mix flour, baking soda, salt, and baking powder. Once combined, set aside.
4. In stand mixer bowl, combine butter, white sugar, and brown sugar until combined. Beat in eggs and vanilla. Beat until fluffy.
5. Mix in dry ingredients, continue to stir until combined.
6. Add chocolate chips and mix thoroughly.
7. Roll 3 tbsp of dough at a time into balls and place them on your cookie sheet. Evenly space them apart, with about 2-3 inches in between each ball.
8. Place cookie sheet directly on the grill grate and bake for 20-25 minutes until the cookies' outside is slightly browned.
9. Remove from grill and allow to rest for 10 minutes. Serve and enjoy!

Nutrition: Calories: 120 Fat: 4 Cholesterol: 7.8 mg Carbohydrate: 22.8 g Fiber: 0.3 g Sugar: 14.4 g Protein: 1.4 g

Smoked Pumpkin Pie

Prep Time: 10 minutes| **Cooking Time**: 50 minutes | **Temperature:** 325F | **Servings**: 8

Ingredients:
o 1 tbsp cinnamon
o 1-1/2 tbsp pumpkin pie spice
o 1, (5 oz) can pumpkin
o 1 (4 oz) can sweeten condensed milk
o 2 beaten eggs
o 1 unbaked pie shell
Topping
o Whipped cream
Directions:
1.   Preheat the grill to 325F. Place a baking sheet in the grill.
2.   Combine all your ingredients in a bowl, except the pie shell, then pour the mixture into a pie crust.
3.   Place the pie on the baking sheet and smoke for 50 to 60 minutes or until a knife comes out clean when inserted.
4.   Remove and cool for 2 hours. Serve with whipped cream topping.
NUTRITION:
Calories: 292|Fat: 11g| Carb: 42g| Protein: 7g

Cheesecake Frypan Brownie

Prep. Time: 10 Mins
Cook Time: 30 Mins
Servings: 2
Ingredients
·   Brownie mix box 1
·   Eggs 2
·   A packet of Cheese cream 1
·   Oil 1/2 Cup
·   Sugar 1/2 Cup
·   Can of blueberry pie filling 1
·   Warm water 1/4 cup
·   Vanilla 1 tsp
Instructions
1. Mix up all of the brownie ingredients. Combine sugar, vanilla, cream, cheese, and egg in a separate dish and beat until smooth.
2. Grease the frypans and pour the brownie batter into them. Top with cheesecake and cherry pie filling, blending with a sharp knife to create a mottled appearance.
3. Preheat the grill to 350°F and bake for 30 mins.

4. Allow cooling for about 10 mins before serving

Smoked Pumpkin Pie

Preparation Time: 10 Minutes
Cooking Time: 50 Minutes
Servings: 8
Ingredients:
·   1tbsp cinnamon
·   1-1/2 tbsp pumpkin pie spice
·   15oz can pumpkin
·   14oz can sweetened condensed milk
·   2beaten eggs
·   1unbaked pie shell
·   Topping: whipped cream
Directions:
1.   Preheat your smoker to 3250F.
2.   Place a baking sheet, rimmed, on the smoker upside down, or use a cake pan.
3.   Combine all your ingredients in a bowl, large, except the pie shell, then pour the mixture into a pie crust.
4.   Place the pie on the baking sheet and smoke for about 50-60 minutes until a knife comes out clean when inserted. Make sure the center is set.
5.   Remove and cool for about 2 hours or refrigerate overnight.
6.   Serve with a whipped cream dollop and enjoy it!
Nutrition: Calories: 292 Total Fat: 11g Total Carbs: 42g Protein: 7g Sugars: 29g Fiber: 5gSodium: 168mg

Grilled Peaches and Cream

Prep Time: 15 minutes| **Cooking Time**: 8 minutes| **Temperature**: 300F| **Servings**: 8
Ingredients:
o 4 halved and pitted peaches
o 1 tbsp vegetable oil
o 2 tbsp clover honey
o 1 cup cream cheese, soft with honey and nuts
Directions:

1. Preheat the grill to 300F.
2. Coat the peaches lightly with oil and place on the grill pit side down.
3. Grill for 5 minutes or until nice grill marks on the surfaces.
4. Turn over the peaches, then drizzle with honey.
5. Spread and add cream cheese dollop where the pit was and grill for 2 to 3 minutes more.
6. Serve.

NUTRITION:

Calories: 139|Fat: 10.2g| Carb: 11.6g| Protein: 1.1g

Banana Trifle (Smoked)

Prep. Time: 25 Mins
Cook Time: 10 Mins
Servings: 8
Ingredients

- Cream cheese 1 cup
- Condensed milk 4 tablespoons
- Whipped Cream 1 cup
- White sugar 4 tablespoons
- Cinnamon 1 tablespoon
- Butter 3 tablespoons
- Brown sugar 4 tablespoons
- Bananas 8
- Wafer cookies 1 package

Instructions

1. In a mixing bowl, combine the cream cheese, sweetened condensed milk, whipped cream and white sugar and mix to make a smooth mixture.

2. Place in mixture in a skillet and, over medium heat, add brown sugar, cinnamon and butter. Keep stirring until bubbles appear. At this point put in 8 chopped bananas. Stir for a couple of minutes then remove from heat.

3. In a jar place a wafer base, then some of the mixture, then the wafer and the mixture

4. Sprinkle with cinnamon and serve immediately or chill in the refrigerator for 24 hours before serving.

Smoked Peach Parfait

Prep Time: 20 minutes| **Cooking Time**: 35 to 45 minutes | **Temperature:** 200F|
Servings: 4
Ingredients:

o 4 barely ripe peaches, halved and pitted
o 1 tbsp. firmly packed brown sugar
o 1-pint vanilla ice cream
o 3 tbsp. honey

Directions:

1. Preheat the grill to 200F.
2. Sprinkle cut peach halves with brown sugar.
3. Transfer them into the grill and smoke for 33 to 45 minutes.
4. Transfer the peach halves to dessert plates and top with vanilla ice cream.
5. Drizzle with honey and serve.

NUTRITION:

Calories: 309|Fat: 27g| Carb: 17g| Protein: 4g

Berry Cobbler on a Pellet Grill

Preparation Time: 15 Minutes
Cooking Time: 35 Minutes
Servings: 8
Ingredients:
For fruit filling

- 3cups frozen mixed berries
- 1lemon juice
- 1cup brown sugar
- 1tbsp vanilla extract
- 1bsp lemon zest, finely grated
- A pinch of salt

For cobbler topping

- 1-1/2 cups all-purpose flour
- 1-1/2 tbsp baking powder
- 3tbsp sugar, granulated
- 1/2 tbsp salt
- 8tbsp cold butter
- 1/2 cup sour cream
- 2tbsp raw sugar

Directions:

1. Set your pellet grill on "smoke" for about 4-5 minutes with the lid open until fire establishes, and your grill starts smoking.

2.   Preheat your grill to 350 for about 10-15 minutes with the grill lid closed.

3.   Meanwhile, combine frozen mixed berries, Lemon juice, brown sugar, vanilla, lemon zest, and salt pinch. Transfer into a skillet and let the fruit sit and thaw.

4.   Mix flour, baking powder, sugar, and salt in a bowl, medium. Cut cold butter into peas sizes using a pastry blender, then add to the mixture. Stir to mix everything.

5.   Stir in sour cream until dough starts coming together.

6.   Pinch small pieces of dough and place over the fruit until fully covered. Splash the top with raw sugar.

7.   Now place the skillet directly on the grill grate, close the lid, cook for about 35 minutes until juices bubble, and a golden-brown dough topping.

8.   Remove the skillet from the pellet grill and cool for several minutes.

9.   Scoop and serve warm.

Nutrition: Calories: 371 Total Fat: 13g Total Carbs: 60g Protein: 3g Sugars: 39g Fiber: 2g Sodium: 269mg

Wood Pellet Grill Smoker Blackberry Pie

Preparation Time: 10 Minutes
Cooking Time: 40 Minutes
Servings: 8
Ingredients:
- Butter, for greasing
- ½ c. all-purpose flour
- ½ c. milk
- Two pints blackberries
- Two c. sugar, divided
- One box of refrigerated piecrusts
- One stick melted butter
- One stick of butter
- Vanilla ice cream

Directions:
1.   Add wood pellets to your smoker and follow your cooker's startup method.

2.   Preheat your smoker, with your lid closed, until it reaches 375.

3.   Unroll the second pie crust and lay it over the skillet.

4.   Lower the lid, then smoke for 15 to 20 minutes or until it is browned and bubbly.

5.   Serve the hot pie with some vanilla ice cream.

Nutrition: Calories: 100 Carbs: 10g Fat: 0g Protein: 15g

Grill Chicken Flatbread

Prep Time: 5 minutes | **Cooking Time**: 30 minutes| **Temperature**: 400F| **Servings**: 6
Ingredients:
o 6 mini breads
o 1-1/2 cups divided buffalo sauce
o 4 cups cooked and cubed chicken breasts
For drizzling
o Mozzarella cheese
Directions:
1.   Preheat the grill to 400F.

2.   Place the breads on a surface, flat, then evenly spread ½ cup buffalo sauce on all breads.

3.   Toss together chicken breasts, and 1 cup buffalo sauce, then top over all the breads evenly.

4.   Top each with mozzarella cheese.

5.   Place the breads directly on the grill but over indirect heat. Close the lid.

6.   Cook for 5 to 7 minutes or until slightly toasty edges and cheese is melted.

7.   Remove and drizzle with cheese. Serve.

NUTRITION:
Calories: 346|Fat: 7.6g| Carb: 33.9g| Protein: 32.5g

Banana Skewers

Prep time: 15 minutes.
Cook time: 6 minutes.
Serves: 2
Ingredients:
- 1 loaf (10 3/4 oz.) cake, cubed
- 2 large bananas, one-inch slices

- ¼ cup butter, melted
- 2 tablespoons brown sugar
- ½ teaspoon vanilla extract
- ⅛ teaspoon ground cinnamon
- 4 cups butter pecan ice cream
- ½ cup butterscotch ice cream topping
- ½ cup chopped pecans, toasted

Preparation:

1. Thread the cake and bananas over the skewers alternately.
2. Whisk butter with cinnamon, vanilla, and brown sugar in a small bowl.
3. Brush this mixture over the skewers liberally.
4. Preheat the Ninja Foodi Grill on the "Grill Mode" at LOW-temperature settings.
5. When the grill is preheated, open its hood and place the banana skewers in it.
6. Cover the grill's hood and grill for 3 minutes per side.
7. Serve with ice cream, pecan, and butterscotch topping on top.

Serving Suggestion: Serve the skewers with maple syrup on top.

Variation Tip: Add crushed chocolate on top of the skewers.

Nutritional Information Per Serving:
Calories 245 | Fat 14g |Sodium 122mg | Carbs 23.3g | Fiber 1.2g | Sugar 12g | Protein 4.3g

Smoked Roasted Apple Pie

Prep. Time: 20 mins
Cook time: 60 mins
Servings: 6

Ingredients

- Cups Apples 8 (cored, peeled and lightly sliced)
- Sugar 3/4 Cup
- Lemon Juice 1 tbsp
- Cinnamon 1 tsp
- Whole Pie Crust 2 (Frozen but Thawed)
- Nutmeg 1/4 tsp
- Heavy Whipping Cream 2 tbsp
- Apple Jelly 1/4 Cup

Instructions

1. In a large mixing bowl, combine the apples, lemon juice, cinnamon, sugar, flour and nutmeg.
2. Cut two 11-inch circles from the pie crust dough. Fill a 9" pie dish with 1 circle, preferably glass. Using the "apple jelly," apply it to the surface. Toss in the "apple mixture" into the pan.
3. Moisten the crust's edge with apple juice. Push the ends of the top crust together to seal them.
4. Trim the pastry and flute the sides if necessary. Make several thin slits on the top crust with a paring knife. Apply a little layer of cream to the top of the pie using a pastry knife.
5. About 15 mins before you're ready to cook, pre-heat the oven to high. Preheat the oven to 350°F and bake for 50–60 mins, or until the apples are tender and the crust is golden brown.
6. Place the cake on a wire rack to cool. Serve warm or at room temperature. Enjoy!
7. *Cook times may vary depending on oven temperature and air temperature.

Moist Carrot Muffins

Prep time: 10 minutes
Cook time: 20 minutes
Serves: 6
Ingredients:

- 1 egg
- ¼ cup brown sugar
- ¼ cup sugar
- 1 cup all-purpose flour
- ¾ cup grated carrots
- 1 teaspoon vanilla
- ¼ cup applesauce
- ½ tablespoon canola oil
- 1 ½ teaspoon baking powder
- ¼ teaspoon nutmeg
- 1 teaspoon cinnamon
- ¼ teaspoon salt

Preparation:

1. Place the cooking pot in the Ninja Foodi Grill Main Unit.

2. Add all ingredients into the bowl and mix until well combined.

3. Pour batter into the greased silicone muffin molds.

4. Press Bake mode, set the temperature to 350°F, and set time to 20 minutes. Press Start.

5. Once a unit is preheated then place muffin molds in the cooking pot.

6. Cover with lid and cook for 20 minutes.

Serving Suggestion: Allow to cool completely then serve.

Variation Tip: Add melted butter if you don't have canola oil.

Nutritional Information per Serving:

Calories 165 | Fat 2.2g |Sodium 120mg | Carbs 33.7g | Fiber 1.3g | Sugar 16.2g | Protein 3.2g

Bacon Chocolate Chip Cookies

Preparation Time: 10 Minutes
Cooking Time: 30 Minutes
Servings: 24
Ingredients:

· Eight slices of cooked and crumbled bacon
· 2 ½ t. apple cider vinegar
· One t. vanilla
· Two c. semisweet chocolate chips
· Two-room temp eggs
· 1 ½ t. baking soda
· One c. granulated sugar
· ½ t. salt
· Two ¾ c. all-purpose flour
· One c. light brown sugar
· 1 ½ stick softened butter

Directions:

1. Mix the flour, baking soda, and salt.

2. Cream the sugar and the butter together. Then lower the speed. Add in the eggs, vinegar, and vanilla.

3. Still on low, slowly add in the flour mixture, bacon pieces, and chocolate chips.

4. Add wood pellets to your smoker and follow your cooker's startup method.

5. Preheat your smoker, with your lid closed, until it reaches 375.

6. Place some parchment on a baking sheet and drop a teaspoonful of cookie batter on the baking sheet. Let them cook on the grill,

7. covered, for approximately 12 minutes or until they are browned. Enjoy.

Nutrition: Calories: 167 Carbs: 21g Fat: 9g Protein: 2g

Baked Caramel Pecan Brownie

Prep Time: 15 minutes| **Cooking Time**: 50 minutes | **Temperature**: 325F| **Servings**: 6
Ingredients:

o 1/2 cup cocoa powder
o 3/4 tsp. baking soda
o 3/4 cup pecans, halves
o 1/4 cup butter
o 1/2 cup brown sugar
o 1/2 cup heavy cream
o 1 cup brown sugar
o 1 cup all-purpose flour
o 1/2 tsp. salt
o 6 tbsp. butter, melted
o 3 eggs
o 1/4 cup heavy cream
o 6-ounce chocolate, chopped

Directions:

1. To make the caramel sauce: toast the pecans in a pan on the stovetop for 5 minutes. Stirring occasionally.

2. Add ½ cup brown sugar and ¼ cup butter to the pecans and mix. Cook until mixed well.

3. Remove the pan from the heat and add ½ cup heavy cream. Return to heat and cook until mixed. Remove from heat and set aside.

4. For the brownies: In a bowl, combine the salt, baking soda, cocoa powder, flour, and brown sugar. Add the eggs, melted butter, and cream and mix well. Fold in the chocolate.

5. Pour the batter over the pecan-caramel mixture.

6. Set the grill temperature to 325F and preheat for 15 minutes with lid closed.

7. Cook the brownies in the grill for 35 to 40 minutes.

8. Remove from the heat and cool a bit. Serve with ice cream.

NUTRITION:
Calories: 844|Fat:52.9g | Carb: 90.5g| Protein: 11.7g

Easy Scalloped Pineapple

Prep time: 10 minutes
Cook time: 30 minutes
Serves: 6
Ingredients:
· 3 eggs, lightly beaten
· 8 ounces can pineapple, crushed
· 1 ½ cup sugar
· 4 cups of bread cubes
· ¼ cup milk
· ½ cup butter, melted
· ½ cup brown sugar
Preparation:
1. Place the cooking pot in the Ninja Foodi Grill Main Unit.
2. In a bowl, mix eggs, milk, pineapple, butter, brown sugar and sugar.
3. Add bread cubes and stir until well coated.
4. Pour mixture into the greased baking dish.
5. Press Bake mode, set the temperature to 350°F, and set time to 30 minutes. Press Start.
6. Once a unit is preheated then place the baking dish in the cooking pot.
7. Cover with lid and cook for 30 minutes.
Serving Suggestion: Serve warm.
Variation Tip: None
Nutritional Information per Serving:
Calories 492 | Fat 17g |Sodium 281mg | Carbs 80g | Fiber 0g | Sugar 66g | Protein 3.4g

Grilled Fruit with Honeyed Lemon Thyme Vinegar

Preparation time:30 minutes
Servings:6
Ingredients:
· 2 medium peaches, chopped
· 2 medium plums
· Lemon thyme vinegar, 2 tbsp.
· 3 medium apricots, halved
· Honey, ¼ cup
· 2 medium nectarines, chopped
· Olive oil
· Vanilla ice cream
Instructions:
· Spray gently with oil before starting a grill. A grill pan can also be used. Stir the Lemon Thyme Vinegar and honey to a low boil in a small saucepan. Prepare the wood pellet grill and lubricate it with oil. Heat for 5 minutes over very low heat.
· Whisk the fruit with 2 tablespoons of oil in a mixing bowl. Heat the fruit for 3 minutes over high heat, rotating once, until golden brown in areas. Serve with ice cream in bowls with honeyed vinegar sprinkled on top.

Sweet Tooth Carving Rhubarb Crunch

Preparation Time: 45 min
Cooking Time: 30 min
Servings: 4
Ingredients:
• 1 tablespoon ground fennel
• Salt and pepper to taste
• 1/2 cup brown sugar
• 1 lb. pork belly, sliced into cubes
Instructions:
1. Preheat your wood pellet grill to 350 degrees F for 15 minutes while the lid is closed.
2. In a bowl, mix the ground fennel, salt, pepper, and brown sugar.
3. Coat the bacon cubes with this mixture.
4. Grill for 30 minutes.
Tips: It's also a good idea to use a foil for cooking the bacon to catch the bacon drippings and reserve for later use.
Nutrition: Calories: 701, Total Fat: 60.35g, Total Carbs: 28.8g, Protein: 11.08g, Sodium: 46mg

Grilled Pound Cake

Prep time: 15 minutes.

Cook time: 5 minutes.
Serves: 4
Ingredients:
· 2 large peaches, sliced
· 2 tbsp. pomegranate molasses
· 2 tbsp. brandy
· ½ tsp. sugar
· 4 1-in.-thick pound cake slices
· About ¼ cup whipped cream
Preparation:
1.	Mix peaches with sugar, brandy, and molasses in a bowl.
2.	Place the cooking pot in the Ninja Foodi Grill then set a grill grate inside.
3.	Select the "Grill" Mode, set the temperature to MED.
4.	Use the arrow keys to set the cooking time to 5 minutes.
5.	Press the START/STOP button to initiate preheating.
6.	Once preheated, place the cake slices in the Ninja Foodi Grill.
7.	Cover the hood and allow the grill to cook.
8.	Flip the cake slices once cooked halfway through.
9.	Top the cake slices with the peach mixture.
10.	Garnish with almonds and whipped cream.
11. Serve.
Serving Suggestion: Serve the pound cake with melted chocolate on top.
Variation Tip: Add crushed nuts to the cake.
Nutritional Information Per Serving:
Calories 118 | Fat 20g |Sodium 192mg | Carbs 26g | Fiber 0.9g | Sugar 19g | Protein 5.2g

Pound Cake

Prep. Time: 10 mins
Cook Time: 60 mins
Servings: 8
Ingredients
· Butter 1/2 Cup
· Sugar 3 Cup
· Cream Cheese 8 Ounce
· Eggs 6
· Lemon Zest 1 tbsp

· Bourbon Vanilla 3 tsp
· Whipped Cream
· Fresh Strawberries
Instructions
1. In a large bowl, combine the cheese, butter and sugar. Add eggs one at a time, beating between each addition. Finally, add the vanilla and lemon zest.
2. Pour the mixture into the cake pan and bake for 60 minutes at 350 degrees.
3. Let cool and adorn the cake with fresh strawberries and cream. Enjoy.

Ninja Foodi Bloomin' Grilled Apples

Prep time: 5 minutes
Cook time: 30 minutes
Serves: 2
Ingredients:
· 4 tablespoons maple cream caramel sauce
· 2 apples
· 2 scoops vanilla ice cream
· 6 teaspoons chopped pecans
Preparation:
1.	Install grill grate in the unit and close hood. Select GRILL, set temperature to MAX, and set time to 30 minutes. Select START/STOP to begin preheating
2.	In the meantime, slice the tops of the apples and scoop out the core.
3.	Place pecans and maple cream caramel sauce in the center of the apples and wrap foil around them.
4.	Place apples in the Ninja Foodi Grill when it says "Add Food" and cook for half an hour.
5.	Serve with vanilla ice cream scoops on top.
6.	Finally, serve and enjoy!
Serving Suggestions: Top with chocolate chips before serving.
Variation Tip: You can also use applesauce to enhance taste.
Nutritional Information per Serving:
Calories: 636 |Fat: 62.4g|Sat Fat: 9.5g|Carbohydrates: 67.8g|Fiber: 10.4g|Sugar: 53.7g|Protein: 8.4g

Ice Cream Bread

Preparation Time: 10 Minutes
Cooking Time: 1 Hour
Servings: 12-16
Ingredients:

· 1 ½ quart full-fat butter pecan ice cream, softened
· One t. salt
· Two c. semisweet chocolate chips
· One c. sugar
· One stick melted butter
· Butter, for greasing
· 4 c. self-rising flour

Directions:

1. Add wood pellets to your smoker and follow your cooker's startup program. Preheat your smoker, with your lid closed, until it reaches 350.
2. Set the cake on the grill, cover, and smoke for 50 minutes to an hour. A toothpick should come out clean.
3. Take the pan off of the grill. For 10 mins., cool the bread.

Nutrition: Calories: 135 Carbs: 0g Fat: 0g Protein: 0g

Fire-Roasted Berry Crostini with Honey Crème Fraiche

Preparation time:30 minutes
Servings:6
Ingredients:

· 3 slices of bread, halved crosswise
· Unsalted butter
· Honey, 1 tbsp.
· Sugar, ¼ cup
· Crème Fraiche, ½ cup
· Mixed fresh berries, 4 cups
· Salt

Instructions:

· Start a fire with hardwood charcoal. In a mixing bowl, combine the crème Fraiche and honey. Prepare the wood pellet grill and lubricate it with oil.
· Spread butter on both sides of the bread pieces and liberally dust with sugar. Cook 3 minutes over moderately high heat, rotating once until the bread is golden and toasted. Move to a serving tray and set aside to cool.
· Mix the berries with 1/4 cup sugar and salt in a medium mixing dish. Heat the berries on a perforated grill sheet or in a grill basket, occasionally stirring, until they start to pop, about 4 minutes. Allow cooling slightly before moving to a bowl.
· Place the berries on the crostini and spread the honey crème Fraiche over the top.

Sweet Brown Sugar Rub

Preparation Time: 10 minutes
Cooking Time: 10 minutes
Servings: 6
Ingredients:

• 2 tablespoons light brown sugar
• 1 teaspoon coarse kosher salt
• 1 teaspoon garlic powder
• 1 teaspoon onion powder
• 1 teaspoon sweet paprika
• ½ teaspoon freshly ground black pepper
• ½ teaspoon cayenne pepper
• ½ teaspoon dried oregano leaves
• ¼ teaspoon smoked paprika

Instructions:

1. In a small airtight container or zip-top bag, combine the brown sugar, salt, garlic powder, onion powder, sweet paprika, black pepper, cayenne, oregano, and smoked paprika.
2. Close the container and shake to mix. Unused rub will keep in an airtight container for months.

Nutrition: Calories: 5, Fats: 0.1g, Carbs: 1.1g, Fiber: 0.4g, Protein: 0.22g, Sodium: 389mg

Berry Smoothie

Preparation Time: 10 minutes
Cooking Time: 1 minutes
Servings: 1
Ingredients:

• 2 scoops Protein Powder

• 2 cups Almond Milk
• 4 cups Mixed Berry
• 2 cups Yoghurt
Instructions:
1. First, place mixed berry, protein powder, yogurt, and almond milk in the blender pitcher.
2. Then, select the 'smoothie' button.
3. Finally, pour the smoothie to the serving glass.
Nutrition: Calories: 112, Fat: 2g, Total Carbs: 26g, Fiber: 0g, Sugar: 0g, Protein: 1g, Cholesterol: 0g

Kodiak Cakes Candied Bacon Crumble Brownies

Prep. Time: 30 Mins
Cook time: 45 Mins
Servings: 6
Ingredients
· Big Bear Brownie 1 Box
· Butter 1 Stick (Melted)
· Eggs 2
· Coconut Oil 2 tbsp
· Cooked Bacon 2 Cups
· Water 2 tbsp
· Sugar ½ Cup
· Almonds ½ Cup (Chopped)
Instructions
1. Pre-heat the to 300°F and keep the lid covered for approximately 15 mins until ready to cook.
2. Brush nonstick frying oil into an 8-inch "baking pan."
3. In a medium mixing cup, pour the brownie mix from the "Kodiak Cake." In a mixing dish, mix the melted butter, coconut oil, eggs, and water. Mix slowly and gently, being careful not to over mix. Pour into a tightly packed pan
4. Place brownies in the center of the grill grate and bake for 45 mins.
5. While the brownies are baking, assemble the bacon crumbles. Melt the honey/sugar in a saucepan over high heat. Toss in the bacon and almonds.

6. Stir for a few mins or until the sugar is completely dissolved. Remove the pan from the heat and let it cool.
7. Take the brownies from the grill and place them on a cooling rack to cool completely. Candied bacon crumbs may be sprinkled on top of brownies. Have fun with it.

Banana Boats

Preparation Time: 30 minutes
Cooking time: 10 minutes
Servings: 4
Ingredients:
· Four green bananas
· Chocolate chips
· Miniature marshmallows
· Peanut butter chips
· Crushed cookies
Directions:
1. Split a banana lengthwise from end to end, leaving the peel intact on the opposite side.
2. Top with desired toppings.
3. Wrap the banana in heavy-duty aluminum foil.
4. Grilling:
5. Place the bananas on a 400F grill and close the dome for 10 minutes.
6. Unwrap and serve topped with vanilla ice cream, whipped cream, or by them.
Nutrition: Calories: 310 Fat: 17 g Carbohydrates: 40 g Protein: 4 g

Banana-Nutella S Mores

Preparation time:
20 minutes
Servings:
4
Ingredients:
· 2 bananas, sliced
· Marshmallow fluff, ¼ cup
· Roasted hazelnuts, salted, 2 tbsp.
· Nutella, ¼ cup
· Four squares of parchment paper

· 8 whole graham crackers
· Four squares of heavy-duty aluminum foil

Instructions:

· Preheat the grill. Prepare the wood pellet grill and lubricate it with oil. Sprinkle Nutella on 4 graham crackers and marshmallow fluff on the remaining 4. Spread the hazelnuts on top of the bananas and mash them into the Nutella. The graham crackers should be put together. Cover them in parchment paper before wrapping them in foil.

· S'mores should be roasted for about 10 minutes over moderate heat, rotating once or twice until the marshmallow fluff is sticky and gently toasted. Serve after lifting the foil and tearing away the parchment.

Baked Pear and Fig Upside Down Cake

Prep. Time: 30 mins
Cook Time: 45 mins
Servings: 6

Ingredients

· Butter unsalted 13 tbsp (at room temp)
· Brown Sugar ½ Cup
· Pear 1 (Cut In 1/8" Thick Slices Length Wise)
· Figs 4 (Cut in half)
· Granulated Sugar ¾ Cup
· Eggs 3 (Whole)
· Vanilla 1 tsp
· Cake Flour ½ Cup
· Baking Powder ¾ tsp
· Baking Soda ¼ tsp
· Sour Cream ½ Cup
· Salt ¼ tsp

Instructions

1. Pre-heat the to 350 degrees F and keep the lid covered for approximately 10 to 15 mins until ready to cook.

2. Butter a 10-inch cast-iron pan or a standard cake pan and put in all the fruit.

3. In a stand mixer, cream together the sugar and butter until light and fluffy. Pound for the next minute after adding the eggs and vanilla essence.

4. In a mixing cup, combine the baking powder, baking soda and sifted rice. Add the sour cream and mix well.

5. Pour the mixture over the fruit and place the pan straight on the grill grate. Pre-heat the oven to 350 degrees Fahrenheit and bake for 35–45 mins.

6. Let the cake rest for 10 mins. Loop a knife around the corners of the cake to remove the sides. Invert the cake onto a serving platter.

7. Cut into slices and serve. Have fun with it.

Blueberry Cobbler

Preparation time: 15 minutes
Cooking time: 30 minutes
Servings: 6
Ingredients:

· 4 cups fresh blueberries
· 1 tsp. grated lemon zest
· 1 cup sugar, plus 2 tbsp.
· 1 cup all-purpose flour, plus 2 tbsp.
· Juice of 1 lemon
· 2 tsp. baking powder
· ¼ teaspoon salt
· Six tablespoons unsalted butter
· ¾ cup whole milk
· 1/8 teaspoon ground cinnamon

Directions:

1. In a prepared medium bowl, combine the blueberries, lemon zest, two tablespoons of sugar, two tablespoons of flour, and lemon juice.

2. In a prepared medium bowl, combine the remaining 1 cup of flour and 1 cup of sugar, baking powder, and salt. Cut the butter into the flour mixture until it forms an even crumb texture. Stir in the milk until a dough form.

3. Select BAKE, set the temperature to 350degrees F, and set the time to 30 minutes. Select START/STOP to begin preheating.

4. Meanwhile, pour the blueberry mixture into the Multi-Purpose Pan, spreading it evenly across the pan. Gently pour the batter over the blueberry mixture, and then sprinkle the cinnamon over the top.

5.   If the unit beeps to signify it has preheated, place the pan directly in the pot. Close the hood and cook for 30 minutes, until lightly golden.

6.   When cooking is complete, serve warm.

Nutrition: Calories: 408 Saturated fat: 8g Carbohydrates: 72g Protein: 5g

Mixed Berry Hobo Packs with Grilled Pound Cake

Preparation time:

20 minutes

Servings:

4

Ingredients:

·   Sugar, ¼ cup
·   Cornstarch, ¾ tsp
·   Lemon juice, 1 tbsp.
·   Unsalted butter, 2 tbsp.
·   Grated lemon zest, 1 tsp
·   Four heavy-duty aluminum foils
·   Blueberries, ½ -pound
·   Four slices of pound cake
·   Strawberries, 1/2-pound
·   Vanilla ice cream

Instructions:

·   Preheat the grill. Prepare the wood pellet grill and lubricate it with oil. Blend the strawberries and blueberries with the lemon zest, lemon juice, sugar, and cornstarch in a medium mixing basin. Place a quarter tablespoon of butter in the core of each sheet of foil, then sprinkle with the fruit. Pull two sides of the foil up over the fruit and bend over the top to form a seam. Pull the final two sides to close the hobo packs fully.

·   Roast the hobo packs for about 10 minutes over medium heat or until the fruit is popping.

·   Sprinkle the remaining 1 tablespoon of butter on both sides of the pound cake and toast for 1 minute, or until browned. Place on serving plates. Remove the berries and juices from the hobo packs and sprinkle them over the pound cake. Serve with a dollop of vanilla ice cream on top.

Grilled Peaches and Cream Popsicle

Prep. Time: 5 mins
Cook Time: 10 mins
Servings: 4
Ingredients
·   Honey 10 tbsp
·   Yogurt 1 Cup (Plain)
·   Peaches 4 Whole (Halved)
·   Cream 1 Cup
·   Vanilla Bean 1 Whole (Split and Scraped)
Instructions
1. When ready to cook, pre-heat the oven to 450 degrees Fahrenheit with the lid covered for 10 to 15 mins.
2. Sprinkle 2 tbsp honey all over the cut-side of the peaches and cook them cut side down.
3. Cook for 10 mins total, or until grill marks appear. Place in a blender once they have been removed from the grill. After pureeing until smooth, set aside.
4. Mix the sugar, cream, yogurt, and "vanilla beans" scraped off the vanilla bean in a medium mixing cup. Whisk the ingredients together to combine them.
5. Fill Popsicle moulds half full of peach puree and half full of cream, leaving a little space at the end.
6. Embed a Popsicle stick into each Popsicle and refrigerate for at least 4 hours. Have fun with it.

Lemony Smokin' Bars

Preparation time: 30 minutes
Total **cooking time**: 60 minutes
Servings: 8-12
Ingredients:
·   ¾ cup lemon juice
·   1½ cup sugar
·   Two eggs
·   Three egg yolk
·   1½ teaspoon cornstarch
·   Pinch sea salt
·   4 tbsp. unsalted butter
·   ¼ cup olive oil
·   ½ tablespoon lemon zest

- 1¼ cup flour
- ¼ cup granulated sugar
- Three tablespoon confectioner's sugar
- 1 tsp. lemon zest
- ¼ teaspoon sea salt, fine
- 10 tbsp. unsalted butter, cut into cubes

Directions:

1. When you're ready to cook, set grill temperature to 180°F (82°C) and preheat, lid closed for 15 minutes.

2. In a prepared small bowl, combine the lemon juice, sugar, eggs and yolks, cornstarch and acceptable sea salt. Pour into a baking sheet or cake pan and place on the grill. Smoke for 30 minutes, whisking the mixture halfway through cooking. Take from grill and set aside.

3. Pour mixture into a small saucepan. Place on a stovetop set to medium heat until boiling. Once boiling, boil for 60 seconds. Take from heat and strain through a mesh strainer into a bowl. Whisk in cold butter, olive oil, and lemon zest.

4. To make a crust, whisk together the flour, granulated sugar, powdered sugar, lemon zest, and salt in a food processor. Add the butter and blend until you get a crumbly dough. Press the dough into a prepared 9 "by 9" baking sheet lined with parchment paper that is long enough to hang on 2 of the sides. When ready to cook, set the pellet grill to 350°F (177°C) and preheat, lid closed for 15 minutes.

5. Bake or cook until crust is very lightly golden brown, about 30 to 35 minutes.

6. Remove from the grill and pour the lemon filling over the crust. Return to grill and continue to bake until filling is just set, about 15 to 20 minutes.

7. Allow to cool at room temperature, then refrigerate until chilled before slicing into bars. Sprinkle with confectioners' sugar and flaky sea salt right before serving. Enjoy!

Nutrition: Energy (calories): 246 kcal Protein: 2.91 g Fat: 14.85 g Carbohydrates: 26.05 g

Baked Cherry Cobbler

Prep. Time: 10 mins
Cook Time: 35 mins
Servings: 8
Ingredients

- Flour ½ Cup (All-Purpose)
- Baking Powder ½ tsp
- Sugar 5 tsp
- Salt ¾ tsp
- Sour Cream ½ Cup
- Unsalted Butter 8 tbsp (Cold)
- Cornstarch 3 tbsp
- Sugar 1 tsp
- Lemon Juice
- Cherries 5 Cup (Pitted)
- One Lemon Zest
- Vanilla Extract 1/2 tsp
- One Orange Zest
- Whipped Cream
- Turbinado Sugar

Instructions

1. In a medium mixing cup, combine flour, 5 sugar, baking powder, and salt to make the topping. With two knives, cut in the chilled butter until the mixture resembles peas and ground-up crackers.

2. Gently fold in the sour cream until it is evenly distributed.

3. In a mixing basin, combine cornstarch and 1 sugar to prepare the filling. Lemon juice, cherries, citrus zest, and vanilla should be set aside.

4. Fill the baking dish with the "cherry filling" and top with the cobbler topping. On top, "turbinado sugar" should be sprinkled.

5. Before you begin cooking, pre-heat as per the manufacturer's instructions. Pre-heat the oven to 350 degrees F and bake with the lid covered for 10-15 mins.

6. Bake for 35-45 mins, or until the cobbler topping is nicely browned and sizzling immediately on the grill. The mixture might as well have thickened to the consistency of syrup.

7. Garnish with whipped cream. Have fun with it.

Baked Honey Cornbread Cake

Prep. Time: 10 mins
Cook Time: 40 mins
Servings: 6
Ingredients
· Vegetable Oil 2/3 Cup
· Large Eggs Four (Lightly Beaten)
· Buttermilk 1/2 Cup
· Butter 5 tbsp (Melted)
· Mayonnaise 1/2 Cup
· Flour 3 Cup
· Honey 2 tbsp
· Baking Powder 2 tbsp
· One Cornmeal
· Salt 1 tsp
· Granulated Sugar 1/2 Cup

Instructions
1. When you're ready, start preparing. Preheat the to 350°F with the cover closed (10-15).
2. In a medium mixing bowl, combine the cooking oil, buttermilk, melted butter, mayonnaise, eggs, and honey. Set aside.
3. Combine the flour, sugar, baking powder, salt, and cornmeal in a large mixing basin.
4. To integrate the wet and dry ingredients, gently fold them together, taking care not to overmix. Spray a 9x13" baking dish with cooking oil.
6. Pour the mixture into the prepared baking dish and bake for 35-40 mins, or until the top of the cornbread starts to brown and crack.
7. Before slicing, take from the and let it cool fully. Cornbread cake may be served with butter and honey. Enjoy yourself.

Brown Sugar Grilled Pineapple

Preparation time:20 minutes
Servings:10
Ingredients:
· Melted butter, 4 tbsp.
· Dark brown sugar, ½ cup
· 1 ripe pineapple
· Ground cinnamon, 1 tsp
Instructions:
· Place pineapple spears in a tray and slice them into vertical spears.

· In a small dish, combine melted butter, brown sugar, and cinnamon; sprinkle over pineapple. To cover all sides of the pineapple spears, roll them over. Prepare the wood pellet grill and lubricate it with oil.
· Heat pineapple for 6 minutes per side on a clean, lightly oiled grill over medium to medium-high heat or until nicely browned.
· Serve warm, either plain or with vanilla ice cream on top.

Baked Apple Turnover

Prep. Time: 35 mins
Cook Time: 30 mins
Servings: 4
Ingredients
· Flour ½ Cup (All-Purpose)
· Cold Water 6 tsp
· Butter ¾ Cup
· Apples 3
· Brown Sugar 3 tbsp
· Sugar 3 tbsp
· Ground Cinnamon ¼ tsp
· Salt ¼ tsp
· Corn Starch ½ tbsp
· Turbinado Sugar 1 tbsp
· Milk

Instructions
1. In a large bowl, whisk together the butter and flour until it resembles cornmeal, then add the water.
2. After mixing, wrap the dough in plastic wrap and chill for 30 mins.
3. While the dough chills, peel, core, and dice the apples, then combine them with butter, brown sugar, cornstarch, salt and cinnamon.
4. When ready to cook, pre-heat the to 325°F with the lid closed for around 15 mins.
5. Dust a cutting board lightly with flour and roll chilled dough into a 1/4" thick round. Place the apple mixture in the center. Invert the corners and fold them inward.
6. Using some milk, wipe the top of the tart and sprinkle with "turbinado sugar."
7. Transfer it to a parchment-lined "sheet pan" or set the parchment directly on the grill.

8. Bake the turnovers for at least 25 to 30 mins.

9. Serve with a dollop of whipped cream or a scoop of ice cream (vanilla) on the side. Have fun with it.

Marbled Brownies with Amaretto & Ricotta

Prep. Time: 5 mins
Cook Time: 30 mins
Servings: 4
Ingredients
· Ricotta Cheese 1 Cup
· Amaretto Liqueur 1 tbsp
· Eggs
· Sugar ¼ Cup
· Vanilla Extract ½ tsp
· Cornstarch 2 tsp
· One Brownie (Mix)

Instructions

1. Prepare a 9x13" Teflon baking pan by spraying it with cooking spray and slathering it with softened butter.

2. Beat the egg, cornstarch, amaretto, sugar, and vanilla together in a medium mixing cup. Remove from the equation.

3. Follow the directions on the package for "brownie mix." Spread the brownie batter evenly onto a prepared platter. Randomly drop the ricotta mixture dollops into the batter.

4. swirl the plastic knife through all the ricotta mixture to give the brownies a marbled appearance.

5. Pre-heat the oven to 350°F and cook for approximately 15 mins with the lid covered.

6. With the brownie batter in the pan, bake for 25 to 30 mins on a grill directly. Put a toothpick into the middle of the brownies to see if they're done: the batter should never be sticky.

7. Place a wire cooling rack over the brownies to cool completely. Cut out the squares.

Smoked Whipped Cream

Prep. Time: 7 hrs.
Cook Time: 40 mins
Servings: 4
Ingredients
· Heavy Cream 3 Cup
· Powdered Sugar 6 tbsp
· Sour Cream, ½ Cup
· Vanilla Extract ½ tbsp

Instructions

1. Pre-heat the oven to 180°F and keep the lid covered for 15 mins until ready to cook.

2. Pour heavy cream into an oven-safe basin or pan. It is not recommended to use cast iron.

3. Cook for 20 mins on the Smoke setting on the grill with the cream. For a great smoke taste, smoke for 40 mins.

4. Remove the cream from the and leave it away to cool at room temperature for 60 mins. Refrigerate for at least 6 hours before serving.

5. In a mixing dish, mix all of the ingredients and fold in the whipped cream. Only whisk the cream until stiff peaks form.

6. Serve it with your favorite fruits or desserts. Have fun with it.

Grilled Banana Boats

Preparation time:45 minutes
Servings:6
Ingredients:
· Chocolate chips, 6 tbsp.
· Chopped pecans, 2 tbsp.
· 6 large ripe bananas
· Miniature marshmallows, 6 tbsp.

Instructions:

· Heavy-duty foil, divided into 6 (12-inch) sheets. Preheat the grill (gas or charcoal) or the oven to 350°F.

· Prepare a deep lengthwise cut along the inside curve of each banana with a sharp knife, taking care not to overdo all the way through. To make a pocket, widen the slit. 1 piece of foil should be pinched and molded around each banana to produce boats.

· Stuff each banana pocket with 2 teaspoons chocolate chips, 2 teaspoons marshmallows, and about 1/2 heaping teaspoon chopped pecans while holding it in your palm.

· Prepare the wood pellet grill and lubricate it with oil. Each banana should be placed to its foil boat. Allow 2 to 3 inches of headroom when closing the top of the foil. Put on a medium-hot grill. Heat for 8 to 10 minutes, or until marshmallows melt, wrapped on the grill. Alternatively, heat 15 to 20 minutes in the oven until marshmallows are tender.

Baked Molten Chocolate Cake

Prep. Time: 20 mins
Cook Time: 20 mins
Servings: 4
Ingredients
· Flour 9 Ounce (All-Purpose)
· Chocolate 6 Ounce (Bittersweet)
· Butter Four Ounce
· Eggs 2
· Sugar ½ Cup
· Egg Yolk 2
· Salt 1 Pinch

Instructions
1. Pre-heat the oven to 450°F and keep the lid covered for around 15 mins until ready to cook.
2. Grease and flour four 6-ounce ramekins. Remove any excess flour. On the baking sheet, keep the ramekins.
3. Melt the butter and chocolate in a double boiler at low pressure. Whisk the eggs, flour, sugar, yolks, and salt together at high speed in a medium mixing cup until thick and pale.
4. Whisk in the chocolate until smooth, then simply incorporate the egg and flour mixture.
5. Spoon the mixture into the ramekins and bake for 20 mins, or until the edges are set but the centers are still soft.
6. Allow 1 minute for each to cool before covering with an overturned dessert pan. Carefully turn each over, then put aside for 10 seconds before unmolding.
7. Serve immediately with Maple Ice Cream and Candied Bacon. Have fun with it.

Baked Irish Creme Cake

Prep. Time: 20 mins
Cook Time: 60 mins
Servings: 4
Ingredients
· Pecans 1 Cup (in pieces)
· Vanilla Pudding 1 (3.4oz) (Instant Package)
· Cake Mix Yellow 1 (Boxed)
· Eggs 4 (Large)
· Vegetable Oil ½ Cup
· Water ½ Cup
· Cream Liquor 1 Cup (Irish)
· Sugar 1 Cup
· Butter ½ Cup

Instructions
1. Butter and flour a 10-inch Bundt pan. Pecans should be distributed throughout the bottom of the pan.
2. Using an electric mixer, combine the yellow cake mix, pudding mix, water, eggs, oil, and Irish Cream liquor in a large mixing basin. Fill the container with the mixture and pour it on top of the nuts.
3. When ready to cook, pre-heat the to 325°F with the top closed for approximately 15 mins.
4. Bake in a Bundt pan on for 60 mins, or until a toothpick injected in the center comes out tidy. Remove from heat and put aside for 10 mins to cool.
5. While the cake is cooling, bring the water, butter, and sugar to a boil. Cook for 5 mins, stirring constantly. Remove the pan from the heat and add the Irish cream liquor to it.
6. Use a bamboo skewer to punch holes in the cold cake. Using a pastry brush, sprinkle the glaze over the cake. Let the glaze seep into the cake for a few mins. Have fun with it.

Grilled Peaches and Plums with Mascarpone

Preparation time:
45 minutes
Servings:
10
Ingredients:
· Lemon juice, 2 tbsp.

- Water, 1 cup
- Unsalted butter, 6 tbsp.
- Sugar, 1 cup
- 10 peaches, halved and pitted
- 24 plums-halved and pitted
- For serving, Mascarpone

Instructions:

- Preheat the grill. Prepare the wood pellet grill and lubricate it with oil. Bring 14 sliced plums, 3/4 cup of the sugar, and the water to a boil in a medium saucepan. Cover and cook over low heat for about 10 minutes or until the plums are very tender.
- Process the plums in a food processor until completely homogeneous. Pour the plum sauce into a bowl, whisk in the lemon juice and put aside.
- Whisk the remaining 1/4 cup sugar into the melted butter in a small bowl.
- Brush the plums and peaches with the butter and proceed to grill, rotating once and spraying again, for about 2 minutes, or until browned and gently seared.
- Place the grilled fruit on plates and top with the plum sauce. Serve with a dollop of mascarpone on top of the fruit.

Maple Bacon Pull Aparts

Prep. Time: 10 mins
Cook Time: 45 mins
Servings: 8
Ingredients

- Bacon 12 Slices
- Maple Syrup 1 Cup
- Biscuits Homestyle 2 Can
- Brown Sugar 1 Cup
- Water ½ Cup
- Butter 1 Cup
- Cinnamon 2 tsp (Ground)

Instructions

1. When ready to cook, warm the on High for approximately 15 mins with the lid closed.
2. Cook the bacon for 5 to 8 mins on one side, according to thickness, then turn and cook for another 5 to 8 mins on the other side. Set aside the crumbled bacon.

3. Remove the biscuits from the container and split them into four halves, then strip each half in half. Take it out of the equation.
4. Combine the butter, honey, brown sugar, and water in a saucepan; bring to a boil, then decrease heat and simmer for 1 minute.
5. Blend in the cinnamon well. Combine biscuit quarters with bacon crumbles and sugar until evenly coated.
6. Pre-heat the grill to 350 degrees Fahrenheit and place the pan on it. Cook, covered, for 30-35 mins, or until the biscuits are done.
7. Place the pan on the serving plate after removing it from the grill.
8. Serve immediately. Have fun with it.

Grilled Watermelon with Yogurt

Preparation time:
20 minutes
Servings:
6
Ingredients:

- Chopped thyme, 1 tsp
- Olive oil
- White wine vinegar, 1 tbsp.
- Salt and pepper
- Lemon juice, 2 tbsp.
- 12 triangular slices seedless red watermelon, 3 inches
- Plain whole-milk Greek yogurt, 1 cup
- Small mint leaves, ¼ cup

Instructions:

- Preheat the grill. Prepare the wood pellet grill and lubricate it with oil. Whisk the lemon juice, yogurt, vinegar, thyme, and 1 tablespoon olive oil in a mixing bowl. Add s alt & pepper to taste.
- Sprinkle the watermelon triangles with salt and pepper after spraying them with olive oil. Heat for 1 minute per side over high heat until thoroughly browned; move to plates.
- Top the watermelon with black pepper and a dollop of yogurt sauce. Serve with a splash of olive oil and a topping of mint.

Christmas Shortbread Cookies

Prep. Time: 45 mins
Cook Time: 12 mins
Servings: 24
Ingredients
- Butter, 8 oz.
- Flour 3/4 cups (all-purpose)
- Corn starch ¼ cup
- Peppermint extract ¼ tsp
- Vanilla extract 1 tsp
- Powdered sugar 2 cups
- Milk 4 tbsp

Instructions

1. Preheat oven to 350°F. Line two sheet pans using parchment paper.
2. In a mixing dish, place the soft butter. Stir everything together with a spatula until it's lovely and smooth. Combine the sugar and vanilla extract in a mixing bowl. Hand-mix until frothy and fully combined.
3. Mix in the flour and cornstarch. Stir until all of the flour is incorporated. Turn the dough out onto a lightly floured board and roll it into a ball.
4. Roll out the dough to a thickness of 3/8 inch on a slightly floured work surface. Keep the dough on the surface, and lightly sprinkle the rolling pin with flour.
5. Cut out the required shapes and place them on the baking sheets. Reroll each scrape until the dough is gone.
6. Refrigerate the cutouts for at least 1 hour.
7. Preheat the grill to 350°F (177°C) when ready to bake by switching to smoke mode, waiting for the fire to catch, and then adjusting to 350°F (177°C). Bake for 12-14 mins, or until the edges are just beginning to turn golden. Allow cooling completely before frosting.
8. To make the mint glaze, whisk together milk, peppermint essence, and powdered sugar in a mixing basin. Blend until completely smooth. Its best if the glaze is thick yet pourable.
9. Dip the tops of the cookies into the glaze to glaze them. Allow any remaining glaze to run back into the basin. Turn the cookie right side up as soon as possible. Allow 15-30 mins for the glaze to dry before serving. Take pleasure in it.

Rum-Macadamia Ice Cream with Coconut and Grilled Pineapple

Preparation time:
10 minutes
Servings:
4
Ingredients:
- Cooking spray
- Rum-Macadamia Ice Cream
- Melted butter, 1 tbsp.
- Flaked sweetened coconut, 4 tsp
- 1 small pineapple, cored

Instructions:

- Prepare the grill to high. Prepare the wood pellet grill and lubricate it with oil.
- Slice the pineapple into 12 slices lengthwise. Using a pastry brush, coat pineapple slices with butter. Heat pineapple for 2 minutes on each side or until completely heated on a grill rack coated with cooking spray. Allow cooling slightly.
- In each of the four bowls, add 3 pineapple slices. Spoon half cup Rum-Macadamia Ice Cream and 1 teaspoon coconut on top of each serving.

Baked Chocolate Brownie Cookies with Egg Nog

Prep. Time: 15 mins
Cook Time: 12 mins
Servings: 6
Ingredients
- Bar bittersweet chocolate 16 Ounce
- Eggs 4
- Unsalted Butter 4 tbsp
- Granulated Sugar 1 Cup
- Flour 1 Cup
- Vanilla Extract 1 tsp
- Semisweet Chocolate Chips 1 Cup
- Baking Powder ½ tsp

Instructions

1. Pre-heat the to 350°F and keep the lid covered for approximately 15 mins until ready to cook.
2. Place two baking sheets on top of the parchment paper.

3. Combine the finely chopped chocolate and butter in a heatproof dish; place over a pan of just boiling water and often stir till the chocolate is totally melted and smooth. Allow it to cool to room temperature.

4. Stir together the eggs, sugar, and vanilla extract in a medium mixing cup. Take it out of the equation.

5. Combine flour and baking powder in a shallow mixing cup. Whisk the egg mixture into the melting chocolate mixture with a rubber spatula until it is completely mixed.

6. Using a spatula, gently fold the flour mixture into the batter in three stages. Mix in the "chocolate chips" until all of the flour has been incorporated.

7. Scoop. Place half a teaspoon of dough on parchment-lined baking sheets. Bake for 10-12 mins or until the edges are firm. Make sure the potatoes aren't overcooked.

8. Take the baking sheets out of the oven and let them cool completely. Have fun with it.

CONCLUSIONS

Whether you're an experienced chef or new to grilling, whether it's smoking, baking, or grilling, Wood pellets are a versatile kitchen appliance that will make it easy for you.

Cooking with a pellet grill allows you to choose your favorite pellet flavor to create your favorite smoke for your food. You can also mix and match your favorite flavors for the final product. Without forgetting that wood pellets grill can have some disadvantages which, however, do not exclude its many advantages.

You can use this wonderful book to prepare your favorite meals for your loved ones, or you can give it to your friends as a gift.

The main advantage of pellet grill is that it makes grilling simpler and easier, especially when it comes to those hard-to-grill foods that don't work well with a traditional outdoor oven, such as turkey or large fish.

Cooking grates are mainly used for cooking grilled foods. Hardwood pellets add amazing flavor to your dishes and your friends will love it!